PRAISE FOR MARY KOLE

"Mary truly is amazing! Thanks to her, I have learned so much about writing. She made me laugh. She made me cry. She made me a better writer!"

M. CHURCHILL

"I've read many books on the craft of writing, and *Writing Irresistible Kidlit* is among the best. I've never been so excited to get to the keyboard."

ALAN HARELL

"The advice is wonderful, thoughtful, and so clearly written that no writer could read *Writing Irresistible Kidlit* and not walk away with something gained from it."

ASHLEE W.

"*Writing Irresistible Kidlit* is hands-down the best writing book I've read in years. It's a masterclass in a book."

ALISON S.

"I can't begin to say how helpful *Writing Irresistible Kidlit* has been for my own writing journey."

JOEL A.

"From now on, if I see a writing craft book with Mary Kole's name on it, I will hit the 'one click purchase' button without a second thought. She respects writers. She feels for writers. She understands writers. She knows exactly what insights writers need as they work. *Writing Irresistible Kidlit* is possibly the very best book on writing craft I have read in twenty-five years."

SPROCKET

"Mary Kole made me feel a renewed enthusiasm toward my writing goals."

SUSAN

"*Writing Irresistible Kidlit* is quite simply, the best 'how to' book on novel writing that I've ever read and probably ever will read in my life."

CAROL

"Mary Kole helped me to find my way. Her suggestions on my query letter are just what I needed to begin fearlessly searching for a place to call my own. I now consider Mary Kole my secret weapon."

TRACY

"*Writing Irresistible Kidlit* is the perfect blend of technical 'how to' guidance mixed with a healthy dose of encouragement. If anything I write in the future ever sells, I feel I may owe Ms. Kole a royalty for her shaping input from this book."

A. GABLE

"Mary Kole knows all that a story needs to be to be successful in today's market."

R. TATE

"I'm a big fan of everything Mary Kole does and this book was no exception. I learned so much reading Mary's feedback on the various components of each query letter in *Irresistible Query Letters*."

"Kole is clearly passionate about her work and the world of kidlit, and that passion spills over the pages of *Writing Irresistible Kidlit*."

WRITING INTERIORITY

CRAFTING IRRESISTIBLE CHARACTERS

MARY KOLE

GOOD
STORY
PUBLISHING

"Writing Interiority: Crafting Irresistible Characters"
By Mary Kole

1. Reference / Writing, Research, and Publishing Guides / Writing

FIRST EDITION
Ebook ISBN: 978-1-939162-10-6
Print ISBN: 978-1-939162-09-0

Cover Design: Jenna Van Rooy
Cupcake Image (page 460): Jenna Van Rooy
Emotional Plot Graph (page 77): Mary Kole
Author Photo: Joe Ferrucci
Editing: Amy Wilson

Theo, Finn, and Ella give meaning to everything I do.

ABOUT THE AUTHOR

A former literary agent, Mary Kole knows the ins and outs of the publishing industry. She founded Mary Kole Editorial in 2013 to provide consulting and developmental editing services to writers across all categories and genres. She started Good Story Company in 2019 to create valuable content like the Good Story Podcast, Good Story YouTube channel, and the Writing Craft Workshop membership community. Her Story Mastermind small group workshop intensives help writers level up their craft, she offers done-for-you revision and ghostwriting with Manuscript Studio, and marketing services with Good Story Marketing. She also develops unique and commercial intellectual property for middle grade, young adult, and adult readers with

Upswell Media and Bittersweet Books, the latter with literary agent John Cusick and #1 *New York Times* best-selling author Julie Murphy.

Mary has appeared at regional, national, and international writing conferences for the SCBWI, Writer's Digest, Penn Writers, Writer's League of Texas, San Francisco Writers Conference, WIFYR, Writing Day, NINC, and many others. Her guest lectures have taken her to Harvard, the Ringling College of Art and Design, the Highlights Foundation, and more. Mary's recorded video classes can be found online at Writing Mastery Academy, Writing Blueprints, Udemy, and LinkedIn Learning.

Mary holds an MFA in Creative Writing and began her publishing career with a literary agency internship and the Kidlit blog, which she started in 2009. She has worked at Chronicle Books, the Andrea Brown Literary Agency, and Movable Type Management. Her books are *Writing Irresistible Kidlit: The Ultimate Guide to Crafting Fiction for Young Adult and Middle Grade Readers* from Writer's Digest Books/Penguin Random House, and *Irresistible Query Letters, Writing Irresistible Picture Books, How to Write a Book Now,* several associated workbooks, and *Writing Interiority: Crafting Irresistible Characters,* all from Good Story Publishing.

Originally from the San Francisco Bay Area, she lives with her three children, husband, two pugs, and a cat, in Minneapolis, MN.

MARY KOLE

"Receiving Mary's feedback on my novel has been one of the best things that has happened to my writing in recent years. Thanks to her, I see the possibilities in my book and also feel like a fire has been lit under me to continue. I know the work is not yet done, but today—*today*—I feel like it's possible."

ANONYMOUS

facebook.com/goodstoryco

x.com/goodstoryco

instagram.com/goodstorycompany

linkedin.com/company/goodstorycompany

pinterest.com/goodstorycompany

tiktok.com/@goodstoryco

youtube.com/goodstory

AI TRANSPARENCY STATEMENT

1. No original text in this book has been *generated* using AI, such as automatic drafting based on an LLM's understanding of existing text.
2. No original text in this book has been *suggested* using AI. This might include asking ChatGPT for an outline.
3. No original text in this book has been *improved* using AI. An example is a system like Grammarly, which offers suggestions to reorder sentences or words to increase a clarity score. The author improved this text the hard way, through human feedback and revision.
4. Original text in this book has been *corrected* using AI (Microsoft Word's standard spelling and grammar check) but suggestions for spelling and grammar have been reviewed, then accepted or rejected, based on the author's human discretion.

Special Circumstances:

This book features excerpts from 56 novels and memoirs. Excerpts are clearly identified and the author cannot make the above warranties for any text that is not original to this guide.

This AI Transparency Statement text is adapted from one Kester Brewin developed and published in *The Guardian*.[a]

TABLE OF CONTENTS

Content Warning   xvii
About the From the Shelves Excerpts   xix
Who Uses Interiority?   xxi
Introduction   xxiii

PART 1
INTERIORITY BASICS

1. What Is Interiority?   3
2. Your Job as a Writer   19
3. Premise and Theme   37
4. Point of View and Plot   59

PART 2
DEEP CHARACTER DEVELOPMENT

5. Backstory and Wound   83
6. Sense of Self   111
7. Objective and Motivation   139
8. Need   165
9. Inner Struggle   197
10. Worldview   225
11. Character Arc   245

PART 3
SUPPORTING STORYTELLING ELEMENTS

12. Secondary Characters   285
13. The Interiority of Relationships   303
14. Information Reveals   325
15. Character Reactions   339
16. The Power of Decisions   355
17. Leveraging Stakes   377
18. Story World   393

PART 4
PUTTING IT ALL TOGETHER

19. Voice and Writing Style   417
20. Stacking the Deck   443
21. Troubleshooting Interiority   455

Conclusion   469
Resources for Writers   471
Wait! Before You Go!   475
Acknowledgments   477
Also By Mary Kole   479
Notes   481
Copyright Notices   495

CONTENT WARNING

This writing guide features excerpts from 56 published works and summarizes contextually relevant elements of their plots. What this means for you: There will be spoilers for certain books. I will generally mention the book's title before discussing it, so if you don't want anything spoiled, skip that section.

More consequentially, these stories deal with a number of potentially difficult topics, as novels and memoirs often reflect and even amplify the most dramatic events life has to offer. These topics include historical human slavery, colonialism, sex and sexuality, domestic and familial violence, infidelity, murder, sexual assault, abortion, child and pregnancy loss, immigration and deportation, mental health crisis, suicidal ideation, and self-harm. Go easy on yourself as you read if you find any of these subjects triggering, and make sure you have support. This is a writing guide, and I would hate for the subject matter in certain excerpts to overshadow their intended educational purpose.

There are also a few references to sexual slang and occasional swear words (theirs and mine—sorry Mom!).

ABOUT THE FROM THE SHELVES EXCERPTS

The theoretical concepts in this writing guide are supported by excerpts from 56 published books (over half released since 2022). My selection process was not very scientific. I gravitated toward popular, bestselling, and/or award-winning stories for various reasons. While some might see certain selections as "lowest common denominator" fiction, or judge these works as derivative and less "literary,"[1] I have an interest in what's selling to the masses and trying to unpack why that might be. I took some recommendations from BookTok, just for the hell of it, because it's a force that has shaped a lot of publishing industry discourse in the last few years. To balance things out, I also found some more niche titles with smaller followings.

I fully admit that some of my reading biases steered my selections. For example, there are many female characters and authors represented in these From the Shelves excerpts. That said, I'm proud to have read widely and intentionally when it came to selecting diverse protagonists and creators. Interiority, after all, is about how human writers put various character experiences on the page. I hope you're compelled and intrigued by the variety of protagonists you'll meet.

One thing to note is that I have, at times, edited the excerpts for

---

1. While "literary" *is* an established publishing genre, the use of this term as a descriptor is quite subjective.

meaning and clarity, including omitting material that would've necessitated additional explanation. My goal with these changes was to focus on the interiority in the sample, while also staying true to the story and my perception of the author's intentions.

Though a few original ellipses (…) do appear in the excerpts themselves, most ellipses that you'll see indicate that I have omitted irrelevant information or taken an opportunity to shorten the sample. If a sentence ends and is followed by an ellipsis, you'll see four dots (….). Any small changes that I made to the text itself, as these were occasionally necessary to tweak the grammar or to explain a reference, appear in [brackets].

In three instances, I chose to excerpt from two novels by the same author. I got on a reading kick with *Milk Fed* and *Death Valley* by Melissa Broder, *How to Sell a Haunted House* and *The Final Girl Support Group* by Grady Hendrix, and *The Nickel Boys* and *The Underground Railroad* by Colson Whitehead, and couldn't help myself.

Full copyright information for these works appears at the end of this guide. All works are used with permission from their respective publishers for all relevant English language territories.

WHO USES INTERIORITY?

This interiority resource will be most helpful to novel writers who are working in any genre and for any target audience, from children (middle grade and young adult)[1] to adult readers. Though only one of the books I've excerpted is a memoir,[2] this guide was also written with the intention of benefitting creative nonfiction writers, especially since contemporary memoirs have a lot of narrative and craft concepts in common with novels.

If your project only has one protagonist, the following caveat is not for you. However, if you're working with multiple point of view characters, read on. For my sanity—and yours—I will refer to any main character who is experiencing the present action of the story in their perspective as the "protagonist" or "character" (singular). If your story has multiple protagonists, know that my advice applies to all of your "protagonists" or "characters" (plural).

---

1. This guide does not address children's books younger than the middle grade age category. (One MG and four YA novels are excerpted here.) If you're writing for those audiences, check out my book, *Writing Irresistible Kidlit: The Ultimate Guide to Crafting Fiction for Young Adult and Middle Grade Readers*. If you're writing for even younger readers, I'm also the author of *Writing Irresistible Picture Books: Insider Insights Into Crafting Compelling Modern Stories for Young Readers*.
2. I had one other selection but wasn't able to obtain a license to reprint materials from a celebrity project.

INTRODUCTION

When you develop a deep understanding of your characters, you get to the root of the creative writing craft itself. Characterization is a means of discovering voice and deepening your storytelling, and the tool of interiority is essential to crafting a compelling protagonist.

Learning and practicing this concept will help you make your individual mark on the industry, whether you want to publish traditionally or try your hand at self-publishing. In this guide, we'll add to your writing toolbox together and explore what interiority can do for you.

This book is written in four parts: Interiority Basics, Deep Character Development, Supporting Storytelling Elements, and Putting It All Together.

Interiority Basics

Kicking off Part 1, I'll start with a detailed presentation of the craft concept of interiority, defined as the deep exploration of a character's thoughts, feelings, reactions, expectations, and inner struggles. Then I'll discuss how to convey these elements on the page. There are also four levels of narrative depth that can be plumbed with interiority, from narration and interpretation on the superficial side, to extrapolation and subsumation as we dive into the soul of character.

I'll define your most important job as a writer in today's crowded marketplace—and it's not wringing out beautiful prose. You must make readers care, and a compelling, multi-faceted, and relatable character is key. I'll also unpack why "show, don't tell," an important maxim in storytelling, has been responsible for leading many well-meaning writers astray and hamstringing character development for generations. I've been teaching characterization, interiority, and voice since 2009, and many writers wonder whether interiority counts as telling. Here, I'll delve into the crucial differences (and commonalities!) between interiority, telling, and showing.

We'll stay zoomed out to discuss premise and theme because all writers must interrogate the stories they choose to tell, the characters and plots they develop, and what their ideas are "about" in the bigger scheme of things. If you haven't made strong choices at the highest levels, you might struggle to craft an intentional story or do deliberate character development. Your theme and premise are part of the unique selling proposition—or USP, to borrow a term from marketing speak—that you bring to the table. Love it or hate it, books are products, and publishers are marketers.[1] We must also pay attention to theme and premise as they relate to reader engagement.

I'll briefly discuss point of view, also called POV, and plot next, though this book is not primarily a narrative structure guide. The bones of your story relate to important character benchmarks, though. And while POV might strike some writers as a rudimentary concept that doesn't merit much exploration, it's also absolutely crucial to our understanding of interiority. Once these foundations are laid, I'll get into the thick of crafting a protagonist.

Deep Character Development

Writers often wonder how much character development they should do. Backstory is crucial to our—and, eventually, readers'—understanding of the protagonist, as it also informs the wound and misbelief. While it may seem odd to tackle backstory so early in this guide, before

---

1. Though many published authors would disagree with this statement, because creators often bear the brunt of book promotion.

we get into the bulk of our character work, I have specific reasons for sequencing the concepts of Part 2 as I have. In these sections, I'll really begin to explore excerpts from 55 novels and one memoir to demonstrate how various contemporary authors apply the technique of interiority.

After you develop your protagonist's formative experiences, you can dig into the character as they exist now, and as they'll appear to readers once your present story gets underway. Next, I'll discuss a character's sense of self, since self-knowledge (or lack thereof) is crucial to how a protagonist comes across on the page, especially in the private world of their thoughts, feelings, reactions, expectations, and inner struggles. After that, I'll teach you how to harness character motivation and objective. The protagonist's inner life will now begin to intersect with your plot. I'll also explore need—what it is, and how it ties into backstory, wound, and misbelief—and the role these interconnected elements play in story.

The last pillar of interiority—internal conflict—gets its own chapter, as we begin to add layers and nuance to the protagonist. Then I'll dig into worldview and how it's established, whether it changes, and how it affects reader engagement. Throughout, I'll explore where and how you can generate maximum emotional impact by leveraging the tentpole plot moments you've already engineered. To cap off Part 2, all of these interiority concepts come together into a comprehensive study of character arc, including deep dives into the trajectories of several From the Shelves protagonists.

Supporting Storytelling Elements

Part 3 is our bridge to the larger ecosystem of the story. Characters don't exist in a vacuum. No matter how specific a protagonist is, they also need to be surrounded by context and put into motion. Once you develop a character full of contradictions, wants, needs, formative experiences, and values, you'll want to populate your story with other similarly interesting secondary characters and antagonists (if applicable) who will play specific roles. I include a special section on romantic relationships, as partner conflicts tend to be very important sources of stakes and tension in many types of stories, not just romances.

I'll then shift to talking about information reveals, since a character's response to events and data allows writers to generate a foundation of stakes and tension. Nuanced reactions at important turning points make the plot resonate at a higher frequency and truly land theme and character arc with audiences. Readers become more engaged, and the choices you've made pay dividends.

Writers often take it too easy on their characters. There are many opportunities for a book to droop, and tension must be threaded through every scene. Interpersonal conflicts, information reveals, reactions, decisions, and stakes matter, as they offer chances for you to hook readers and keep engaging them for the long haul. Interiority allows you to juice maximum impact from the plot you've created. I'll also discuss the context of a story's world and how world-building can be used to enhance and deepen character development.

Putting It All Together

Now that the details of your protagonist's characterization and scene-to-scene experience have been established, I'll wrap up our journey with Part 4 and the all-important topics of voice and writing style. I'll explore the enigmatic voice questions that all writers have: What is voice? Do I have it? If not, how do I get it?

It's important to remember that interiority is a gray-area tool, with no set parameters or, until now, clear definition. When used effectively, it takes a manuscript to the next level. In the penultimate chapter, I'll go through several longer scenes and showcase how interiority is used to accomplish multiple nuanced objectives at once. By delving into some meatier excerpts, I'll stack the deck and bring every concept in this guide together.

Writers face several common issues when learning to use interiority. That's why I'll end on a troubleshooting chapter that identifies interiority pitfalls and answers the most popular questions I've received over the years.

Finally, I'll circle around to the well-established idea that our call to arms as writers is to make readers care. By harnessing the power of interiority and caring more deeply about your protagonist and other *dramatis personae,* you will create irresistible characters for the passionate readers who are waiting for *your* story.

This is the book I've wanted to write for over a decade. I'm so thrilled to finally take you on this journey. Read on, and here's to a good story!

PART 1

INTERIORITY BASICS

1

WHAT IS INTERIORITY?

Interiority is a brilliant creative writing concept because it's the most effective way to develop your protagonist. It's universal and useful across all writing styles, target audiences, and genres. If you want to write compelling characters and connect on a deep level with your readers, I'll offer a top-line definition here. Don't worry if this doesn't click perfectly yet. It will.

Interiority: The on-the-page, in-the-moment rendering of your character's thoughts, feelings, reactions, expectations, and inner struggles, whether conscious or subconscious, either anchored in present time or outside of it. Interiority reveals all manner of character insights, including ideas tied to theme, premise, backstory, objective and motivation, need, worldview and morality, character relationships, perspectives on other people, reactions to plot events and information, decisions, stakes, and the story world. Interiority is also inherently tied to voice and writing style.

You should know that interiority isn't just for novels! This tool is especially useful when applied to memoir and narrative nonfiction projects, and even some picture books, which is great news for writers who work in multiple categories. Once you learn interiority and its many nuances, you'll spend the rest of your storytelling life using it, no matter what you're working on.

The Five Pillars of Interiority

Though my specific terminology and conceptualization might be new, interiority is a familiar concept. Writers have been exploring this area of the craft for as long as pen has been put to paper. That said, this guide codifies interiority into five pillars, which encompass a character's:

- Thoughts
- Feelings
- Reactions
- Expectations
- Inner Struggles

Sounds simple, right? Well, it can be, but skill, self-inquiry, and intention are required to truly leverage these ideas. Especially since a character's thoughts, feelings, reactions, expectations, and inner struggles can also be conscious or subconscious, and based in the present moment or elsewhere in time. All of these distinctions will be explored in detail throughout this guide.

Interiority can, honestly, be anything. A reaction to what's happening. A joke or bit of character uniqueness coming through. A worry about the past or future. An observation that's tinged with emotion. A reminder of what the character wants. A change of heart after a difficult conversation. All of these ideas are available to you. Adding such layers to your work serves your premise, propels the plot, raises stakes and tension, and enriches character development. Luckily, interiority can be learned.

It's important to note that while interiority happens inside the mind, heart, and intuition of a character, their reactions can be triggered from within (internal conflict) or without (external conflict), or, often, both. For example, a plot point generates a reaction, or an inner struggle inspires the character to make a choice that changes the trajectory of the story. As we'll see later in this guide, character and plot are interwoven like a DNA double helix.

Great interiority adds emotion and perspective to your novel or memoir, plain and simple. Instead of "He was annoyed," you open yourself up to much more interesting prose, like, "He couldn't believe that dumpster-fire-on-wheels needed fixing again. A lemon so sour, it couldn't even make lemonade." The emotion in this example is communicated to readers clearly and without explanation or condescension.

To understand this technique, think about the existence you have inside your own head. Unless you have perfected the art of mindfulness, you probably don't spend every single second perfectly embedded in the present moment. You are often "time traveling" to your memories of the past, imagined scenarios you wish had happened, or your hopes, dreams, anxieties, and fears for the future. You're constantly reliving, revising, telescoping into various possibilities, and otherwise jumping around in reality and what one of our From the Shelves characters calls "the counterlife."[1]

As such, our definition of interiority can be expanded to consider your character's various ideas about time—past, present, future—and the level of information they're integrating about the plot, other characters, and the story world. This is all part of being alive, so why would a protagonist's internal processes lack this type of richness and nuance? As writers, we should strive to express a character's mental and emotional experience as richly as we experience our own. We can further explore interiority across four levels of narrative depth.

The Four Levels of Narrative Depth

A lot needs to be conveyed in the course of storytelling, from the most superficial ideas to the most profound. Character is the lens through which everything is channeled, as we'll see in Chapter 4. Information can be deployed using four broad types of writing, and interiority is generally found at the three levels of self-expression which lie beneath

---

1. See Chapter 9.

simple objective statements. Here are four distinct approaches to rendering information, listed from the most superficial to the deepest:

1. **Narration:** The reporting of events *without reaction or interpretation*, as if the character is a security camera and seeing the scene with no specific slant. Though narration is usually going to be filtered through a concrete point of view, which is inherently biased, this portrayal of events is about as neutral as you can get. Narration can be played out in a full scene, or compressed into a summary—like a progress montage in a movie. *Most narration is not considered interiority.*

2. **Interpretation:** Character perspective on a scene from a specific emotional or intellectual angle, with commentary and context that add a personality layer to what's being shown and experienced. Interpretation can be applied to small and big story moments to develop a character and their unique point of view. We'll mostly find interiority containing thoughts, feelings, and reactions at this level of depth.

3. **Extrapolation:** A character making meaning from scene-based stimulus. They can remember something relevant from the past, change their perception of the present or future, or decide something about the self or another character. Extrapolation is usually reserved for more pivotal moments of protagonist development, or attached to a reaction or decision which will angle the plot in a different direction due to cause-and-effect logic. In addition to being shown through thoughts, feelings, and reactions, extrapolation is closely related to setting, resetting, and analyzing expectations. At this level of depth, characters can also ask questions, reexamine their positions, and otherwise dig into what a specific event, relationship, or piece of information means to them.

4. **Subsumation:** A protagonist using information or stimulus to perform self-reflection and integrate new data or emotional development into their sense of identity. Subsumation exposes something hitherto unknown about a character's subconscious and shows growth or change on a deeper level. For example, extrapolation might inspire a protagonist to take a different action, based on perception and interpretation, but

subsumation might inspire a character to behave differently from a moral perspective. All five pillars of interiority can come into play at this deepest level, but extrapolation is especially relevant to inner struggle.

If we review the above list, we'll notice that narration is going to almost always be present as protagonists experience scenes and move the plot along. It's crucial to acknowledge that not every moment needs interiority, as you'll see throughout this guide. Sometimes, narration is sufficient. But when we start to go deeper into character perspective with interpretation, extrapolation, and subsumation, we'll find ourselves adding different layers of connection and meaning. This is the realm of interiority.

By exploring these narrative depths, writers have the opportunity to connect with their own point of view character first, and then, eventually, foster a relationship with their audience. Basically, by using the tool of interiority, you are adding emotional context for what your character is experiencing in the moment (and, as we now realize, outside of it, too). This is key.

A Psychology Interlude

In terms of the human brain's function, interiority straddles the Executive Control Network (ECN) and the Default Mode Network (DMN). When your brain is using its ECN wiring, you are actively engaged, noticing, responding, considering, reacting, and experiencing intentional thought processes. When your consciousness enters the DMN, you are daydreaming, remembering, and otherwise unplugged from the present moment.

The study of how people think, what they think about, and how the mind interfaces with the body and vice versa, has come a very long way in the last century. We are far beyond simplistic (and largely discredited) ideas like a "left brain" or "right brain" personality.[2]

---

2. While most brains are structurally divided into left and right hemispheres, neuropsychology has moved past the notion that a "left-brained type of person" is logical and a "right-brained type of person" is creative.

Let's expand our understanding of thoughts and thinking a bit more. You might be tempted to skip this section because you didn't sign up for a neurology or psychology lecture, but since characters are modeled on people, I find these topics fascinating.

If we go back to the brain and the ECN, we can also understand the kind of though processes related to this mode:

- Setting and achieving goals
- Understanding the perspectives of others
- Communicating and collaborating
- Problem-solving
- Taking on challenges[a]

This sounds a lot like what a proactive protagonist does in storytelling. That said, you'll also want to balance this active, hard-driving ECN activation with moments spent in a DMN state, as a character retreats into their mind to remember, reflect, and subsume what events might mean.[3]

While the Executive Control Network is outward-facing, the Default Mode Network is much more inward-facing. Both have a place in our own brain-based experiences as humans, and both should feature in your character's interiority.

There are also other types of cognitive operations that you might want to show your characters doing. This list is adapted to storytelling and character from concepts that appear in *The Breakthrough Years* by Ellen Galinsky, a nonfiction parenting psychology book:

---

3. It's interesting to note that not all people "think" the same way, literally. (Obviously *what* someone thinks about is unique to each individual, but *how* they think can vary, too.) It's emerging that some people think in vividly detailed mental images and have the capacity to visualize whatever they hear or learn. On the opposite end of the spectrum, some people hear an internal voice in a visual void. (That's me! My head is full of darkness … literally and figuratively.) Others, such as people diagnosed with synesthesia, experience sensory inputs in unexpected combinations, like sounds interpreted as colors. Since we're using the written medium to express what's happening in the minds of our point of view characters, we'll generally convey interiority in words and occasional descriptions of mental images.

- **Deductive reasoning:** testing a theory by starting with a conclusion and discovering what makes it true;
- **Inductive reasoning:** assessing facts in combination and coming to a conclusion about them;
- **Abstract thinking:** considering ephemeral concepts rather than concrete objects;
- **Hypothetical thinking:** imagining possibilities and exploring potential consequences (very helpful for developing stakes, as we'll see in Chapter 17!);
- **Meaning-making and autobiographical reasoning:** deriving significance from one's experiences (much more about this when we discuss a character's sense of self in Chapter 6);
- **Perspective taking:** understanding (or attempting to understand) others' lived experiences and how they differ from or align with our own (very helpful in relationships, as we'll see in Chapter 13); and
- **Metacognition:** awareness of one's own thought processes, and thinking about thinking. (Believe it or not, we'll explore this in Chapter 9.)

We can also consider convergent or divergent mental processes, especially when it comes to how characters interface with information and make their way through the plot by experiencing inputs and deciding on their next course of action. Convergent thinking means that a protagonist will use cause-and-effect logic to arrive at a creative solution to a problem. Divergent thinking cycles through ideas that seemingly have nothing to do with one another at face value, then arriving at an a-ha! moment (similar to deductive and inductive reasoning, discussed on the previous page). Convergent thinking is more streamlined and logical, which makes it useful to track in interiority so that a character's thought process is clear to readers. (Especially in a mystery, thriller, or other type of story that relies on information and deduction. As we'll see in Chapter 14, a character simply realizing the correct answer, perhaps using divergent thinking, can exclude readers.)

It might be helpful for you to consider *how* your character thinks, how their mind works, and what audiences will experience in your rendering of their interiority. You'll notice some of these concepts threaded throughout this guide, as our characters can and should be informed by real human mental patterns and processes.

And? So?

If all the psychology mumbo-jumbo is a little technical for you, there are two helpful and *simple* questions that can also help you access deeper levels of character and interiority: "And? So?"

If you find that you're having trouble getting to the bottom of your protagonist's experience, stop and ask yourself what's really going on, or how you can make additional meaning from that moment. Here's an example of how to use "And? So?" when training yourself to think more profoundly about your character's expectations, reactions, and choices.

Let's say we have a scene where the protagonist is merely attending a work meeting before anything disruptive happens. (If nothing disruptive *ever* happens, of course, you may want to consider whether the scene is pulling its weight.) We'll get some narration of people filtering in, but that's not exactly story-worthy, so let's start digging.

And?

Well, what if[4] the big promotion will be announced at this meeting?

So?

Sonia wants it.

And?

If Sonia doesn't get it, she'll be humiliated.

So?

She'll have to save face.

And?

In front of her boss …

---

4. "What if?" is another marvelous storytelling question that can help you get unstuck, especially when you're casting around for a dynamic plot point or source of conflict.

So?

Sonia's father.

Of course, this is exactly why Sonia probably won't get the promotion. The optics are too dicey, and both father and daughter want to avoid nepotism accusations. For this scene to really sparkle, though, Sonia should either be kept in the dark or actively misled about her chances (by Daddy himself or one of his sycophants). That way, her expectations at the beginning of the scene will generate tension and inner struggle, making the outcome seem to matter more. Notice how "And? So?" keeps us focused on continually digging deeper and raising the stakes of the situation.

At the surface narrative level, Sonia sits in a conference room, watching her colleagues get settled. But once significant events start happening, interiority kicks in to convey some of the wrinkles we just discovered with "And? So?" Interpretation should become involved, at the very least, but maybe some extrapolation and subsumation, too.

Sonia might leave the present moment and start worrying about how events will impact her, or go back in time and replay a gaffe she now fears will doom her. She'll fixate on every conversation she's had with her father in the last few weeks, sifting around for clues. But job and family aside, what about Sonia's deeper sense of self?

Let's say she's a workaholic. Her achievements are a major part of her identity.[5] Whatever happens with this promotion is going to either elevate Sonia's self-worth or plunge her into despair. There's also the potential for a twist, because success is sometimes more fraught than failure.

If she does get the job, will she always wonder whether she truly *earned* it? Will Sonia forever have to watch her back against jealous colleagues? Are her so-called achievements even *hers*, or has Daddy been pulling strings behind the scenes since kindergarten?

What started as a pretty normal meeting narrative can now act as an inciting incident, midpoint, act break, crisis, or climax scene (we'll

---

5. I personally wouldn't know a thing about this. (Obvious sarcasm.)

identify some key plot points that really benefit from additional interiority in Chapter 4). If this moment ends up being pivotal, and Sonia is confronted with the loss of her job or becomes Dad's scapegoat to demonstrate a commitment to corporate fairness, she's also set up for some very interesting reactions and decisions.

This hypothetical scenario brings me to a crucial question that many writers have about the logistics of interiority. When is interiority appropriate, and how much do various moments need?

When and How Much Interiority to Use

To address this question, I like to pull out my favorite idea of the writer as a spotlight operator. Imagine a darkened theatre and a proscenium framing a stage. There's a dance number playing out, and then, suddenly ... a beam of light shines on the soloist. The audience looks there automatically.

As a writer, it's your job to identify the important parts of your story. By directing reader attention to an event, impression, or interpretation, you are, in essence, shining a bright spotlight (in the form of additional interiority) and making a big statement: *Look over here! Remember this! It's a big deal! This matters!*

The more time, description, reaction, and emotion you lavish on a story element, the more a reader will believe that this thing, person, event, or idea is important. Spotlight moments in the plot are major turning points, instances of character change, events that alter the trajectory of a protagonist's objective, motivation, or need, and other places where character, plot, and the project's big-picture theme intersect. Interiority is often used to brighten and focus that spotlight at these junctures.

You've gone through the trouble of creating *this* plot for *this* character. (That's right, the plot should intentionally showcase your protagonist development.) Make the important moments more impactful with interiority and juice maximum emotion from the events you've engineered.

Another great time to use interiority is when you're establishing who your character is, their past, their present, and their imagined or expected future. No, I don't mean an info-dumping chapter of backstory right as the manuscript is trying to get off the ground (more on this in Chapter 4). Opening exposition is very much frowned upon in most contemporary writing that aims for traditional publication.

Instead, I want you to identify story elements that could use more context. As a character's mind changes on an issue, is there any background that becomes especially relevant? Do we deepen interiority as the protagonist vacillates or decides to go against their moral compass? As they're worrying about the future, is their inner memory zooming back to some past event that makes the present even more poignant? We'll see how interiority is deployed at key moments in many of our From the Shelves excerpts.

As you get more comfortable with this tool, you can also play around with the type of interiority you use, offering superficial narration and coupling it with deeper extrapolation to enhance a moment, for example. Sometimes great meaning can be made with a few sentences of additional insight—a dash of seasoning instead of a whole side dish.

The more important the scene, the more impactful it will be to character, and the more interiority you might want to apply. I should note that the most important instances of interiority, those at the extrapolation and subsumation levels of narrative depth, don't necessarily contribute a lot of word count to their respective stories.

When I initially sampled 56 published works for this project, I ended up extracting excerpts which ranged from 15 words to 1,751. Of course, most of these narratives had interiority threaded throughout, in small moments and big ones, but it's noteworthy that I extracted only 511 words on average from each book when it came to *exemplary* material.

While some writers might not find this math useful and will argue (correctly) that different genres and categories of stories require different approaches to interiority, this data might help some of you zoom way out and see that you really can accomplish a lot with material that makes up maybe 3% of your total word count (say, 2,000 words out of 70,000, which is a pretty standard manuscript length for adult audiences).

It's not how much interiority you use—it's what you do with it.

Characterizing Details

One idea I'll keep returning to is that our thoughts, interpretations, extrapolations, hopes, dreams, fears, etc., are specific. Instead of offering random information in interiority, you will want to develop characterizing details, which lend additional insight into the premise, theme, and, of course, protagonist.

Characterizing Detail: Data that fundamentally informs a point of view protagonist's personality, objective, motivation, or reaction to stimulus, rather than irrelevant tidbits. For example, that your character's favorite movie is *Shrek* is a random fact, unless they are a champion *Shrek* cosplayer and this is crucial to your world-building and plot. On the other hand, the fact that your character only goes to watch movies in the middle of the day, when the theater is more likely to be empty, is an interesting characterizing detail. It suggests something about the character that readers have to interpret. Maybe the protagonist likes to be alone, enjoys their own company, or puts a premium on escapism. If the various attributes you're choosing for them (and which appear in their interpretations of various secondary characters) don't do some kind of double duty and deliver deeper insights, put some more thought into selecting characterizing details that do. Don't pull random preferences and facts out of a hat and call the resulting amalgamation a character.

If you think about, well, thinking, in the context of your own mental processes, you'll find that specificity makes sense. We don't often get *generally* nervous, unless we suffer from certain types of anxiety or experience a pervasive sense of doom. Usually, what we're afraid of is detailed and presented with context. If someone leaves a threatening message under the windshield wiper of your car one day, your mind probably won't stop at the vague question of, "Who did this?"

Instead, you might consider your longstanding enemies,[6] as well as anybody you may have been in conflict with recently. Is this the work of your high school bully, who just got back into town? Or the woman whose parking space you accidentally stole in the Target lot the other day? You don't want to ruminate like this for pages and pages in a novel, but notice how this specificity reminds you of a more human and relatable extrapolation than the generic rhetorical question of, "Who could it be?" Specific thoughts pack more punch, too.

Obviously, detailed consideration does add to the word count. You might notice that you'll be expanding moments, rather than streamlining them, especially when you first start using interiority. However, it's entirely possible to learn the ropes, practice, and become more precise in how you use various aspects of interiority, so that you're not contributing a ton of additional material with each instance. (Outside of major events that demand a bigger reaction, of course.)

So far, we've defined interiority and discussed where and when to use it (in big and small moments that serve plot or character development). We've also touched upon how much you'll include, though you'll see both short and long examples of interiority in the From the Shelves excerpts throughout this guide. But missing so far is a sense of what, exactly, interiority looks like on the page. How do we format this stuff? Is it just italicized verbatim thought? You'll find these answers in the next section.

Formatting Interiority

There are a few set interiority formatting conventions, but their ultimate use is up to you. Like voice and writing style, which we'll discuss in Chapter 19, interiority and its formatting are nebulous higher-order writing craft concepts. I want you to embrace this nebulousness, even though uncertainty can sometimes feel uncomfortable, especially when a lot of writing guides are full of set formulas and rubrics.

Interiority generally appears either folded into the narration or in italics, whether in a quiet moment of reflection or in the midst of scene

---

6. Everyone has these. Right, guys? Right?!

and action. The first option means narrating as normal and incorporating interiority into the flow of the text itself, without any special formatting. This can work in either first or third person, as we'll discuss in Chapter 4. The second option renders the verbatim text of the thought, impression, reaction, or interpretation, then separates the content of that interiority with either italics or a "thought" tag. Again, this is common in both the first and third person.

If we're folding the interiority into narration alongside some dialogue, it might look like this:

> "This is so yummy," she said, wondering how she might sneak away to the bathroom and spit out the gummy, flabby steak. This would be risky, and Jim would no doubt notice. What a disaster.

If we're using italicized verbatim thought or "thought" tags, it might look like this:

> "Oh, so this is your favorite steak place?" she asked, forcing a smile. *Maybe the kitchen's having an off night?* But Jim seemed to be enjoying the food. *Maybe this guy's taste buds are broken,* she thought.

In the modern publishing marketplace, more writers weave interiority into the narrative without offsetting it, as we saw in the first example. This is the primary style of interiority that you'll see in our From the Shelves excerpts.

However, there are still some authors who choose to use italics or a "thought" tag, as demonstrated in the second example. In fact, I used italics *and* a "thought" tag, which is unusual (but you'll still see this at least once in our published From the Shelves excerpts).

You can also add the "thought" tag the first few times you offer verbatim though, then let the italics formatting stand alone. This approach tends to be more common in third person, as in first person, everything the character thinks is biased and slanted through their lens, so the argument could be made that it's *all* interiority.

How you format your interiority might vary, even from project to project, though I would urge you to keep your formatting choices consistent *within* each manuscript. If you've woven interiority throughout narrative for the most part, readers might be jarred to suddenly see italicized verbatim thought and "thought" tags.

The more interiority you read—or the more you start to notice it—the more you'll internalize how to use it within the flow of your own writing. It's important to note the overlap of interiority and voice here. Both rely on writing style, syntax, and word choice. By practicing one, you will always be homing in on the other, as we'll see in Chapter 19.

Today's emotionally intelligent and nuanced fiction and memoir readers put a premium on getting to know your characters deeply. Interiority is your best bet for adding vulnerability and authenticity, which are huge factors that pull audiences into a story. At this turning point in our culture, when humans can be found pouring out their feelings, perspectives, and identities left and right via social media,[7] readers want more access to a protagonist's inner life. They prefer entertainment that thinks deeply and asks big questions.

At moments grand and small, today's most successful fiction and memoir authors use interiority to establish and deepen their characters. My goal is that you'll notice opportunities for this in your own writing.

Now that you're beginning to understand what interiority is, from the big-picture, heady concept level to the logistical how-to brass tacks, I hope you find yourself getting excited to dig in. Before we get into detail on individual interiority-related craft concepts, let's set our intention by meditating on a writer's most important job.

---

7. It's important to remember that social media shares are biased, almost always existing at the levels of interpretation, extrapolation, or subsumation.

2

YOUR JOB AS A WRITER

Writing can be a private and intimate creative practice, full of experimentation and false starts. Some aspiring authors naturally want to avoid crass market talk, especially at first. I'd argue, however, that it's very important for you to know what (and why!) you're creating, the earlier the better. Especially to successfully sustain yourself through a first-draft manuscript and several rounds of revision.

> "The first draft is just you telling yourself the story."
>
> TERRY PRATCHETT

This means you'll have a pretty intensive conversation with yourself before you bring anyone else on board.[1] Ignore the market, luxuriate in the creative cocoon, and figure out what you're doing.[2] At some point, though, you'll have to share what you've been working on, unless you

---

1. It's also important to note that many would-be writers never get this far, despite claiming very loudly that they have a book inside them. If you've finished a project, no matter how short it is, or how badly you believe it's written, you're far ahead of the pack already!

2. Not "what you're doing with your life," as some critical family members might ask. What you're doing with your *book*.

intend to keep it for yourself (which is also perfectly valid, but I know that a lot of you hope to one day traditionally or independently publish).

Once we pivot to desiring publication, we need to take our target reader into account, perhaps for the first time. At this inflection point, I strongly believe your only job is to make that audience care.

You obviously care about your book very much, especially if it's a memoir, since it is your *literal* life story. (If you find that *you* don't care, I'd wager that you have some deeper challenges to overcome before you start thinking of pleasing an external reader.) You may even have some very complimentary early feedback from loved ones, though this can be problematic because your nearest and dearest will make an effort to be nice about your creative output, even if it's not yet ready for prime time.[3]

Unfortunately, most readers won't know you from Adam (yet!). They have no built-in reason to care about your book or to give up hours of their lives to read it. (In traditional publishing, this also goes for gate-keepers like literary agents and acquiring editors—you *especially* need to make them care if you want a shot at reaching that wider readership.)

Even well-known authors with rabid fan bases need to hook their audiences with each new book. Basically, good or bad, expert or novice, you need to *earn* those eyeballs. The good news is you can learn how.

How Readers Read

First, let's define how readers read, and why, since these ideas tie back directly into making audiences care and solidifying that reader-protagonist connection using interiority.

Readers are detectives. They want something to do when they show up

---

3. The solution here is to develop workshop or critique relationships with other writers working in your category or genre, or to add feedback from a freelance editor to your drafting and revision workflow. Check out my guide, *How to Write a Book Now: Craft Concepts, Mindset Shifts, and Encouragement to Inspire Your Creative Writing*, for more on these topics.

to the page. The big joy of reading doesn't only come from sinking into a different world and experience, it also stems from learning, analyzing, and making judgments—in other words, engaging intentionally and critically.[4] This means audiences want to understand how a character reveals themselves and participates in plot over the course of the story.

Readers might *look* like they're just sitting there, turning pages, but they're actually playing a very active role, as our protagonists should be (more on that later in this chapter).

The big high of reading[5] is the joy of discovery. By telling an eager audience a story, you are inviting their participation, empathy, time, attention, and emotional investment. Happily, a reader is already primed to give you all that, and more, but you have to know what you're doing when you say you intend to take them on a story journey.

Interiority Insight: "Empathy" differs from "sympathy." With empathy, readers are on the same level as the character and relating to them, maybe even pulling from their own life experiences to understand what a protagonist is going through. Sympathy puts the reader on a level above the character, where audiences look at a protagonist and feel pity or concern, rather than true understanding. You're aiming to create empathy for your character in most cases, though sympathy might also arise when conflicts spike and the going gets tough.

From the jump, you'll want to develop a clever premise and hook which pique audience interest and curiosity. Of course, some reader desires will vary by genre and category, so it's important that you know something about the current publishing market. That's what we'll talk about next.

---

4. I mean "critical thinking" here, not "criticism," though the denizens of Goodreads might disagree.
5. One of them, anyway.

Writing to Market

Your very idea is part of the hook that might draw an eager reader in, as we'll see when we discuss premise in Chapter 3 and plot in Chapter 4. Oddly, some writers might not truly understand their own project until it's time to write a query letter or pitch for an upcoming writer's conference. This isn't ideal if you want to work smarter, not harder. Your central story concept should be a foundational part of your book's design from the very beginning. (If this didn't happen prior to your current draft, that's okay. There's always revision!)

When we talk about audience, book category, or genre, we're already starting to think about the kind of premise that specific readers tend to enjoy. Now, before you start to vomit, or go off on a rant about how art is *art* and there are no certain *types* of art, artists, or art appreciators, I'll tell you that I know how you're feeling. It's pretty gross to slice and dice your creativity into neat little boxes or try to label it. That said, publishing categories and genres *do* exist, so it'd be silly to pretend otherwise.

Category: You may notice that I use the terms "genre" and "category" separately and intentionally. Genre refers to a story's broad stylistic conventions and content expectations, whether it's fantasy, historical, or romance. Category refers to the target audience, such as middle grade (MG) for children ages nine to thirteen, young adult (YA) for teens ages fourteen to eighteen, or adult for anyone who has aged out of reading kidlit (though many adults still gravitate toward YA novels). It wouldn't be industry standard to call middle grade a "genre," as you can have a fantasy middle grade, or a historical middle grade, for example.

Some writers roundly reject the idea of writing to market and scoff at genre expectations, but I think these ideas are worth considering, especially if your goal is traditional publication with a Big Five house or success within a self-publishing niche.

For better, but largely worse, these ideas are becoming more relevant than ever, since today's publishing industry is characterized by conglomerates and mergers,[6] which unfortunately means there's a preference for mainstream projects, which are sometimes called "high concept" or "upmarket."

As alluded to in the previous chapter, publishing is a business, and books are products. If you think you can escape these notions by self-publishing, just wait until you encounter the 4,000 different Amazon categories that you'll be asked to choose from before you can list your book for sale. Since this is our current reality, there's power in understanding your intended reader and, in broad strokes, what they might be looking for.

Writing to Market: This can be a somewhat controversial idea, but "writing to market" simply means crafting a story to fit perceived category desires. A classic example is the expectation of an HEA or "happily ever after" (or at least a "happy for now") ending in romance. If you aim to write a mainstream genre romance for traditional or independent publication, you pretty much have to fulfill this at the end of your story (or you better have a very good reason why you don't). Your readers may not respond well otherwise. Even if you don't start out writing to market to reflect perceived trends and realities, you will want to research, understand, and pay attention to the larger publishing landscape at some point in your career (depending on your goals, of course). Writing to market isn't a requirement. Some people write whatever they want and ignore trends, which can be a very healthy approach. Your philosophy may also change with time.

High Concept: Various publishing industry gatekeepers often express a preference for "high concept" projects. This means that

---

6. For more on this, see *Big Fiction: How Conglomeration Changed the Publishing Industry and American Literature* by Dan Sinykin.

the premise is easily expressed, and the ensuing story does exactly what it says on the box. Imagine the type of narrative that often gets made into a movie. A kid is left home alone for the holidays (the *Home Alone* franchise). Dinosaurs are resurrected from DNA samples for entertainment, until this backfires (the *Jurassic Park* franchise). The idea doesn't require nuanced explanation for someone to "get it." Compare this to "a newly single parent comes to terms with life." The latter is not necessarily a *bad* story, it's just not a high concept one. A lot of action and adventure narrative, fantasies, thrillers, and romcoms get the high concept label, but this description can apply within any genre and category.

Upmarket: This is a slightly more nuanced term than "high concept" and is sometimes called "book club fiction." It reflects a bent toward female audiences and tends to be realistic, literary, and romantic or comedic (or both). These books often explore relationships, journeys of self-actualization, and intergenerational conflicts. For examples, check out the various book club endorsements, from Oprah to Reese Witherspoon to Good Morning America. The "single parent" example, above, might get this label instead, depending on its voice and plot.

I don't want to be utterly reductive, but an upmarket fiction reader will probably reach for a book with a woman on the cover, bright colors, and maybe a Hello Sunshine stamp of approval. Writers and books can contain multitudes, and so can readers, of course, but my point is that a book designed to attract an upmarket or women's fiction fan is unlikely to feature blood-splattered dragons front and center.[7]

This discussion could merit its own writing guide, so I'll wrap it up by

---

7. *Fourth Wing* by Rebecca Yarros has, in fact, been a huge crossover romantasy (a portmanteau of "romance" and "fantasy") hit with some upmarket and women's fiction readers, but you'll notice that the book's packaging is quite subtle, so as not to overwhelm the delicate sensibilities of someone coming over to dragon smut from, say, *Tom Lake* by Ann Patchett.

saying that different broad types of readers tend to gravitate toward different broad types of stories. As you think about your premise and intended audience—whether that's fans of historical military fiction, self-help junkies for your memoir of resilience and redemption, or kids ages nine to twelve for your sweet coming-of-age novel helmed by a plucky young protagonist—you can acknowledge that all readers have tastes, and those tastes make them engage with certain ideas more favorably than others.

More importantly, once you understand your audience, you might have a leg up in making your characters more relatable to *them*. Not perfect, not even consistently sympathetic, but *relatable*.

Character Relatability

Character introductions always stress writers out, even memoir writers, who theoretically know their protagonists inside and out. That's because the all-important first meeting between the reader and protagonist has to be artfully done. Gone are the days of, "Hi, my name is Ruby. I'm in middle management, and my favorite outside-of-work hobby is birdwatching." Sorry. This kind of direct exposition is distinctly out of style, and it's also telling about the core essence of your character, which is, indeed, the kind of telling your English teacher warned you about (as we'll see toward the end of this chapter). When you introduce your protagonist, prioritize relatability over demographic data.

Relatability: A protagonist quality designed to engender reader empathy, connection, and a sense of commonality between the character and audience. Relatability arises from a number of choices that writers make, like giving the protagonist recognizable flaws and foibles, vulnerabilities and values, driving wants and needs, specific characterizing details and quirks that are observed from real life, or any combination of these. The goal is to get readers to care about the protagonist, even if they don't always make the right choices or aren't consistently sympathetic.

Your job as a writer, especially at the beginning of your story, is to thrust the reader into story, introduce just enough context to make the present action clear and consequential, hit upon some main characterizing details, and plant a seed or two of future tension, which I'll talk about more in the following chapter.

Today's savvy audiences are more interested in the big questions. What is a character's ... well, character?[8] What's their sense of purpose? Which roles do they play in their life and world, and do they accept or reject these? What "kind of person" do they feel they are, and who might they want to be, if they're still evolving? These are the types of things that you should be thinking about as you design your point-of-view protagonist.

The keys to inspiring relatability and reader connection are multifold. My first warning here is to avoid trying to create someone "everyone" will like.[9] This sounds like surprising advice if relatability, empathy, and mass connection are your goals, but stick with me. Medieval plays used to feature overt Everyman characters so audiences could project themselves onto the blank canvas of a bland hero. In modern times, I see a trend toward very specific and even polarizing protagonists. How can two such different approaches lead to the same outcome of audience engagement?

As contemporary storytelling craft and style have emerged, writers are capturing audiences by keenly observing human mannerisms, foibles, and behaviors. One of my favorite experiences as a reader happens when a small thought, reaction, interpretation, or impulse displayed by a character in action or interiority rings so true that I feel a surprising kinship with them. Other people think and feel this way? I'm not alone? This type of connection is the gold you're digging for.

Even if a character is inherently different from their reader, it's still possible for opposites to attract. Especially if the writer has taken pains

---

8. David Brooks has an amazing book on this topic: *How to Know a Person: The Art of Seeing Others Deeply and Being Deeply Seen*. It's self-improvement nonfiction for humans, and not even a little bit about developing fictional characters, but I found it brimming with ideas that can apply to the writing craft.
9. There's no such thing as universal appeal, anyway. Even oxygen is poisonous to anaerobic bacteria.

to fully render the protagonist, define their value system, empower them with specific wants and needs, offer a peek at formative and emotional backstory, and raise the stakes so the present journey matters. It's also a good idea to make a character fundamentally good inside, even if they are flawed, make mistakes, have shaky self-worth, or seem damaged or unhinged. Their good and valiant qualities should generally outnumber the negative ones, but perfection is *not expected*. In fact, it's boring and doesn't make for a good story, unless the protagonist is a recovering perfectionist who's waging a small war against social convention, like Grace in *Amazing Grace Adams* by Fran Littlewood.

The best and easiest way to get readers on board with a character is by showing audiences what they care about. For Mare in *Red Queen* by Victoria Aveyard, it's her childhood best friend, Kilorn, who she wants to save from the draft. For the wild and temperamental Isabel in *The Nightingale* by Kristin Hannah, it's *"liberté, égalité, fraternité"* as she challenges the Nazi occupation of France during World War II. In *Remarkably Bright Creatures* by Shelby Van Pelt, Tova is a retiring, walled-off stickler. She and I, at face value, have little in common. But when she develops an unexpected friendship with Marcellus, a giant Pacific octopus at the aquarium where she works, and he seems to *respond*, I'm immediately intrigued.[10]

Many relatable characters also operate with misbeliefs or self-doubts that readers can empathize with, which we'll unpack more in Chapter 6 and Chapter 9. Over the course of the plot, these protagonists are likely to confront and consciously wrangle with their limiting beliefs, which puts them on a redemptive growth trajectory that audiences tend to find aspirational. Most importantly, readers care about characters who care about something. Wanting is universally relatable, as we'll see in Chapter 7.

In order to write interiority and authentically connect with readers, writers aspiring to create intelligent, relatable, and consumable fiction for the contemporary market need to get very comfortable with

---

10. This book also uses octopus point of view, which is an inspired choice. (As long as it's done well!)

emotion and vulnerability—their characters' *and* their own. By feeling deeply first, you can access a protagonist deeply enough to convey your themes and ideas to audiences. So prepare to go on a personal journey, even as you're plumbing the depths of a fictional person.

You should also expect to put your character into action early—and keep them there throughout the story. Creating a proactive protagonist goes a long way to compelling readers into turning pages.

Putting the "Pro" in Proactive and Protagonist

At the center of every good story is a relatable character who's hard at work doing ... something. Actually, *what* they're doing doesn't matter nearly as much as the fact they're doing it in the first place. They don't even have to do it successfully! In fact, they can fail in small or major ways throughout your plot, and all of this will add to their perceived charm. Readers love a proactive protagonist. Ideally, this go-getter quality will propel your character throughout the entire narrative, because there's nothing worse than a "character-driven" story that's not driven by character at all.

Proactive Protagonist: A protagonist who pursues internal and external objectives and needs over the course of a story. Even if yours is primarily a plot-driven novel, like a thriller, or a memoir where you're stringing together seemingly unrelated events into a cohesive structure, there should be a sense that the character is in forward motion toward one or several goals, from scene to scene, and act to act. While characters can and should react to external conflict at times, their primary progress through the story must aim toward the realization of their small and large goals. Interiority is used to add cause-and-effect logic and create stakes, tension, and growth. With a proactive protagonist, plot is steered and affected by decisions they make, as we'll see in Chapter 16.

The reason readers attach to a proactive protagonist has a lot to do with audiences and their real lives (which they are fleeing to spend time in books). Many modern readers may feel out of control in between bouts of doom-scrolling and feeling overburdened with their non-reading responsibilities. As a result, they might dream of inhabiting the consciousness of kick-ass heroes who aren't quite so constrained. Writers themselves can absolutely relate to these feelings, with the relative loss of control inherent in the publishing process. Why not add a healthy dose of aspirational wish fulfillment as you design your characters and premises?

Remember that readers want to care. But they also want to live vicariously through larger-than-life events elevated into something meaningful. Even though reactive/passive protagonists can be relatable and realistic, your goal is to aim higher. Find ways to put your character into the driver's seat in a way that makes sense for the story. The goal is a protagonist who makes the plot happen, rather than letting it happen to them. (We'll learn how to combine external events and character agency at key plot points in Chapter 4.)

Psychologists Richard Ryan, PhD, and Edwards Deci, PhD, developed something called Self-determination Theory, which basically means that actualized humans need to feel:

- **Related:** connected, valued and loved by others, a sense of belonging;
- **Autonomous:** able to make one's own choices rather than being pressured or coerced; and
- **Competent:** effective, capable, able to affect one's world.

I bet you can relate to these driving needs, so give them to your characters, too. If you keep the above in mind, you might get closer to creating a proactive protagonist who pursues their own wants and needs over the course of a story (a lot more on these two craft elements in Chapter 7 and Chapter 8).

Self-determination Theory ties into the idea of the "locus of control," which simply means that some people believe that events are outside of their influence (an "external locus of control"), while others assume they have power over their lives and situations (an "internal locus of control"). For a powerful protagonist, you'll want to focus on the latter.

To that end, put your character into proactive action from the very first pages of your story, whether you knock them down or show them climbing. Why? Because both failing and striving are incredibly relatable.

To round out this chapter, I'll challenge a perfectly well-meaning and extremely pervasive piece of writing advice. The familiar paradigm of "show, don't tell" has been wrecking prose and making writers neurotic[11] for centuries. Instead, it's better to use an expert combination of showing *and* telling, and this is my hill to die on. Interiority occupies the gray area between these approaches.

It's Okay to Show *and* Tell

The old craft chestnut of "show, don't tell" has some wisdom behind it. But since it's considered "Writing 101," many writers follow it blindly without digging any deeper. This is a mistake. There are actually multiple types of telling. That's right, not all telling is created equal.

Many writers already know that "telling" simply means stating emotion, objective, motivation, characterization, etc., in the text itself. Think, "She was angry," and, "He is a nice guy, the kind who'd give a buddy the shirt off his back." Meanwhile, "showing" is the practice of demonstrating some of these same ideas, emotions, and character traits through action. Think, "She balled her fists up into tight knots," and the narrative description of the character giving someone the shirt off his literal back.

Telling: Explicit statements of story and character realities, where the author or narrator speaks directly to the reader in an expository or explanatory manner. This gets in the way of reader extrapolation and discovery by overtly expressing thematic, character, and plot elements. There is wisdom to the advice of "show, don't tell," which steers writers away from passive telling, but some telling is

---

11. Of course, one can argue that neuroticism is a pre-condition of becoming a writer, but like the chicken or the egg, I suppose we may never know which comes first.

appropriate and warranted, as long as it occurs in concert with showing and leaves room for audiences to participate.

Showing: An action-based method of displaying a character's inner life via external means, from dialogue to movement to the sensation in their physical body. This allows readers to participate actively by interpreting what's happening below the surface and extrapolating why. It also reminds writers to keep their stories active with narrative and scene. But if you're only showing throughout your story, this approach can present some unique challenges and get in the way of deeper character exploration.

Here are some very derivative examples of showing and telling, side by side, which are intended to make a very obvious point. The telling instances will be aligned to the left, while showing is on the right:

He was angry.

> He huffed and slammed the door.

She was nervous.

> Her stomach fluttered with butterflies.

She fell head over heels in love.

> Her heart hammered in her chest.

He was nice.

> He pulled the cat out of the storm drain.

Think of our detective readers, who like to be actively involved in uncovering and interpreting information. If you simply tell them everything you want them to know, you risk them feeling like outsiders with no stake in the story. "She was angry" might be true and clear, but it doesn't ask anything of the audience. It's disposable information that doesn't elicit empathy, either. Reading the word "angry" won't make me feel angry (though the flagrant emotional telling might!). It won't even make me think, and that's the issue.

Contrast "She was angry" with, "If that no-good, rotten jerk ever darkens my doorstep again, I'll knock him into next Thursday." This communicates anger in a colorful and engaging way, using interiority and voice. It lets the reader draw the connection between the prose and the emotion of "angry." Leaving an opening for interpretation invites the audience to reach out, emote, and relate to a character's feelings. As a result, readers take personal ownership of the storytelling process, which is key.

Telling, at its core, is incredibly condescending. It doesn't trust the reader to do their job—and in the case of most people who actively choose to be readers, it's a job they love. Egregious telling in a manuscript feels like a pat on the head. It also (perhaps unintentionally) communicates a lack of writing confidence. It's as if the writer doesn't think they've done a good job of making the story speak for itself. You shouldn't approach your reader relationship from this place of insecurity. I know, I know, that's easier said than done.[12] But once you realize that you don't *have to* explain, you can trust yourself to tell the story and trust your reader to follow. It's a terrifying and liberating breakthrough, and something I hope you experience as you start applying the concepts in this guide to your own work.

But here's where things get more nuanced: The simple "show, don't tell" dichotomy doesn't give writers or readers the full story. If you unlearn what you think you know about this advice, you might start noticing telling all over published books. Has there been some kind of massive error? Does publishing have a huge double standard, enabling a shady cabal of writers who are "allowed" to tell? No. Because there are multiple types of telling, and not all are bad. In fact, some are

---

12. Yes, writing a book is hard, and rejection makes writers feel vulnerable. But don't take it out on the reader. You are in full control of how much you learn and practice your craft. Reading guides like this one is a great way to help yourself feel more empowered, no matter what happens in the slush pile.

downright necessary. This is where I draw a distinction between what I call "bad telling" and "good telling."[13]

First, let's discuss bad telling and the writing elements you should avoid simply telling about:

- **Inherent Personality Traits:** Don't outright explain personality traits that are central to your character's core identity, whether the protagonist is a "good sport" or a "loose cannon."
- **Emotions:** When readers hear that someone is "hurt" or "sad" or even "happy," this is the most superficial expression of that emotion. The "why" behind a feeling is almost always more interesting than the feeling itself, which is either provided in context within the scene or communicated using interiority. There's also the thought that triggers the feeling, and its aftermath. None of these juicy ideas can be explored if you're merely labeling the emotion.

Take, for example:

> Tina was a loyal person, but this latest fight had hurt her very badly. James had been her friend since the second grade, and Tina didn't want to jeopardize such a longstanding and meaningful relationship. Still, she found herself undecided.

This is straightforward bad telling. It delivers information but there's no sense of voice or emotional inflection. You'll notice that "hurt" and "undecided" don't really do much justice to the betrayal that Tina might be feeling. The information lies on the page like roadkill on the turnpike.

Contrast it with this:

> She wanted to hate James, everyone said she should. But Tina couldn't throw away eleven years of friendship. Could she?

Not only are the ideas of "hurt" and "undecided" communicated with

---

13. That's right, I'm really using my creative writing MFA with these terms!

more nuance—as the reader must work to unearth them from the prose —but we get information about the length of the friendship in context. Thanks to interiority, the data is seamlessly inserted without calling much overt attention to itself.

This second example involves good telling, which you may not have felt comfortable exploring before. However, it can be perfectly appropriate to make factual statements in creative writing, as long as these are balanced with action. Certain categories of information can and *should* be conveyed with interiority and narration. Sometimes, there's really no good way to say it … except to say it. The below story elements fit under the good telling umbrella:

- **Backstory:** What are some significant past events that have shaped a character, for better or worse (or both)? (See Chapter 5 for more on weaving these into the present.)
- **Context:** What's happening for your character in their current place in their growth arc and the overall plot? Why is it important? (See Chapter 11.)
- **Objective:** What does the character want and why do they want it? (See Chapter 7.)
- **Self-Perception:** How does the protagonist see themselves? Is this in conflict with anything or anyone else? Does their self-perception change as they go through the story? Do they shift from their objective to their need, and what are the ramifications of this transition? (We'll discuss these issues in detail in Chapter 6 and Chapter 8.)
- **Inner Struggle:** What's the biggest thing they're grappling with, on a personal level (in general) or in difficult times (in particular)? (More on this in Chapter 9.)
- **Plot Tension and Conflict:** What are the story's sources of external, plot-based conflict?
- **Stakes:** What are the consequences of a specific event or choice? What happens if the character is successful or unsuccessful in a present or future action? (More on this in Chapter 17.)
- **Historical World-Building and Magic System Context:** If you're writing in a speculative, fantasy, science fiction, or historical genre, you'll want to include details about the world

or era, why it works the way it does, and how these issues affect character development and plot. (See Chapter 18.)

If you were paying attention to the previous chapter, you might start to recognize that a lot of these story elements intersect with the broader definition of interiority. Yep, that's right. Interiority is good telling.

I often find myself writing *"Interiority instead!"* in the margins of client manuscripts, especially when I notice too much showing (or bad telling). There's certain information that's difficult to transmit to readers without it being explicitly stated *somewhere*.

Funnily enough, the writers who are showing too much—doing the "right" type of writing!—are sometimes the most lacking in the interiority department. Their characters display the same cluster of physical clichés for emotion—hammering hearts, stomach butterflies, white-knuckle fingers on steering wheels—over and over, with no deeper insights for readers to explore.

A major benefit of strong interiority is its ability to provide seamless context. Writers often struggle with establishing information and backstory. It can be tough to draw the line between good and bad telling. They know that a character needs extra dimension but are often unsure how to provide it without hitting readers over the head. Interiority is an elegant way to deploy not only emotion but information, and offer reasons why both matter. This guide hinges on this distinction.

So if you keep a wreath of Post-its around your computer monitor, or reminders above your writing desk, you might want to add the soon-to-be-second-nature comments and questions of "Interiority instead!" and "And? So?" to your vision board.

The point is simple. I don't really care *that* a character is crying. Tears shown on someone's face aren't going to make me commiserate. I also especially don't care *that* a character is merely thinking. This is a big one. "Thoughts whirled around in her head." Okay. That's nice. Anything more specific? And? So?

Specificity is key. Characters are individuals. Everyone experiences emotions and events differently. When I'm sad, I might look like I'm hungry (because I'm eating so much junk food). When you're sad, it might look like you're angry (because you're pounding the wall). If you're only showing those actions, a whole layer is missing. Relying on the visual presentation of an emotion leaves no room for nuance. Why is the character crying? What's the thought that touched off the tears? We all know what it's like to be overcome with emotion, but it's often a very specific thought or image that sparks the waterworks. The physical body can only tell us so much. Then we have to dig deeper.

This is why interiority transcends the limitations of both telling *and* showing, and why it's such a crucial tool to add to your ever-expanding understanding of writing and storytelling. Though many of you are grown-ass adults[14] and don't need *anyone's* permission to do *anything*, I'll give it anyway: It's okay to both show *and* tell, as long as you focus on good telling. Just in case this helps you feel more comfortable.

Next, you need to decide what your story is about and whether your idea promises enough potential for character and plot development, as well as reader engagement. This is where premise and theme enter the conversation, and that's what I'll explore next.

---

14. And if you're a young writer reading this guide, I applaud your commitment to learning your craft!

3

___

PREMISE AND THEME

Before we get into the deep work of character development, let's talk about the idea that's going to support your protagonist and plot. A lot of stories have several interconnected ideas operating behind the scenes. Together these can be called theme and premise. In practice, theme often supports the early story concept and its evolution, while premise is the audience-facing expression of your story idea, which is more relevant during the revision and pitching process.

___

Theme: The "core emotional experience" of the story, or what it's about on a human level. This is the topic, assertion, or argument that you keep at the front of your mind while writing and that you want your audience to consider while reading. Though the theme is ever-present in a story, it's rarely stated outright. For most of the narrative, it is hidden below the surface, yet powers the project, like an electric current.

___

___

Premise: This is the audience-facing explanation of your story that can pull together character, plot, and theme. For the purpose of this guide, I generally use "premise" to mean a short summary of your main character and plot points. In the larger publishing industry, a "premise" can also refer to a formal elevator pitch or logline statement that's used to succinctly present a manuscript or published book. Many of these terms are used interchangeably, which can be confusing. (For more on submission, query letters, and other aspects of pitching, check out my book, *Irresistible Query Letters: 40+ Real World Query Letters With Literary Agent Feedback*.) Premise also factors heavily in the packaging of a finished book—the marketing copy, cover image, and blurbs—so that readers know what to expect.

The fact is, stories are all about *something*, whether a clever premise or a protagonist's emotional growth arc. Memoirs also have a theme, or at least they should. A life story from the cradle to the present day is an autobiography, and these can be extremely hard to sell to traditional publishers unless you're a household name. The overwhelming majority of contemporary memoirs encapsulate events and reflections around a specific theme—love after loss, triumph over adversity, a unique family dynamic, etc.—which helps writers be selective with their focus when shaping a narrative from millions of lived experiences.

If you have a story idea that you're developing, there's probably a nugget, image, character, or scene that first came to mind and inspired you to expand it into a novel or memoir. Very few productive concepts are developed by writers who say something vague like, "I want to write a Hero's Journey coming-of-age novel." If this is where you are right now, push yourself to discover a more concrete angle.

While you should be specific, you also shouldn't pressure yourself to create something singular. There are no new stories to tell. At some point in recorded or forgotten history, someone has probably played with similar characters, plot points, and ideas. There are many familiar notions floating around in brains and slush piles; on hard drives and shelves. There are only so many different types of clay in the world but look at the incredible variety of pottery that comes from the imaginations and hands of individual creators. You may not win solely on your book *idea*. Instead, you might win on your character, writing style, and interiority.

Idea-Execution Dichotomy: The theme, premise, and idea constitute just one part of a novel or memoir. It's notable that you can't copyright a book idea. The execution—how that idea is expressed and explored on the page—is where you can really leave your mark. And that's what we copyright: the words that comprise the written work itself. Successful novels and memoirs combine both a good, relatable, and interesting idea that's likely to resonate with their target audiences, and an execution that demonstrates intentional writing craft on every page.

Every writer is capable of creating a specific and nuanced character, and *they* can be your unique selling proposition. Other writers may be working with a similar premise to yours right now, but only you are capable of giving it *your* spin.

Developing Theme and Premise

To that end, you will want to answer the following question as soon as possible, ideally before you sit down to draft: What's your story about? Be specific. It's also helpful to know who your intended audience is and which thematic ideas you're hoping to explore.

A lot of our From the Shelves books have strong core themes around which their respective stories revolve, and from which their premises evolve. If you follow the *Save the Cat Writes a Novel* methodology taught by Jessica Brody, you'll notice there's a beat called "Theme Stated." This usually happens early in the story and comes from a secondary character (we'll see an example later in this chapter). The wisdom of the theme, and the mentor who's delivering this statement, is generally rejected by the protagonist at this point in their development, but it's there for readers to appreciate.

This helps to set up the character's growth arc, as audiences can understand the protagonist's early worldview and intuit how far they have to go to realize a more evolved outlook. From there, explorations of the theme and premise appear throughout. These elements reinforce the book's essence to the writer, at first, then to agents and other publishing gatekeepers, and finally, to readers.

I strongly suggest that you get clear on these major ideas—even if you don't have all of your plot ingredients and narrative choices hammered out yet—because your ideation, writing, revision, and pitching process will be easier.[1]

The Promise of the Premise

You may have heard about this concept on the conference circuit, in forums, or in other writing craft books. When you're designing the premise of your story and thinking about your plot (more on that in Chapter 4), consider what might be engaging and aspirational about it.

Promise of the Premise: This depends on your genre, audience expectations, and story idea. You'll want to develop storytelling sequences that show off the unique attributes of your novel or memoir and which will plunge your readers more deeply into your particular idea. Think of what's aspirational, inspirational, or noteworthy about your premise, then play it up with your settings, plot obstacles, and how "big" you let your protagonist go in the pursuit of their objective and need. Even ordinary characters and lives can offer fun sequences of wish-fulfillment or high emotional stakes. What kinds of scenarios and experiences are only available in your story world and to your particular protagonist?

For example, an established but potentially fading trend in today's market is "dark academia." What's the appeal of this? For a certain type of reader, there's a real attraction to privilege, power, secret societies, ivy-slung campus buildings, and the kind of edgy, romantic fun and trouble that young people get up to when they're away at boarding school or college for the first time.

If you're writing something that can be considered dark academia, you'll want to offer plot and character elements that live up to the

---

1. Not *easy*, mind you, but potentially easier.

promise of the premise. This means protagonists who stay up all night falling in love or debating big ideas, parties in secret chambers, hushed libraries with soaring ceilings, new best friends, fresh foes, and an atmosphere of extreme academic and social pressure that promises either acceptance or bitter rejection. One of the worst outcomes for a young person in this kind of environment is to feel irrelevant. The stakes are high, especially if you're weaving in speculative or fantasy elements, and this is exactly what a dark academia audience will be drawn to.

As mentioned in Chapter 2, you don't have to let the market decide *everything* you write, but the kind of book you're crafting tends to come with certain expectations. Audiences flock to memoirs of resilience and triumph over adversity because they're probably going through something themselves. Even if they aren't planning to travel the world (*Eat, Pray, Love* by Elizabeth Gilbert) or hike the Pacific Crest Trail (*Wild* by Cheryl Strayed), they'll find insights, solace, and solidarity in memoirs of this stripe. There's something compelling about seeing our own human foibles, feelings, and struggles writ large across a story that's elevated almost to a tall tale. This is why extraordinary lives make great backdrops for stories of growth and personal development.

Now imagine if *Eat, Pray, Love* was about a freshly divorced woman who went to the bakery to eat, the church down the street to pray, then signed up for a dating app to pursue new love. Not nearly as entertaining or engaging as a travelogue across Italy, India, and Bali, right? If we simply followed this character on her errands around the neighborhood, we wouldn't be getting a very juicy promise of the premise.

Ideally, you've come up with a good novel idea that will showcase an exciting sequence of events, or lived a series of interesting experiences that can become a memoir. Show these off and have fun! Figure the theme out, then use it as your North Star while drafting and revising. It's actually quite easy to boil down the essence of a story, as long as you've arrived at that clarity in your own mind first. This is especially relevant when it comes to deeper issues of character sense of self, objective, and need, all of which we'll explore in Part 2 of this guide.

Let's pivot to some From the Shelves excerpts, which will show how interiority is used to convey the theme and premise. It's quite astounding how easily these books can be characterized by their essences, often in small moments that are pulled straight from the pages.

First, I'll take a bird's-eye view of external premise and theme examples. Next, we'll explore some themes related to character relationships. Finally, I'll flow into internal premise and theme, which have more to do with the character journeys embedded within the stories, and which really anchor the protagonist-reader relationship.

I especially love starting this guide with theme and premise excerpts, since this also lets me overview some of the books we'll end up discussing in depth. Here, we'll also find our first taste of true interiority and finally make this theoretical tool feel more concrete.

External Premise and Theme

Let's kick off with an excerpt from *Within These Wicked Walls* by Lauren Blackwood, a young adult fantasy that's also a fairly well-disguised *Jane Eyre* retelling. Protagonist Andi is a "debterra," a kind of exorcist skilled in resolving demonic possessions. She shows up to a haunted mansion, desperate for work, and thinks:

> Eventually I learned that the world was scarier than anything
> the Evil Eye could manifest.[a]

Andi is a loner who's been abandoned by her birth parents and father-figure mentor. She's forced to make her way in the world alone. It's no surprise that she finds facing reality more challenging than battling supernatural forces.

The Vaster Wilds by Lauren Groff is a fascinating literary novel that's basically *all* interiority, as we primarily see the untouched North American wilderness from the perspective of a teenage girl. Lamentations was brought over to the colonies as a servant, but soon escapes to live life on her own terms. Her experience of the woods—and her encounters with animals, trees, and the occasional human—shapes the entire narrative, which is also interspersed with flashbacks to her old life. While Lamentations is a teenager, this is very much a novel for adult readers, rather than a story for the YA market. The book can basically be summed up with the following thematic statement:

The wilderness had so moved upon her that she would never be young again.[b]

While it's generally unusual for a teenager to take this position of future nostalgia,[2] Lamentations has nothing but time to think. Each day of her existence is so precarious that it adds urgency to her thematic position.

We'll continue with the adult thriller *All the Dangerous Things* by Stacey Willingham. The main character, Isabelle, is left reeling after, Mason, her baby, is stolen from his crib in the night. She hasn't stopped campaigning for his return and, in the process, becomes something of a curiosity on the true crime conference circuit. This is her observation about the world in which she finds herself:

> I've experienced firsthand the sick fascination people have with other people's pain.… As if they could possibly know what they'd do in my shoes. How they would feel.[c]

The judgments leveled at Isabelle—in public, in private, and those she reserves for herself—play a key thematic role in this book. Isabelle feels judged, maybe even freakish, and like she can't exist among regular people anymore. She blows off steam by villainizing her perceived audience. This interiority hints that she resents them, but needs them, too.

Interiority Insight: You can show how a character sees themselves in the way they project their own feelings onto others. How they believe they're viewed also demonstrates their inner sense of self.

The world of the uber-rich is the backdrop for adult literary novel *The Glass Hotel* by Emily St. John Mandel. In it, multiple POV characters have various relationships to money. First, there's Vincent, who comes

---

2. Extrapolating an imagined future while already feeling bittersweet about the recent past or present.

from humble beginnings and starts dating hedge fund manager, Jonathan Alkaitis. There's also Alkaitis himself, who is actually running a Ponzi scheme that collapses in spectacular fashion and lands him in prison.

In these excerpts, we will hear from both characters and see how their yearning for money has defined their lives. In our first excerpt, Vincent marvels at finding herself in the "Kingdom of Money," as she calls it, and resolves to stay there, even though she'll have to settle for a trans-actional existence (as we'll see later in Chapter 13):

> What kept her in the kingdom was the previously unimaginable condition of not having to think about money, because that's what money gives you: the freedom to stop thinking about money.[d]

Interiority Insight: Sometimes interiority reveals a character's wishful thinking, but that's all it is. Here, Vincent claims "freedom" from considering money, but her hyper-vigilance about it shows that money still keeps her in its thrall.

On the other hand, Jonathan has now escaped the Kingdom of Money, but not by choice. He has lost his fortune and is incarcerated, though he's actually finding it ... quite soothing:

> In the outside world, he used to lie awake at night worrying about being sent to prison, but he sleeps fairly well here, between head counts. There is exquisite lightness in waking each morning with the knowledge that the worst has already happened.[e]

Various tensions surrounding the theme of money—what it's like to make it, keep it, and lose it—are central to this book.

Similar themes appear is the adult novel *The Guest* by Emma Cline, though the premise is different. This story actually features a character who devolves, rather than evolving. Alex goes from limited self-awareness into almost total delusion, as we'll see in Chapter 11. After escaping her pathetic city life, she ends up living in a wealthy man's Hamptons mansion for the summer.

When she alienates Simon and he kicks her out, she decides that she just has to bide her time for a week before making her sparkling return and reclaiming her borrowed life. Meanwhile, she unironically looks down on people who flee the city for a quick trip to the Hamptons, seemingly unaware that she may as well be speaking into a mirror:

> They would leave here Monday night, imagining they had
> gotten close to something, had some rarefied experience.[f]

It's exactly this rarefied experience that Alex covets, but the irony is for the reader to appreciate, as she almost never reaches the levels of extrapolation or subsumation, at least not in any truly insightful way.

Interiority Insight: Notice that characters *lie*! Either willfully, by omission, or because they haven't yet gone on their own growth journeys. What's your protagonist's relationship to the theme initially? At the midpoint? Toward the end? Is it always straightforward and, most importantly, honest?

In another example of how the story world informs character and theme, we'll see Felicity declare her deepest desires in the adult fantasy novel *The Fair Folk* by Su Bristow. While Felicity's journey stretches from childhood into her twenties, this book is not what I'd call middle grade or young adult. It's a coming-of-age story, but for older audiences, similar to *The Vaster Wilds*, discussed earlier.

In *The Fair Folk*, Felicity discovers fairies in the woods behind her house and is immediately drawn to them because of her own loneliness. They seize upon this and snare her in their web. As is common with fae stories, this "kindness" has consequences. In this thematic excerpt, Felicity is fully under their spell, and their charms are working as intended. Shortly after she returns from the woods, she looks down at a treat that her mother has given her:

I have feasted with the fairies, I thought. *You can give me nothing that I want.*[g]

Earthly pleasures seem to have lost their appeal, but as with all "too good to be true" things, Felicity will face a very difficult choice once the fairies demand repayment for their gifts. (Notice that this instance of interiority features italicized verbatim thought as well as a "thought" tag, demonstrating some formatting options.)

Interiority Insight: As we'll see throughout this guide, a character's level of self-awareness varies wildly and can also shift over time, especially if they have a more pronounced growth arc, as demonstrated in Chapter 11.

In a similar example of a protagonist grappling with fairy magic, Miryem is a teenage girl who has taken over her family's debt collection business in the young adult historical fantasy novel, *Spinning Silver* by Naomi Novik. Her village sits on the edge of a wood, where a cruel fairy king, the Staryk, is encroaching on the people and crops with a never-ending winter. When he discovers that she can magically turn silver coins into gold, he propositions her to help him build his wealth. Even in this short description, Miryem seems to intuit that the task comes with strings attached:

He held another purse out to me, clinking like chains.[h]

As she's roped deeper—first, into the world of recouping debts (a man's job in this time and place), then into working for the Staryk—Miryem continues to chafe against the restrictions placed on her as a young girl in a patriarchal society. She also has this to say, which typifies the experience of many female characters:

What I wanted didn't matter. [i]

Interiority Insight: As we'll see in Chapter 10, on worldview, characters can use interiority to agree or disagree with the status quo.

Fantasy and science-fiction stories are obviously world-building heavy, but historical novels are also deeply concerned with their story worlds.

The Nightingale is a sweeping World War II epic adult novel by Kristin Hannah that's framed by present-day narration. Two sisters are forced to undergo great risk and transformation to survive the war. Vianne's husband is shipped off to the front and she must host Nazi officers in her home. Isabelle joins the resistance, escorting downed British airmen through the mountains to Spain. The war is a character in and of itself, especially as described in this premise statement:

> There was no opponent for [Vianne] to fight, just loss on both sides.[j]

And this one, about the kinds of decisions available to the women:

> Bad choices. That was all there were anymore.[k]

Not only does the war change these characters, it also changes the trajectories of their lives. Similar to Miryem in *Spinning Silver*, above, the protagonists of *The Nightingale* aren't in command of their own destinies. As a result, they have to really clarify what their values and boundaries are, and who they will become during (and after) the all-consuming war. Now, we're starting to explore how the social and cultural atmosphere of the story affects character wants, needs, and sense of self.

Zooming back to the modern world, let's look at the adult upmarket novel *Amazing Grace Adams* by Fran Littlewood. Grace, the titular character, is having a bit of a ... breakdown. It's triggered by backstory that's withheld for most of the plot, as we'll see in Chapter 5. She's also presently estranged from her husband and teen daughter. It's a midlife crisis bound between two covers, and utterly relatable to its intended audience.

The story starts with Grace leaving her car parked in the middle of the road. In fact, the main stakes of the plot involve her getting her daughter a birthday cake, even though she's been asked not to come to the party. Unlike the life-or-death situations in *The Nightingale*, this sounds entirely inconsequential. But Grace's interiority manages to make this errand into a big deal. (Stakes don't have to life-or-death, as we'll see in Chapter 17.)

Grace has been following the rules her entire life, until she realizes (in a pivotal scene excerpted in Chapter 17 as well) that maybe she … doesn't have to. Here's that moment:

> Such potency in a simple act. Quietly, calmly, she has taken the bolt cutters to social convention. She has set herself free.[1]

This thematic statement invites the reader to daydream about rebelling against their own invisible prisons of social convention, which is exactly the kind of subversive spark that upmarket book club fiction can offer.

Interiority Insight: Interiority can be used to showcase how theme ties into the promise of the premise, too.

Let's stick with examples of protagonists rejecting prevailing cultural norms. Anna, the main character in the adult novel *Aesthetica* by Allie Rowbottom, is hung over from the high of being a social media influencer. During her dubious career, she rigorously edited her looks with cosmetic surgery. Now, washed out and approaching middle age, she's about to undergo a revolutionary (fictional) procedure, called Aesthetica, which will reverse all of her nips and tucks, restoring her true, age-appropriate appearance. Several timelines are woven together, interspersing scenes from her past with the present-moment run-up to the surgery.

Though this might read as justification to some, Anna is always very clear that she *chose* her path. She grew up feeling powerless and started creating different versions of herself as a way of taking back control:

For women, so often robbed of agency … it was empowering to decide which version I preferred.[m]

She also recalls her first bikini wax, which started her down the path of altering her image:

My first wax, first act of self-care, self-directed violence.[n]

Whether readers agree with Anna or not, her struggle with herself in the current beauty paradigm epitomizes the novel.

Interiority Insight: Specificity in character development can be polarizing—and engaging. Vagueness (Everyman Syndrome) is neither.

A similar literary adult novel, *Tell Me I'm an Artist* by Chelsea Martin, features Joey, a young woman discovering herself in art school. This is her interpretation of contemporary culture:

It's funny that the world just keeps going. Seems impossible that there hasn't been a moment yet where humanity is collectively like, Can we pause for a sec and reassess what we are doing here? Cuz something feels off.[o]

Much of the story grapples with whether it's selfish to make art, what being an artist means, and how art fits into daily life.

Finally, there's Cassie, in the adult literary novel *Ripe* by Sarah Rose Etter. She experiences a lot of the same conflicts as Anna and Joey do, especially when it comes to late-stage capitalism culture. She's an anonymous tech worker in Silicon Valley and becoming aware of the yawning gap between expectation and reality:

Isn't that always the way adult life begins? You think you'll become something different, something new.[p]

Cassie feels tricked into falling for a coming-of-age self-actualization fantasy. She wonders why nobody warned her, or maybe she thought she would be the exception, which is a bit of magical thinking.

Magical Thinking: A character's tendency to engage in some light denial, which we'll explore in Chapter 9. This is what-if wish fulfillment. A protagonist with magical thinking impulses may not actually believe their imagined situation is true, or even possible, but they often use this thought experiment to reveal their hopes, dreams, or regrets.

A second thematic interiority excerpt from *Ripe* typifies Cassie's reluctance to unplug and feel her feelings, which represents a battle between self-awareness and self-medication via today's digital distractions:

Sober, with the screens tucked away, a great ache surfaces. In the awful stillness, I can hear the deafening river of melancholy roaring through the dark red cave of my heart.[q]

So far, a lot of these thematic statements have dealt with what it's like to exist in various story worlds, whether fantastical, historical, or contemporary. A similar sense of ennui is expressed by Adrian, the male romantic lead in adult romance *Guy's Girl* by Emma Noyes:

Adrian wonders if every twentysomething feels the way he does. Untethered. Searching for a home.[r]

It's fascinating how many common threads I found while collecting From the Shelves theme and premise examples. This goes to reinforce the notion that there are only so many different ideas to explore, but endless executions available. Books with the same theme (in principle) might never be compared to one another (in practice). Ideas are a dime a dozen,[3] but *your specific book-length execution of an idea* is your USP.

---

3. This is a spicy take indeed, but for more on this line of thinking, check out my book,

As we dive deeper into examples of thematic interiority that address the self, going from external to internal, let's zoom in on relationships —the smaller environments that impact a protagonist's identity. After all, these are the bubbles in which characters exist, by birth or choice, and they say a lot about who someone is and what they experience in their day-to-day lives.

Relationship Premise and Theme

Most novels and memoirs are character, plot, and world stories, but they're also relationship stories. It is inherently human to be in relationships with others—or to crave those connections, if a protagonist is missing them.

Relationships with nuclear family, chosen family, friends, enemies, and romantic interests can lift characters and people to the heights of the human experience or plunge them into the depths of despair. Therefore it's no surprise that a novel or memoir's theme can involve these complicated entanglements. (We'll dive deeper into the complexities of interiority as it's used to explore secondary characters and relationship dynamics in Chapter 12 and Chapter 13, respectively.)

Two quotes from two different books provide an eerily similar take on romantic love. In one, from adult literary novel *Milk Fed* by Melissa Broder, the loss of identity that can happen within a relationship is seen as desirable. Rachel, the protagonist, has just broken up with Miriam, her situationship and first female lover. Here, she's reflecting on other losses she's experienced (we will hear more about Rachel's longing for her mother in Chapter 5):

> I wanted to lose the edges of myself and blend with a woman, enter the amniotic sac and melt away. I wanted a love that was bottomless, unconditional, with zero repercussions.[5]

Of course, a relationship like the one described is an impossible fantasy, but this sets Rachel up to grow and deepen her understanding of life and self.

Interiority Insight: Interiority can be used as a time capsule, freezing certain wants, thoughts, and feelings in one amber bead that's strung next to others into a growth arc.

Meanwhile, in adult literary novel *Wellness* by Nathan Hill, Elizabeth is dealing with a failing marriage. She works as a sociology researcher, and here's how her mentor and boss, Dr. Sandborne, talks about love:

"The boundaries of the self ooze toward [the partner], like an amoeba.... You glom on to [a partner] and surround them and subsume them, until ... you pull [them] within the conceptual borders of your own self. And the subjective experience of this process, the delusion the mind serves up to explain it, this is what we've given the name 'love.'"[t]

That's definitely one way to look at it! Notice that there's no interiority in this excerpt, since Dr. Sandborne's worldview is voiced in dialogue, but this moment is a great example of a "Theme Stated" beat which comes from a secondary character.

Notice how interesting it is that Rachel craves exactly this kind of merging with a partner, while Dr. Sandborne seems to judge it as human folly. Both novels have all-consuming relationships at their cores, so these are relevant thematic meditations.

Remember Felicity from *The Fair Folk*, who became enchanted by vindictive fairies to the point that everything in the real world lost its appeal? Well, she eventually goes to Cambridge University and falls in love with Sebastian, a handsome aspiring actor. As she makes her own way in the world, she realizes that non-magical things can be powerful, too. For the first time, she imagines letting her childish forest games go:

This was grown up magic. This was real.[u]

With every high comes a crash, especially in fiction and memoir love stories. Whether you're a Rachel or a Dr. Sandborne, you can't ignore the fact that human bonds involve potential conflict.

In the adult romance *Before I Let Go* by Kennedy Ryan, we meet Josiah and Yasmen, divorced spouses and co-parents who still work together. They have walled up their respective hearts but can't seem to fully give up on one another. Yasmen hurt Josiah deeply, and he gets especially defensive as expresses his position:

> Love and life occur just beyond the reach of our control. There is only one letter of difference between love and lose, and somewhere along the way, for me they became synonymous.... I started measuring how much I loved people in terms of how much it would hurt to lose them.[v]

Let's go back to Cassie from *Ripe*, whose disillusionment we saw in the previous section. She tries to fill the void by getting involved with a chef who has a girlfriend. This is probably not the best idea if she craves lasting happiness, but she admits:

> My mind can make love out of anything, even the smallest of shards.[w]

Similarly, Ginny, the female romantic lead from *Guy's Girl*, has kept her group of male friends at arm's length. She's caught in the swirl of an eating disorder amid a job transition and recognizes that she tends to neglect herself whenever she gets involved with someone else:

> By the time she finishes distributing every ounce of love within her, she has none left for herself.[x]

Interiority Insight: The interesting interiority angles in these thematic statements reveal that a character's philosophy about relationships can also reflect how they feel about themselves and life in general. Many bigger-picture implications can be conveyed by a thematic statement.

But before we get too cynical, let's acknowledge that there are also great love relationships in literature. For positive examples of love themes, specifically, let's look to the aptly named adult romcom *Romantic Comedy* by Curtis Sittenfeld, in which awkward comedy writer protagonist, Sally, finally consummates an unlikely relationship. Here, she waxes poetic about what it would mean to find love with romantic lead Noah:

> It would be the best thing that had ever happened to me, and if this was all I ever got, I'd never stop wanting more of it.[y]

Interiority Insight: Interiority can leverage hyperbole to make a point and direct reader attention to character wants and needs.

Let's leave the world of romantic love behind and explore how relationships with other characters can impact a protagonist's worldview and sense of self, too.

Next, we'll meet June, the self-aware but also incredibly evasive and delusional narrator of upmarket adult novel *Yellowface* by R.F. Kuang. June is a failed writer who hides behind an obsession with Athena Liu, a former friend and successful "hot young thing" on the New York literary scene. June pretty much defines her entire self unfavorably in comparison to Athena. Early on, she gets a golden opportunity when Athena dies and leaves behind an unfinished manuscript. (June was with her and says it was an accident but readers must take her word for it. As you'll learn, she's not very reliable.)

Boldly, she decides to pass the book off as her own and shoot into the literary stratosphere that Athena enjoyed, even though Athena is AAPI and writing Asian characters, and June is white.[4] Early in the story, June makes this thematic statement, which actually reveals more about her than the other anonymous writers she's referring to:

---

4. See Chapter 21 for more on the hot topic of writing outside your own lived experience.

I've found that jealousy, to writers, feels more like fear.[z]

Interiority Insight: Just because a character is capable of deep insight doesn't mean they'll use it to grow and change.

Relationships also introduce the concept of power dynamics, which are ideally present in every interpersonal bond. If two characters are perfectly matched, with no inequalities of status or perceived value between them, there is less room for tension. Imagine if June was as successful as Athena, and perfectly at peace with herself in *Yellowface*. There'd be no story.

In a similar vein, Joey from *Tell Me I'm an Artist* grapples with her own difficult family dynamics—a drug addict sister and a mother who constantly guilts and shames her for going off to college and getting a frivolous[5] art degree. Joey is caught between her malleable present and the fixed past:

Making art is my way of tricking myself into believing that the past is something I can continue shaping.[aa]

Yet for all the pain and suffering involved in relationships, humans and characters persist in cultivating connections. We've already heard from Vianne in *The Nightingale*, now let's hear from her sister, Isabelle, as she thinks of the distance between her and their father. She characterizes their bond as:

Unbearable but unbreakable.[bb]

For our penultimate example of relationship-based thematic statements, let's look to adult thriller *The New House* by Tess Stimson,[6] which is full of broken people who have come together over an

---

5. I don't necessarily espouse this view, but many people do, including this mother character.
6. This book was originally published in the U.K., so you'll notice some British English spelling in its excerpts.

attempted real estate transaction. We'll learn more about Millie's tragic backstory in Chapter 5, but it involves sneaking out of bed to watch her father beat her mother. Here, she expresses why she did it:

> I needed to see: to remind myself what happened when you ceded your power to a man.[cc]

Interiority Insight: Power dynamics tend to generate significant tension, especially if the character feels powerless. More on this in Chapter 13.

In a different universe entirely, the character of Sona, from the young adult science fiction novel, *Gearbreakers* by Zoe Hana Mikuta, is an elite Windup pilot, driving giant mechanicals. Even though she's already one of the top recruits, she knows that she must constantly assert herself, especially when it comes time to enact her real plan and destroy the authoritarian regime from within. She expresses her strategy here:

> Power comes from finishing fights, not starting them.[dd]

Whether they're full of love or hate, or both, relationships are key thematic components in many stories. Sometimes the entire backbone of a novel or memoir is a marriage, as in *Wellness* and *Before I Let Go*, a friendship, as in *Yellowface*, or an upbringing, as in *The Fair Folk*.

Even more foundational, though, is the main POV character's essential relationship to their innermost sense of self. I'll round out this chapter with excerpts of thematic statements that pertain to the protagonist's core identity.

Internal Premise and Theme

Let's dive into premise and theme as they apply to a character's inner self. An uncertain sense of identity is a sticking point for Roman, one of the love interests in the young adult romantasy *Divine Rivals* by Rebecca Ross. Roman is a privileged upper-crust boy who's been handed a cushy newspaper job and an arranged marriage. His parents don't care what he wants (which happens to be our other romantic lead, Iris). At first, he merely wonders whether he can possibly stand up for himself, as his sense of identity is wrapped up in wanting to please his family:

> How do you make your life your own and not feel guilt over it?[ee]

After the midpoint, he gains perspective and is much bolder with his wants and needs. He also discards the notion of keep his feelings under wraps, having become emboldened when Iris accepts him for who he is. His rejection of an emotionally diminished but socially acceptable life is key to his growth arc.

Sometimes identity-specific themes are less pointed and even less decisive. That's okay, too. We've already met Rachel from *Milk Fed*, who wishes to merge with the divine feminine. Her counterpart in Melissa Broder's next adult literary novel, *Death Valley*, is an unnamed woman who's so neurotic that she doesn't even know *how* to exist:

> But how do you just experience things?[ff]

Interiority Insight: Don't be afraid of existentialism. Theme can sometimes be nebulous. You'll need to ground these thoughts in scene, action, and plot, though, to keep them from floating away into complete abstraction.

Themes can be presented at any point in a story, and they're commonly marked during big character transitions. It's important to note that a protagonist doesn't *have* to be lost to think about theme, and they don't need to be on a major growth arc to express thematic development, either. Indeed, our innermost identity can be a mutable thing, and thoughts about theme can pop up whenever.

Hannah, from adult thriller *The It Girl* by Ruth Ware, finds herself at Oxford, feeling like an ugly duckling compared to her glamorous heiress roommate, April. With some measure of self-awareness, yet a dose of naïve hope, Hannah defines her objective as she begins her college career:

> She, Hannah, could reinvent herself here.[gg]

On the other hand, sometimes a character knows exactly who they are, even if that personality isn't ideal or socially acceptable. That's Millie, the surgeon from *The New House* who can't bear to cede power, as expressed in the previous section. The thematic resonance of good versus evil is especially relevant in any kind of mystery, thriller, and suspense story. With that in mind, Millie reflects on her sense of self here:

> Usually I keep my darker angel on a very short tether ... she holds herself in check and agrees not to set my world on fire.... I never lose my temper. But sometimes I choose to unleash it.[hh]

Interiority Insight: Theme often lives at the intersection of character, plot, and premise, tinged with a nod to genre expectations, if applicable.

As you can see, theme and premise are threaded through these story worlds, character relationships, and moments of protagonist self-interpretation. Up next, I'll finish out Part 1 by tracking how premise and theme translate into point of view and plot.

4

POINT OF VIEW AND PLOT

Interiority is inherently tied to the concept of point of view. If you've been intuitively feeling your way around POV in your writing without making conscious choices, this could be a mistake. The more intentional your use of point of view, the clearer your storytelling. Within the confines of perspective, you'll find great control and order. Sometimes, creative constraints actually illuminate a clear path forward. Point of view is one such craft element. I'll also briefly mention tense in this chapter, because it's often discussed in the same breath as POV.

Then I'll dig into what makes a compelling plot, with a specific focus on finding opportunities for character development. I'll also explore how interiority operates alongside the events of the story themselves. Instead of offering a robust plotting and outlining framework, I'll concentrate primarily on seven major tentpole moments that are found in many novels and memoirs. Plot involves a lot of moving parts. While this isn't a point of view guide, or a structure framework, I want us to be aligned about how these elements inform character and vice versa. It's important to note that this is largely a theory chapter, without excerpts, as big story moments often need a lot of context and explanation.

Point of View

Since point of view is, in essence, the perspective through which story is told, it's incredibly relevant to our study of interiority. As discussed in Chapter 1, all interiority is biased—meaning it's filtered through the lens of character, often at the levels of interpretation, extrapolation, and subsumation. You should also, practically speaking, think about POV early because it's an important decision that you must make, the sooner, the better. Sure, it's possible to revise POV after a manuscript is finished, but trust me, it's a huge pain in the you-know-what.[1]

Point of View: If your novel is a movie, the POV is the camera lens that's recording the action, conveying a sense of narrative distance that separates the reader from the story. Is the audience inside a primary character's head, as close as possible ("first person")? Is the camera zoomed out a bit, but with access to one character's inner life ("close third person" or "third-person limited")? Or does the camera zoom around above the action, able to see and know all ("omniscient")? Multiple POV, where different sections or chapters are told from distinct perspectives (with each character written in either first or third) is also an option. There are other choices, which tend to be more niche, like the "you" perspective ("second-person direct address"), that's used in our From the Shelves adult thriller novel *You* by Caroline Kepnes (alongside first-person for the narrator, Joe). If you ever go into or suppose the experience of multiple characters at once, like a group of kids reacting to an assembly, this is "joint" or "fourth" point of view, also called the "first- or third-person plural." It's rarely used for the entirety of a novel (this can also be said for second-person POV), because it's unlikely a group of characters is feeling and thinking the same exact thing simultaneously. But joint POV can sometimes help to flesh out scenes where a lot of people need to offer a perspective. *Brutes* by Dizz Tate, one of our adult literary From the Shelves

---

1. If you find yourself considering a change, take your first chapter and rewrite it from the new point of view. Read the two attempts side by side. It's always better to do a test run before you commit to overhauling an entire draft on a whim.

novels, uses the joint POV of several teen girls for part of the narrative. The overwhelming preference, though, is to inhabit a distinct point of view per scene or chapter. Each POV choice also has storytelling benefits and limitations to consider.

This definition brings up a few related craft concepts.

Narrative Distance: Also sometimes called "psychic distance." Compare the view from inside your specific brain to the perspective that a deity might have, floating above their charges and observing. The "narrative distance" is much closer to the action in the first instance than it is in the second, especially if the deity doesn't have access to individual people's interiority. The current novel and memoir market prefers closer narrative distance, while the omniscient point of view, which offers greater distance, is considered more outdated or specialized. It's important to know that you can always close the narrative distance gap and access your characters on a deeper level with interiority. In fact, that's what this tool is for! Writers using third person close or omniscient might find they need to work harder to overcome narrative distance and stay attuned to their point of view characters' experiences.

Breaking the Fourth Wall: A character or narrator seeming to speak directly to the audience. You'll see an example of June, from *Yellowface*, addressing the reader in Chapter 9. It's important to note that second-person direct address can be used occasionally without the entire story being in the second person, like *You* is. As a point of contrast, interiority shows how characters make observations or generalizations to themselves in private without them consciously speaking to the reader.

Let's discuss your generally available point-of-view options in more detail. The first-person POV is the preferred perspective for certain categories, like children's books and some upmarket. This might make first person appealing, sure, but be careful, because some agents and publishers claim first-person POV exhaustion. The obvious benefit is that readers get immediate access to your character with very little narrative distance, which engenders closeness and connection. It can also help writers get into their protagonist's mindset and experiences more easily. There are, however, some downsides.

For example, if dry voice is a known struggle of yours, watch out (and see Chapter 19). First-person POV clashes with formal or distant voice and tends to make the writing style feel disjointed and awkward. You're also locked into your character's perspective in first, with no way to separate the narrative from a protagonist's experience. If you need to reveal information to the reader but not the character—say in a thriller or mystery novel—you're out of luck. Your character is your camera, and they can't record anything they're not privy to.

First person is the expected point of view for memoir since you're writing as yourself and sharing your deep experiences, realizations, and reflections. It's generally unusual to find third person close in a memoir, like an attempt to go into a family member's perspective, for example. The cast of other characters is filtered through the memoirist's perspective, complete with the point-of-view character's impressions, assumptions, and judgments (see Chapter 12 for more).

Close-third POV is also very popular, especially in genre and literary fiction, and a lot of agents and publishers are actively seeking well-executed examples. This means that the camera follows your protagonist closely but can also break away and "zoom out" onto other action. We're observing the protagonist "outside in" instead of "inside out" (as in first person). Every time you go into the third person, you have to work harder to grant the reader access to your POV character and close the narrative distance. There's an inherent divide between the "I" (first) and the "she," "he," or "they" (third) perspective, and this must be overcome. The work of interiority becomes all the more important in third person. You'll see beautiful examples throughout this guide.

Omniscient third is quite difficult to do and requires substantial focus and intentionality. Certain categories—like high fantasy, hard sci-fi, some thriller, and literary fiction—lend themselves well to this narrative choice. In its wildest form, this POV allows the camera to wander around in the action, potentially diving into any character perspective that the writer sees fit. One of the benefits of omniscient is the ability to create a really strong narrative voice, a writing style that almost becomes a separate character in and of itself. (We'll see examples of authorial intrusion in Chapter 10, with excerpts from the adult upmarket novel *Anxious People* by Fredrik Backman.)

Unfortunately, omniscient POV is very difficult to do *well*, so a lot of agents and publishers don't actively seek it. You can certainly try this technique, but your choices should be in harmony with the requirements of each scene. Don't float into a nearby chipmunk's head just because you can. One upside of omniscient, which is also possible with multiple POVs, is that you can reveal important information to readers and certain characters but exclude others.

In collecting our From the Shelves excerpts, I tried to find compelling examples of all kinds of POVs. For an in-depth look at this topic, check out *Writing the Intimate Character* by Jordan Rosenfeld. It contains many more point of view exercises and considerations than this guide can offer.

Multiple Point of View Narrative Options

Some writers don't think point of view is all that important because they're working with a single protagonist. Their decision is generally very simple: first or third. But what if your narrative structure is shaping up to be more ambitious,[2] and you want to do this whole "writing a book" thing on hard mode?

Well, you can always experiment with more than one chronology and multiple point-of-view protagonists. For example, we might catch chapters from your antagonist or killer's perspective in a fantasy or thriller. Or you'll get into the heads of many family members in an

---

2. Single-POV stories are not inherently less ambitious, though!

intergenerational story, which happens in the adult literary novel *Sing, Unburied, Sing* by Jesmyn Ward.

If advanced narrative technique is calling you, know that the market very much prefers a multiple-POV project with a more organized approach. This can mean entire sections or, more commonly, chapters told in either first or third person as you follow various characters around. The divide between POVs is neat and orderly, and the reader never feels confused, unless that's your intended effect.[3]

The benefit of multiple POVs and chronologies is that you can play with different styles of storytelling and do a lot of neat plot tricks, like ending on a cliffhanger in one character's POV, then zooming away to unrelated action, all while keeping both threads taut with various open loops and curiosity hooks working simultaneously.

But these techniques have to be executed *well*. That means I should be able to flip your multiple-POV narrative to a random page and know exactly whose head I'm in. If all of your "different" voices sound the same, an agent or publisher has a very easy reason to pass.

Curiosity Hooks: Small mysteries or questions that can also be called "open loops" and will mostly be resolved over the course of the plot. The purpose is to keep readers curious, unsettled, or unsatisfied (in this case, a good thing!). When an outstanding question is answered, we "close the loop." Expert writers never stop opening new loops or planting hooks (especially in a series idea) so there's always at least one dangling carrot enticing readers or grabbing audiences.

How do you know if advanced narrative techniques are for you? Well, if your story is coming across as quite flat with one protagonist, and

---

3. I discourage you from making readers disoriented unless it's done for a very specific purpose (the character is coming to after blacking out, are on drugs or otherwise compromised, etc.). Clarity is actually a very desirable quality that helps readers connect to your storytelling. The plot can mislead, but this must be orchestrated intentionally, meaning the writer should always be in control of their story's impact.

there are other characters you want to explore, perhaps those who have their own subplots or complications, consider adding their points of view. You don't have to lock yourself into any set pattern, either. You can have a primary protagonist, who might use first-person POV, but also give point-of-view access to people from their friend group, who all have their own secondary character arcs. They chime in every few chapters with close-third perspective. You are literally only limited by your imagination here.

One common question I get from writers working with multiple POVs is: How do I choose which character "owns" the perspective in a particular moment? Easy. Consider who has the most dynamic emotional experience in the scene at hand, who stands to gain or lose the most, who's doggedly pursuing an objective or need, or who's poised at a big turning point—internally, externally, or both. They should probably be your main perspective.

Something called "head-hopping" tends to happen if you give multiple characters point-of-view access in one scene without delineating between POVs with section or chapter breaks, and this can become needlessly complicated. I strongly recommend structurally separating each perspective, especially if you're trying multiple points of view for the first time. This will also allow you to close the narrative distance on your point-of-view character in that particular section and sink more deeply into their experience. If you're constrained to one protagonist's POV at a time, you are more likely to explore it fully.

If every writer who comes to me for editorial services could consider this information before drafting, I would pre-empt about 15% of the feedback I give on a daily basis. Point-of-view issues are everywhere, especially head-hopping and gaping narrative distance that develops from a lack of interiority. That's, in part, why this guide exists.

A word of caution: If you have multiple POV characters who are present for an event, you don't want to show the same scene from each perspective. Sure, each individual character might be experiencing something new, but readers have seen the given moment play out before. Whenever you repeat an event or a piece of information, remember what audiences already know. Trust them to retain what they've learned. Instead of repeating, add layers, nuance, data, or make fresh meaning from the plot.

Should you decide to replay a scene readers have already witnessed in another POV, you can always show new information only available in the relevant viewpoint, like the butler slipping poison into the wineglass. The earl missed it, to his peril, but the maid saw it and, significantly, didn't say anything.

If you want to see your options for multiple POVs and explore various narrative structures that take advantage of bringing more than one perspective or timeline to the table, check out the following From the Shelves titles: *The New House* by Tess Stimson, *Spinning Silver* by Naomi Novik, *Before I Let Go* by Kennedy Ryan, *Wellness* by Nathan Hill, *Lovecraft Country* by Matt Ruff, *The Villa* by Rachel Hawkins, *Everyone Here Is Lying* by Shari Lapena, *Brutes* by Dizz Tate, *Sing, Unburied, Sing* by Jesmyn Ward, and *Americanah* by Chimamanda Ngozi Adichie.

Working With Tense

Tense is another decision that writers have to make for each project, but your options are very straightforward: past or present. (Future tense exists but isn't usually used for an entire project.) Some writers gravitate to one or the other tense naturally, while some prefer to match tense to the character or plot at hand. This decision is a bit less *in-tense*[4] than your selection of POV. But if you make the wrong call here, it's even more of a pain in the you-know-what to change the tense of every sentence in an 80,000-word manuscript. If you're at all on the fence, try the advice in the POV section: Write the first chapter in past tense, then write it in present tense. Read them both aloud. Which flows and sounds better to your ear?

Tense: Your two options are past tense ("I ran") and present tense ("I run"). Both can be used across all available POVs. Present tense tends to bring immediacy and tension to the narrative, while past

---

4. Har har har. Wait until you see my jokes about stakes!

tense can feel more contemplative or even-keel, and is considered the classic choice.

When you consider which tense to use, think about how well it might play with the POV you've chosen. You have the in-your-face immediacy of first-person present tense, and the more removed third-person past tense. What kind of effect are you trying to achieve? What does your audience expect? Know that each tense has its pitfalls. First-person present tense can be exhausting, especially when paired with a brisk plot. When combined with an especially slow or nonexistent plot, it can create an odd dissonance. Present tense can also generate a flurry of "-ing" verbs, or present participles, which can become grating to read.

Past tense can have its own issues. When you go further into past action in past tense via a flashback, for example, you might fall into the dreaded past-perfect verb trap, or the "had had." This does awful things for voice, and I suggest being very clear in your chronological transitions, then continuing in normal past tense, as usual, for the flashback material itself.

No matter what you choose, keep it consistent. Shifting tense is perhaps one of the sneakiest errors I see in client manuscripts. Whether a writer started in one tense and changed it halfway through, or their sentences and paragraphs veer from one tense to another without much rhyme or reason, these projects are easy to reject in the slush pile.

POV and Tense By the Numbers

If you're curious about these broad storytelling concepts as they appear in our From the Shelves excerpts, here are the POV breakdowns:

- First person POV: 28 out of 56, or 50%
- Third person POV: 21 out of 56, or 37.5%
- Mix of third and first person POV (including occasional chapters in second and fourth): 7 out of 56, or 12.5%
- Of the above, instances of multiple POVs: 26 out of 56, or 46.43%

As you can see, first and third person are pretty evenly split, and almost half of the books use multiple perspectives.

Here's a breakdown of tense:

- Past tense: 36 out of 56, or 64.29%
- Present tense: 20 out of 56, or 35.71%

It seems that past tense is preferred by the majority. It's important to note that YA and thriller stories are overwhelmingly represented within the present tense cohort.

Now that the "how" of your storytelling is decided, let's focus on the "what" you're including in your book. We've already talked about theme and premise, so let's turn our attention to plot.

Seeing the Plot Through a Character Lens

The rest of this chapter delves into what makes a compelling plot, from a character perspective, and how interiority is the mortar that holds its events together.

It's certainly possible to write a book full of character and voice without much action. But plot is such an integral part of the fiction and memoir reading experience—and an important draw for today's audience—that I'd challenge you to develop some big events and obstacles for your characters to experience, stumble on, and/or overcome. You'll also need to consider your story's ideal structure.

Structure: The *sequence* of plot events as they're presented to the reader.

The next two sections will focus on a story's opening, then seven tentpole moments or sequences that not only support a robust plot but offer great opportunities to challenge and activate your protagonist as they struggle to realize their full potential. The goal is to imagine an external story that is relevant to character, especially their inner struggle and growth trajectory, no matter your other genre or world-building choices.

Starting Your Story

The first few pages of a novel or memoir are often the most anxiety-provoking passages on any writer's to-do list. They are written and rewritten, workshopped and critiqued, and, though you might hate to hear it, often thrown out altogether and redone. Why? A lot is expected of the writer in the opening of a book-length project.

At the very beginning of a novel—and here, I'm talking about the first few *words*—there's a skewed power dynamic. The writer has all of the information, the reader has none. But the reader *wants* information. After all, how else are they supposed to plunge into the tale?

Unfortunately, the writer can't just shovel a bunch of data onto the page as if they're lecturing to a captive audience—simply because the audience isn't captive just yet. They may still be browsing in the bookstore or library and flipping to the first page of several options to see if anything catches their eye. If you start with an "info-dump" on the first page, odds are high your potential reader will put your offering down. (Odds are even higher that you're not in the bookstore or library in the first place, because an agent or publisher has passed regretfully on your static beginning.) Action and tension are all-important, and they facilitate that crucial initial audience connection. While the premise is, in and of itself, a hook, the burden to bear it out in action falls on your opening page, then chapter, then first act.

This is the most critical spot in the manuscript and your only job is to make your reader care. All of the superficial elements of communicating premise—like your query pitch, or the cover and marketing copy of a published book—are like the alluring nectar inside the Venus fly trap. They will deliver readers who are predisposed to enjoy your idea to the threshold of your story. It's then your manuscript's job to spring the trap. If you don't have an explosive opening planned, you can plant seeds and promise bigger conflict to come. All I ask is that you approach this challenge intentionally.

We close those glistening Venus flytrap jaws—while offering readers something to care about—in a number of ways. While this isn't a guide on first pages or chapters, I do recommend these best practices:

- Offer access to your main point-of-view protagonist right away, ideally as they're doing something relatable, interesting, or jarring (depending on your genre). Start in scene, with dialogue, action, and some smaller-scale tension. This will suck readers in;
- Suggest or express your theme in a covert way so readers know what—in the broadest possible terms—they'll be reading "about";
- Open some loops and embed some hooks, which can be as simple as: an intriguing envelope arriving with no postmark; the question of who the character should take to prom; or a reference to a past event that seems so dramatic that readers will immediately want the scoop. As long as this doesn't seem like it's being done cheaply, just to play on a reader's innate curiosity and string them along, it's a very compelling initial gambit; and
- Avoid using a prologue unless you absolutely need one. These can read as a high-stakes bait and switch, especially if the real the first chapter feels like a giant energetic comedown.

In case you aren't familiar with prologues, let's take a moment to define them.

Prologue: Short chapters that appear at the beginning of some story structures to either deliver backstory or flash forward to an exciting event that happens later in the plot. This teases readers with a curiosity hook, especially if it shows off a high-stakes moment selected from the sequence before the climax. Prologues are more common in certain genres, like fantasy, science-fiction, thriller, and adventure, and categories, like MG and YA. Agents and publishers tend to be very mixed on them, though, because they're often used to make the first few pages of a manuscript seem compelling before dropping tantalized readers into a slow or boring first chapter. If you suspect this is the case with your project, remove the prologue and add more action, scene, tension, conflict, and, of course, interiority to your actual chronological beginning.

To wrap some of the above ideas together, consider Donald Maass's idea of the "bridging conflict" from *Writing the Breakout Novel*.

Bridging Conflict: An initial source of tension that's introduced in the first chapter as a means of engaging readers right away. It doesn't necessarily have to hook into the larger external plot conflict that will end up driving the book after the inciting incident, but it should offer readers a glimpse into some inner tension that the character deals with throughout. There are multiple ways to showcase a character's thematic experience of self-doubt, for example. You don't have to dive right into a high-stakes test of the character's mettle in a pivotal plot point. For the bridging conflict, you can show them wanting to speak up in an important moment but chickening out.

I'd caution you against starting with level-ten conflict on the first page. The reader doesn't care about your character or story yet, so it's hard to sell life-or-death stakes immediately. If I'm reading about a random death in the paper, I feel sympathy about the tragedy, sure, but I'm not inclined to be immediately gutted. If an alien planet is in danger, but I just learned its name two sentences ago, same thing.

The bridging conflict can either be irrelevant to the larger plot, or the beginning of a much bigger and more consequential series of events. For example, preparing for an important job interview in the first chapter can be an isolated incident and just one demonstration of the character's search for purpose. Or the job can be an entry point into an elite cohort that the protagonist will spend the rest of the novel trying to join.

Even if you don't start your story with a big-bang event-based introduction to the project's main themes and ideas, you should know what
those are and express them overtly or covertly in the opening chapters.
As you plan your beginning, your character will ideally already be in
turmoil. Interiority is very helpful in conveying this. Even though your
opening introduces plot, which is happening outside your character,
you get to play with their thoughts about, expectations for, interpretations of, and reactions to the early events of your story. As we saw in
Chapter 3, you can also pull in thematic ideas to prepare readers for
what's to come.

For other tips on grabbing a reader right away with a manuscript opening, check out Les Edgerton's *Hooked*. But since this is primarily a character book, and interiority is a character-specific tool, let's move on to
other ways to make readers care. Conflict and tension serve this goal
nicely, especially when combined with plot.

Conflict: Any fiction and memoir event, character relationship,
inner struggle, or obstacle that translates to difficulty for the
protagonist. It can be internal or external, as small as a paper cut
and as large as the decision to take a dystopian society down from
within. Conflict often involves uncomfortable growth or pain, frustrated objectives, unmet needs, and, of course, physical pain or
harm that comes from external action. Conflict generally gains
meaning and resonance from stakes, which we'll discuss at length
in Chapter 17.

Tension: Tension is the gas in your story engine and keeps readers
engaged. You don't just need conflict in your story. You must also
use interiority to underscore *why* certain obstacles and struggles
matter to your character on a deeper level. Conflict generates a
sense of tension within a protagonist (and for readers), as the hero
grapples with internal or external issues and proactively works
toward something that will bring them back to equilibrium or
resolve the problem at hand. Tension applies at the scene level and
across the larger plot. All conflict creates tension, but not all

tension involves outright conflict. Whether you use interiority to extrapolate or subsume internal tension, setting and imagery to add a sense of unease to a scene, or dramatic irony to bridge the gap between the conscious and unconscious, you'll want to find a source of tension for every chapter, scene, and even paragraph. If you think hard enough, and consider all angles, there's always tension to stir up. Try using "And? So?" here.

Your plot will ideally be structured in a way that generates maximum conflict and tension for your main character. In the following section, I'll offer seven specific sequences you can focus on.

The Seven Major Plot Tentpoles

The following is a bulleted list of the seven main plot tentpoles that are often present in story, with definitions and a focus on interiority and character development:

- **Inciting Incident:** An event early in the plot that ramps up stakes and gets readers invested in the character and story. The first major conflict in your structure, the inciting incident changes the character's status from "normal"[5] to "abnormal" in a way that creates tension that they—and the reader— become invested in resolving. This is a "one-way door" in the narrative, because once a character engages with the inciting incident, there's usually no going back to how things were. This event asks a lot of your protagonist internally, and they may be reluctant to get involved at first, but they do so anyway (or there's no story).
- **Escalating Obstacles:** This is a large swath of the plot that covers parts of the first and second acts, if you're working with a traditional three-act structure. On the emotional plot graph

---

5. You'll see throughout that I will put "normal" in quotes when referring to characters and their personalities. This is to acknowledge that there's no such thing as "normal," which is pretty much one of the main points of this guide. Everyone's experience is unique to them, and aside from obviously amoral or immoral behavior, there's no right or wrong approach to being alive.

reproduced later in this chapter, this is the gradual yet steady slide into despair as your character attempts to achieve their objective, fails, realizes they have growth to do, struggles with said growth, grapples with their vulnerability, and otherwise goes from confident to insecure. Driven by their objective and misbelief, they generally aren't aware of the extent of their internal struggle, the power wielded by the antagonist, the flimsiness of their plan, or all of the above. This section strips away their hopes that the solution to their conflict will come to them quickly and easily, or that they'll be able to succeed without changing or sacrificing some of the personal misbeliefs and qualities that brought them to conflict's doorstep in the first place. Of course, there should be some victories embedded in this period of the story to encourage characters and entertain readers, or it'll be a slog.

- **Midpoint:** Many writers struggle with the "muddy middle" of a manuscript because they might have clearly visualized their beginning, climax, and ending, while the rest of the story looks more like an opaque gray mist. One way around this plotting obstacle is to approach the midpoint from the perspective of character development. The midpoint is actually a very crucial moment in most stories. It's when pretensions and illusions fall away and the true nature of the plot's conflict and the protagonist's vulnerability is revealed. (To the protagonist, at least. Readers who've been paying attention can usually identify the character's flaws and imagine their remedies by this point.) It may take protagonists a bit longer to realize the gravity of what's to come, or what they'll need to do or be to succeed. Around the midpoint, the character goes from "solving the problem the wrong way"[6] by relying on their limited understanding of their selves and the story they're in, to digging down deep and steeling themselves to "solve the problem the right way" in the second half, as conflicts and stakes escalate toward the climax. The midpoint requires

---

6. Credit for this phrasing and way of talking about plot goes to Jessica Brody and *Save the Cat Writes a Novel*, which was inspired by Blake Snyder's original *Save The Cat! The Last Book on Screenwriting You'll Ever Need*.

humility and courage in equal parts, and this is where the protagonist starts to truly become a "hero worthy of their story."[7] Surrounding this sequence will be false victories, defeats, and other developments that will test your protagonist's mettle, including relationship changes, allies falling away, and the deaths (literal or figurative) of old guides and ideas. The midpoint also represents a sea change as the character begins to realize what's holding them back and the effect their wounds and needs have had on their present behavior, choices, and experiences. This is when they might start to let go of their flaw or misbelief, access reserves of courage and commitment they didn't know they possessed, and truly engage with the story on its terms, rather than their own.

- **Crisis:** There's often an "Act II crisis" in structure where a character is truly tested before they're cleared for the final climax. This is like a run-up to the major event of the story, where things hang in the balance but the character flounders or doubts themselves, going back to old patterns and not quite nailing the transition from pursuing their want to going after their need. There isn't just one big action or danger sequence in a narrative. You'll want to start generously devastating the character after the midpoint and before they reach the next stage of conflict.

- **Dark Night of the Soul:** Tension is highest leading up to this character development point, which generally precedes or coincides with the climax. As the protagonist approaches the most high-stakes and dangerous (physically, emotionally, or both) synthesis climax moment in the story, they take stock. Whether they crumple in self-doubt, a plan is pulled out from under them, or a betrayal rocks their sense of what they believe to be true, this is a final test they must overcome from within. If they're about to engage in the climax, the dark night of the soul is their last chance to either back out or commit. If they've been unsuccessful during the climactic action thus far, they will

---

7. As my editorial colleague Kristen Overman likes to say.

plunge into despair and try to scrape themselves together for one last effort.

- **Synthesis Climax:** The protagonist just did deep inquiry and resolved to give the conflict their all. Now, they're surprised to learn that they can actually triumph by marshaling what they've learned or leaning into what was once perceived as their weakness. The character, using all of their spark, wherewithal, and even reframed flaws, has been engaging with the plot in new ways since the midpoint. They synthesize the virtuous and problematic parts of themselves to claim plot victory or, at the very least, a new level of selfhood that they never would've achieved otherwise. If this sounds like a cheesy "the magic was inside them all along" moral, that's actually spot on. While you'd never overtly explain it this way in a novel or memoir worth its storytelling salt, this tentpole moment is all about the character realizing that they are enough during the most dire circumstances of your plot.

- **Ending:** In most instances, your character will eventually triumph. They'll sacrifice, suffer losses, and reach deeper into themselves than ever before, but they will triumph. If they don't, you are technically writing a tragedy, like *Ripe*, and that's all fine and good, as long as this ending is intentional. The final image of your project generally echoes the beginning, comes full circle, or reverses expectations. It also creates a sense of how the protagonist might move forward in the short- and medium-term in the reader's mind. Your character will have other conflicts, they will still fail and flounder, but now that they've achieved synthesis, solved the present conflict, and somewhat resolved their need and wound, they're much better prepared for anything else the future brings. If engineered well, the climax and ending bring everything together, and all of the turbulence and trouble a writer has created for their protagonist seems worth it to both character *and* reader. Goals are realized (or not), stakes come to pass (or don't), relationships are ironed out (for the most part), and the protagonist reaches a new level of mastery or understanding of themselves and their lives. The inner struggle crests and resolves (though maybe not in the way that readers and characters expected), and readers leave more or less emotionally satisfied (even if you're planning a series).

These are obviously broad strokes examples of how these tentpole moments relate to character, and I've written them to be as widely applicable to as many types of stories as possible. What should emerge from this chapter is the idea that plot is the crucible in which your protagonist confronts not only external tensions and conflicts, but internal ones, too. What they do and how they do it matters, but so does who they are and who they become. I'll talk a lot more about character arc and development in Chapter 11, and, spoiler alert, I really do believe that a character should grow, change, or even devolve. Otherwise, what's the point?

To remind yourself that the character's experience influences the reader's, you might also find it helpful to follow the emotional plot framework.

Emotional Plot: This idea comes from my book, *Writing Irresistible Kidlit: The Ultimate Guide to Crafting Fiction for Young Adult and Middle Grade Readers*. You'll see it on the opposing page, and it's basically a visualization of your character's emotional experience as they go through the structure.

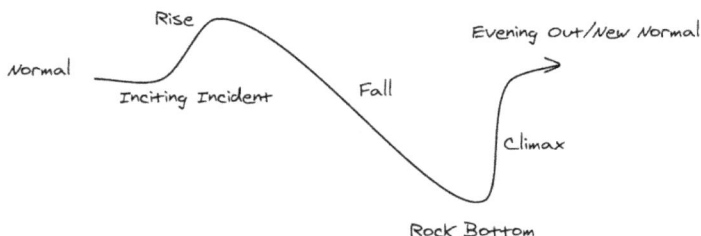

The protagonist starts off somewhat level (though their "normal" has inherent problems, otherwise, there'd be no story). Then their feelings can edge up as the excitement of the inciting incident kicks in. However, the majority of the plot is a race toward emotional rock bottom. Though there are highs and lows at the scene and chapter levels—or "polarity shifts," as Robert McKee calls them in *Story*—the character's emotional journey usually keeps getting worse until the dark night of the soul. After that, if the character prevails, they experience a new normal and an evening out of their baseline. That's an "*even*-ing," rather than an "evening out on the town," meaning that they enter a new phase of their life after the climax and synthesis

If you struggle with weaving this many elements into one narrative, as many of us do, you might consider outlining or getting into the "plotter" mindset, as opposed to the "pantser" approach to drafting. If you've never tried it before or are abstaining on principle, you literally have nothing to lose except for a few hours of your time.

A Case for Outlining: Do you *have to* outline your novel or memoir? No. I won't tell anyone if you choose to skip it. That said, I can personally say that my creative process blossomed beyond my wildest dreams when I started outlining. There are fewer dead ends and higher motivation to sit down for "butt in chair" time on a regular basis because I always have a general idea of where I'm going next. The main benefit? The thinking is already done, for the most part, so the writing process is simply more fluid and fun. (Remember? This whole thing is supposed to be enjoyable? Yeah, me neither.) There are many structures and formats to choose from, like the aforementioned *Save the Cat Writes a Novel* by Jessica Brody, *Story Grid* by Shawn Coyne, and *The Story Solution* by Erik Edson. I've also developed an outline framework for my small group writing workshop intensive, Story Mastermind. Download a free copy here: https://bit.ly/novel-outline

---

As you navigate character in the context of plot, you may find yourself struggling to find a balance of internal and external conflict, and that's okay. You may also be suffering from a lack of external plot, especially if you're writing a character-led literary novel. Or you might have the opposite problem in an action-driven fantasy or thriller. Ironically, plots which often fail due to passive protagonist issues are sometimes the biggest, with the highest stakes. That's because their writers spend all of their energy on plot and neglect character development, especially at key junctures.

Have you given enough reason for the character to keep fighting when the going gets tough? Have you enticed readers to root for the protagonist, even if they fail, make mistakes, and forget their values? These are the questions you should ask as you design a bespoke journey for your character to travel.

Crucially, you also need to think about the order of events and how everything fits together. Since this is a guide that sees storytelling through the lens of character, I want you to keep in mind that your plot and character arcs should operate with cause-and-effect logic.[8]

By using interiority, you can chart a character's expectations and objectives going into a scene or chapter, their attempts to succeed as the action progresses, their reactions to what other characters do or don't do, and how they reset their thinking or change strategies after the event plays out. This will set up their next course of action, and the following scene will build upon what the protagonist previously experienced. (A lot more on this in Chapter 15.)

Interiority is tied intrinsically to character logic. Readers not only want to know what a protagonist is going through, but *why*. Why are they reacting a certain way? Why do they want what they want? Characters can be prickly and standoffish with every other person in the manuscript, if they so choose, but not with the reader. A certain measure of self-awareness and vulnerability is required as they *guide* audiences through their experiences, a path that's illuminated by interiority.

This is how you get readers to care. As the protagonist moves through the story, they have to overcome ups and downs while battling an

---

8. This is the hill another one of my editorial colleagues, Amy Wilson, will die on. If you ever want a logic check, go see Amy.

increasingly difficult downward emotional trajectory. It's important to give your character some successes in order to keep them motivated to continue, or to offer them respite in the form of friendship, love, or guidance, so they don't have to act, feel, and suffer alone. That being said, their reactions and decisions need to be examined at every major plot turn to keep the action moving forward and the logic clean.

Keep in mind that scenes and chapters should matter—they should introduce, reinforce, or change the reader's understanding of the protagonist, story, plot, relationships with other characters, or all of the above. If a plot point is there simply because you love it, seriously consider whether you need it or if it can be combined with a more revelatory scene or chapter. Even "promise of the premise" sections where you're having fun with your idea should simultaneously advance the story.

Now that we know the lens through which we'll see the main character and the seven crucial tentpoles of plot, let's craft that protagonist in earnest and do our deep focus on interiority. We'll start by developing the crucial underpinnings of backstory and wound. A character's personal history, and how it affects the action of the present, is what we'll discuss as we rocket into Part 2.

PART 2

DEEP CHARACTER DEVELOPMENT

5

BACKSTORY AND WOUND

Some creative writing workbooks are full of exercises for getting to know your character better. This is not one of them. I believe in working smarter, not harder. Filling a journal or spreadsheet with arbitrary facts about your protagonist is not actually helpful in your pursuit of understanding that character's essence. I'm interested primarily in developing characterizing details, so that you're anchoring your protagonist to the deep, foundational information that matters. Once you understand your character as a person, you can use interiority to allow them to express themselves.

It may surprise you that I'm starting our Part 2 character focus by discussing backstory, which gets a bad rap in the writing world. I want to be clear, right away, that this is information you need to know for your own purposes as you're creating your protagonist. How much of it actually ends up on the page, when, and where, is another question entirely. This is the work of exposition, which must be undertaken lightly and gracefully. First, let's define the major topics at hand.

Backstory: Every character has a collection of past events that have informed their identity leading up to the present. It's the writer's job to decide what this entails, how detailed it gets, how much is used, when, and how. Not all aspects of a character's past are relevant, even though everyone has a lot of material (years or decades!) in their rearview mirrors.[1] To be effective, backstory must relate to the present and give readers added insight into character. As such, it should be used selectively and layered into a story gradually as the plot unfolds. Avoid large info-dumps of backstory, especially in the first few chapters, where dense information can easily crush your forward momentum. Backstory can be summarized in compressed narration, alluded to in a moment of interiority, or rendered in scene via flashback.

For our purposes, backstory is crucial to know and think about because it offers insight into a character's wound and misbelief. These elements will be embedded deeply within your protagonist and largely unconscious … at first.

Wound: You may have heard this called the "shard of glass" if you follow the *Save the Cat Writes a Novel* methodology. In essence, this is a specific situation, event, or relationship in the past that's consciously or unconsciously keeping your character from realizing their full potential in the present. This can be as simple and diffuse as a middle child feeling like they can never get enough attention within their family system, or a car accident or similar moment of tragedy that starkly divides a protagonist's life into a "before" and "after." You can get specific about developing the circumstances that first plant the character's wound within their psyche. These events generally happen in childhood or around puberty. Even if a character believes they've healed—or compartmentalized—their trauma, their past will interfere with their ability to reach their objectives (see Chapter 7) and remind them of their underlying need (see Chapter 8). Your primary question when developing the wound is: How does it help or hamper the character *now*? Wounds can also affect the protagonist in positive ways by contributing important character assets, not just liabilities. In fact, after the midpoint, characters might become more comfortable

---

1. Especially memoir writers, who have a lifetime to choose from! They must be ruthlessly focused on their theme and premise as they select and structure their content.

with leveraging their so-called flaws or the hard-won lessons of their early wounding experiences. This can be a lovely way to synthesize all of their various parts.

Misbelief: This term can be used interchangeably with the idea of a character flaw, and is ideally connected to the wound, so that all of your character's "damage" is cohesive. Your protagonist might believe that they are broken, not good enough, cowardly, power-less, or any other shameful deeply held idea. This messaging might take root during the wounding circumstances. Misbeliefs can also relate to a character's gender, physical body, qualities, abilities, successes, and failures. Characters and humans have a sense of self (see Chapter 6) and specific worldviews (see Chapter 10), and the latter could be connected to prevailing cultural or social norms (see Chapter 18). Not all of these beliefs are positive, proactive, or productive. A compelling plot is designed to, at least in part, bring your protagonist to confront, change, or overcome their wound and misbelief. Ideally, that same plot will allow them to meet their deeper need in the process.

More likely than not, your character will be operating with certain past experiences that will dictate or interfere with the present narrative. Of course, not every protagonist needs a *tragic* backstory, wound, misbe-lief, or flaw. Tragedy for the sake of tragedy—used to ramp up stakes, tension, and reader empathy—can be a bit of a cliché choice. Alas, most humans don't make it out of childhood and their families of origin without some suffering. If you're going to use an especially traumatic backstory, make sure you're prepared to make these aspects specific, deeply felt, and respectfully rendered. You don't need to be extensive when deciding on your character's wound and misbelief, but you should be prepared to examine it and allow it to drive some of your protagonist's behavior for the rest of the story. Choose a backstory that you really want to work with and can explore without resorting to stereotype.

Now that we understand the kinds of elements that make up the substance of backstory, and the type of character development that you'll want to do around your protagonist's past, let's talk about putting these ideas onto the page.

Bringing Backstory Into the Present

A character's backstory matters to the present narrative, whether they like it or not. Protagonists should grapple with their backstory, wound, and misbelief, but their goal isn't necessarily to heal themselves forever. It's to integrate this early trauma so they're no longer held back (or held back as seriously) by what happened and who they became as a result. They aren't aiming for perfection, but to move forward with their heads held high and their needs nurtured at long last, which is no small task, either.

"The past is not yet dead. It's not even past."

WILLIAM FAULKNER

To that end, you'll want to consider introducing important backstory elements early on—but with restraint. I'd recommend dispensing this information in a series of small bites throughout the first act. Sometimes you'll invite the past into the present narration, especially if you're writing multiple timelines. *The Villa* by Rachel Hawkins and *Bright Young Women* by Jessica Knoll use this technique.

In other instances, a piece of backstory is so shattering and incendiary that the author has built the entire book's structure around a shock twist or reveal that takes place toward the end (more about this in Chapter 14). In this case, curiosity hooks about what happened are everywhere. Other times, wounds and painful backstory events are merely alluded to, discussed, or thought about, but never explicitly shown on the page. Finally, flashback can be used to narrate crucial past events in scene.

Flashback: The narrative transitions to an encapsulated memory for a set period of time, whether one paragraph, a scene, or several chapters (though the latter is rare outside of a frame[2] structure). There's a beginning and end to this event, and the point of the flashback is to reveal important backstory. Flashbacks are useful for *showing* past events or characters who aren't available in the present, for whatever reason. This technique is effective when you have a fully realized moment that can be sustained, rather than a lot of quick, well, flashes. In essence, flashback is *how* you do it, and backstory is *what* you provide once there.

Flashbacks are helpful for showing readers the character's perspective of formative backstory events firsthand, but you should also use these sparingly. If a character is too caught up in their past and spends most of their present ruminating, your readers may disengage because the story is *too* backward-facing. After all, those events can no longer be changed, so the result can be a passive narrative. The past is most relevant when it helps or hinders the present, so you'll want to make sure the majority of the story has yet to be lived. (Memoirs are obviously exempt from this, as so much of their action happens in retrospect.) If you find your story's past more interesting than its present, why not shift your structure? You might be starting too late in the character's life and getting away from what's juicy to you.

If a character who played a formative role in your protagonist's life is dead or unavailable in the present moment because they're incarcerated, estranged, or otherwise unreachable, flashback is a great tool for putting them on the page, showing them in action, and letting readers "meet" them, play detective, and bring their own interpretations to the story. While flashback has a bad reputation if introduced too early or overused, it can absolutely serve an important function in narrative.

---

2. "Frame" stories play out mostly in the past or future, with present narration appearing only at the beginning and end. That past section, which contains most of the plot, isn't necessarily considered a flashback. *The Nightingale* is an example from our shelves.

Now let's discuss when and how to include backstory, and then we'll explore some From the Shelves examples.

How and When to Use Backstory

The wound and backstory you explore will depend on the kind of project you're writing. In memoir, the past is very relevant and can take up the bulk of a manuscript. In romcom, we usually get a sense of romantic wounding in one or both characters' backstories, and this interferes with their current ability to love or trust. Upmarket, women's, and literary fiction can also feature backstory elements, but these may or may not get a lot of attention in the present, unless there's a crucial thematic element of trauma or grief.

In mystery, thriller, suspense, and horror, various individual wounds tend to loom large in both the psychology of the victim(s) and the perpetrator of the danger. Backstory elements provide salient clues to the "whodunit" plot mechanic of a mystery story, or the "whydunit"[3] dramatic question of thriller. In fact, the past may be re-examined several times once new information emerges, as characters explore theories and clues, after twists, and when instances of misdirection pile up before the climactic reveal.

Writers often wonder how much backstory to develop for their main characters, and how much of that should end up on the page. The answer is: It varies. Especially if you're the flavor of writer who has journals and journals devoted to everything from your character's early life experiences to their favorite ice cream flavor. That's valid work, but some of it won't see the outside of those journals and you have to be okay with that. Too much information, especially to start, is, well, a non-starter. It's too dense. Audiences don't care about your character yet, so they certainly don't care about earlier versions of them. I admire that you've done this writing homework. That shows dedication. But most of it will end up on the cutting room floor with the other dead darlings.

A novel or memoir often rides the delicate balance between action and

---

3. This term comes from Jessica Brody's *Save the Cat Writes a Novel*.

information. Yet with backstory and flashback, you have 100% information to give, even if it's shown in scene. Why can't you simply explain it? Well, just like the spoonful of sugar that helps the medicine go down, you need a delivery medium that won't make your target gag. Information, by itself, isn't built to engage. With a cold, hard start, it's unreasonable to expect your readers to suddenly plug into a list of biographical details about your character. Turn up your action, however, and the story gets rolling. It's that vital mix of showing *and* telling. You'll notice in my chapters on reactions (Chapter 15), decisions (Chapter 16), and stakes (Chapter 17), that small doses of data can trigger big character and plot changes. Your goal should be to strike a balance of action and information.

Balance of Action and Information: Action moves quickly, while information tends to be dense and slow. Both are necessary for story (and to convey a compelling character on the page), but too much of either is a potential liability. Action tends to be "slippery" and doesn't engender much empathy, emotion, reflection, and understanding. Information is quite "sticky" in that it provides context but can also sink your pacing, which is the perceived speed at which your narrative moves. You should play around with the balance of these elements, adding small instances of context, backstory, and reaction to scenes, then interspersing high-stakes action with moments of reflection, memory, and strategy. Both action and information ebb and flow throughout a structure. If you find yourself indulging in too much data or interiority, or hitting readers with scene after scene of conflict, introduce some action to break up heavy info-dumps, or find places to fold in some information, respectively. How you'll strike this balance is an individual choice that depends on your writing style, category, and genre, and it might take some trial and error as you draft and revise.

In terms of introducing backstory and deploying it throughout the narrative, sometimes the most direct way is best. In other words, you'll do some telling, but the good kind. After all, how else is a reader supposed to know that characters practice mage magic on your planet, but the protagonist's powers failed to awaken? Or that a woman's bachelorette party was last Friday, but nobody showed up? Definitely don't show the bride pointing at a calendar with the date conspicuously circled, then crying and throwing away bags of unused party favors in a misguided attempt to "show, don't tell." She's not a mime.

With backstory, specifically, the reader needs to know the immediate context of who the character is, what they're doing, and why, if possible. A few quick bursts of exposition to get audiences started will be welcome.

To "tell" is not a four-letter word in these instances, especially if the reader gets just enough data to understand what's going on. The ramifications of the backstory, whether traumatic or formative, will undergird the present-day character's behavior, wants, needs, worldview, and actions. Once readers know the history, they can speculate about its effects. A character wouldn't have meaningful present action without a sense of the future (in the form of objective, motivation, and need). Likewise, they would lack serious substance without the past and its attendant identity-shaping wounds and misbeliefs.

I'm not going to give a rule of thumb here, but I would *strongly suggest* (ahem, ahem, *very strongly*)[4] that you avoid flashback and backstory in, at minimum, your first scene. Instead, begin your story with action (are you tired of hearing that yet?), and in present-day narrative you can sustain for at least two or three pages. Just because you introduce a best friend character in this scene does *not* mean that you need to go zooming off to a quick flashback of how the friendship was cemented over mud pies in kindergarten. Don't do it! There's time for that context later, if this specific backstory is key to the reader's understanding of the present or future. Sometimes saying "childhood friend" and showing the current relationship is enough. This is where the advice to "kill your darlings" needs to be followed in an especially cold-blooded way. Each instance of flashback, memory, and backstory needs to serve a very specific purpose.

Once the present action is established and running smoothly, you can start thinking about *how* to layer in backstory. Less is more. We don't

---

4. This is me trying to be forceful while respecting your creative autonomy.

need the character's whole life story, Mom and Dad's history, and the family dog's provenance, unless this is an intergenerational saga. Generally, the earlier you are in your structure, the more often the backstory and wound are teased as a curiosity hook. Events are referenced but readers don't have context for them yet, which keeps audiences wondering: What happened? Why does it matter? Later in the story, more information is revealed and additional layers of meaning and understanding are added. In some genres, the whole puzzle doesn't snap together until the end.

In pulling this chapter's excerpts, I found that backstory generally runs the gamut from traumatic to formative. Sometimes it's both—the event was tough for the protagonist to overcome, but they have really grown as a result, in a way that wouldn't have been possible without their wounding experience. Backstory can also be raw or mostly healed and can come from the recent or distant past.

The following From the Shelves examples demonstrate that tension is the spark that brings flashback and backstory to life. There are obviously long scenes of flashback in some of these stories that I could've included, but the big point I want to make is that it really *is* possible to do a lot with a little. Most of these books offer past context with impeccable restraint. It should go without saying, but there will be a lot of spoilers revealed in the following sections.

Traumatic Backstory

Even if a person or character has a tranquil life or well-adjusted personality, they will still have challenging seasons. Unfortunately for our fiction and memoir protagonists, they probably haven't had the most peaceful existences, because there's a bias that selects for tension, struggle, and hardship in storytelling. Nowhere is that truer than in a character's traumatic backstory and wound.

Snow, a fox spirit in the beautiful adult historical fantasy novel *The Fox Wife* by Yangsze Choo, has lost her daughter. Alas, dead children are a big wound in certain narratives, because few can imagine anything more painful than losing a child.[5] We meet Snow as she is trying to track down the person she holds responsible for her daughter's death. In the process, she runs into Kuro, another fox spirit, who she knows from her very long past (fox spirits live for hundreds of years).

At this point, Snow is merely hinting at a few dangerous backstory elements, so this is less of a reveal and more of a curiosity hook:

> The good thing about Kuro is that he doesn't ask questions. The bad thing is that you never know what he's thinking. But that was all right; I didn't need to know. He'd promised in the past to stay out of my way, and was, I reminded myself, generally good about keeping promises (*except one time*, though I didn't wish to remember it; no, I would not think of it).[a]

Snow references Kuro again about 50 pages later, building on the mystery:

> Of course, being told not to do something is like salt herring left out to dry for foxes. An almost irresistible bait…. My face was burning. From indignation, I told myself, though I knew deep down that it was from Kuro's voice. That low, dark voice that has haunted my dreams and nightmares, and that I never wished to hear.[b]

Are you curious about what happened between them? It'd be hard not to wonder. I also love the image of "salt herring left out to dry" and can imagine how it must tempt foxes. This small turn of phrase plunges readers right into the story world of fox spirits.

Let's zoom over to Mari, from the historical portion of *The Villa*, an adult thriller by Rachel Hawkins. She has joined her stepsister, Lara, and her technically married partner, Pierce, at a sleazy recording artist's rented villa in Italy. She finds herself really struggling with Pierce, who routinely cheats on her (including with Lara!). Mari believes it's because their baby son died several years before:

---

5. I have experienced this myself. If you have any desire to read about my first daughter, Nora, I love sharing her story: https://kidlit.com/nora-pepper/

Pierce is not faithful, Mari knows that, and she also knows she can't reasonably expect him to be, given that he still has a wife. Sweet, noble Frances, out in some village in Surrey, pining away for him, hoping he'll come to his senses and come back to her. But he swears it was just one time with Lara, and it was after Billy had died, when Mari had felt lost in her grief, wondering how she was supposed to get out of bed when someone she loved so much was gone forever. Wondering if her baby dying was the universe's way of settling the score, since Mari's birth had killed her mother. They were dark thoughts, awful thoughts.[c]

This is Mari telling herself *about* herself, which is a powerful example of interiority and also manages to convey her distorted worldview. Pierce, "catch" that he is, abandoned his wife to be with Mari. Readers also get the backstory that Mari's own mother died in childbirth. This is multi-generational trauma that just keeps pushing out carnage.

Interiority Insight: The above is an example of self-reflective story-telling, which we'll learn more about in Chapter 6.

In *Amazing Grace Adams*, Grace has come—generously speaking—unhinged. Throughout the story, readers put together pieces about her previous mental breakdown. Underpinning both is a horrible wound, which drove Grace from her husband and made her feel inadequate as a mother to her teen daughter. It's the death of her second child, which she can't even admit to herself (or readers) until the climax.

At the beginning, though, we see this ominous memory—a flashback to Grace cradling a baby. The author's intention is for audiences to assume it's the living daughter. Only later, readers can think back to this moment and realize that this was the lost child all along. The clue is right there, masterfully played for maximum impact only in hindsight:

A memory swoops, snares her. And she is standing in the middle of the park, a heavy-soft parcel of baby on her hip as she points up at a tree struck by sunshine. *Look at the leaves*, she's saying. *Look*. But she's talking as much to herself as the child in her arms.... And then her mind shifts sideways and she's remembering, she's remembering ... and it's too late, she's seen it: she has glimpsed the dark rip in the fabric of things.[d]

Notice how all three of these excerpts show characters rejecting their painful memories and thoughts, practically forcing them back into the unconscious.

Unfortunately, our exploration of dead child wounds doesn't end here. *Before I Let Go*, which plays with a second-chance romance trope, features POV access to two divorced partners who can't seem to quit one another. They broke up when Yasmen suffered a traumatic pregnancy loss and shut down, leaving Josiah to grieve alone. Here, we hear from Josiah about how this tragedy tore their marriage apart. He reveals that he abandoned Yasmen after he felt abandoned himself. This interiority shows him wrestling with endless what-ifs, long after the fact:

Did I make Yasmen feel weak? With my expectations? With my impatience to get our lives back and to move on, with my inability to deal with all we had lost, did I *add* to Yasmen's pain?[e]

Interiority Insight: Characters who demonstrate empathy toward others—especially in difficult circumstances, or after being hurt themselves—will attract the same from readers.

While Josiah pushing Yasmen to move on might've contributed to the situation, he feels accountability, which redeems him. (Josiah's hurt is compounded by the death of another beloved family member around the same time.) It's no surprise that his perspective on love and life is tainted afterward:

Not for the first time, the frustration, the helplessness of all I've lost, burns in my gut. The chaos of life and how you can calculate and project and plan and save … and then the ones you love die. There can be hope growing inside of the woman you love more than life itself, and in a moment, that hope can be lost. That future, snuffed out.[f]

He goes from optimism to utter hopelessness. This, in turn, defines who he is as a character in the present timeline, as he struggles to decide whether to give his heart to Yasmen once more. Here, the wound informs both his worldview and relationships.

Death is ever-present in wounds and backstories. In the speculative adult novel *Family Meal* by Bryan Washington,[6] we meet Cam, a gay man moves back to his hometown from Los Angeles after his boyfriend, Kai, dies. Cam is incredibly broken, as we'll see again in Chapter 8, and he's been going from hookup to hookup on Grindr, trying to numb his grief with sex. His wound is hinted at, to start, as we see in this conversation that Cam has with Kai in his head. He imagines Kai ridiculing his choices, which reflects Cam's personified shame:

Fucking ridiculous, says Kai.

You and I weren't exactly chaste, I say.

This is different, says Kai. There's a cost.

But you aren't here to stop me, I say.[g]

Readers haven't learned a lot about Kai up until this point, so hearing "you aren't here to stop me" is a moment that demands attention and clearly establishes that Cam is deeper in the trauma hole than he pretends.

Interiority Insight: In *Family Meal* by Bryan Washington, *Sing,*

---

6. As you'll see in this and other excerpts from *Family Meal*, the author chooses not to format dialogue using quotation marks. Certain works, often literary-leaning ones, make this stylistic choice. If you decide to do something similar, know that it can be polarizing.

Unburied, Sing by Jesmyn Ward, and Eleanor Oliphant Is Completely Fine by Gail Honeyman, we see characters in mental discourse with dead loved (or hated) ones. This also occurs as protagonists imagine former incarnations of themselves. This technique, similar to a therapy scene, can be used to apply interiority to especially painful topics.

A character who's similarly negatively affected by a traumatic past event (in this case, a rape) is Eden, from the young adult novel *The Way I Used to Be* by Amber Smith. Only her experience isn't withheld from readers—everyone knows what happened right away. Her sense of identity is demolished, as we'll see in Chapter 6, and this is shown as she looks at a picture of her younger, more naïve self with disgust:

> I want to slap the girl ... because as the girl smiles demurely, I look in [her] eyes and I see now what the girl couldn't then: ... he knew not only that he would do it, but that she would let him get away with it.[h]

It isn't until page 321 that we see a flashback to the rape and how Eden dissociated from her body as it was happening, signifying how she first split from "the girl" who existed before, to the person she becomes after:

> I had felt plenty ugly before, in general. But never ugly like this. Never as insignificant and repulsive and hated as he made me feel then, with his eyes on me.... He wasn't even holding me down. Not physically. But he was holding me in some other way, a way that was somehow stronger than muscle and arms and legs. I couldn't even feel my body anymore, not even the hurt, but I could feel ... all the ways I didn't matter.[i]

Here, she subsumes the event—how could she not?—and makes meaning about herself. Eden decides that she has no value. Unfortunately, sexual assault can really interfere with a character's ability to form an identity or function in their day-to-day. It's a common wound, and a heartbreakingly prevalent phenomenon off the page, as well.

Interiority Insight: Sometimes a wound doesn't just explain the past, it gives a character a map back to themselves in the present. Protagonists (and people) often realize that they have strayed down the wrong path, or lost their true selves, only by reflecting on what truly mattered to them once upon a time. It takes great courage and insight to make a course-correction, so not everyone is capable of it.

Leonie from adult literary novel *Sing, Unburied, Sing* by Jesmyn Ward is traumatized by a number of things, from her incredibly low self-esteem to her partner, Michael's, incarceration, to her brother, Given, getting shot. Here, she's spiraling after his death, doing drugs while pregnant, and seeing his ghost (a magical realism element in this otherwise non-speculative novel):

Three years ago, I did a line and saw Given for the first time. It wasn't my first line, but Michael had just gone to jail. I had started doing it often.... I knew I shouldn't have: I was pregnant. But I couldn't help wanting to feel the coke go up my nose, shoot straight to my brain, and burn up all the sorrow and despair I felt.... The first time Given showed up ... my brother walked through there with no bullet holes in his chest or in his neck.[j]

Reality continues to blur for Leonie, especially because she works to actively reject it, as we'll see throughout this guide.

Interiority Insight: As much as interiority can be used to establish specific information, it can also embrace the nebulous and enter the realm of fugue and fantasy.

A character who exists in a similarly blurry reality is Joe from adult thriller novel *You* by Caroline Kepnes. Something is clearly very wrong with him because he's killed multiple people and keeps obsessively fixating on Beck, a vivacious young woman who comes into the book-store where he works.

We see him stalk her with dark results. Instead of talking about himself, though, he projects his own hurts onto her (in part to justify the idea that he knows what's best). While we don't learn a lot about his upbringing, he has no problem imagining that Beck's father's death has broken her, making her weak and needy. Joe proceeds to paint himself—in all of his "exceptionalism"—as her savior:

> [Other men] don't understand what you want, someone to make you pancakes. You don't care about money. You don't want to be spanked. You want love. Your father had a red ladle and now I have a red ladle and I will make you the pancakes you want so badly, the pancakes you haven't tasted since he died.[k]

Make no mistake, this excerpt is about Joe, not Beck's backstory (especially since we later find out she lied about having a dead father, so Joe miscalculates even his delusions of grandeur).

Interiority Insight: Some backstory and wound information is stated outright, but other instances require inference from readers.

It's common to read about wounds and backstory tied to specific events, but we also see past hurts that have accumulated like a sword forged from a thousand cuts. Rachel, in *Milk Fed*, has mommy issues. Instead of giving readers a specific instance as an example, she generalizes the ongoing animosity between the women:

> I could feel her opening an emotional spreadsheet that began in the womb. This was why I never confronted her. Now we'd have to go traipsing through it together, cell by cell, until I retracted everything.[l]

Interiority Insight: Interiority about wounds, especially those that were perpetrated by others, is inherently biased. Some stories show both sides, with a lot of inherent conflict to explore. But most are slanted toward the perspective of the POV protagonist.

Family members, especially mothers and fathers, offer a ton of wounding potential. (Very disheartening for those of us who are parents!) These troubled bonds provide a relatively easy explanation for ongoing character dysfunction, as childhood is well known to be fertile ground for trauma.

For Cora, from adult speculative historical novel *The Underground Railroad* by Colson Whitehead, her family wound is compounded by the harrowing experience of attempting to escape slavery. When she does eventually run away, with a kind man's help, she pauses to ruefully remember how her mother abandoned her in the process of her own flight, years prior:

> After landing in South Carolina, she realized that she had banished her mother not from sadness but from rage. She hated her. Having tasted freedom's bounty, it was incomprehensible to Cora that Mabel had abandoned her to that hell. A child. Her company would have made the escape more difficult, but Cora hadn't been a baby. If she could pick cotton, she could run. She would have died in that place, after untold brutalities, if Caesar had not come along. In the train, in the deathless tunnel, she had finally asked him why he brought her with him. Caesar said, "Because I knew you could do it."[m]

At face value, this passage is about Cora's terrible backstory and bad relationship with her mother, but as with so many other instances of interiority, a deeper need is suggested. In this case, it's to have someone believe in her, because she *can* do it. This idea is revealed in the wish to go back and prove herself to Mabel, who sold her short. Even though Caesar has championed Cora, and Mabel doesn't deserve her, wounds don't often respond to logic. Though she becomes free, as we'll see in Chapter 17, Cora might never fully heal from this early insult, even if the pain mellows with time.

> **Interiority Insight:** Even if the character prevails in circumstances similar to the wounding event, their past can tinge the present with regret and the unmet desire to have had things play out differently in the first place. In the world of traumatic wounds and backstories, there is a lot of power in the feeling of regret. Characters can regret things they've done or circumstances that have befallen them. They can also regret things they haven't done or which didn't happen.

Let's now pivot to wounds and backstories that aren't solely traumatic, but formative and galvanizing as well. Yes, characters might become hardened or jaded as a result of their experiences, but the lessons wounds teach can also help protagonists thrive (eventually). In this next set of excerpts, the wounds are both painful *and* act as a launch pad for growth.

Character-Defining Backstory

Some protagonists rise from the ashes of their past traumatic experiences, or are at least able to synthesize these events with their present selves. The backstory might still affect them, but they are able to look toward their objective, motivation, and need.

Eleanor Oliphant in upmarket adult novel *Eleanor Oliphant Is Completely Fine* by Gail Honeyman is a stunning character study, and we will explore her story in great detail in Chapter 11. The book is predicated on the slow-burn reveal of what happened to Eleanor. Readers initially learn that she was in foster care and had a terrible relationship with Mummy, who she talks to and whose voice echoes in her thoughts. Pieces are filled in very gradually. For example, Eleanor is covered in scars, but audiences won't know their origin until much later:

> It doesn't bother me at all when people react to my face, to the ridged, white contours of scar tissue that slither across my right cheek, starting at my temple and running all the way down to my chin. I am stared at, whispered about; I turn heads.[n]

Though she's gone through something terrible, Eleanor acts as though it doesn't affect her all that much. (Spoiler alert: It does.) She makes a joke about turning heads, but this is a shield she builds around her vulnerability.

Interiority Insight: Coping mechanisms, which we'll discuss in Chapter 9, can hinder characters, but they can also help protagonists function until they're healthy enough to try and heal.

Eleanor projects some of her needs on a plant she's tended to since childhood, rather than speaking about herself directly, just as Joe projects his wound on Beck in *You,* as we saw in the previous section:

> She came with me from my childhood bedroom, survived the foster placements and children's homes and, like me, she's still here. I've looked after her, tended to her, picked her up and repotted her.... She likes light, and she's thirsty. Apart from that, she requires minimal care and attention, and largely looks after herself. I talk to her sometimes, I'm not ashamed to admit it. When the silence and the aloneness press down and around me, crushing me, carving through me like ice, I *need* to speak aloud sometimes, if only for proof of life.[o]

This vagueness holds pretty well, until we start to get flashbacks embedded in the narrative. At first, they are compartmentalized and Eleanor works hard to make them so. Vodka helps, as we'll see:

> Vodka is, for me, merely a household necessity.... The very best thing about it is that it helps me to sleep. Sometimes, when night comes, I lie there in the darkness and I can't prevent myself from remembering: fear, and pressure, but mostly fear. On nights like those, Mummy's voice hisses inside my head, and another voice, a smaller, timid one ... it breaks apart, pleading: *Eleanor, please help me, Eleanor* ... over and over and over again. On those nights I need the vodka, or else I'd break apart too.[p]

This "another voice" is important, but readers don't yet understand why. In this section, which is about 130 pages into the novel, Eleanor also hints at a night that changed everything:

> Apparently talking was good; it helped to keep anxieties in perspective.... *Talk to someone, do you want to talk about it, tell me how you feel, anything you want to share with the group, Eleanor? You do not have to say anything, but it may harm your defense if you do not mention when questioned something which you later rely on in court. Miss Oliphant, can you tell us in your own words what you recall of the events that took place during that evening?* I felt a tiny trickle of sweat run down my back, and a fluttering in my chest like a trapped bird.[q]

The writing style suddenly takes on the formal hallmarks of a court interrogation, which is notable. One hundred pages later, readers aren't much closer to the truth, but the author works diligently to keep tension tight. We get a major hint that Eleanor actually had a family, aside from Mummy and the plant:

> I wondered if that's what it would be like in a family—if you had parents, or a sister, say, who would be there, no matter what. It wasn't that you could take them for granted ... it was simply that you would know, almost unthinkingly, that they'd be there if you needed them.... I'm not prone to envy, as a rule, but I must confess I felt a twinge when I thought about this. Envy was a minor emotion, however, in comparison to the sorrow I felt at never having a chance to experience this ... what was it? Unconditional love, I supposed.[r]

We'll learn what really happened to Eleanor Oliphant in Chapter 11. What's important here is that she carries on despite her trauma, but can't fully break through to the next level of her development until she admits to it and integrates her past with her present.

We've already met Millie from *The New House*, and she's not shy about her backstory. Far from it. Her damage includes watching her father beat her mother (as seen in Chapter 3). Here's detailed interiority about how these events affected her:

If I allowed myself to feel, the emotion uppermost would be rage.

Rage at my father, a violent narcissist who took pleasure in reducing my mother to a cowering wreck with his fist and his words. Rage at my mother, for letting herself be used as a punchbag and coming back for more again and again.[s]

The interiority of "if I allowed myself to feel" is especially telling.

Interiority Insight: Knowing with the head, intellectually, can mean a character putting distance between themselves and the painful event. Truly feeling with the heart and body is different, more visceral, and can be all-consuming. Some protagonists (and people) keep pain at arm's length without truly experiencing it. Sometimes this silo holds, and sometimes it breaks.

Clearly, this backstory has inspired Millie, but she hasn't yet healed these jagged formative edges. Here's a bit more:

I despised my mother, even at the age of five. I despised her for her weakness: not her physical inability to stand up to him … but for willingly ceding him her power in return for the ring on her finger. She was a beautiful woman, a *smart woman*. As young as I was, I could see she had other weapons in her arsenal. She could have made him love her. She could have made him love *me*.

I wasn't weak like my mother.[t]

This seems to lay the blame on Mom. Millie resorts to the magical thinking that her father's love was actually attainable, when it likely wasn't. Characters (and people) like him tend to keep "moving the goalposts" to exert control, diminish others, and keep them starving for approval that will never come.

Moving the Goalposts: A pop psychology term for the phenomenon of changing a goal once it's finally attained (or about to be). Other characters can establish the rules, then move the goalposts on a protagonist—such as parents who claim they'll finally be appeased if a child achieves X, Y, or Z. More notably, however, people and characters can move the goalposts on themselves— such as writers who fully believe that their entire lives will change if they achieve a traditional publishing contract. (Spoiler alert: Publishing will not fix your personal problems. It may actually introduce more issues, but at least they'll be different from the unpublished writer problems you might be mired in now.)

The formative experience of watching her mother and father fight plants a stake in the ground for Millie. She will *not* be the same kind of woman. We get a mini-flashback to another night of violence and are privy to her interiority:

> I wondered if he'd kill her this time. I wondered if I was strong enough yet to kill him if he did.[11]

It's jarring and heartbreaking to imagine a child thinking this way— cool and calculating, devoid of emotion and innocence. Maybe young Millie really did act and think this way, or maybe the contemporary Millie's coldness colors her memories.

Interiority Insight: There have been a lot of studies done about subjective memory, including behavioral theories that suggest people react to how they feel *about* a memory, rather than the memory itself. Memories also change over time, especially as people invent naturally biased narratives surrounding these stories in an attempt to make meaning. When recalled, memories tend to have more in common with the self-reflective narrative than the original event. Very few memories are actually objective outside of certain factual details that can be corroborated (setting, time, etc.).

Shockingly, Millie does actually kill her father by stabbing him in the femoral artery. Very fitting for a future surgeon, but also sad for the child who felt pushed to such drastic action. A reader might see how she was driven to it and empathize with her pain, redeeming her for technically being a murderer.

Interiority Insight: Tragic backstory shouldn't be used as a blatant sympathy play, but if it's respectfully done, a "sob story" can indeed inspire reader connection.

Violent and deranged parents are obviously going to wreak havoc on a childhood. But distant, neglectful, or simply nonexistent parents can also be problematic. In *Within These Wicked Walls*, Andi struggles because she doesn't know her birth parents and feels she missed out on love, especially since her mentor, Jember, who raised her, has also kept his distance. She mourns what she never had, and it all comes pouring out as she sees him for the first time after leaving home:

> I threw up my hands, barely holding in a scream of frustration ...
> concealing something that hurt so much worse.... My blood
> rushed through my veins, and I gripped my fists to try and take
> back control.... "I care about what *you* think of me," I snapped.
> "You. Because you're my—" I choked on an unexpected sob.
> "You're the closest thing I'll ever have to a father." ... He wasn't
> going to say he cared for me. That he ... loved me. Because
> maybe he didn't.... And maybe ... maybe my new survival
> habit needed to be that I didn't care.[v]

Here, she seems to fully embrace denial as a coping strategy, but this results in a misbelief. Through this extrapolation in interiority, readers are treated to some cause-and-effect logic that makes sense to Andi in the moment. Audiences might empathize with her, even if they see the short-sightedness of her plan. (In fact, the plot purposefully attacks her determination not to care.)

> **Interiority Insight:** Breaking points in the present can lead to breakthroughs about the past, or a decision to approach the future in a new way.

Later, Andi starts to fall for Magnus, her patron, and reflects on how her backstory affects her sense of what she has to offer in relationships:

> *Say something, Andi. Anything.* Anything to comfort [Magnus], to show him everything would be all right. Instead I just let him cry on me, loving him the only way I was truly good at—taking care of people who were in pain. It was a specific type of love I'd developed because it had been the only way I was allowed to love Jember. And, for me, I'd needed to love someone for my own survival.[w]

These two excerpts chart her personal growth as a character, from rejecting love to knowing she needs to practice it for her own sake, even though she doesn't yet trust that it'll be returned.

Let's pivot to a character who's more able to take her past in stride, at least superficially. This is Hannah Brooks from adult romantic comedy *The Bodyguard* by Katherine Center. Hannah's mother dies at the beginning of the story, but our intrepid protagonist wants everyone to know that she's perfectly fine, and that emotions can't and won't affect her, thankyouverymuch. She has thrown herself so fully into her career that even her backstory is only discussed in terms of what it has allowed her to achieve:

> Growing up as my mother's child had forced me to learn the opposite of language: all the things we say without words. I had turned it into a pretty great career, to be honest. But if you asked me if it was a blessing or a curse, I wouldn't know what to say.[x]

> **Interiority Insight:** Depending on worldview and theme, wounding backstory can be perceived as a curse or a blessing.

In *The City We Became,* an adult fantasy novel by N.K. Jemisin, the five boroughs of New York City are represented by individual POV characters, plus a sixth who stands in for the Spirit of New York. Bronca, the avatar for the Bronx, pulls not only from her personal backstory to anchor her present-day self, but from her ancestral trauma and indigenous identity. She's Lenape, descended from the nation that inhabited the land that became Manhattan and its environs. Traumatic Dutch colonization from centuries ago still informs aspects of Bronca's current life, though she doesn't always keep the lessons of the past in mind:

> Her people have survived by hiding in plain sight for generations, passing as Black or Hispanic or whatever worked, but all that time pretending has left its mark. She tries to always remember that the way of the Lenape is cooperation, but it's a struggle sometimes.[y]

Interiority Insight: Does your character come from a culture where the "collective unconscious"[7] adds a layer to their identity or present struggle? Consider exploring this possibility.

Let's now shift to backstory and wounds that are more galvanizing in nature. That means they either failed to destroy a character's sense of self, or the protagonist has already done serious healing. The characters in the following section now use their backstory as fuel for their objectives, motivations, and needs, instead of as dead weight that pulls them down.

Formative Backstory

To demonstrate how a wound or backstory element can be formative, let's meet Jim from adult upmarket novel *Anxious People* by Fredrik Backman. This character lost his wife years ago, and while he's not

---

7. An idea initially codified by Carl Jung for a foundational type of joint memory that comes "pre-loaded" in each brain like system software: https://www.britannica.com/science/collective-unconscious

overtly traumatized by it, he shows no interest in moving on, despite his son, Jack's, prodding:

> When the old policeman—and he's never felt older than he does right now—lifts his hand, he toys with his wedding ring. An old habit, but scant comfort.... Jack mentions the ring once every six months or so, saying: "Dad, isn't it time you took that off?" His dad nods, as if he's forgotten about it, tugs it a little as if it fits more tightly than it usually does, and mumbles: "I will, I will." He never does.[z]

Her death is now simply a fact of life.

Interiority Insight: Not all backstory needs to be dramatic or traumatic.

How Far the Light Reaches is a hybrid memoir and nonfiction essay collection by Sabrina Imbler. Parts of the project pull from the author's life, showing formative moments as they inform Sabrina's nonbinary and queer identity. In this excerpt, they recount a memory by talking to their former self in second-person direct address:

> You and M first saw each other in the library and officially met in a queer theory class (a cliché, obviously). You were ghosted that summer by the first girl you slept with (tacky!), a separation that left you depressed, unsure if you were in love, or if you were gay or straight, because you, young idiot, were under the impression that sexuality could exist beyond the binary for everyone but you. You felt afraid to return to dating men, that it would prove your first girlfriend right. You were also afraid to date people who were not men, that perhaps you were not queer but only wanted to be.[aa]

Readers see some deep feelings and vulnerabilities here, but not in a way that paints these moments as necessarily traumatic. Instead, a seed of inquiry is planted. The self-deprecating humor helps to add this dimension.

Interiority Insight: If your character could write a letter to their younger self, what would they say? If the past and present selves met, what would they think of one another? (Also, would they help and console each another or ditch the interaction because they have nothing in common anymore?) Second-person direct address asides can add voice and engagement, but should be used consistently if this is a stylistic choice you make.

A change in circumstance brings Vincent from *The Glass Hotel* into contact with her imagined past selves. She has started dating a financier and enjoying the Kingdom of Money (as we saw in Chapter 3), and in this scene, she marvels to a new friend:

> "Do you find that shopping is actually incredibly boring?"
> Vincent felt guilty saying this aloud ... [but] Mirella hadn't come from money either. Ghosts of Vincent's earlier selves flocked around the table and stared at the beautiful clothes she was wearing.[bb]

These aren't ghosts or avatars of some horrific tragedy, but Vincent acknowledges she has now separated from them and launched into a new identity.

Interiority Insight: Notice the tone of inquiry and curiosity in these excerpts, which is a departure from some of the grief and horror featured earlier in this chapter.

Fathers come into the picture with seemingly a bit more emotional distance than mothers, at least as far as these From the Shelves selections go. Louise from adult horror novel *The Final Girl Support Group* by Grady

Hendrix remembers her father but acknowledges that she might see the past through rose-colored glasses. As she reads over her old journals, she's surprised by her teenage self's anger, which has since mellowed:

> Dad had been in the army and had definite ideas about law and order. Maybe he was stricter than he needed to be, but I don't remember hating him [that] much.... I sanded down our rough times and polished up Dad's halo until it's bright enough to blind me to the past.[cc]

Interiority Insight: Remember, all memory perspectives are inherently biased. Even as characters recall events and people in their lives (or past versions of those people, who may have changed since), these are merely interpretations, extrapolations, and subsumations. Backstories often reveal more about the protagonist than the actual subject of the memory.

Finally, June from *Yellowface* shares an anecdote from college, in which she told her frenemy, Athena, about being sexually assaulted on campus. Later, she claims that Athena wrote a piece that heavily borrowed from this story, told in confidence. Readers are left to wonder whether June shares this memory in a calculated attempt to justify eventually appropriating Athena's manuscript:

> She'd stolen my story. I was convinced of it. She'd stolen my words.[dd]

Whether this is an excuse or June's genuine recollection, this excerpt shows that trauma and backstory can either fester inside of a character or be used to drive the protagonist forward. The past, especially, informs a character's sense of self. This last point hits at the beating heart of interiority, how we use it, and why it matters—this craft tool allows us to express a protagonist's deepest identity. That's what I'll explore in the following chapter.

6

_____

SENSE OF SELF

Most humans have a deep and private identity, and so do our characters. How does a protagonist think *to* and *about* themselves? Their true opinions, insecurities, and reflections are often at odds with whatever the audience might see externally. A great way to demonstrate sense of self to readers is to have protagonists engage in self-assessment and self-inquiry, early and often, especially at consequential moments in the plot.

Audiences are going to form their own opinions of your character, and you absolutely want to encourage this process. Remember, a reader wants to be an active participant by thinking critically and generating their own impressions, which you will either confirm or subvert. However, this can only happen if you're aware of how your protagonist comes across in the first place. Interiority is especially suited to characters expressing how they feel about themselves, in their own words and thoughts.

This opens up a lot of interesting potential. Is your protagonist reliable, or perhaps unreliable, in their self-assessment? Too nice and maybe even delusional? Too harsh and perhaps suffering from their own misbelief or someone else's unfair expectations? Do they have low self-awareness or high? Low self-esteem or high? Do these attributes change over time? Their identity is also subject to internal tension, as we'll see in Chapter 9.

Personality types and styles are one jumping off-point into a character's sense of self. An example is the concept of fixed or growth mindsets, codified by Carol Dweck in *Mindset: The New Psychology of Success*. Her research centers on the idea that some people have a fixed mindset and tend to believe that identity characteristics are set. This often correlates with lower self-awareness and passivity. Other people have a growth mindset (which I sometimes call "flexible" because I like the alliteration with "fixed"), which opens them up to self-awareness, self-improvement, and proactive behavior. This has also been called a "possibilities" versus an "adversity" mindset. The latter type of person focuses on all the reasons something is impossible, rather than finding opportunities to prevail. The former type believes in the potential for self-driven change and growth. There are also people and characters who ascribe positive motivation to others, and those who are more distrusting or suspicious. (More on relationship mindsets in Chapter 13.)

There are many, many frameworks out there for fleshing out your protagonist's sense of self. One new trend in parenting circles divides children into "orchid" or "dandelion" personalities to conceptualize levels of resilience. Some writers explore character through the lens of a Myers-Briggs type or enneagram number. Others are drawn to figuring out personality through star charts and zodiac placements. But keep in mind that these are broad categories and shouldn't replace a fully developed, multi-layered character.

More importantly, what kind of story does your character tell themselves *about* themselves?[1] Is the protagonist able to explore their own narrative identity and develop a nuanced self-understanding? Do they make meaning from experiences then extrapolate and subsume those insights into their sense of being? Are they able to overcome their difficulties and achieve a redemptive growth arc (more on this in Chapter 11)? Or do they allow their moods and most recent successes and failures influence their self-perception?

You don't have to answer all of these questions, but you should be

---

1. In psychology, this is called the "internalized story of self."

aware that these options exist for characters, just as they do for human beings.

The Foundation of Everything

The character's relationship to their inner self guides the reader's relationship to character. One of the benefits of being human is that we have the capacity for self-awareness—not that everyone uses theirs! As such, most sentient beings have longstanding and nuanced ideas of who they are. These notions guide their actions and thoughts, and can also be flexible as protagonists change and grow (or, less often, regress). Remember, your character might present to the world very differently from how they function internally. Interiority is a wonderful tool for giving readers a peek at these layers.

In this chapter, you'll get a nuanced and, more importantly, self-expressed overview of most of the characters from our 56 books. Still, not every person or protagonist is created equal when it comes to sense of self. Some personality types seem to go through life without thinking about it too hard.[2] These characters don't always make for terribly interesting POV protagonists. If there's no depth or "there" there, readers may not become or remain as engaged as they could be.

So how can you create a fictional character—or package your real self into a protagonist for the purposes of a memoir—in a way that feels as rich and layered as the voice in your own head? A winning strategy involves deploying interiority as characters examine themselves and comment on what they find.

Let's begin with some examples of characters who define themselves in comparison to others. This line of inquiry is often biased by a misbelief that everyone else has everything figured out. These protagonists also tend to be acutely vulnerable to their perception of how others might see them. Sometimes characters accept these assumed labels, and sometimes, they reject them. This externally defined sense of self is perhaps the least evolved, so we'll start there.

---

2. Several of Melissa Broder's characters and I would like to know their secret!

Self as Defined by Others

If low self-esteem was a person, it might be Patrick from *The Glass Hotel*. (We've already met his sister, Vincent.) In the scene below, he's giving out drugs at a club to try and attract a woman, but isn't too optimistic about his odds:

> "Anyway, they're yours if you want them," he said, to this
> group that like all of the other groups he'd ever encountered in
> his life was going to reject him.[a]

Things hit a new low when one of his pills kills the woman's friend. Though Patrick is an insecure character who has been laid low by the plot, readers may wonder whether his misbelief and worldview are hindering him, too. If he goes into a situation expecting rejection in interiority, he might be creating a self-fulfilling prophecy.[3]

Interiority Insight: Worldviews can technically change, though this kind of growth takes a lot of courage, energy, and willingness to imagine that other options exist.

Rachel, from *Milk Fed*, is still sore after her breakup with her first girlfriend, Miriam, who she doesn't really respect. Instead of feeling bad about herself, per se, she seems to dread what Miriam's rejection says about her status instead:

> I felt in that moment that I did not know myself at all.... Miriam
> had traveled fewer places than I had. She still lived with her
> family and had no grand plans for any kind of career. Yet some-
> how, she seemed to be moving forward more freely than I was,
> or if not forward, then deeper and higher, in a series of infinite
> crescendos. While I was aggressively pedaling nowhere, she was
> orbiting peacefully.[b]

---

3. He should also probably stop handing out adulterated drugs.

Interiority Insight: A character with a fragile sense of self might not be able to come to their own conclusions, instead wondering: What will others think about me now?

The question of identity and community intertwines in *The City We Became*, where each of the main POV protagonists is tasked with protecting NYC from destruction. (The less-than-subtle suggestion is that the antagonist is an avatar for gentrification itself, and often appears under aliases like the Woman in White and Dr. White.) Manny, a mixed-race representation of Manhattan, is acting rowdy in public and scares off a white woman. He imagines himself through her eyes in this excerpt:

> She'll never sleep easily again in New York, never walk to work without looking over her shoulder. He's in her head now, waving at her from the little box of assumptions that she carries about Certain Kinds of People ... [and he] hates that he's just confirmed her stereotypes.[c]

This quote raises the question of who a character is versus who they appear to be, and whether those are the same thing. Manny seems to make a foregone conclusion about racism and how his skin tone colors every encounter, at least with white people. He's unhappy with the situation, but he's also convinced that this is reality, like it or not. Is he actually one of those "Certain Kinds of People"? If he's not, on a deeper level, would it even matter to this woman? Or has she made up her mind about him already, so it's not worth the energy to try and convince her otherwise? Does her perception reflect on him in any way or not? Does he stand by the way he acted, or is there some shame there, too?

Interiority Insight: Consider "code-switching," which means that characters act differently in specific situations and with various groups of people. Does your character display certain behaviors with family that they'd never dare show their friends? In a profes-

---

sional setting versus while goofing off? How does this factor into their identity and presentation? How do they feel about it?

Another character in this novel is Bronca, who represents the Bronx. We saw her channel her Lenape heritage in Chapter 5. Now, she explores her sense of self in comparison to Veneza, the avatar for Jersey City:

> Bronca realizes all of a sudden that she's facing a choice about how to deal with Veneza.... Veneza is so much of what Bronca could have been, if she'd come up in a better world—and so much of what Bronca is now, because the world is still a goddamn shitshow. Bronca wants so badly to protect her.[d]

In both instances, Manny and Bronca indulge in racial, cultural, and socioeconomic commentary as they compare themselves to others. Though *The City We Became* is a fantasy novel, it very much amplifies real, contemporary concerns in American society. (We'll discuss world-building in more detail in Chapter 18.)

As first noted in Chapter 3, Roman from *Divine Rivals* struggles to live up to his parents' expectations. One of his deeper issues is that he doesn't trust his own emotions. This is him trying to imagine what his family might see when they look at him, which reveals some misbeliefs about his shortcomings:

> Do you ever feel as if you wear armor, day after day? That when people look at you, they see only the shine of steel that you've so carefully encased yourself in? They see what they want to see in you ... all the times you've failed, all the times you've hurt them or disappointed them. As if that is all you will ever be in their eyes.[e]

Of course, this interiority also suggests that he doesn't want to live this way anymore, which sets up his growth trajectory.

> **Interiority Insight:** Going from feeling defined by others to standing by your own sense of self is actually a huge leap. This kind of growth arc is very common in middle grade, young adult, memoir, and some women's fiction, where more profound transformation is often expected.

Another character struggling with family dynamics is Hazel, one of the main narrators in adult literary novel *Brutes* by Dizz Tate. With an astute level of self-awareness, she seems to define herself in relation to her sister, Jody:

> I've been ignoring Jody's messages for months.... Silence pushed to its limits on both sides. We have never been good at talking about our feelings. We are not those types of sisters, or people. Emotions are competitive for us, like everything else.[f]

> **Interiority Insight:** A protagonist's role within their larger interpersonal framework is an interesting identity layer, as we'll see in Chapter 12. Consider birth order and sibling rivalry. Studies have found differences between only children and those with siblings; first children, middle children, and younger children; and in children from big families and small ones. How might various family roles inform your character's identity?

An amazing character study is June from *Yellowface*. After stealing Athena's manuscript, passing it off as her own, and rising to fame, June ends up with everything she ever wanted. However, her secret comes out, and she starts losing her precious (but ill-gotten) literary cachet. In this excerpt, she teaches a writing workshop under her pen name, Juniper Song. When she overhears the students gossiping about what a fraud she is, she viciously rips their work apart in retaliation. This is how she unpacks her decision to go for the jugular (figuratively, we hope):

I've won. It's a pathetic victory, sure, but it's better than sitting here and suffering their mocking glares. That hot, vicious satisfaction stays with me through the rest of the morning. I conclude the critique circle, assign homework, and watch them flee wordlessly out the door. I've only made things worse, I know. Now I'll have to sit before their resentful, condescending faces for another week and a half. I'm sure that, behind the scenes, they'll bitch about me endlessly until this workshop is over. I'm sure they'll join the chorus of Juniper Song haters online. But I've at least made myself into a terror rather than a punch line, and for now, I'm all right with that.[g]

She knows it's wrong, on the one hand, but like the competitive siblings, Hazel and Jody, from the previous excerpt, she will sacrifice anything to "win." (One could argue her moral code has always been self-serving, given that she stole "her" breakthrough manuscript.) It seems June would rather be "a terror" than admit to any fault or engage the students in meaningful dialogue, whether out of shame, ego, or both.

She does acknowledge this, which, believe it or not, is a measure of some growth. After she enjoys the highs of fame and the "promise of the premise" of this novel, the truth starts catching up to her, and the trajectory of the plot changes from wish fulfillment to thriller.

I'll talk a lot about the masterful adult literary novel *Americanah* by Chimamanda Ngozi Adichie throughout this guide. In this passage, we meet Nigerian native Obinze, who's been living as an illegal immigrant in England. He has a lot more trouble suppressing his moral compass than June does, and this reflects his dignity and self-esteem, even in a low moment. He has just told his public defender that he'll agree to be deported, a decision we'll see excerpted in Chapter 16. Once his fate is sealed, he ruefully thinks about the others sitting beside him in an immigration holding cell:

Obinze envied them for what they were, men who casually changed names and passports, who would plan and come back and do it over again because they had nothing to lose.... He was ashamed to be with them, among them. They did not have his shame and even this, too, he envied.[h]

His interiority reveals that he'll go home to Nigeria, ashamed and empty-handed, and that his primary concern is keeping his integrity intact.

Interiority Insight: Moral code. Values. Integrity. These are all things to consider as you build out who your protagonist is at their deepest core.

Mare Barrow, from the young adult fantasy novel, *Red Queen* by Victoria Aveyard, is wrestling with her ethics, too. As we'll also see in Chapter 16, she's trying to survive in a challenging authoritarian world where impoverished Reds live in a separate echelon of society, rungs below the privileged Silvers. There's a ton of other magic, danger, and intrigue, of course, but this is the basic gist.

In trying to improve her situation and prevent her and her best friend from being drafted, Mare sneaks into a Silver stronghold but ends up accidentally exposing herself and endangering her sister's livelihood.

Horrified by this turn of events, she goes back to thieving, believing she can't do better for anyone involved, not even herself. Here, she sees her identity through the lens of mistakes made and harm done to others:

I caused so much harm today, so much hurt to the ones I love most. I should turn around and go home, to face everyone with at least some courage. But instead I settle against the shadows of the inn, content to remain in darkness.

I guess causing pain is all I'm good for.... No one notices, no one even cares, when I fade away again. I'm a shadow, and no one remembers shadows.[i]

Interiority Insight: Intentional actions reflect on the self. Unintentional actions, failed attempts, and mistakes do, too. Identity can be shaped by both presence and absence—what did happen, and what didn't.

Like Obinze, Mare's ashamed, but unlike him, she feels she can't go home and face reality. In fact, she doesn't even get the chance, because she meets Cal, a powerful Silver prince in disguise, outside the tavern where she's picking pockets.

He "rescues her" from the draft, but she'll have to pretend to be a lost Silver heiress, live at the palace, and leave her entire life behind. (What nobody knows at this point is that she has very rare Silver-type powers.) Though she saves herself, Mare can't stomach the Silver lifestyle and mindset. When she and Cal venture out of the palace again, she joins the resistance—the Scarlet Guard.

Like the sisters in *The Nightingale*, Mare has no good choices available to her, only hard ones. In the first excerpt, she was ashamed to face her family after ruining her sister's career. Now, she can't look Cal in the eye as a new Scarlet Guard recruit. At some point, she's going to have to choose a side. In the meantime, she is very mindful of how the world sees her in all of the various roles she plays:

> Maybe it's a military tactic he picked up in one of his books: *let the enemy come to you.*
>
> *Because that's what I am now. His enemy.*[j]

Interiority Insight: Your protagonist might not be in dire straits, like Mare, but they may still have a private and a public self. This can generate a lot of internal tension, which we'll read about in Chapter 9.

Of course, a character doesn't simply define themselves by the opinions of others. They also have an inherent concept of their identity. Self-awareness and self-esteem exist on a spectrum, from low to high. Keep in mind that low self-awareness and low self-esteem are not the same thing. In fact, some of the most self-aware characters can have the lowest self-esteem. Many of the following excerpts appear at the beginnings of their respective stories, leaving room for growth. Other times, a character sinks deeper and deeper into delusion as their stories progresses, like Alex from *The Guest* and June from *Yellowface*.

Low Self-Awareness and Low Self-Esteem

We've already met Leonie from *Sing, Unburied, Sing*, and she's basically a masterclass in delusion, evasiveness, and self-loathing. Surprisingly, readers manage to (somewhat) root for her, even as they might judge her choices and worldviews.

Leonie is a character I'd like to grab by the shoulders and shake some sense and self-love into. Knowing her backstory, which we learned in the previous chapter, I don't particularly blame her for being a porous kind of character who's only happy when the light of someone else's love shines on her. This makes her vulnerable to being taken advantage of, and to feeling miserable and lonely whenever she's left to her own devices. After she perceives rejection by her on-again-off-again partner, Michael, she turns that agony inward in interiority:

> I would throw up everything. All of it out: food and bile and stomach and intestines and esophagus, organs all, bones and muscle, until all that was left was skin. And then maybe that could turn inside out, and I wouldn't be nothing no more. Not this skin, not this body. Maybe Michael could step on my heart, stop its beating. Then burn everything to cinders.[k]

Interiority Insight: Imagery and hyperbole can be used to create high emotional conflict, as long as this doesn't veer into melodrama (see Chapter 16).

A character who's similarly hard on herself is Aislyn from *The City We Became*. Aislyn represents Staten Island and lives a sheltered life. She tries to leave on the ferry and suffers a panic attack, due to her paranormal connection with her borough. Here, she wishes for a more glamorous existence:

> She's lonely and ashamed and she hasn't given up hope for a
> life of excitement and sophistication, somewhere and sometime.
> But this is the sort of lie that she needs, especially in the wake of
> her disastrous attempt to board the ferry.[1]

We see a glimmer of self-awareness in this interiority, as Aislyn deludes herself and seems to acknowledge it. It's also easy to imagine her—technically a part of New York City—merely gazing at a glittering Manhattan across the water and feeling left out.

We now pivot to the queen of self-delusion: June from *Yellowface*. This is an expanded version of the excerpt, on jealousy, that originally appeared in Chapter 3. She's reflecting on what Athena's success might mean for her own sense of self:

> Jealousy is the spike in my heart rate when I glimpse news of
> Athena's success on Twitter—another book contract, awards
> nominations, special editions, foreign rights deals. Jealousy is
> constantly comparing myself to her and coming up short; is
> panicking that I'm not writing well enough or fast enough, that I
> am not, and never will be, enough. Jealousy means that even
> just learning that Athena's signing a six-figure option deal with
> Netflix means that I'll be derailed for days, unable to focus on
> my own work, mired by shame and self-disgust every time I see
> one of her books in a bookstore display.[m]

June is aware of her tendency to be blinded by despair when her friend achieves something noteworthy, of how much she covets this kind of validation for herself. But, similar to Leonie, June is unlikely to feel fulfilled by anyone else's love, or any publisher's seal of approval.[4]

---

4. Are you listening, aspiring writers?

Neither character seems to realize that they need to love themselves first.

Interiority Insight: It's up to you to decide whether your struggling characters will redeem themselves with morally solid choices. Protagonists like Leonie and June can still engage readers despite their behavior, but fostering this connection may be tougher.

We continue our rather dismal exploration of characters with low self-awareness and/or low self-esteem with Olivia from *The Glass Hotel*. Years ago, she was a notable young artist, beautiful and acclaimed. As she ages and tries to participate in the world of taste and money once more, she attempts some of her old tricks, only to get a reality check:

> "You won't remember me," she said … and immediately wished she'd said something different. The trouble with that line was that it had worked when she was young because when she was young, she was beautiful, also fierce in a calculated manner that she'd believed to be attractive, which had lent a certain irony to the suggestion that anyone could have possibly forgotten her—*Oh, you know, just another gorgeous magnetic fresh young talent with gallery representation*—but lately she'd found that the line sometimes elicited a tactful silence, and she'd realized that often people did not, in fact, remember her.[11]

In this instance of interiority, Olivia seems to derive her worth from the opinions of others, and is mortified to realize that her self-deprecating humor no longer plays as intended. She has become what she once feared—old and irrelevant—and this suggests a big turning point in her sense of self.

The inability to feel good without validation is a common conflict, and reminds me of Hannah from *The It Girl*, who sees herself as successful only if her wealthy and glamorous new friends accept her:

> She wasn't as spiky or witty as Emily, or as cheeky and sarcastic

as Ryan. But she could be someone else. Someone new. Maybe
… and here she swallowed, a shiver of longing running across
her bare skin beneath the kimono. Maybe she could even be a
girl that someone like Will would look twice at.[o]

When Hannah does manage to find her way into this social group, she
finally feels good about herself, but she'd do well to develop a sense of
internal worth. Hannah seems to succeed at leaving Dodsworth, her
working-class hometown, behind, but this might be a shallow victory:

Every day she spent with April she felt increasingly dissociated
from her old self, the gulf between this gilded existence and
humdrum Dodsworth gaping wider and wider until it seemed
that no train could bridge it.[p]

Underpinning Hannah's need to fit in is the vulnerable question of
whether this new reality is "too good" for her, per her low self-esteem.
Her external circumstances lead her to subsume ideas about her value.
By believing she belongs, she's able to feel a kind of acceptance she's
not able to offer herself. Unfortunately, becoming part of this clique
also gets her involved in April's murder, so there's a steep price to pay.

Interiority Insight: There's an old adage: "Wherever you go, there
you are." Some characters, especially those with low self-esteem,
will pursue the objective of leaving their "old self" or "old life"
behind. This tends to be an early-story misbelief, as meaningful
transformation is not as easy as a location change.

Finally, here's Rachel from *Milk Fed*, who believes she is damaged at
the soul level, which is an incredibly heavy and shameful thing to feel:

I was scared of my soul. What if my soul was monstrous? If a
person had a monstrous soul, should she still follow it?[q]

Interiority Insight: Characters often present with a dreary sense of self and feel damaged when they consider their backstory wounds or act outside of their values.

Luckily, a lot of our low self-esteem and/or low self-awareness protagonists don't remain in these states for long. There are also many characters who are already on a growth trajectory when readers meet them, and they populate our next slate of examples.

Growing Self-Awareness and Self-Esteem

Characters who evolve and engage in self-inquiry are dynamic and fun to read. Eden, the protagonist in *The Way I Used to Be,* starts off quite low. She was raped by Kevin, a friend of her older sibling. She thought Kevin was a safe person and that her home was a safe place. When he assaults her, she becomes willing to do anything to numb the pain. At the beginning of her story, she doesn't show any self-worth:

> I feel it tingling in my bones and skin and blood—something barbaric, something animal.... If I don't move, I'm afraid I might do something crazy, something really bad.... I'm dangerous, criminally dangerous.[r]

Later, though, Eden slowly pulls out of her nosedive. Once she's able to process her trauma and actually speak the truth of what happened, she reclaims her power:

> The Earth is still intact. I'm still alive. The floor didn't open up and swallow me whole. I haven't spontaneously combusted. I didn't know what I thought would happen if I told ... but I didn't expect nothing to happen. Everything is just as it was. No giant meteors collided with the planet and completely wiped out the entire human race.... My heart, it's still beating, and my lungs, I test them, in and out, yes, still breathing.[s]

Notice that this is the beginning of self-awareness and self-advocacy for Eden. Her worst-case scenario—an anticipated disaster revealed in interiority (more on the concept of stakes in Chapter 17)—doesn't happen. She achieves delayed growth, but growth nonetheless.

Interiority Insight: Not all story obstacles are external. Plenty of characters put internal obstacles in their own way, consciously or not, due to fear, vulnerability, or self-defeating tendencies. Sometimes this is understandable and warranted, but it's detrimental all the same.

Lily, from adult literary novel *Bad Fruit* by Ellie King, is a really interesting character study, especially at the beginning of her story. She's cursed with an overbearing mother who demands that biracial Lily behave and look a certain way (more Chinese, like Mama herself).

Lily finds herself in the unenviable role of Mama's emotional support animal and keeper of family peace at any price. Unfortunately, she's also self-aware and suffers greatly as a result. Here's a classic mirror scene, in which she regards herself while taking off the make-up she wears to fit Mama's ideal:

> Usually, I linger over this Chinese version of me.... I reach for my pack of wipes, scrub off the yellow-undertoned makeup, sweep out the tinted contact lenses, and look again. White skin. One hazel eye. One brown. My hair is still that cheap black, but when I examine my hairline, the brown is already pushing through.
>
> I sit back, relieved. Despite everything Mama has done to bring out the Chinese in me, I remain resolutely myself, her whitest child.
>
> *I'm not the same as her.*[1]

Interiority Insight: Some writers like to be very specific about a character's appearance, while others take a lighter approach and let readers fill in the blanks. At some point, though, no matter your preference, you will have to provide a physical description of your protagonist, so try to avoid well-known contrivances. In the above excerpt, Lily *is* looking in the mirror and relaying what she sees, which is perhaps the biggest cliché of all. But what she notices about herself—and how she subsumes it—makes this self-description in interiority feel fresh. This moment is characterizing and does double duty. Also note that appearance information is often more awkward to provide in first person POV than in third. In fact, "third-person-style" self-description in first person can be a huge voice issue. Consider this: "I swept my bangs aside with my left hand, looking for all the world like the light in my eyes had gone out." This sounds like something a *narrator* might say *about* a character, but I'm hard-pressed to imagine someone saying this *about themselves*. How often do we think about the basic stats of what we look like, after all? It's too overly self-conscious. If you're guilty of this in your first-person writing, decide how you want to tackle the question of describing the character's external actions and qualities, and whether your efforts sound organic. You may also want to do less with descriptions of individual physical actions, or "play-by-play choreography," as I like to call it. In the above example, do we *really* need to know which hand was used to touch the bangs? No. These details are often superficial and less interesting than what interiority can convey. Keep them to a minimum.

Lily keeps straining against the bonds of Mom's expectations. She wants to make her own decisions but doesn't feel she can:

> When Mama and I go shopping, I play this game. I give myself a choice between two things and ask myself if she weren't there, what would I choose? … If choosing is a muscle, mine has atrophied from disuse and although I keep practicing, I don't think I'll ever be able to do it. You have to picture yourself when you choose an outfit or a piece of jewelry, imagine your-

self wearing this or that, but when I think of myself, I see only
… me in Mama's imagination, and then I don't want to think
anymore.[u]

Lily's need to choose and be herself is emerging, and she will eventually have to confront her mother. "When I think of myself, I see only me … in Mama's imagination" would also make a great thematic statement.

Interiority Insight: The above is a great example of stating the situation in interiority, then digging deeper into the underlying psychology, as if using "And? So?" to extrapolate the ramifications. For the moment, Lily remains stymied but she's also developed a hypothetical situation in her head that's ruled by fear.

Similar self-inquiry gets a slightly lighter touch with Rachel from *Milk Fed*. She becomes aware of her mommy issues but doesn't know what to do with that knowledge. This reaction is very relatable and underscores that growth is a process:

I wondered whether there was a deadline for when a person had
to finally stop blaming her mother for her own thoughts. I
thought I'd hit that age, then hit it again. At nineteen, twenty, I
decided: *Okay, this is enough. You are a grown-up. Time to take
responsibility for your own mind.* At twenty-one, *I am over it.* At
twenty-two, *I understand why she did what she did.* At twenty-
three, *I forgive. But now what?*[v]

As we'll see in Chapter 11 and Chapter 16, growth isn't always linear. Decisions can generally take place after a fraught process instead of occurring in a single moment. It's okay not to know, as long as the character ends up somewhere more definitive, especially since a total question mark can be unsatisfying for readers.

Moving on from moms and daughters, let's track Sona, the Windup from *Gearbreakers,* and her evolving sense of self. She trained for a coveted mech pilot job and underwent an extremely brutal surgery.

Now that it's too late to change her mind, she realizes what the role actually entails. It's a watershed moment:

> My fingernails curl into my sides, seeking an invisible seam or a ridge … to dip into and tear back. There is nothing—it is me, it is all me, humming, glowing, pretending to gasp for breath. I am not steadfast; I am not something rigid. I am a child who must kill today, and it makes me scared for myself.[w]

Notice that she, a tough teen, also identifies herself as "a child" for the first time, instead of the soldier she has physically become. She also admits to some difficult truths.

Throughout the story, Sona ends up fighting against her own feelings, first denying them, then compartmentalizing them. When Sona meets the rebel Gearbreakers, led by Eris, "the girl" referred to, below, she realizes that those messy feelings make her life worth living:

> Comforting people is new to me…. Suddenly, now, there are people around me that I do not want to hurt, and I do not know how to take my hard edges out, how to say the right things, how to comfort the girl who gave me living, breathing people to fight for.[x]

This kind of painful, vulnerable growth elevates Sona as a compelling protagonist.

Interiority Insight: It's also possible to define a character's sense of self in a positive, proactive way, and show them standing up for their valuable qualities and beliefs. If a character becomes more authentic and principled, the story may offer readers a desirable and aspirational experience.

The characters in the upmarket adult novel *Bright Young Women* by Jessica Knoll are thrown into chaos when a murderer breaks into a sorority house and kills chapter president Pamela's best friend, Denise. This puts Pamela on a collision course with a woman named Tina, who believes the same person once slayed her partner, Ruth. Before Tina arrives with this clue, Pamela is left to her own devices and needs to show the world that she can handle things. But early in her arc, she's floundering:

> All day, I'd felt wretched at the thought of Sheriff Cruso in our rooms, touching our things, going through our drawers. But then, when his men did leave a week later, I had to suppress the urge to chase them down the street and beg them to come back. *Don't leave me in charge. Please. I can't do this alone.*[y]

It's juicy to see Pamela, who has a very exacting and rule-following personality, throw up the white flag and admit helplessness. This interiority goes completely against her established sense of self.

Ruth, the previous murder victim, gets a point of view, as this novel weaves together several chronologies. When she was alive, Ruth struggled with cystic acne and her mother made her feel useless. When Ruth gets out of the house to group therapy, her priority is to look as good as possible to the other women there (including her future partner, Tina):

> When it was my turn to talk about my support system, I led with my ex-husband. I didn't want the women to get the wrong idea about me. I was having a bad breakout, but I didn't always look like this. Someone had married me and had sex with me. "We had a lot of problems in our marriage," I said, leaving out the part that my ex-husband was having an affair. I didn't need them thinking, *Well, of course he did, can you imagine waking up to that face without makeup in the morning?*[z]

Her self-loathing is clear, and the interiority to that effect is formatted in both narration and verbatim thought. Later, as Ruth begins a relationship with Tina and finds her own place in the world, she begins to literally see herself in a new light. The following excerpt demonstrates her evolving sense of self:

> I'd come up here to splash water on my face, to get ahold of myself.... I felt some of my self-loathing dissipate. I had my

problems, my weaknesses, and succumbing to them had contributed to the lousy belief that I did not belong anywhere.[aa]

Interiority Insight: Tracking a character's perspective on any attribute or flaw that makes them miserable over the course of several scenes is an opportunity to clearly communicate their growth trajectory.

A character's transformation can be tremendous, but it is often parceled out in small moments. These instances can carry intense emotional stakes.

As we move toward characters with higher self-esteem and awareness, let's meet Ariana Ruiz, also known as Ari, from the young adult novel *The Luis Ortega Survival Club* by Sonora Reyes. Ari has autism and selective mutism, which are exacerbated when she's raped by a classmate, the titular Luis Ortega. As Ari learns her limits and begins to self-advocate, she realizes that she can't *also* play therapist for her problematic mother. Remember that Ari doesn't usually speak, a symptom of her grief and trauma. When she does open her mouth, it's with great purpose:

> "I think you should get therapy," I say, not meaning to sound harsh. It's a genuine suggestion. She really needs someone to talk to, and as an autistic selectively mute teenager with an increasingly soiled reputation and a million problems of my own, I'm hardly qualified.[bb]

The interiority that accompanies the dialogue adds depth. Ari identifies the roles she and Mom play and reveals how she characterizes herself.

Finally, on a high point in her growth as an independent young woman, Joey has the following to say in *Tell Me I'm an Artist*. She cheekily admits that she'd rather sulk but this excerpt reminds readers that it's important to track the highs, not just the lows, and that both are part of her evolving identity:

How was I supposed to continue to feel sorry for myself if I kept getting everything I wanted? What if the secret to success was, instead of wallowing in self-pity, vocalizing the things I needed to people who had the ability to help? What if, instead of feeling guilty about everything all the time, I just . . . didn't?[cc]

Sailing on from this high note, let's look at some of those rare and inspiring characters with high self-awareness and/or high self-esteem. Unfortunately, they don't often have things easy, as we'll see in the following section. They tend to agonize over moral choices that may buck against the socially-sanctioned "proper way" of doing things. Such is the flip side of having a clear and strong sense of self. Our final cohort is quite conflicted, and, of course, very engaging to read about.

High Self-Awareness and High Self-Esteem

As mentioned earlier in this chapter, people with high self-awareness can have low self-esteem. This makes them interesting because they have the capacity to suffer greatly while being profoundly aware of their innermost selves, unmet expectations, and unfulfilled desires. As such, self-knowledge can sometimes be a barrier to happiness, increasing tension throughout the story. We saw some characters flourishing toward the end of the previous section, but let's start over with the worst of all worlds—misery *and* an acute awareness of it!

Let's look at Jack, the husband in *Wellness*. Not only is he grappling with a fractured marriage and deep trauma, which we'll learn about in Chapter 20, but he's also getting older and feels conflicted about it:

Did he hate the young man he once was? That selfish and cocky brat? Or did he hate the older man he had become? In a way, he hated both. He saw his older self through the eyes of his younger self, and he felt betrayed. He had a mortgage now, and a 401(k), a job that he dressed nicely for, a marriage, a child. His older self had abandoned all his younger self's principles. He cut coupons. He woke up early. He wore slacks. He owned a watch. And he regretted his tattoo.

How could two such dissimilar people ever inhabit the same body?[dd]

This interiority raises some really interesting questions. Are we our younger selves? Our older selves? Both? How do we integrate such drastically different identities? Jack doesn't seem to see his older self positively, and there's a touch of longing and perhaps romanticizing of the past here.

Millie from *The New House* has a very strong sense of identity, but high self-awareness and self-esteem can breed their own neuroses:

> The dark wolf in me is strong, but I've worked hard all my life to starve him into submission. My childhood forced me to armour myself against the world, to detach myself emotionally for my own self-preservation. But I'm not a psychopath: if I were, I wouldn't distinguish between the good wolf and the bad. I wouldn't even know they were different.[ee]

Millie claims mastery over her "dark wolf," but has also made great sacrifices for this kind of rigid self-control, including denying herself meaningful relationships, as we'll see in Chapter 13.

Another character who's self-aware and conscious to the point of cynicism is Vincent in *The Glass Hotel*, who we saw musing about the Kingdom of Money in Chapter 5. She gets into a relationship with wealthy (for now) Jonathan Alkaitis:

> "You're so poised," Jonathan said.
>
> … *That's my job*, Vincent didn't say in return. Calling it a job seemed uncharitable, because she really did like him. It wasn't the romance of the century, but it didn't have to be; if you genuinely enjoy someone's company, she'd been thinking lately, if you enjoy your life with them and don't mind sleeping with them, isn't that enough? Do you have to actually be in love for a relationship to be real, whatever real means, so long as there's respect and something like friendship? She spent more time thinking about this than she would have liked, which suggested

that it was an unresolved question, but she felt certain that she could go on this way for a long time, years probably.[ff]

Vincent asserts that she doesn't want a real relationship and even seems to look down on the idea. I have to wonder, though, whether she's only pretending to be okay with lowering her expectations. Is part of her sad that she's not able to find an authentic love relationship? Or does she really, truly not care?

Interiority Insight: Sometimes it's revelatory to go into verbatim thought to show readers what a character purposefully leaves *out* of dialogue. There's a juicy contrast between the spoken and unspoken.

In our search for self-aware but damaged characters, we might gravitate to the unnamed narrator of *Death Valley*, who is a struggling novelist. (Bookstore shelves are littered with writers and other literary characters, for obvious reasons.) Here she is, musing about her writing process and reacting to how she's perceived. It's a sobering portrait of anxiety and self-loathing, yet many of us may be able to relate and forgive her some navel-gazing:

When interviewed about my "writing process," I always say that I don't believe a person has to suffer to make art. But that's only because I imagine it's true for others (also, I don't want to be accused of inspiring teen suicide). If ever I attempt to make the inside of my skull a softer place to live (i.e., by saying kind and gentle words to myself), a counter-alert pops up inside my head that says, This is dangerous. Do not tread here. Also, you're wrong. The counter-alert comes from a primal place.... Its message may ultimately be more destructive than helpful, but it feels like protection: self-preservation through self-flagellation. It's as though I'm wired to believe that if I say something nice to myself, cut myself any slack, it will lead to me dying.[gg]

For the sake of formatting, notice that we have the content of verbatim thoughts without italics here. This is a stylistic choice.

Interiority Insight: It's one thing for a character to *know* how they might improve their inner selves and lives, or at least give themselves some grace. It's another for them to actually put self-love or self-actualization into practice. Simply having the idea will often represent some progress, though that growth may remain theoretical, depending on the character.

Lamentations in *The Vaster Wilds* seems to see herself through the lens of change as well, but she's a bit more charitable with her subsumation of what her experiences say about her identity. It's interesting to note here that she doesn't know her real age because of the realistic constraints of her lower-class upbringing in a historical setting:

> The soreness in her body from her six days running was such that she felt infinitely older than her years, a wizened hag, and she knew that, even should she have long months of only rest, there had been things in her body that had been changed forever. She was but sixteen or seventeen or perhaps eighteen years of age, but the wilderness had so moved upon her that she would never be young again.[hh]

You'll recognize part of this longer excerpt from the theme discussion in Chapter 3. It's notable that Lamentations feels older, "changed forever." Story is often described as a journey "from innocence to experience," which can also apply to every character who's on a growth trajectory.

Our following two characters emerge as having very healthy self-esteem. One, Miryem in *Spinning Silver*, comes to it honestly after she takes over her father's debt collecting business. She finds it tough to be treated seriously, but once she has asserted herself, she subsumes her hard-won success:

> I liked to feel their eyes on me, weighing me like a purse, and

being able to hold my head up when they did it, feeling my own worth.[ii]

There's some sleek foreshadowing here about Miryem's ability to turn silver into gold and a play on words about her personal worth versus the worth of the purses she will soon be filling.

A more complex character perspective that suggests self-worth belongs to Ruby in adult horror fantasy novel *Lovecraft Country* by Matt Ruff. Ruby is a religious Black girl who struggles with her conscience as she judges her mother's side hustle of telling fortunes in the back of her hair salon. Ruby has a strong moral compass and takes a position that makes her unpopular in her own family:

> Maybe Momma could make a distinction between strangers she
> took advantage of and friends and acquaintances she helped,
> but Ruby didn't know how to draw that line, and refused to
> learn, no matter how angry Momma got. And Momma got very
> angry towards the end, calling Ruby an ungrateful child, a
> foolish child, too, passing up the chance to assume her mother's
> vocation; she'd come to nothing in this life, being such a fool.
> Fine, Ruby said, throwing it back at her, let me come to nothing.
> At least when I go to meet Jesus I won't have to explain why I
> cheated people in His name.[ji]

Ruby's basically saying that she can hold her head high for eternity, no matter what Momma says. She's chosen her own values, even if this makes her an outcast. Some might argue that having such a clear sense of self—and being able to stand up for it—is one of the highest expressions of both self-awareness and self-esteem.

Though her self-declaration might create conflict in the moment, this interiority shows readers that Ruby values herself and her moral high ground. Of course, Ruby ends up tempted by magic in this world, as we'll see in Chapter 18. Do you think her ethics will hold up?

A protagonist's interpretation of themselves—and their perception of what others think—isn't the only ingredient in fleshing out the essence of character. And often, a protagonist's sense of self is not static or straightforward. As you'll see in Chapter 9, a lot of nuance emerges in moments of internal conflict.

But first, let's look at some more practical declarations of identity and purpose. One external way to put sense of self into action is to give your character a goal with its own reasoning and trajectory. We'll talk about these all-important driving forces of objective and motivation in the following chapter.

7

OBJECTIVE AND MOTIVATION

Simply put, readers care about characters who care about something. The idea of striving toward an outcome, big or small, is universally relatable. This excerpt from Filipino-mythology-inflected middle grade fantasy *The Spirit Glass* by Roshani Chokshi exemplifies why character wants are so electrifying:

> Wanting something very, very much is a lot like trying to touch the horizon. Reaching it seems impossible. But what if one day you were dropped inches from that burning red line where the sun disappeared from the sky? And you could feel the heat of it, that scalding rush of the thing you most wanted.[a]

A protagonist's objective matters and tends to make them proactive, to boot. The origin of a compelling desire is often tied to a character's backstory, whether they're aware of it or not. An objective, and the driving logic behind it, can also change and deepen over the course of a story. Let's do a quick definition round on objective and motivation.

Objective: What a character wants. This can be superficial (generally seen toward the beginning of a story) or substantial (generally seen as the character's sense of self evolves). The want can be internal or external, or both. Characters can have multiple wants in various areas of their lives, but these should be cohesive and characterizing, meaning they reveal aspects of the protagonist that deepen reader understanding. Often, the objective transitions toward a more foundational need, which either supports or contradicts the original want. This shift tends to happen around the midpoint of the plot, if we look back to the tentpole moments defined in Chapter 4. Need is such an important character element that it has its own focus in the following chapter.

Motivation: The reason a character wants what they do. Sometimes this logic is conscious, sometimes, unconscious. Motivations can also transition as characters grow, change, or become more self-aware. Objective and motivation are usually coupled together, though the same motivation can drive multiple objectives. For example, if the character's motivation is to be a hero, they will take many different actions or cycle through various objectives in the service of this driving force (take down one villain, then another, open a new public park in Gotham City, etc.).

The concepts of objective and motivation will help readers understand what a character is doing, why, and how these elements circle back to their sense of self. If a reader understands the reason a protagonist does or says something, or acts a certain way in a certain context, they will be more compelled. Interiority is fantastic at conveying these layers. Even a story's villains should have supporting logic driving their choices, which I'll talk about again in Chapter 12.

Objective and motivation also help clarify a character's expectations when they go into a scene, and suggest what they imagine (or fear) will happen during and after. By following along with what a protagonist wants and knowing why they want it, readers will also be able to extrapolate how the outcome of each attempt might affect the character and their trajectory. This brings me to a key point: Readers must often infer objective and, especially, motivation from interiority. Since we're now drilling into deeper layers of protagonist development, we aren't going to find too many overt statements that blatantly explain these concepts.

This is where your audience will really start doing their detective work —and it's an opportunity to keep enticing them with your masterful use of interiority. Objective and motivation should also leverage the character's backstory, as we saw in Chapter 5, because your protagonist can only seek to achieve their goals in the present or future, which is great for forward plot momentum, too.

Sometimes objectives that a character actively pursues are called "approach," and those they avoid in order to stave off consequences are called "avoidance." Imagine running toward something versus running away. We can also call them "positive" and "negative" objectives. I strongly suggest that you choose to focus on building positive approach objectives rather than giving protagonists negative avoidance ones. Characters who pursue something rather than trying to hide from consequences tend to read as much more proactive and heroic.

Now that theme, plot, character background, and selfhood have been established, it's time to kick everything into motion. The most powerful tools for putting rocket boosters on a story, especially in the beginning, are character objective and motivation.

Lessons From the Theatre

Allow me a small digression. In addition to my English BA, I made the very financially savvy decision of majoring in theatre.[1] In that program, I was introduced to the story and acting theory of Konstantin Stanislavsky, a famous Russian director whose methods are still taught today. One of his most important thought experiments for actors—the "seven questions"—is very relevant for writers, too, especially when it comes to crafting character. Here are five[2] of the seven questions:

---

1. Obvious sarcasm on the financially savvy part. Also, you can identify a theatre major if they spell it "theatre" instead of "theater," like the rest of the world does.
2. The other two questions deal more with scene-setting, which is still relevant to written characters but obviously more crucial to actors appearing in a specific time and place in the physical realm.

1. Who am I?
2. What do I want?
3. Why do I want it?
4. How will I get what I want?
5. What must I overcome to get what I want?

It's immediately obvious that objective ("What do I want?") and motivation ("Why do I want it?") form, at least for Konstantin Stanislavsky and his legions of acting students, the very basis of who a character is. (I'd also make a case for wound and need as important elements.)

The interesting common thread to consider is that "acting" is all about "action." They even share the same prefix ("act"), just as "proactive" and "protagonist" do ("pro"). When you're on stage, you aren't *playing a character*, you are *playing an action* in the service of an objective. This concept was hammered into our skulls in class. Theatre scenes, then, have this in common with written scenes.

When Stanley calls for Stella in a famous moment from *A Streetcar Named Desire* by Tennessee Williams,[3] each instance of him yelling her name offers the opportunity to play a new action. Does he "rage" with the word? Does he "implore"? Does he "seduce"? On stage, each action —or "beat," a term also used in writing—can look and sound different in terms of tone of voice and body language. Every attempt can be selected to potentially affect Stella in a different way, in order to achieve the objective of having her come down the stairs to him, which is Stanley's desire in this scene.

In books, readers don't have the benefit of being able to interpret tone of voice or body language. We don't have an actor in front of us, making the text come alive. Film and theatre depend on an actor's physical instrument to flesh out and convey character, as these are almost entirely mediums of showing. In fact, interiority is relatively uncommon in film and theatre and would be rendered in voiceover or monologue and song, respectively.

---

3. A small love note to Justus Vierra here. He was our Stanley and left us far too soon. A lot of people love and miss you, friend. Also, a wink to the luminous Rachel Zampelli, our Blanche.

Body language and tone of voice are an externally focused display of characterization. They don't translate as well into the written medium, which isn't great at conveying visual data. "A picture is worth a thousand words," right? So in a novel, memoir, or short story, writers need to create character without play-by-play (see Chapter 6), physical clichés (see Chapter 2), or filling dialogue tags with tone of voice indicators. This is why I tend to discourage writers from communicating point of view character experiences exclusively with body and voice descriptions, or pure showing. (Secondary characters whose interiority we can't access are an exception, as I'll discuss in Chapter 12.) This is where interiority comes in.

To be clear, a novel or memoir is in no way "less than" these other forms of artistic expression. In fact, the great benefit of the written word is that readers *can* plunge deeply into character, and audiences *are* invited to bring their own interpretation to the page. This connection just happens via a different channel (reading versus sensing). Both storytelling pathways evoke feeling and reaction, and that's what matters.

Okay, back to our scheduled writing guide!

Using Objective and Motivation

Stay active in your development of a character's objective and motivation. Every time an objective or motivation shifts, track it. Put some interiority on the page about the change of heart. This is a turning point, which you'll read more about in Chapter 15. Give the reader enough data to understand the character's logic. Objective and motivation can change independently of one another or shift together. They can morph as a result of small moments and big ones. These transitions can come quickly or gradually, connected to plot tentpoles or spread over the course of an entire story, similar to a character arc (see Chapter 11).

In the beginning, you should establish objective and motivation as early as is natural. Initial character drivers are likely to be superficial, and that's okay. This is similar to the idea of bridging conflict, discussed in Chapter 4. As long as readers get a sense that your character is actively pursuing something, ideally something relevant to the larger plot, you are doing your job and offering audiences a sense of immediate context and conflict. Have the protagonist look to the future and share their dreams or expectations.

In psychology, we find the idea of extrinsic and intrinsic motivation. The former refers to people and characters who choose to do something because they perceive that it will have external value (climbing the career ladder, donating to charity with the goal of getting acclaim, etc.). The latter refers to activities that people and characters choose to do because they consider them internally motivating, interesting, or fulfilling. Here, we can see the distinction between an external objective and a deeper need.

A slightly different delineation compares external objectives (to save my love, to survive the fight, etc.) and internal ones (to prove I can write and revise a book, to like the way I look in the mirror, etc.). Only you know which objectives and motivations matter to your character, to what degree, and why. Direct reader attention to the highest-stakes desires with interiority.

Remember to also track the character's experience as they give up certain objectives or outgrow them. How do they talk to themselves about what they wanted once upon a time and didn't get, or are actively abandoning? What are some selfish or superficial emotions this might stir up? Many layers of thoughts, feelings, reactions, expectations, and inner struggles underpin a character's wants and needs. As you start building conflicts for your characters, these antagonizing forces can especially target their objectives.

Here's a description of how humans tend to work toward objectives, which appears in *The Breakthrough Years*. You might find it helpful as you consider how your characters might pursue their goals:

- Use what you know to explore your dreams and desires—what do you really want to accomplish (working memory);
- Figure out whether the goals you have are realistic and how they can be achieved (reflection);
- Think flexibly and respond to changing circumstances as you pursue goals (cognitive flexibility); and

- Stay the course, resisting temptations and distractions and addressing obstacles (inhibitory control).[b]

Finally, an objective should be feasible, even if it's unlikely. A goal that's obviously impossible within the framework of the character, plot, or world will not get buy-in from readers. The objective must be something a protagonist has control over. This is why genies can't make people fall in love with one another.[4] Avoid giving your character a desire that solely depends on someone else, like "make my aunt tell me how my father really died." There are other ways to find this out, but if the aunt is the only option, the protagonist (and story) might hit a dead end pretty quickly if she outright refuses.

I've organized this chapter's From the Shelves excerpts along a spectrum from the most superficial (or superficial-seeming) objectives, to those that demonstrate character growth, and then to the deepest and most evolved desires. Pay special attention to how the following characters both express their objectives and motivations, and analyze how well or badly their quests are going. Also, notice that readers really do have to extrapolate what the protagonists truly want, and why, from the interiority.

Superficial Objective and Motivation

Notably, few characters are seeking a simple external physical *object* (the treasure, car, money, etc.).[5] Even though the below objective and motivation examples are superficial in nature, the vast majority of them offer glimpses into the deep subconscious layers of each character's psychology. This is a good moment to remind you that interiority can permeate your story, rather than being reserved for only Big and Important Moments.

For example, Leti from *Lovecraft Country* is a Black woman who has accomplished something amazing, especially for her time period: She has bought a house in a predominantly white neighborhood in

---

4. Rewatch *Aladdin* if you need a reminder!
5. And if they are, it's often a MacGuffin—a storytelling term for a symbolic item that acts as a focal point and plot driver.

Chicago. Of course, there's a catch with this too-good-to-be-true opportunity, and it's a supernatural one, since this is a speculative novel. The house is incredibly haunted and has ties to the villain, though Leti (and readers) don't know that yet. Here, after her first experience with the phenomenon, she thinks quite practically about her next steps:

> Back inside the Winthrop House all was quiet, for now.... Is this going to be an everyday affair? Twice weekly? I'll take whatever you throw at me, but I need tenants, too, and even South Siders might draw the line at nightly earthquakes. Then again, people rent apartments next to the L tracks all the time.[c]

Her objective is external: She needs to take on tenants to afford the house. Her motivation can also be interpreted as external: She's going to have to sell if she can't find any boarders. Of course, there's a deeper layer here, too. Can she justify misleading innocent people? Or will she do anything to cling to her property, even if she has to live—and convince others to live—with a violent poltergeist? Even the most external-seeming wants have nuance.

Elizabeth, the wife and mother from *Wellness*, is also having Chicago problems. She and her husband, Jack, have recently transitioned their son, Toby, to a new school in a wealthy neighborhood. Toby has some behavioral issues, and Elizabeth lives in fear that the school (and its social circle) will reject him (and, by proxy, her). When Brandie, the PTA president, first asks for a very personal favor that would force Elizabeth to bend her moral code and endanger her job, she declines. But then she vacillates:

> Elizabeth considered it for a moment, what it would mean for Brandie to owe her a favor. Elizabeth's latent worry since moving Toby to Park Shore Country Day was that he might start having his meltdowns and tantrums in school, and while public schools had resources and professionals devoted to addressing behavioral problems, private schools tended to have a little less tolerance. They could simply insist that problematic students not return next term, no questions asked. And this fact troubled Elizabeth, that Toby might be summarily expelled and then forced to endure the new-kid-in-school ordeal all over again,

somewhere else. But if Brandie were in her corner? The leader of the Park Shore PTA? The school's biggest fundraiser? The administration might be a little more accommodating, if Brandie asked them to be.[d]

Elizabeth's interiority is focused on Toby and his experience, but there are also selfish motives at play. Logistically, she wants social insurance in case her worst fears come true. She gives Brandie what she wants and, of course, this ends up backfiring spectacularly. (We'll see many more moments of characters wrestling with decisions in Chapter 16.)

In *The Fair Folk*, Felicity desperately wants to be accepted by the fairies, unaware that her father promised her to the fae before she was even born. She fully believes that she somehow charmed the fairy queen, Elfrida, on her own. Here, Felicity shows her desire for the fairy crown (a physical objective):

> The scent drifts around me as I put it on. Is that the wrong thing to do? Nothing ventured, nothing gained; and I've come this far, after all ... [Elfrida] left it for me, and that must mean something.[e]

But what Felicity *really* wants is to be accepted somewhere. She wants to subsume the stamp of approval represented by the crown. I would argue that this deeper objective is superficial as well, simply because Felicity is naïve. Her misbelief is that living a fantasy with the fairies will make her feel better about herself and life in general. Here, she states another superficial goal, imagined as a response to questions about her future:

> So if I told the truth when they asked me what I wanted to do when I grew up ... if I said what I really thought in my secret inside self (which I never did, because they just got angry or laughed at me), it would have been this:
>
> "I don't want to grow up. Ever."[f]

Her lack of understanding and insight into her own desires will be tested over the course of the plot.

> **Interiority Insight:** As you consider a protagonist's early objec-
> tive(s), you might want to start by reverse engineering them from
> what the character ends up achieving at the end (even if the final
> prize is largely internal). As you build these elements, do a cohe-
> siveness test and ensure the protagonist's growth arc aligns with
> your theme and premise.

We've already met Joey from *Tell Me I'm an Artist* and, unsurprisingly,
she has some very superficial objectives and motivations. In fact, if you
consider the title, you realize that she's largely extrinsically motivated
by outside sources of validation. She also operates with a fixed mindset: She's either accepted or not, labeled an artist or not, etc.

The plot involves Joey struggling with a capstone project that she
doesn't even seem to like. Readers might wonder whether she actually
wants to be an artist or if she's simply attracted to the lifestyle. With
that in mind, let's start with two objective and motivation statements
from her:

> I have always had a deep desire to be a "regular" somewhere. I
> wanted to be the type of person who would go to a bar or
> restaurant so often that when I walked up to the counter, the
> cashier would say, "The usual?" ... But I couldn't afford to go
> anywhere frequently enough that employees could come to
> know me.[g]

Joey has a pretty rough family life, so I don't blame her for wanting to
get away from it and find herself. That being said, this desire to be a
"regular," be known, and have a "usual" means, to me, that she badly
wants to belong and be seen as important. This is insecurity talking. A
very similar idea is expressed a bit later, as she drifts through a party,
feeling self-conscious:

> Emboldened by the wine in my system ... I found two
> unopened beer bottles in the fridge. I opened both and then
> wove through the party in a manner I thought would suggest

the confidence of someone retrieving two beers for themselves
and a friend.[h]

She wants people to perceive her a certain way, to the point that she'll
carry two beers around to play the role of "casual girl with friends."
Notice that these are scene-specific statements of objective, but the
motivation behind each remains the same.

Similarly, Ifemelu from *Americanah* moves to America from Nigeria and
wants to adopt not only the American lifestyle, but the sense of happiness and confidence that she observes in those who already "belong":

> She liked, most of all, that in this place of affluent ease, she
> could pretend to be someone else, someone specially admitted
> into a hallowed American club, someone adorned with
> certainty.[i]

The "affluent ease" of the "American club" is, of course, an assumption. This interiority demonstrates Ifemelu's ill-informed view of her
new world, and this excerpt appears on the third page of the book.
Ifemelu is in for a rude awakening, mostly due to her naïve precon-
ceived notions and expectations.

I'll now cite a few objectives and motivations that are superficial but
point more obviously to the protagonist's underlying motivations,
though the characters might not yet know what's driving them. They
are either not yet self-aware enough to understand themselves or
actively in denial but okay with it. Compartmentalizing emotions can
be easier than dealing with them. (We'll dive more into internal conflict
in Chapter 9.)

Let's meet some characters who are in denial and *unaware* of it, a superficial starting point. Konstantin is a corrupt priest who's banished to
the countryside in *The Bear and the Nightingale* by Katherine Arden, a
historical fantasy for adult readers. And he's miserable. In Moscow, he
had worshippers (though he seems convinced they were worshipping
him). In this small village, the people believe in spirits and demons.
Konstantin thinks he's being punished for his popularity (the monastic
equivalent of "my haters are just jealous"):

Most of all he ached for the people, for their love and hunger and half-frightened rapture, for the way their hands stretched out to his.... And now he was exiled, for no other reason than that people preferred him.[j]

He wants to go back to Moscow and reclaim his parishioners. A straightforward objective and motivation, easy-peasy. But the village and its denizens—human and supernatural—have other plans for him.

Chloe Brown starts out similarly stunted in her understanding of herself in adult romcom *Get a Life, Chloe Brown* by Talia Hibbert. She believes that if she can only follow a list, she will escape her limited existence, which has been defined, thus far, by a chronic pain condition. Her true objective is cheekily summarized in the book's title, but the way she pursues "getting a life" is, at least at first, quite superficial:

She had not yet transformed her life, but she was in the process of doing so.... Someday soon, she would emerge as a beautiful butterfly who did cool and fabulous things all the time, regardless of whether or not said things had been previously scheduled. All she had to do was follow the list.[k]

The idea that one neat little list can completely shift an entire life and frame of mind is, obviously, something Chloe needs to ditch over the course of the story.

One of the most interesting character studies of denial and shallow objectives deepening into real growth appears in *Eleanor Oliphant Is Completely Fine*. There's even denial in the title, because the first thing it suggests is that she's not actually "fine."

Interiority Insight: Notice how the two titles referenced here—*Get a Life, Chloe Brown* and *Eleanor Oliphant Is Completely Fine*—perfectly communicate their respective premises. This is also the promise of the premise in action.

We first meet Eleanor as she's unable to own her emotions and past trauma, which is considerable. In order to please Mummy's ever-present critical voice, which Eleanor has internalized, she decides to "legitimize" herself by getting a husband. For some inexplicable reason, she fixates on a local musician and truly seems to believe that falling in love with him will solve all of her problems:

> It was luck that he'd come along at precisely the right time. It was fate that, after tonight, my Eleanor pieces would finally start to fit together.

> How exquisite the anticipation—a pain, a churning pain inside me. I did not know how to assuage it—I felt, instinctively, that vodka would not work. I would simply have to bear it until we met, and that was the nature of this peculiar, blissful burden. Only a little longer to wait now, a matter of hours. Tonight, I was going to meet the man whose love would change my life.

> I was ready to rise from the ashes and be reborn.[l]

This, as you can imagine, falls apart in spectacular fashion and propels Eleanor into what might be called a psychotic break. Though she starts therapy on the heels of said crisis, Eleanor still has major work to do. She begins the therapeutic relationship in her typical guarded and performative fashion, while fully acknowledging to herself (and to readers!) that she's withholding information:

> I would tell her almost everything, I'd decided, but I wasn't going to mention the little stockpile of pills … and I had also decided to say nothing about the chats with Mummy.… Mummy always said that information should be divulged to professional busybodies on a need-to-know basis.… All the doctor needed to understand was that I was very unhappy, so that she could advise me how best to go about changing that. We didn't need to start digging around in the past, talking about things that couldn't be changed.[m]

Her objective is to wave a magic wand and fix her unhappiness without doing the work or letting any skeletons out of her closet. Of course, this isn't realistic and she's about to be bitterly disappointed. These early attempts and failures are important, though. They set Eleanor up to finally rise from the ashes, but in a much deeper and more meaningful way.

Interiority Insight: Therapy is a very well-know and frequently used plot contrivance for unpacking tricky character development. Use it with caution so it doesn't come across as a cliché excuse to simply present backstory. There are many other characters who can provide support to your protagonist, like allies and romantic partners, as we'll see in Chapter 13. A character opening up to an antagonist, whether on purpose or by accident, is also a high-stakes possibility. You'll see several therapy sessions in our From the Shelves excerpts. The internal tension generated during these visits helps them earn their keep.

Hannah from *The Bodyguard* has just lost her mom. Instead of grieving or feeling her feelings, she does what she's been doing for years—throws herself fully into work. In this scene, she's about to ask for a new assignment. She seems perfectly aware that she's hiding but is also, notably, fine with it:

The last thing I wanted to do was *stay home and think about it.*

I was going to talk [my boss] into letting me come back to work if it killed us both.[n]

Of course, she doesn't get to keep her head stuck in the proverbial sand. The plot is very much engineered to force a confrontation with vulnerability, which often happens in romantic comedies, as we'll see in Chapter 13.

> **Interiority Insight:** As you can tell from these excerpts, initial superficial objectives don't tend to hold up. Sooner or later, events or emotions (repressed or otherwise) become so unbearable that characters start to change, discard their initial goals and motivations, and grow.

As a segue to our examples of self-aware objectives and motivations, I pulled this excerpt from *Bright Young Women*. Here's Pamela furiously working to maintain her illusion that everything will somehow be okay after the sorority stabbing and Denise's death:

> I hurried out, eager to help, to get all this sorted so I could go and see Denise at the hospital and rush back here to tidy up before the alumnae arrived.... The alumnae would no doubt be ... impressed that the tour still went off without a hitch. I imagined them reporting back to the governing council that the women of the FSU chapter showed extraordinary poise in the face of a harrowing ordeal. I followed the officer downstairs, fevered with hope.°

Pamela cares what the alumnae think, how she's viewed, and about visiting Denise "in the hospital" (even though she has already seen that Denise is dead). Our only hint that Pamela *knows* she's delusional is one word: "fevered." She's not "floating" with hope, she's not "buoyed" by hope. "Fevered" connotes sickness, hallucination, and a break from reality. Her objective to impress these alumnae needs to be abandoned before she can deal with what happened.

Objective and Motivation Growth Trajectories

We'll still see some characters in denial about their true motives in this section, as well as a few external and superficial objectives, but the following protagonists are generally more self-aware and growth-oriented.

For example, the unnamed narrator of *Death Valley* has an external objective, but she'll be the first to tell readers it's bullshit. Her transparency is refreshing compared to assertions by Alex in *The Guest* or early-stage Eleanor Oliphant. This character is trying to escape herself and her feelings after her father falls into a coma, only to realize she can't:

> I'm here at the Best Western for a week under the pretext of figuring out "the desert section" of my next novel. If I'm honest, I came to escape a feeling—an attempt that's already going poorly, because unfortunately I've brought myself with me.... I am still the kind of person who makes another person's coma all about me.[p]

She's engaging in some delusional thinking, but she admits it. Whether she'll deal with her deeper struggles is another story.

In *Divine Rivals*, Roman starts out as Iris's competitor at the newspaper, even though he admires her writing and thinks she's better suited for the work. He starts corresponding with her anonymously via magical means and realizes he can trick her into opening up to him. They eventually fall in love, as this romance uses an enemies-to-lovers trope, but at this early point in the story, Roman still prioritizes external success and uses Isis to this end:

> *I should tell her now,* he thought ... *should tell her it's me. This is the point of no return. If I don't tell her now, I will never be able to.*
>
> But the more he thought of it, the more he realized he didn't want to. If he told her, she would stop writing. He would lose his tactical advantage.[q]

Interiority Insight: The above is another instance of interiority rendered in narration *and* italicized verbatim thought.

He's consciously stringing her along for selfish purposes. This isn't exactly sympathetic, but it makes him a compelling enemy—as that's his current role in the story.

In a different reality, Elwood, a Black kid in Colson Whitehead's adult historical literary novel *The Nickel Boys*, is sent to a troubled boys' home, where atrocities quickly come to light. The novel jumps back and forth in time to track a group of survivors from their past experiences to how are were affected into adulthood. When Elwood first arrives, he chooses a simple objective: to do well and get sent home. But he's also aware enough to treat this action as his resistance against the place. He will behave in an unimpeachable way so his environment won't wear him down. Or so he thinks:

> I am stuck here, but I'll make the best of it, Elwood told himself.... Everybody back home knew him as even, dependable—Nickel would soon understand that about him, too. At dinner, he'd ask Desmond how many points he needed to move out of Grub, how long it took most people to advance and graduate. Then he'd do it twice as fast. This was his resistance.[r]

Interiority Insight: Notice the interiority formatting of "told himself" in this excerpt, which hints at some self-delusion.

In Holly Black's young adult fantasy, *The Cruel Prince*, Jude and Taryn are twin human sisters who have been kidnapped by a fairy general to live in that world with their older half-sister, Vivi, who has fairy blood. At one point, Vivi nudges them to go back to the mortal world:

> She's suggesting we live like the wild fey, among mortals, but not of them. We'd steal the cream from their cups and the coins from their pockets. But we wouldn't settle down and get boring jobs.[s]

Jude balks because Vivi has no idea what the mortal world is like, and doesn't realize she's pitching a fantasy. Part of Jude, though, seems tempted by this, even if she knows it's a daydream. Vivi's suggestions are relayed with a certain glow and seem especially appealing because the dangers of the fairy world are heating up. Instead, Jude's growth as a character is demonstrated when she decides to not only stay in the realm, which has never fully accepted her, but defy Dain, the fairy prince who emerges as the antagonist:

> I think of all the vows I made to Dain, including the one I never spoke out loud: *Instead of being afraid, I will become something to fear.* If Dain isn't going to give me power, then I am going to take it for myself.[t]

Indulging in fantasy is one thing, but Jude choosing to engage and live with her reality is a sign of mature growth.

Interiority Insight: Accepting one's lot in life can actually be a proactive choice, rather than a failure. Leaving (mentally, emotionally, or physically) can sometimes be easier than staying, hence the siren song of denial.

Sona from *Gearbreakers*, who underwent the surgery to become a Windup, also has a grand objective: to honor her family and gain power in her society. Then she realizes that these external goals are shallow and won't satisfy:

> For just a moment, a glittering, happy moment, I thought it was all worth it. That this was how I could avenge my parents. This was how I could avenge myself.... For weeks I have known I can do damage ... and for weeks, I have known that I cannot do enough. I am just one girl. I have just one Windup. And I was so drunk on the mere *thought* of having power that I allowed myself to be made into this.[u]

Interiority Insight: Even as a character gets closer to their objective —*especially* as they do—their journey can be made more dynamic if they second-guess themselves or ask big questions. They might not have the answers yet, but their line of inquiry engages readers.

Corazon, the main character in *The Spirit Glass*, whose quote about yearning kicked off this chapter, has a great objective growth trajectory. She's been raised to believe that she will develop spirit guide and healer powers. Not getting them seems unfathomable:

> All her life she had been told that she would be a great babay-
> lan. She just had to wait. But she'd been waiting for years, and
> in two days she would be twelve! That's when most babaylans
> started their official training … and Corazon still had no sign
> that her magic was anywhere near waking up.[v]

The prospect of remaining powerless is made even scarier by the notion that Corazon won't be able to communicate with the spirit world, which includes her dead parents. What Corazon *actually* wants the most is to go beyond the veil and not only see them … but bring them home. If her powers don't come, her parents are lost to her forever. She elaborates here:

> How could it be a bad thing for them to come back? All she had
> to do was figure out how to make it happen. Magic operated
> with bargains and balances. There had to be something in the
> world that could correct the imbalance that had led to that car
> accident three years ago.[w]

Not only are readers starting to understand what's really driving Cora-zon, but she's able to interrogate her objective and motivation and explore her real reasons for wanting what she does. She also expresses an interesting additional motivation: to see a magical injustice righted.

Bronca demonstrates objective and motivation growth on either side of a big decision in *The City We Became*. She helms the Bronx Art Center, a museum run for and by people of color. She's approached by Dr. White, a mysterious philanthropist (and the antagonist in disguise), who dangles a giant donation carrot and asks Bronca to display some art that goes against the institution's values. Bronca vacillates:

> Trying to reason with bigots is always a losing game. And
> Bronca can already tell there's going to be an epic explosion
> from the board if she refuses the donation.… It is a small conces-

sion to make, isn't it? A few terrible paintings on the walls for a few weeks, in exchange for enough money to keep the Center running at peak for years, even if the city reduces its funding. With that kind of money, Bronca could make a real difference.[x]

Bronca's objective, to "make a real difference," is noble. But capitulating to this offer would come with a lot of strings attached. Finally, after Bronca sees the taint of evil in both the proposed art and artists, she comes to her senses and responds with growth, confidence, and an f-bomb:

These *people*. They have come into her borough, her territory, and ripped down good art. They've tried to force her to accept their disgusting mediocre bullshit instead. And here is this white woman, who is not a white woman at all but who has tried to manipulate mechanisms of power against Bronca just like the worst of them, demanding that Bronca capitulate. Like *fuck* she will.[y]

This interiority is used to cement Bronca's position, except now she has to tell the villain the bad news, which sets readers up for a battle sequence.

Interiority Insight: Objective, but more importantly, motivation, can be *very* galvanizing, especially after the midpoint in a character's growth arc.

August is on an emotional journey in the adult romantic comedy *One Last Stop* by Casey McQuiston. She goes from not wanting to open herself up—to *anyone*—to engaging with her feelings. (Paging Rachel from *Milk Fed* and Hannah from *The Bodyguard*!) Unfortunately, the person who cracks August's heart open is Jane, a woman who has been trapped on the Q line of the NYC subway since the '70s, which is this novel's speculative twist.

Jane could vanish at any moment, since nobody knows how she's suspended in time, and therefore represents the most unattainable partner possible. As we transition into deeper objective and motivation and reach a fuller expression of a character's growth arc, let's see August decide whether she wants to take this emotional risk:

> August feels alive. She feels *present*, somehow, *here*. Exactly, really here. She smears a messy kiss across the top of Jane's cheek and feels like Jane is the first thing she's ever touched in her life.[z]

Interiority Insight: For the sake of writing a proactive protagonist, consider having your main character make the first move.

This is also a lovely moment of interiority that shows the stakes of love and need, and how intense and immediate they can feel. As a protagonist's objectives and motivations become characterizing and personal, they can offer readers more to care about.

Deep Objective and Motivation

Let's start with an example of an external but substantial objective and motivation from *Amazing Grace Adams*. Though the want here seems superficial—to win a competition—it represents deep character growth. In fact, Grace has previously chickened out of entering this linguistics championship for three years running. After she works up the nerve to participate, she realizes how much she lost because of her own self-denial:

> Every year for the past three she has almost entered the contest, but something always stopped her, a sense that maybe she wouldn't be good enough. She even filled in the forms last year, but in the end didn't send them. Now that she's here, she can't believe she talked herself out of it. And suddenly she wants this. She wants, more than anything, to win.[aa]

Interiority Insight: Look at that lovely "she wants, more than anything" interiority here. These are the kinds of stakes that powerful objectives and motivations bring to story. How does your character think about their desire? Do they attach deep meaning to it? How might you enhance this resonance?

In the next excerpt, from the multi-POV adult thriller *Everyone Here Is Lying* by Shari Lapena, Alice's objective and motivation are straightforward but hint at a much deeper goal. This character is a neighbor whose son, Derek, is suspected of behaving inappropriately with Avery, a missing child. The cops are loudly wondering whether he kidnapped her. After Alice tells them that Derek is innocent and sends them away, she decides to search the house:

> For a long moment she can't think at all. But then her mind clears. She must look, before the police do. She will search the entire house, and she will find nothing. Then she will know that Derek had nothing to do with this.... And chances are, Avery's never coming back to say anything different.[bb]

Alice doesn't just want the house evidence-free for the police. Her interiority reveals something else. As Derek's mother, she desperately wants to prove his innocence to herself, first and foremost. As we move toward the end of this chapter on objective and motivation, you'll notice these deeper instances slant away from want and angle toward need. This is significant, because need is often the force underpinning, creating, or even contradicting overtly stated objectives.

Ginny in *Guy's Girl* has previously suffered from anorexia, an eating disorder. Now she's developing bulimic behaviors after a period of recovery. Her explicit want here is obvious:

> She can feel it, when the gluttonous part of her brain turns on. It's a switch.... It comes alive, this deep hunger, all instinct and animal, and it demolishes Ginny's every impulse toward self-restraint.

We all have a beast. They might desire different things—some crave sex, some power, some chemically induced happiness. And Ginny? Well. After five years of feeding herself just enough to get by, just enough for the pain to be chronic but livable, and one more year of throwing up almost everything that went into her body—

Well. Her beast wants to eat.[cc]

But under the surface is a desperate desire for control. Ginny needs to be able to satisfy something—even if it's her hunger—because she feels like she's failing in other areas of her life. She's not entirely aware of these drivers at this point in the story, but this excerpt offers a good reminder that a want isn't always just a want.

Rachel from *Milk Fed* is very self-aware, so she realizes that her stated want is impossible:

I was not really longing for my mother, who certainly was no mama. I wanted another mama, a fictional one. I thought about what my dream mama would look and feel like…. If it were possible to create the mama I'd wished for, I wasn't even sure who she would be. My wish for that mama had always been a response to an absence.[dd]

In this case, Rachel knows she can't have the kind of mother she's always dreamed of, as this individual doesn't exist. Her objective and motivation come across as bittersweet and wistful in interiority, which helps endear her to readers.

Interiority Insight: Putting fantasy or wish fulfillment on the page allows characters to share their deeper needs covertly and invite readers into a more vulnerable version of themselves and their wounds. There's some semblance of safety in pretending that they're merely expressing a "fantasy" instead of admitting what they truly want.

Isabelle in *All the Dangerous Things* is no stranger to wanting what seems impossible. After her sister died in childhood and her baby, Mason, was taken from his crib, she has become a regular on the true crime conference and interview circuit, her identity synonymous with tragedy. When she gets sick of everyone judging her, she decides to let a podcaster, Waylon, into her inner circle to try and set the record straight:

> I'm so used to calculating my statements, trying so hard to please whoever is on the receiving end of them—saying only the right things, the good things—and how, still, it never seems to matter. Waylon appears to see through that, though. He somehow knows when I'm not being entirely truthful.[ee]

Unfortunately, while Isabelle wants to control the narrative, make the world see her a certain way, and have someone in her corner, for once, these difficult objectives also require honesty. By wanting something so massive, Isabelle is forced to reckon with her behavior and values in interiority. Readers are inspired to wonder what she's willing to sacrifice to get what she wants. And what she's hiding.

Let's go even deeper. Ari from *The Luis Ortega Survival Club* was raped at a party. When she thinks about what she actually wants from her assailant, she's conflicted:

> I don't *think* what I want is to get back at Luis. I do want him to apologize to me. For what, I don't know. Maybe for not asking before taking my clothes off. For not giving me any kind of warning. But how can I blame him when I couldn't even bring myself to tell him to stop?
>
> … He should have asked.
>
> But I don't want revenge. I want an apology.… I want him to feel bad on his own about what he did, just because he cares about me. Deep down, I know it's a long shot, but a girl can hope, right?[ff]

For a character who has been through a lot and is dealing with other challenges—notably autism and selective mutism—Ari is incredibly self-aware. She's able to strip her ego and superficial desires away in this simple interiority-based declaration of objective and motivation.

She wants an apology. She wants to be seen. She wants him to acknowledge her hurt and be accountable for causing it. She also wants him to arrive at these ideas on his own, which is, unfortunately, unlikely and completely outside of her control. More than anything, though, she wants to handle this with dignity and maybe even a little bit of hope. This objective and motivation say a lot about her and are beautifully expressed.

Now that we're playing on a deeper level, one that's occasionally beneath a character's own awareness, let's go back to our understanding of backstory and wound. Once we combine those concepts with objective and motivation, we'll create yet another crucial character driver: need.

8

NEED

You'll have to excuse me for being cheeky, but a character's need is an expression of what they ... need. It's as simple and as complex as that, since a protagonist's need can be straightforward or anything but.

I'll invoke Maslow's Hierarchy of Needs here. This idea is often depicted as a pyramid, with the most basic needs at the bottom level. I'll list them in order of immediate importance here, with the base of the pyramid defined first:

1. **Physiological needs:** air, shelter, water, food, sleep;
2. **Safety and security:** health, employment, property, family, social bonds (more on this on the following level);
3. **Love and belonging:** a sense of connection with friends and family, intimacy, relationship;
4. **Self-esteem:** uniqueness, identity, respect, individuality; and
5. **Self-actualization:** creativity, morality, purpose, meaning, inner potential, and achievement.

Of course, we all have basic needs—air, shelter, food, water. But these are typically not the kinds of needs that characters concern themselves with, except in scenes of acute danger, when all other problems and internal tensions fall away. Once a person's or character's physical needs are taken care of, they become more concerned with striving forward, interpersonal relationships, and developing a deep and fulfilled sense of self.

This goes back to the idea of a proactive protagonist, one who has an internal locus of control, is intrinsically motivated, and actively drives their destiny. There is no more powerful way to become fulfilled. Needs that serve character creation and growth are emotional in nature and get to the very marrow of a protagonist's identity, maturation, and sense of achievement and proactivity over the course of the story.

Need: While the objective is what the character might *want*, the need is what they *should* pursue to become complete. The need often emerges once writers and readers understand the protagonist's identity-specific desire, which is created by their backstory and wound. Need is much more vulnerable than objective, and more important for characters to achieve. If they don't, they might not become the most actualized possible version of themselves. As we saw in Chapter 4, a protagonist's transition from pursuing the objective to pursuing the need tends to happen around the midpoint.

Needs can be centered on other characters—like Rachel's desire for an ideal mother in *Milk Fed*—but if we dig a bit deeper, we'll see that they're generally reflections of a protagonist's relationship with themselves. Often, this crucial sense of self is broken, and the plot is at least partially about understanding this and attempting to repair it, or at least come to terms with it.

This excerpt from *Eleanor Oliphant Is Completely Fine* is the perfect quote to kick off our exploration of needs, just as Corazon from *The Spirit Glass* set the tone for the objective and motivation chapter:

I feel sorry for beautiful people. Beauty, from the moment you possess it, is already slipping away, ephemeral. That must be difficult. Always having to prove that there's more to you, wanting people to see beneath the surface, to be loved for yourself.[a]

Contrary to what she says, Eleanor actually *does* want to be beautiful, deep down, or at least to be treated like a beautiful person by society. Eleanor's face and hands are covered in burn scars, and she has already expressed displeasure about them—or at least self-consciousness that people might see her as strange or ugly.

By reading into[1] this interiority, I wonder whether she might actually be happiest if human culture did away with the notion of beauty altogether, so that people could walk around as their essential selves, rather than their external skins. But that's magical thinking and impossible. Eleanor might need to become more comfortable as herself to feel a similar peace.

From what seems like a superficial statement, at first blush, readers can glean a lot of insight into the protagonist. This is the nature of need. It demands that audiences put on their thinking caps and dive right in, as these pearls must be retrieved from the depths.

Needs at Work

For a character to express a need, they must have self-awareness and do self-inquiry. For a reader to infer a need, they will have to do extrapolation and bring their sense of empathy to the page. That's why need is so crucial to character development, and such a juicy way to use interiority. Once you hit upon a compelling character need and plant it at the core of your protagonist, you will motivate readers to engage on the most intimate level yet.

Secrets are powerful forces in storytelling, creating curiosity hooks, conflict, and intrigue. A need is like a secret that your characters keep under heavy lock and key, sometimes even from themselves. Need-generating wounds often start out as painful or shameful events. You can use secrets to create plot tension, as we'll see in Chapter 14, and you can use needs as wellsprings of character inner tension.

In Chapter 5, we discussed backstory, flashback, and wound—which is

---

1. The phrase "reading into" perfectly encapsulates an audience's role. By interpreting, they are "reading into" the author's intentions and the character's self-revelations in interiority.

intimately tied to a character's need. If the wound is an absence of love in childhood, the character might crave love and chase it for the first half of the story. Unfortunately, they could also unknowingly recreate false beliefs and flawed ideas about love. By trying to correct for a distant parent who withheld affection, they might date a very sweet partner who's always around. Of course, this could prove to be the wrong approach and leave the character feeling smothered. They'll then have to interrogate their notion of love, which might involve self-inquiry and, ideally, healing.

It's not until the protagonist tries to "solve the problem the wrong way" first that they might realize the deeper ramifications of what's driving their need. This hypothetical character could come to understand their wound's origin—it wasn't Mom and Dad's distance, but their conditional love. Growing up, the protagonist had to perfectly anticipate and execute on expectations, or the parents would withhold affection and approval. The objective might be "love," but the need might be something more specific: *unconditional* love. And beneath that: *self*-love.

By searching out the latter two qualities in the second half of the story, the character will truly be addressing the wound at the core of their formative experiences as they start to heal it and "solve the problem the right way" instead. In doing so, they stand a better chance of meeting their need, either by getting involved with a truly loving partner, or by accepting themselves.

Objective and motivation might initially spring your character into action, but need is what keeps them going through the toughest and most discouraging parts of the plot, especially once they come to realize what's really happening below the surface. (A lot of the theme and premise statements discussed in Chapter 3 also hint at or express the protagonist's need—it's *that* important to story.)

Most novels and memoirs are about change, including what's happening within a character's psyche as they become more aware of the reasoning behind their choices, actions, and desires. Showing this transformation from objective to need is very powerful, and it allows readers to feel that much more connected to your character.

There are a few interesting patterns I noticed while reading From the Shelves books to assess their protagonists' needs, I'll unpack these before we go spelunking within the excerpts.

Need Patterns

Character and human desires tend to define who we are on the most profound levels. If you think about needs in terms of conscious and unconscious, external and internal, you might start to notice what I like to call "want versus need," which is what someone *wishes* was true about themselves, but isn't.

This is similar to the phenomenon, seen in Chapter 6, of a character defining themselves by what they believe others perceive about them. For example, they *want* to be easygoing, but are easily ruffled. This creates a problem only when they convince themselves that it's "better" to be easygoing. This misbelief can come from other characters judging them, or their subsumation of cultural and social messaging.

A character arriving at this worldview is influenced by the kinds of people and ideas they're surrounding themselves with. If they listen to a lot of "hustle culture" podcasts, they might start to believe that rest and play are slothful and frivolous. On the other hand, they could see "the cult of busyness" as driving a burnout epidemic. If a protagonist perceives part of their personality as a flaw and extrapolates the idea that something's "wrong" with them, they might attempt to "fix" the attribute in question. They might also convince themselves that other people don't struggle with the same issue, or struggle *as much*. This is often a misbelief.

What the protagonist wants is to be "normal," or more socially acceptable, and this fights their profound need to accept themselves or lean into their natural traits.[2] You might find a character whose objective and motivation do a big 180 when they switch to being driven by their need because they realize that their goal was founded on false principles to begin with.

---

2. Of course, if the original attribute is pathological, like extreme "stickler" behavior turning out to be OCD, the character might want to get to a healthier place and reach balance instead of embracing a maladaptive aspect of their personality.

Denial of one's needs—which requires conscious awareness of the need, then a rejection of it—is often seen in romcom, romance, and women's fiction. These are character-driven categories and genres where protagonists have to overcome certain hurdles within themselves in order to reach their full potential and a sense of present happiness, outside of close relationships *and* within them.

To this end, needs don't always inspire action, especially if a character becomes aware of their need before they're fully capable of meeting it or addressing their wound. We'll meet many internally conflicted characters in Chapter 9, and see them run the other way until they're more prepared to tackle the real nature of their problems. They see the shadow of a sea monster lurking beneath the surface and, instead, choose to jump back up to the pier—and to perceived safety. The pier is full of superficial objectives to chase, but if they were to plunge into the depths again, they might realize that the shadow was actually a cave mouth, glimmering with treasure.

Needs, like objectives, often exist within a larger context rather than in isolation. A protagonist's growth journey typically involves letting go of their requirements for others (acceptance, validation, etc.) and working to be their own hero. After all, people and characters can only control themselves (and not always!), and the more they rely on other people for fulfillment, the more likely they are to be disappointed. Not because other people will always let us down (this sounds like a worldview statement from Chapter 10!), but because the deepest necessities must be met internally.

Some characters, of course, are broken by their wounds and past or current experiences. They don't hold out much hope for realizing their own needs, let alone getting them met. I'll begin our From the Shelves excerpts with a section featuring broken people to showcase how characters act out as a result of unaddressed desires. In almost all cases, the real issue is a lack of self-worth and self-love. Though self-actualization is high on Maslow's hierarchy, which means it's rare and difficult, it's also the most sacred gift most characters (and people) can give themselves.

I find that needs are best demonstrated using examples, so let's dig in. What I said in the previous chapter still applies here: While objectives and motivations are sometimes stated outright, needs are created in the reader's mind largely through interiority interpretation. We'll dip into our gallery of broken souls, then track instances of growing need awareness, and, finally, explore some characters' most vulnerable statements of need.

Superficial Needs and Broken People

The poster child for superficial needs hidden far below the surface is Alex from *The Guest*. She's the character who shacks up with a sugar daddy in the Hamptons only to alienate him, then spends the rest of the story trying to claw her way back into his life as if nothing happened. Hers is a reverse growth arc because she dives completely into her fantasy world by the end. It makes sense, then, that a glimpse into her true need appears early in the story instead of in the final moments:

> There had been others before her, Alex knew, other young women with weekend bags and hopeful, careful bodies, other women who drifted into the kitchen at ten in the morning to drink coffee someone else had made for them.... Thin girls in camisoles who ate yogurt standing up. But Alex had outlasted them, had passed into another, more permanent realm. They were ghosts; she was real. Alex lived here; her clothes were in the closet. For the rest of the summer, anyway. She was no longer vulnerable.[b]

Here, she's thinking about what makes her different from Simon's "other young women." Alex explicitly states that she has bested them and "passed into another, more permanent realm." This is, of course, a misbelief. She's as disposable as the rest, which Simon demonstrates almost immediately after Alex relaxes and convinces herself she's "no longer vulnerable." What she claims to already *have* (permanence, security) is what she *needs*.

If Alex felt confident, comfortable, and like she truly inhabited this reality, she wouldn't need to say these things to and about herself. In fact, she feels like a ghost, and seems to be acutely aware of her precarious position. Her deepest fear is vulnerability, and that's why she suffers a complete break from reality when things don't go her way.

Aislyn is our personified Staten Island in *The City We Became*. She's vulnerable to the antagonist's temptation because she's lonely and feels trapped, as described in Chapter 6. The characters who represent the boroughs must work together, but Aislyn brings trouble to their doorstep by attracting the antagonist, called "the Woman" here:

> The Woman has said that she wants to help Aislyn—and somehow she seems to know about the strange voices in Aislyn's head and the strange compulsion that drove her to the ferry station. It makes Aislyn feel more sympathetic than she ordinarily would be.[c]

Aislyn has a long way to go in terms of self-awareness. She doesn't yet realize that she needs a friend—or just basic human contact—so badly that she will take anyone, unknowingly endangering everyone.

This excerpt, from the point of view of Jojo, Leonie's son, in *Sing, Unburied, Sing*, is heartbreaking in its simplicity. He says "wish," but I think this interiority better reflects his need to be happy:

> But by the time we get out of the car in the parking lot, the birds have turned north, fluttered over the horizon.... I wish I could feel their excitement, feel the joy of the rising, the swinging into the blue, the great flight, the return home, but all I feel is a solid ball of something in my gut, heavy as the head of a hammer.[d]

By watching the birds and figuratively attaching himself to them, Jojo is finding an outlet for admitting that he needs to get away from his family. Of course, he's a child, and he can't. That's why he indulges in this fantasy before he comes crashing abruptly back to earth ... and his current situation.

A simpler and less tragic need within the context of other characters is expressed by Jim, the aging father cop in *Anxious People*. He's pretending to have status to impress some visiting hostage negotiators from the big city:

Naturally, Jim did his best to act like he definitely had experience, seeing as dads like teaching their sons things, because the moment we can no longer do that is when they stop being our responsibility and we become theirs.[e]

He needs to be needed, which he actually admits elsewhere in the book. He also needs to be seen as experienced and necessary. He is, after all, in the twilight of his career, so his desire stems from the fear of slowly becoming irrelevant, a common theme in midlife and beyond.

Joey from *Tell Me I'm an Artist* appears in many of my discussions of superficial characters, but I actually enjoyed the book quite a bit. She's a young college student—of course she's going to have some naïve ideas! Here, she unpacks her expectation for making art, and how it clashes with reality. At least she's self-aware enough to label her thought process:

> Expectation: A little inner turmoil, which you make art about.
> Reality: So much inner turmoil that it has found a way to multiply, becoming so massive and relentless that any art you attempt to make about your inner turmoil becomes another source that fuels it.[f]

She's able to realize that she wants to make art, but that she needs the art to come easily. This must not feel nice—or graceful—to admit. When mind-blowing creativity doesn't flow as expected, she gets much less excited for the whole endeavor.[3]

Felicity in *The Fair Folk* is in the middle of her development when she takes a big coming-of-age risk. She has disengaged from the fairies who helped her get through a tough childhood and now she's at Cambridge to live life on her own terms.

Of course, separating from the fairies for good is (almost) impossible. They're like vampires—once you invite them in, they are never truly gone. When she's not getting actual visits from the fairies, she's thinking about them. Unfortunately, she doesn't feel she can tell

---

3. Many writers can relate!

anyone, so this leaves her feeling lonely and tempted to run back to their familiar embrace:

> She made her choice, and the gates to fairyland had closed behind her. At the time she thought that was it. She'd chosen the everyday world, and was free to immerse herself in it. Only she wasn't, of course. The things she couldn't say would always get in the way.[8]

Felicity desperately needs to tell someone the truth about what she's experienced but feels she can't. At college, she's surrounded by people she believes are normal and unbothered by desperate longing for a different realm. She doesn't want to "other" herself ... until she meets a teacher who might share her secret. This only confirms she's out of her depth, and we'll see her struggle to individuate herself later in this guide.

Interiority Insight: Some needs are stupid, or petty, or backward. But characters who admit to having these can, conversely, earn sympathy or empathy from readers who know that not all necessities are noble.

If we stick in the world of fairies and wood sprites, we'll find ourselves following Vasya as she runs through the forest in *The Bear and the Nightingale*. We've previously met Konstantin, the prideful priest. Vasya is a young girl with a witchy lineage who communes with the folk spirits. As organized religion descends on her backwoods community, she wrestles with her true essence. After her father announces that he's sending her away to a convent, she flees:

> The night drew on, and Vasya shivered as she walked.... A small part of her had thought—hoped—that there would be some help in the woods. Some destiny—some magic. She had hoped the firebird would come, or the Horse with the Golden Mane, or the raven who was really a prince.... *Foolish girl to believe in fairy tales.* The winter wood was indifferent to men and women; the

chyerti slept in winter, and there was no such thing as a raven-prince.[h]

She says she "wants" help in this interiority, but her real necessity is deeper than that. She *needs* her beliefs and childhood lived experiences to be true because she cannot deny her reality. Is she a magic-adjacent creature of the woods, a friend of the unseen, or is she a "foolish girl"? The latter is society's opinion, and society is currently winning. In this interiority, readers get the clear sense that Vasya wants to be affirmed—especially in the hour of her need—and rewarded by the chyerti for her unwavering faith in them.

In a similar fantasy forest world, we have Miryem from *Spinning Silver*, who can transform silver into gold at the behest of the Staryk, a winter fairy king. Once she becomes jaded with her magic—and the strings attached to it—she mourns her former naïve self:

> Whatever magic the silver had to enchant those around it either faded with use or couldn't touch me any longer; I wished that it could, and that my eyes could be dazzled enough to care for nothing else.[i]

This is an interesting demonstration of need. Miryem wants her old self back, the one who believed in magic and could be easily impressed. Despite her incredible power, she finds that it makes her weary. If readers dig into the interiority, they might understand that she needs to be that simple girl again. It would fulfill her craving for an uncomplicated life, one that's no longer an option.

Interiority Insight: Needs can sometimes be basic, reductive, and weak-seeming, especially in the face of increasing plot challenges. But they don't have to be elaborate. Most needs aren't, which is why they have the potential to trigger empathy from readers.

Hannah, from *The Bodyguard*, has a similar moment of "I wish it wasn't true, but it is" as she details her mindset after working personal security for high-value targets:

Once you learn to look at the world from a perspective of personal security, you can't look at it any other way. I couldn't walk into a restaurant, for example, without assessing the threat level in the room—even if I was off duty.... Once you know how terrible the world is, you can't *un*know.

No matter how much you might want to.[j]

The first paragraph simply describes her specific worldview, which doesn't seem to address need. It's not until the last sentence that her interiority suggests that maybe she *doesn't* want to believe the world is terrible.

Maybe she wishes it wasn't. It pains her deeply to have seen the things she's seen and done the things she's done. Perhaps she didn't start out *this* cynical but circumstances and experience forced her hand.

If things were different, maybe she would be a bit softer, a bit more open. It hurts, after all, to constantly be on edge. While she blames external conditions for the way she is, I can't help but interpret longing here, too. Who could Hannah be if she didn't carry these burdens?

Interiority Insight: One line of interiority can enhance a whole paragraph ... or more.

Let's dive deeper into some more obviously broken people who have completely subverted their needs. These protagonists can be the most interesting types of characters to read and write. They tempt writers to show their readers redemption, which feels gratifying for audiences, but isn't always possible.

This section reads like a collection of cautionary tales: Look what happens when a character ignores their needs or pretends they don't have any. See how warped life becomes if protagonists lose faith in their needs ever being addressed.

Let's go back to Hannah from *The Bodyguard*. She's very professional, but that's also because she's compartmentalized her humanity away.

Unfortunately for her, she's in for one heck of a wake-up call through a fake dating scheme. Her personal security client—and big-deal Hollywood actor, Jack—is being threatened as he returns to his Texas hometown to deal with a family issue.

Hannah warily agrees to assume cover as his girlfriend, but feels safe because she believes feelings won't come into the equation. Until—*big sigh*—they do:

> And then I realized something else, as Jack pulled the cuff off his shirtsleeve over the heel of his hand, lifted it to my face, and started dabbing at my cheeks.
>
> I was crying.
>
> My eyes were wet, at least. Without my permission.[k]

The "without my permission" gets me every time. You can practically see the steam coming out of her ears as Hannah works to squash her feelings down. But needs can't remain unmet forever, especially in a romcom.

Switching genres to a domestic women's fiction thriller, we meet an ensemble cast of, honestly, terrible and broken people in *The New House*. The husband, Tom, has narcissistic tendencies. The wife, Millie, like Hannah in *The Bodyguard*, has walled off her feelings to such an extent that she's basically a robot. Their son, Peter, is a diagnosed psychopath. Stacey, a TV personality and the owner of the house Millie and Tom are trying to buy, is the actual murderer. Not a lot of warm fuzzies with this crew.[4] Here's how Stacey sees herself, especially in the context of other people:

---

4. Nobody asked for this, but my hot take is that too many thriller and mystery stories rely on extremely rare "dark tetrad" psychological diagnoses like psychopathy, Machiavellianism, sadism, and narcissistic personality disorder to explain their characters' actions. Luckily, there are relatively few true psychopaths walking among us. Yet every contemporary thriller seems to have a handful. By inventing complex wounds and needs for your thriller antagonists, you can motivate their behavior in more interesting ways than simply labeling them a sociopath and calling it a day.

> She doesn't really have friends.... The women she meets outside
> of work ... pretend her fame is irrelevant, but of course it
> colours every aspect of the relationship. They're either star-
> struck fans, or beneath their veneer of amity they're envious and
> resentful.[1]

There's an implication here that Stacey is actually talking about herself and projecting her flaws onto these "bad friends." This is another example of "everyone's just jealous," which I first joked about in Chapter 7. Are all the women she meets either star-struck or envious? Probably not. Stacey clearly has an over-inflated opinion of herself, which is how she later justifies murder.

Millie ends up being the hero of the story, though she's also an extremely broken person. Meanwhile, her husband is becoming entangled with a woman named Harper, an influencer who wants to buy their current house. Let's see how Tom presents himself through a lens of self-deprecating humor:

> If I wanted to try my luck, I don't think I'd be slapped down.
> Except [Harper's] nearly fifteen years younger than me, and I'm
> hardly a sex symbol: more Gérard Depardieu than Timothée
> Chalamet. Even if I didn't love my wife, I'm not that much of an
> old fool. Whatever daddy issues Harper has going on, a fling
> with me isn't going to solve her problems.[m]

While this looks somewhat noble, if you squint, the conflict between Tom's self-awareness and desire also reveals sour grapes. He's listing all the reasons Harper wouldn't go for him, I suspect, out of fear that he *would* actually get burned if he made a play. Well, he can't get shot down if he rejects her first, so that's what he does.

Notice how he also seems to see himself as Harper's savior, similar to Joe from *You*, who treats Beck like an object. How noble of Tom to believe his penis is the answer! Broken-person thinking at its finest.

> **Interiority Insight:** How a POV character sees others reveals a lot about themselves. More on that in Chapter 12.

Here's another, more tragic, instance of "you can't fire me because I quit." Cam is broken seemingly beyond repair by his boyfriend, Kai's, death in *Family Meal*. As he thinks about their relationship, he displays a rare glimmer of vulnerability and need:

> I meant to ask Kai what he'd seen in me.
>
> What love looked like to him.
>
> It was a stupid fucking question and I never got around to it.[n]

The self-loathing is painful here, and the need is clear, even though Cam insists that this question doesn't matter. Cam is desperate to believe he had worth in Kai's eyes because he isn't able to love himself. Unfortunately, Kai is dead, and now Cam hopelessly numbs these deep feelings with anonymous hook-ups. He can't bring himself to care, as this would open his emotional floodgates, so he finds distraction through disposable encounters with others who don't care, either.

He moves back to his hometown, starts working at a bar, and boards with its married owners, Fern and Jake. In a grand act of self-sabotage, he hooks up with Jake, only to immediately banish himself:

> I don't give Jake time to say anything: I turn toward the kitchen, wash the mess off under the faucet, and then I'm out the door, before he's calling my name from the porch—and by the time I look up again, I'm already down the road, thumbing through my phone for a hookup, calling a Lyft to take me literally anywhere else.[o]

Cam desperately believes that running away will soothe his own feelings of shame and self-hatred. What he needs, though, is for someone to see him, love him, and ask him to stay.

Irrational belief is also demonstrated in *All the Dangerous Things*:

> It started as a desperate need to stay awake in case Mason came
> back. Someone had taken my baby, after all. Someone had taken
> him from me, and I had slept through it all. What kind of
> mother does that? ... So for those first few nights, I told myself
> I'd stay awake, just in case. That maybe, in the middle of the
> night, I'd peek into his nursery, and there he'd be: sitting up
> straight in his crib like he never even left. That he would crack
> that gummy little smile when he saw me. That he would reach
> for me, fingers curled around his favorite stuffed animal, and
> finally feel safe.[p]

Isabelle's pain is obvious when she says, "What kind of mother does
that?" The abduction wasn't her fault, but she seems to think it would
never have happened if she'd somehow been a better mom or even
person. (We'll learn more about the wound causing these misbeliefs in
Chapter 16.)

She's self-aware enough to know what she's doing is illogical but this
insight doesn't stop her. It also doesn't prevent her from subsuming the
abduction as a personal failure.

What she needs is someone to tell her (or for her own intuition to
believe) that she did everything she could and this wasn't her fault.
Nothing she did or didn't do could've prevented Mason's kidnapping,
and it's a waste of time to engage in what-ifs.

Let's revisit Stacey from *The New House* here. Remember, she ends up
being the murderer and finds herself drawn to Peter, Millie and Tom's
psychopathic son:

> She wanted to teach Peter everything she knew, to mentor him,
> to protect him, to see him flourish and become who he was born
> to be. For the first time in her life she understood what it was to
> feel like a mother.[q]

This is a twisted version of "motherhood," made ironic because Stacey
actually has her own son. When she takes Peter under her wing, it's not

to instill positive values, it's to nurture his darkness. She frames her goals in aspirational terms—"to see him flourish and become who he was born to be"—but the truth is much more sinister. She's investing in Peter, who she sees as a kindred spirit, because she seeks solace with someone as depraved as her.

The character of Anna from *Aesthetica* is broken, too, though she seems to know and accept it. She's worked her whole life to attain the perfect image through plastic surgery. This pursuit becomes more desperate after she has a short and mediocre "career" as an influencer. A snippet from this longer excerpt first appeared in Chapter 3:

> The longer I looked, the more I wondered if image alteration might actually be empowering. For women, so often robbed of agency, was there some freedom in controlling how the world saw our bodies, consumed our bodies? My final project for that Photoshop course was my own image, edited every which way. A smile where there'd been a frown. Smooth skin where there'd been acne scars. Absence where there'd been fat and flesh. Fat and flesh where there'd been absence. Yeah, it was empowering to decide which version I preferred.[1]

We'll see several characters expressing deep, self-reflective, and evolving needs later in this chapter. Anna, though, is still a bit stunted, as she depends on these "tweakments" (real and computerized) to enhance her *self-image*, not just her physical appearance. We can almost see her talking herself into the idea that the external matters more than the internal as she makes a feminist-sounding argument for her actions being "empowering."

I'd argue that the restless self-modification is instead a symptom of body dysmorphia or a similar condition, which reveals that Anna still needs to work on her self-acceptance first, starting from the inside out, instead of the opposite.

The world of *Brutes* is full of broken and delusional characters, most of whom possess an almost jaded self-awareness. This section is written in the joint point of view (defined in Chapter 4) of several teen girls waiting to be discovered by talent scouts[5] at a mall. The "we" can also be taken to mean any number of nameless and identity-hungry teens and tweens:

> Mia and Sammy recruited girls for the Star Search class. We watched them carefully. We desperately wanted to be picked. We tracked them around the mall and the grocery store and at the movies. We counted how many Star Search business cards they had in their back pockets, checking there were enough for all of us, though secretly we believed only one of us had what it took. We all believed we were the one. We knew this would be the end of us, and we did not care.... We wanted to be loved the most.[5]

As a reminder, sometimes a need hides behind "want" language in interiority, which can be confusing. Here, the narrators admit that they would throw all of their besties under a bus to be "discovered." They need validation, or maybe they just need better friends. Each teen is speaking as if they're the only one who matters, and this self-centeredness, while developmentally appropriate for the age group, runs counter to community-building. This novel paints a grim but very relatable portrait of the shifting loyalties of teens, and how it feels to age into young adulthood without many meaningful life experiences.

Now that we've had a chance to explore the electric needs underneath some truly unrealized characters, let's pivot to protagonists who are becoming clued into their desires or are actively working to meet them.

Growth Arc Needs

As we explore how needs emerge into character consciousness, I want to refer back to some protagonists who, in an earlier state of development, were blind to what really drove them.

Sona from *Gearbreakers* has been welcomed into the rebel fold and is now expected to destroy the autocratic regime to which she used to

---

5. Ironically, the "scouts" are just some older teens who've been given this small measure of authority.

belong. When Sona joins this newfound family, she also meets rebel leader, Eris, a future love interest. Eris has something very foundational in common with Sona: a kind of hardened vulnerability avoidance. In fact, this exact sentiment could've come from Sona herself, but we're in Eris's POV as she thinks about her comrades-in-arms:

> A bleeding heart doesn't really fit into this line of work ... so I don't think about them dying too much, just like I don't think about loving all of them too much. Thinking about one always feeds the other, and then my heart feels like a sinkhole in my chest, and in all honesty, screw *that*.[t]

Of course, by saying that she "doesn't think" about her peers dying, or how much she cares for them, Eris is sneakily admitting to readers—if not to herself yet—that she needs them to be safe.

Interiority Insight: A character can't narrate what they don't perceive or experience, so if they say it, even in the context of denial, that's a clue to readers who are paying attention.

Hannah, from *The Bodyguard*, is an expert at shoving down her needs. Eventually, she starts to crack open and admit her feelings for Jake, as we first saw in the previous section:

> I hesitated. It really was time to go. There was a tiny part of me that thought I should tell Jack something real. That I liked him. That I'd fallen for him. That even though it had been fake— maybe even because it had been fake—it had somehow become the most real thing in my life.
>
> But how humiliating was that?[u]

Even though this happens later in Hannah's growth arc, notice that she tells the truth—"That I'd fallen for him"—only to immediately slam the door with a self-deprecating quip: "But how humiliating was that?" She's not yet ready to admit her need but is also testing the waters by thinking these thoughts. At the beginning of the story, she wouldn't have dared.

Another character caught mid-development is Vasya, from *The Bear and the Nightingale*, who second-guessed her faith in the previous section. Here, she realizes she needs one of her siblings to believe her, to validate her experience without punishing her:

> Vasya's head hurt with thinking. If the domovoi wasn't real, then what about the others? The vodyanoy in the river, the twig-man in the trees? The rusalka, the polevik, the dvorovoi? Had she imagined them all? Was she mad? ... She wished she could ask Olya or Sasha. They would know, and neither of them would ever strike her.[v]

Interiority Insight: If a need is currently unattainable due to a character's circumstances, that raises stakes. In the above example, Vasya is forbidden from discussing her fringe beliefs and is beaten when she does.

Someone else who spends a lot of time reflecting on her past and present selves is Eden in *The Way I Used to Be* (this struggle is even highlighted in the title). When she looks at a picture of herself before the assault, she thinks the following:

> I envy her, that awkward, not-quite-ugly-not-quite-pretty girl. Wish I could start over. Be her again. I look deeply into her eyes as if she holds some special secret, a way to get back to her.... The plan was to get better, to feel better, by any means. But I don't feel better, I feel empty, empty and broken, still.[w]

This interiority shows Eden's desperate need to feel okay, be "better," and recognize herself again. Like Vasya, she wishes for a simpler life, which is unavailable now that her eyes have been opened to the ways of the world. Cynical people, after all, can become so after deep disappointment or heartbreak.

Eden also externalizes her struggles and blames her family and friends for not supporting her. She had low self-esteem, even before the rape, but that's not necessarily unusual for a teen girl. What's notable here is that she also wishes someone had helped her recognize her own value:

> Why didn't they ever teach me to stand up for myself? … They let it happen by allowing him to be here and making me believe that everyone else in the entire world knows what's good for me better than I do. If I hate them, I hate them for that.[x]

The need operating below the surface in this interiority is that Eden sees herself as a lost opportunity, someone who could've stood up to Kevin if only she had a support system. Had someone nurtured her potential instead of leaving her to fend for herself, Eden believes she might have been spared. Remember, it's more proactive and powerful to meet our own needs than to put that burden on others, but in this case, it makes sense that she feels let down. Teenagers don't come equipped with all the tools necessary to develop robust self-worth. The process takes a lot of trial, error, and life experience.

The following excerpts track a character becoming aware of their neglected needs. In *How Far the Light Reaches*, the author and narrator's mother drags them to a weight-loss consultation:

> My mother explained to Karen that I would like to lose weight. Karen looked me up and down and nodded. "You're lucky— you don't have to lose much," she told me, her teeth flashing. I felt both relieved and, unexpectedly, distressed. I hadn't realized a small part of me was hoping the nutritionist would tell me that, actually, I was fine. That, actually, I could just exist in my current body, and the real work was to love it.[y]

"The real work was to love it" is an amazing realization at any stage in life, but it's exceptional wisdom to gain at such a young age. The deeper need here is self-acceptance, rather than the desire for "the perfect body" or "to lose weight." Realizing that self-love is the key doesn't magically translate into the narrator's ability to practice that self-love, though. But this idea is, at the very least, the beginning of a new and more nuanced sense of identity.

Interiority Insight: It's important to note that humans and characters have realizations, backslide, vacillate, and act against their best interests, which we'll explore more in Chapter 15. Realizations and even transformative a-ha! moments don't function like an on/off switch that gets thrown once and stays that way forever. After a character has an epiphany, it's tougher for them to go back to the way they were, pursue the same objectives, and cling to misbeliefs. But forward progress isn't necessarily easy or linear, either.

Needs assert themselves over the course of a character growth arc in fits and starts, and a successful protagonist must step outside of their comfort zone to explore new ways of being. Living differently initially feels much tougher than going back to the status quo. Unfortunately, a character can only attain what they truly need if they take this risk.

Let's stick with the narrator of *How Far the Light Reaches*, who is not only genderqueer and nonbinary but mixed race (white and AAPI). The author is very conflicted about "The Question" they often get asked: "What *are* you?" They resent feeling like a curiosity but, paradoxically, they also find themselves wondering the same thing about other mixed-race people. Here, they explore their own seeming hypocrisy:

> It is tempting to ... advocate for a future in which mixed-race people are no longer intriguing ciphers to be unscrambled on the sidewalk, in which we can simply exist, unbothered.... But I can't. Because whenever I meet a mixed person who looks something like me, I want to ask them The Question. I want to know what kind of Asian they are. I want to know how their parents met. I want to know what words they use to identify themselves. I want to know how close or distanced they feel to their own whiteness. I want to ask them the questions I don't want strangers to ask me.... Maybe it's because I grew up longing for role models, surrounded by dozens of white and Asian families like mine but no mixed-Asian adults. We were all children, a new and blurry generation, all of us ogling the oldest

of us for some glimpse into our uncertain futures, some idea of who we might grow up to be.[z]

The deeper need operating below the surface in this interiority is to know one's people and theoretically get closer to knowing oneself.

I want to connect this excerpt to another racially inflected meditation, this time from Bronca in *The City We Became*. Here, she's thinking about Manny (the personification of Manhattan) through the lens of her ancestry. Within this context, she perceives him as both familiar and dangerously unknowable:

> Manhattan is no better, with his friendly smile that shows too many teeth. She thinks at first that he might be kin; something about the set of his features feels familiar, even though he's obviously so multiracial that he could be anything. Then she finds herself leaning toward him, listening to him a little more than the others as he speaks, and belatedly she gets it. Maybe the Dutch smiled like that when they gave trinkets to people of the Canarsee—a band of the Lenape—and laid sole claim to what all others had shared for millennia. Probably every ethnic group he meets thinks he's one of theirs, at least partially. It's a subtle, manipulative bit of magic, and Bronca resents the fuck out of it as soon as she figures it out.[aa]

Interiority Insight: Two deep needs are context and trust—a character knowing where they stand and whether they're secure there.

Bronca needs to know her people, too. At this point in the story, as alliances are being forged and broken between the characters representing each borough, she needs to understand who she can trust and uses the filter of race and ancestry to glean that insight. Interpreting Manny in this way shows Bronca's growing awareness of the dynamics developing around her.

Let's stick with Bronca again, but this time, as she needs to understand

who she is and whether her identity is aligned with her job at the
Bronx Art Center:

> It's easy for a nonprofit administrator to lose touch with her
> purpose. Life can become nothing but grant applications and
> payroll problems, supply orders and fund-raising schmoozes, if
> one isn't careful. Bronca's an artist, so she takes pains to keep art
> foremost in her routine, if not her mind, every day.[bb]

This is a reminder that Bronca needs to be her essential self, as well as a
significant character insight. Seeing Bronca grow and claim her desires
sets us up perfectly for this chapter's final section of excerpts, in which
protagonists confront their deepest selves and needs in interiority.

Foundational Needs

We'll begin with excerpts that show how some protagonists first realize
their drivers, then show characters grappling with their deepest necessities. After all, epiphanies can come suddenly or emerge with time,
like an image darkening in a developer bath. The following paired
quotes represent similar turning points. Some moments are whispers,
but these are screams, literally.

We've already met poor Mari from the historical portion of *The Villa*:
Her baby died and her musician partner can't seem to keep it in his
pants. Feeling trapped in a glamorous vacation house—and paradoxically miserable in even the most ideal-seeming circumstances—she lets
loose a primal scream:

> Tipping her head back, she looks up, where clouds are already
> beginning to form, promising yet another evening trapped
> inside the house.... Mari can't help it. She opens her mouth wide
> and screams, literally screams at the sky, a howl of frustration
> that hurts her throat, but at least relieves some of the pressure in
> her chest.[cc]

The need here is to blow her valve and have some say. But Mari also
makes a powerful statement: "I will honor my needs instead of keeping
them bottled up."

Let's see an echo of this kind of moment from *Brutes*, this time as Britney, a cater-waiter, demands attention from the blue-blooded drones attending a glamorous gala:

> I have always loved breaking glass. It is so easy ... it is like the glass wants to break. It wants to be free. It wants to be a thousand flecks of shrieking glitter, announcing an entrance, a star of the show.
>
> People scream as the tray falls from my hand. They throw up their bejeweled fingers to protect their eyes from the splinters of glass. The champagne creates a yellow puddle in the middle of the shining floor, like dog piss.
>
> The men and the women and the waitresses back away from me like I am something rabid. They look like they expect me to cry. I almost do. I think about laughing, too, but in the end, I do neither. I toe the yellow liquid wider with my sneaker. The silence is gorgeous. It ripples out of me like the most brilliant piece of art.[dd]

Interiority Insight: Is there a single moment in your story when a character makes a bold statement of need or demonstrates it in action, no matter how daring?

While Mari's declaration of need is desperate, Britney's is empowering. She aligns herself with the glass (which "wants to break," in her interpretation), and sees herself as "the most brilliant piece of art." Both characters have reached a tipping point with their sense of self and realize they need change and release.

Deep desire can also emerge during acute action, rather than as a result of thinking and growth. Nahri, a grifter from adult fantasy *The City of Brass* by S.A. Chakraborty, has been making her living as a healer, palm reader, and exorcist (performing what're called "zars"). When she's trapped in a creepy cemetery, having encountered a terrifying undead creature, she becomes vulnerable and begs:

I can't stay here. But Nahri could see nothing but tombs in front of her and had no idea how to get back to the streets.... *Please, God ... or whoever is listening,* she prayed. *Just get me out of this, and I swear I'll ask Yaqub for a bridegroom tomorrow. And I'll never do another zar.*[ee]

Interiority Insight: If a character is brought low and reduced to begging, what would they sacrifice under duress? Once things calm down, would they actually follow through, or would they try to recant their offer?

A similar moment of dangerous realization hits Jude, from *The Cruel Prince*, as she sizes up the venomous Prince Cardan:

He stares at me as though I am a stranger, but I have never felt less like one. For the first time, we are both unmasked.[ff]

Jude realizes that she might be capable of standing up to him and recommits to remaining an outsider in a fairy kingdom that wants her gone. Sometimes, positive reactions and motivations proactively point characters in the direction of their true destinies. Other times, a negative reaction or aversion signals the way forward, even if going that path will be riskier. For Jude, staying in this world feels hard, but returning to the human realm is impossible:

I mostly don't like to imagine the life I could have had, the one without magic in it. The one where I went to a regular school and learned regular things. The one where I had a living father and mother. The one where ... I wasn't so angry. Where my hands weren't stained with blood. I picture it now, and I feel strange, tense all over, my stomach churning.

What I feel is panic.[gg]

Remember this moment, as it'll be relevant in Chapter 20.

Interiority Insight: Indulging in a what-if fantasy can sometimes clarify what a character needs.

A very similar interiority-based realization of need appears in *The Glass Hotel*. The hotel's owner, financier Leon Prevant, is finally able to admit, in the darkness of his own mind, that he might be sitting on a throne of financial lies due to his involvement in Jonathan Alkaitis's Ponzi scheme. He's with his wife, Marie, in an intimate space, but she's asleep, which adds to Leon's sense of loneliness. Compounding this is the idea that he's unable to speak the truth aloud:

> He'd purposefully drunk one whiskey too many with the thought that this might make it possible to fall asleep, but it was if … a crack [had opened] in the night, through which all his fears flooded in. If pressed he might have admitted to Marie that he was worried about money, but worried wasn't strong enough. Leon was afraid.[hh]

Leon is an outwardly success-driven older male character who was likely socialized to avoid feeling—and certainly expressing—his vulnerabilities. For him, merely admitting fear is a monumental feat. In fact, Leon is only able to access his deeper self after getting drunk, which suggests he has insight into his needs, but not the courage to act on them.

Most of these deep moments of need acknowledgement have been negative, as characters tend to automatically reject things that seem difficult, or which contradict the lives and mindsets they've carefully constructed. This is the resistance to change that often keeps characters (and people) from pursuing their true paths.

But realizations can be positive, too, as we see with Ifemelu, from *Americanah*, once she meets Obinze:

> She rested her head against his and felt, for the first time, what she would often feel with him: a self-affection. He made her like

herself. With him, she was at ease; her skin felt as though it was her right size.[ii]

Not only does Ifemelu acknowledge her need for romantic love, but a deeper desire for self-affection, too. This connection makes her more herself. Unfortunately, this relationship is an ongoing struggle for both characters, as we'll see elsewhere in this guide.

Lily from *Bad Fruit* seems very susceptible to her mother's opinions (and shifting moods), but she also maintains a strong sense of self. Unfortunately, she feels she must keep it secret (you'll recognize this snippet from a longer excerpt featured in Chapter 6):

> I sit back, relieved. Despite everything Mama has done to bring out the Chinese in me, I remain resolutely myself, her whitest child.

> *I'm not the same as her.*[ii]

Mama wants her to look more Chinese, yet Lily needs to maintain an autonomous identity, even if she's unable to voice this yet. Many characters access their deepest needs and vulnerabilities in the context of their relationships. Interpersonal connections can either help bring protagonists closer to fulfillment, or push them further away.

Interiority Insight: The decision to live in fuller alignment with one's true self can touch off a period of great struggle, which is very high stakes. When might your protagonist find the courage to overcome their misbelief? How might they begin to demonstrate their new self in action? Who, if anyone, is most interested in them remaining stuck and unrealized? Does the protagonist ever confront this person?

Grace from *Amazing Grace Adams* has been struggling with a misbelief her entire life. When she was young, she overheard her mother express regret about having children. In a bombshell moment, the adult Grace realizes what her mother actually meant. Rectifying this misunderstanding not only allows her to reinterpret her backstory, but arms her with the courage to be a better mother herself:

> Grace stares at her mobile … sees her face reflected in the black screen. Her eyes are round with fresh knowledge.… For the first time she understands why her mum said what she did all those years ago. It was because of the guilt. The same guilt Grace feels. The universal mothering guilt that is surely implanted in the delivery room along with that Pitocin shot. One out, one in. This crazed truth that no matter how hard they try, mothers feel they have failed their kids, that they are not good enough, not quite up for the job. When her mum said she wished she'd never had children, she didn't mean it, Grace thinks. Of course she didn't, and it's like a revelation that should have come years ago.[kk]

Here, Grace allows herself to hold two truths at once and experiences a new realization that heals a childhood wound. She needs to understand this, and I love the following image: "her eyes are round with fresh knowledge." Sometimes all we can do is marvel at an epiphany, and this interiority demonstrates that.

Motherhood is tough (as is fatherhood, of course, though a lot more women's, upmarket, and literary fiction tends to be written about a mother's shifting identity). Even in a paranormal adult novel, *How to Sell a Haunted House* by Grady Hendrix, we hear a grounded statement of deep need, as one of the narrators, Louise, holds her sick daughter:

> Louise held Poppy's feverish, limp body for hours, wishing harder than she'd ever wished before that for just sixty seconds someone would hold her, but no one holds moms.[ll]

In this matter-of-fact instance of interiority, Louise reveals that all she needs is to be held. Unfortunately, she also believes that's unlikely to happen because she has crossed the identity threshold into the role of "carer." Due to her mindset, Louise might be cutting off the opportunity to be nurtured, at least according to her definition of motherhood.

Family obligations also play a part in the adult historical novel *Home-*

going by Yaa Gyasi. Here, James, a white English colonizer living in Africa,[6] laments that he doesn't have agency over his own life:

> He was the son of a Big Man. There were things he had to do. Things he had to be seen doing so that everyone would know that his family was still important. What he wanted, what he most wanted, was to disappear. His father had seven other sons who could carry on the Otcher-Collins legacy. He wanted to be a man without a name.[mm]

Though it's difficult to empathize with a privileged white man who's subjugating African people on their own land, James offers a relatable insight. I like this fantasy of being "a man without a name" and shaking off the burdens and responsibilities of the life he finds himself living. Fantasies are a means of expressing deep need, especially when it comes to relationships and social roles. This kind of escapism is catnip for a lot of readers, as discussed in Chapter 2. It's also a popular method used to reveal a character's most vulnerable inner necessities, as we saw earlier in this chapter.

The next excerpt comes from Cassie in *Ripe*, who imagines a romance with the unavailable chef:

> A brief fantasy carries me away: driving to the sea with the chef again, gesturing at the waves as I list all the blues for him: cerulean, turquoise, azure … handing him my dripping heart with our bare feet in the sand. My mind can make love out of anything, even the smallest of shards.[nn]

The level of self-awareness contained in that last sentence is excruciatingly honest, so you can see why I also chose it as a thematic statement in Chapter 3. This interiority is so full of need and vulnerability that I immediately empathize with Cassie, even as I recognize she's making self-defeating choices. She's aware of the issues at play yet seems unable to stand up for herself. Rejecting this relationship might allow

---

6. The schadenfreude is almost too much, though, because neither do the people he is enslaving. He doesn't acknowledge that his power only comes from society's interpretation of skin color.

her the opportunity to get her love needs met by someone who's capable of doing so, but Cassie doesn't see that as an option. She cannot have the chef, but she clings to him anyway. Perhaps she's sabotaging herself subconsciously because she doesn't believe she's worthy of happiness.

Ari from *The Luis Ortega Survival Club* is able to make the distinction between what others think of her, how they treat her, and her own needs. This is a very mature insight for a teenage character, especially one who has undergone a horrific sexual assault:

> He picked me for a reason. He knew I was lonely and desperate
> for someone to notice me, and he took advantage of it. This
> whole time I thought I wasn't really over him. But what I'm
> really not over is what he did to me.[oo]

Ari realizes that she needs to heal herself, rather than depending on anyone else to do it for her. But even if the perpetrator takes accountability—which is unlikely—Ari suspects that only she can make herself okay again. Things can't return to the way they were, but by honoring her needs and her selfhood, she might be able to move forward.

Finally, our last example centers on a bit of beautiful writing from *The Vaster Wilds*. Lamentations, who has fled indentured servitude, goes through the wringer and almost dies several times after escaping into the wilderness. In this interiority, her life is entirely her own and she finds a kind of joy in that notion:

> Sometimes she stopped in her labors and saw with a thrill how
> beautiful the world was, how exquisite the purple mountains
> sometimes rising, a trick of optics, at the edge of sight, how
> joyous the blue birds chasing each other like scraps of wind-
> blown sky.
>
> A pureness of happiness coursed through her and left her
> ravished.[pp]

While this high of being reduced to her most essential self is unlikely to last, and danger lurks all around, she needs to mark this moment. May we all have even a glimpse of such rapture in our lives, no matter how hard-won or fleeting. This reminds writers and readers that a character's most essential needs can be met in big and small ways. When they are, protagonists experience growth, resolution of their internal conflicts, and true harmony.

Our exploration of objective, motivation, and, now, need, has centered on a character's growth and development over time. Next, I'll add the layer of inner tension, which is a natural side effect of a protagonist in motion. Change and growth hurt, especially when the character feels conflicted or otherwise experiences internal turbulence. Transformation doesn't flow in a straight line from stimulus to realization to new reality. This kind of situation-specific inner struggle is the subject of our next chapter.

9

INNER STRUGGLE

One of the five main pillars of interiority, as defined in Chapter 1, is inner struggle, or the emotional friction your character feels as they experience the plot.

Are they in denial? Do they indulge in coping mechanisms? Are their wants at odds with their needs? Can they even admit to their true desires? Are they acting in alignment with their values? Is their behavior consistent with the type of person they believe they are, or want to be? Are they wrong or is someone else wrong (including, possibly, the entire story world and its culture)?

You will absolutely want to introduce an element of your character's inner struggle in the first chapter of your novel or memoir, if you can. This is easy to do, since the protagonist is usually spinning their wheels in their "normal" before the inciting incident, superficially presenting as okay but somehow dissatisfied. (This is what often sets them up to go on a journey of internal and, often, external transformation to begin with.) The flavor of this internal conflict should align with the backstory, wound, objective, and need, but you have many options to choose from, as you'll see in this chapter's excerpts.

The Importance of Inner Struggle

Every character wrestles with something internally. In Lisa Cron's *Story Genius*, she calls inner struggle a story's "third rail" because it powers everything else your protagonist goes through. What is your character's big internal turmoil? How you present it matters, too, as straightforward explanation probably isn't the best strategy. Readers want to see the protagonist actually wrestling with an idea. This is what interiority was *made* for, so take it out for a spin.

You'll want to limit your character's expression of inner struggle to short yet revealing moments, nothing too ponderous. In other words, no protagonists navel-gazing while sitting around in their rooms, thinking about how much their life sucks. Do real-world humans—your readers—do this? Absolutely. Especially if you're writing for middle grade and young adult audiences, your characters will whine and moan. My life from ages twelve to fifteen was probably one giant sulk. But endless complaining isn't the best approach to conveying juicy inner struggle.

We all have to use the restroom several times a day, for example. That's realistic and relatable. But do you put each instance on the page? Probably not. Unless your character goes to the restroom only to encounter a terrifying tentacled monster, which happens in *The City We Became*. In that case, Bronca's biological urge combines with a consequential plot point, which elevates the action out of the basement of mundane necessity. You can shape realistic behavior into larger-than-life story by adding proactive character drive, generating forward momentum, and having characters search for ways to meet their needs.

Early on, let your character have a moment that encapsulates their inner struggle but within the context of the opening scene. After the plot is rolling, don't stop finding opportunities to add internal tension and nuance. You can even play with interiority and choices that outright contradict a reader's understanding of your protagonist. To be clear, the character's actions and reactions must be supported by specific logic that readers can follow and understand. While a protagonist won't always be rational, they must always present a *rationale*.[1]

Sometimes, characters work to convince themselves. Other times, they're trying to convince others, including the audience. Unless protagonists intentionally "break the fourth wall," it's assumed they don't know they're being "watched" when they're in their own heads. Internal struggle deals a lot with appearance versus reality and whether a protagonist is especially vulnerable to "saving face" or comparing themselves to others. The prevalence of inner conflict can also depend on whether things are going well or poorly in the present action.

Interiority Insight: Characters have moods! Your character has a general temperament and emotional baseline, but they should also have variable moods, just like you do. Some will be reasonable, some not. How much bandwidth a protagonist has available to deal with tension in any specific moment may also fluctuate. When they have a short fuse, they're less likely to manage conflict well or respond admirably. Consider, also, their general state of health. If they are sick or hindered by acute physical or mental challenges, they might not approach situations with the same mindset as they would if they were functioning as usual. Don't forget chronic issues which inform their sense of well-being, either.

Showing a character's inner struggle on the page exposes readers to your protagonist's deepest self. We'll find variable self-awareness when it comes to internal conflict because characters can be more or less prepared to confront tough issues, depending on their mood, the context of the scene at hand, and where they are in their growth arcs (see Chapter 11). How a character commands their awareness of their own inner tension demonstrates their trajectory.

---

1. Thank you from the bottom of my heart to Scott Marasigan for this marvelous turn of phrase. We'll always have the Solage!

Opportunities to Create Inner Struggle

You'll see some examples of characters trapped between their wants and needs, as well as those who are grappling with denial. Per Chapter 3, denial can be a powerful tool for revealing character dimension, but it shouldn't go on for too long, lest readers lose patience or empathy for the protagonist. This can be a difficult balancing act. Writers often have to introduce information (which we covered in Chapter 4 and will explore again in Chapter 14) without directing too much reader attention to it or making it Obviously Important Later.

If a character notices something, only to deny it, readers usually realize what's going on before the protagonist does. But audiences can only exist in this kind of limbo for so long before they start itching for the hero to catch up and acknowledge what's already clear.

Many characters are designed to be smart or otherwise exceptional, something that makes them interesting and engaging. Readers want a protagonist who's perceptive and capable of critical thinking. Audiences want to participate in a character's internal process, logic, and reasoning. Some genres tolerate more denial than others (like romantic denial, which we'll talk about in Chapter 13), but overall, if you use denial, let the character be at least somewhat aware that they're rejecting reality, then have them come around quickly.

Consider the following examples of cognitive bias[2] that can also come into play as characters struggle with themselves and others:[3]

- **Tunnel vision:** focusing on part of a threat at the expense of other information;
- **Confirmation bias:** believing only those pieces of information that confirm one's viewpoint or perspective, ignoring everything else;
- **Egocentricity:** discounting others' perspectives; and
- **Attribution bias:** attributing the problem to someone else, rather than taking accountability or a more balanced view.

---

2. For more on this topic, check out *The Age of Magical Overthinking: Notes on Modern Irrationality* by Amanda Montell.

3. This list is adapted for storytelling purposes from *The Breakthrough Years*.

The juiciest moments of internal tension occur when a character's actions and choices conflict with their morality, value system, or true identity.

The following From the Shelves examples demonstrate some brief instances of interiority that crystallize the turmoil inside each protagonist. First, we'll see sections that focus on largely unconscious inner tension, then the conflict between want and need (originally introduced in the previous chapter) at crucial moments, and, finally, what conscious or self-aware inner tension looks like on the page. Let's start with our most guarded and unevolved characters.

Unconscious Inner Struggle

Denial ain't just a river in Egypt, as they say. Even seemingly smart characters are vulnerable to it, especially if it offers them a benefit: protection, image, power, or control. Of course, when these safe harbors are "achieved" with denial, they don't often last. Usually, protagonists are forced to confront whatever they're avoiding, especially if you construct your plot to bring them into direct conflict with their wounds and needs.

Indulging in delusion positions a character within the context of their growth arc. We've heard from poor Cam in *Family Meal* a number of times already. He's about as unaware as you can get, hardly able to admit that he's completely lost in grief. Here, his childhood best friend, TJ, confronts him. This is a brave act on TJ's part, especially since the two aren't on good terms, but Cam can hardly utter a response:

> I think something is going on with you … [TJ] says, and when he turns to look my way, I don't say anything to that.

> … I won't even pretend to understand what you're dealing with, because there's no way I could. That just wouldn't be possible. And I can't imagine the burden of it all. But I think you're still trying to deal. And I think what you're going through is really, really hard. And I just think, you know, it might help to find resources for navigating it? Something to help you?

Okay, I say.

The word feels like a hook in my throat. I have to cough it out. And I feel fucking nauseous.[a]

Cam's true feelings only appear in that final sentence of interiority. Why do characters act in self-defeating ways? It's usually because they detect a threat to their current reality, belief system, sense of self, understanding of the past, or goals and dreams for the future.

Interiority Insight: Every instance of protagonist denial should serve a purpose and hint at what's really going on below the surface.

Cam doesn't give enthusiastic buy-in to the idea of therapy, meaning he's unlikely to embrace help at this point in his growth arc. But at least he's one step beyond outright disavowal of the truth.

Here's another incident of denial, as Father Konstantin from *The Bear and the Nightingale* wrestles with whether the village is actually full of folk spirits. He's been sent to wipe out this kind of archaic thinking, yet he experiences secret worries that contradict his mission, faith, and training:

That night, Father Konstantin lay on his narrow cot and shivered and could not sleep. In the north, the wind had teeth that bit after sunset, even in summer.... There was something hostile about the nighttime house. Almost, it seemed to breathe.... *What foolishness*, thought Konstantin.[b]

Konstantin shouldn't let his guard down just yet. There is, indeed, ancient magic in the village, and it doesn't take kindly to threats.

Interiority Insight: Believing that everyone else is the problem (attribution bias, as defined in the previous section) can signal a character with low self-awareness and a fixed mindset, who blames external factors for their problems. They'd rather avoid change and accountability at all costs, even if it means they'll berate the sun for shining, rather than putting on a hat. Paradoxically, the behavior of blaming external factors can also indicate a character with high self-awareness who is questioning the larger framework of the world around them. If your protagonist takes action as a result of this inner struggle, risking themselves to confront—and potentially change—the issues in their society, they're in the latter group. Only the most self-actualized characters choose to do this, while everyone else stews and complains.

Sometimes characters dive under the blanket of denial in order to shield themselves from something they dread. Other times, they wall themselves off from potentially positive developments, because to allow themselves to hope and love represents a risk as well.

Let's shift over to the world of romance, as delusion and denial run rampant in this genre, much to the chagrin of some readers. The following two examples showcase the romance beats of "there's no way I like this person" and "we simply *can't* have a relationship because XYZ."[4]

The first excerpt comes from Red, the romantic interest in *Get a Life, Chloe Brown*. Red takes a more relaxed view of life and is convinced that Chloe is too uptight and fussy:

> Even if she was rude and she made him feel like a monster of a man, he could not be a dick to Chloe Brown, not anymore …
> they weren't in a relationship and never would be. So there. He was safe.[c]

This idea of "He was safe" is central to romantic denial. Red *needs* to believe that Chloe isn't a viable partner. Why? Because he knows that her standards are high, and he's afraid of her rejection. This interpretation in interiority helps him feel insulated from any potential vulnerability.

---

4. Insert any number of justifications here.

A similar mistaken assumption operates beneath the surface as Jude finds herself in a romantic clinch with the villainous Prince Cardan in *The Cruel Prince*:

> Cardan's cruel mouth is surprisingly soft, and for a long moment after our lips touch, he's still as a statue. His eyes close, lashes brushing my cheek. I shudder, as you're supposed to when someone walks over your grave.... If I didn't know better, I'd say his touch was reverent, but I do know better. His hands are moving slowly because he is trying to stop himself. He doesn't want this. He doesn't want to want this.[d]

Jude tells readers that Cardan "is trying to stop himself. He doesn't want this." She can't know, of course, since she doesn't have access to his POV. Ironically, she insists "I do know better," which is usually a denial red flag. She's coming to the most negative possible assumption because it's the one she *must* believe. Maybe she's self-conscious or has low self-esteem. However, she's *also* not supposed to want him, which complicates things. Is she speaking about Prince Cardan, whose inner life she can't know? Or is she projecting her own feelings? My money's on the latter.

Many romantic plots and subplots are strung together with this kind of misdirection, assumption, interpretation, and denial. As we'll see in Chapter 13, a protagonist opening their hearts to love can be one of the most evolved and vulnerable things they'll ever do. It's no wonder so many characters avoid it, especially early in their arcs.

In these cases, protagonists mislead themselves away from fundamentally good things. But delusion can also lead to self-destruction, as anyone who has ever become addicted—to food, alcohol, drugs, nicotine, sex, online shopping, gambling, work, etc.—knows. The rationalization thought pattern usually goes something like this: *This vice feels good and feeling good can't be bad. Besides, I deserve it. Others might have a problem stopping but I'll have the fortitude and self-discipline to quit whenever I want.*

Checking in with Eleanor from *Eleanor Oliphant Is Completely Fine*, we see how she soothes herself after an unsuccessful encounter with the musician she believes she's "in love" with, which comes from a longer excerpt that will appear in Chapter 11:

> Come on, Eleanor, I told myself. Tonight was simply not meant to be.... I assuaged my disappointment with the consoling thought that, when it did finally happen, the encounter would be perfect.[e]

At face value, this is encouraging self-talk and could be considered positive and soothing. Dramatic tension arises, however, as readers suspect that her obsession with the musician is unhealthy and won't end well. (Spoiler alert: It does not.) Eleanor can be very self-aware (when she wants to be). Here, she brushes this off as "disappointment," when it's so much more than that. She delusionally pins all her hopes for having a "normal" life (whatever that means) on this random stranger. This sets her up for an inevitable fall.

Let's wrap up our exploration of unconscious inner tension with my favorite delusional character from these shelves, June from *Yellowface*. June may or may not have caused Athena's death—I don't entirely trust her account of what happened, since she was the only witness—but she's certainly guilty of stealing Athena's manuscript. She knows it's wrong on some level. But instead of dwelling on her feelings of shame and inadequacy, which many characters (and people) use as guardrails that encourage them to do the right thing in morally ambiguous situations, she adopts a suspiciously positive view instead:

> But the truth is, I was too excited.
>
> For the first time in months, I was happy about writing again. I felt like I'd been given a second chance. I was starting to believe in the dream again—that if you hone your craft and tell a good story, the industry will take care of the rest. That all you have to do is put a pen to paper, that if you work hard enough and write well enough, the Powers That Be will transform you overnight into a literary star.[f]

In this instance, she not only feels entitled to literary stardom, but she reasons that the shortcuts she's taking by appropriating Athena's project are an achievement! June is like a magician, flashing her excitement in the reader's face and hoping they don't look at what her hands are doing—stealing, cheating, and lying. On a subconscious level, I suspect June is mostly reassuring *herself* in this instance of interiority.

Interiority Insight: Characters and people are unlikely to see themselves as the antagonists of their own stories, as we'll see in Chapter 12. They'll either insist they're upholding a moral high ground, fighting for a vision of the world that matches their values, or are a misunderstood hero who has been unfairly cast as a villain. Beneath this is a deep and relatable need to be in alignment with oneself, and to explain away those feelings and/or actions that make the character feel ashamed. Even a somewhat implausible-sounding rationalization is better to such an antagonist than admitting they're wrong or have done something bad. This delusion and internal tension operate on two levels: Characters attempt to fool others (including readers) and they attempt to fool themselves.

Internal tension doesn't stay buried in the subconscious for long, though. As we start to bring inner tension closer to the surface of a protagonist's awareness, their conflict can become more overt, and they can begin to confront the gap between their wants and needs more actively.

Wants in Conflict With Needs

An early indicator of internal conflict is a character's realization that their objective chafes against what they suspect—or know outright—they need. When these two forces clash, a protagonist might realize, for perhaps the first time, that they're not in alignment with their true selves, and, troublingly, that they might have to choose a path or make some sacrifices. This awareness tends to kick in after the inciting incident, when a character's "normal" is first challenged or subverted.

We can see this at play in the Kingdom of Money, which we recognize from *The Glass Hotel*. Oskar, a Polish employee of Jonathan Alkaitis's

Ponzi scheme, is finally realizing that the house of cards is about to fall. The first half of the excerpt is written in the style of notes from the eventual court case, once his online search history is revealed, and the second half transitions to interiority:

> Oskar spent a full ninety minutes looking up real estate prices in Warsaw, then seven minutes researching which countries had extradition treaties with the United States, then another twenty-three minutes looking up real estate prices in Kazakhstan, where he had a couple of cousins, before finally logging out and leaving the office.... It was only mid-afternoon, but he thought that he wouldn't mind being fired.[g]

Oskar seems torn between whether or not he plans to accept reality. Part of him realizes that he's in a lot of trouble, hence researching countries without extradition treaties and looking at real estate. Here, he does some interpretation and extrapolation.

Interiority Insight: Difficult decisions are great for showing character growth (or lack thereof) with interiority. We'll see more examples of pivotal instances in Chapter 16.

Another part of him, the part that "wouldn't mind being fired" is imagining that there's still a way out of this situation, as if termination could retroactively shield him from the legal ramifications of what he's already done.

Interiority Insight: Magical thinking and naïveté are human, even if some protagonists want to believe they're above these self-preservation mechanisms. But, let's face it, characters who never vacillate or doubt are boring. Nobody's perfect and vulnerability in a pivotal moment helps protagonists become relatable. If you find yourself wondering "What would I do in this situation?" about your protagonist, you can put that moment of indecision on the page, too. Decisions aren't always instant, either. The higher the

---

stakes, the more you'll want to explore the character's vacillation, but you're okay to summarize it instead of unleashing a lengthy inner monologue.

The internal conflict between want and need plays out in moments of tension, when a character must pretend or wrangle their vulnerability into a show of strength.

In *Red Queen*, Mare, a Red, resents her new life as a Silver pretender. But instead of showing weakness, she becomes strategic. In this scene, the Silver girls are pitted against one another in a paranormal power showcase to secure a proposal from one of the crown princes:

> *Yes*, I want to scream. *Yes, I am scared*. But Silvers don't admit things like that. Silvers have their pride, their strength—and nothing else. "When I fight, I intend to win," I say instead.[h]

While it's Mare's assumption that Silvers never admit fear or insecurity, she uses that idea to muster her own bravado. That's what she feels she must do, at least early on, to "make it" and forestall exposing who—and what—she really is.

Interiority Insight: Differentiating between what your character feels or thinks internally and what they communicate externally can be a wonderful way to show internal struggle on the page.

Sometimes a character will know what they want. Other times they'll know what they *don't* want, even if they subsume that there's something wrong with them. Here, Millie, from *The New House*, judges herself for being unable to fall into female friendship as easily as those around her seem to:

> Stacey showed me a glimpse of the mysterious and intimate world of female friendship from which I'd excluded myself for so long, and I finally understood what I'd been missing. I dared

to dream I might be allowed to be part of it, to have what
everyone else took for granted.[i]

Millie isn't speaking from a place of experience. Instead, she has denied
herself these potentially vulnerable relationships, opening up only to
shut down once more. After trying to befriend Stacey, she realizes that
she needs to keep people at arm's length—which ultimately ends up
being the right decision, at least where Stacey is concerned. But Millie's
loneliness and self-judgment also stoke reader empathy, because the
inner struggle and psychic toll of living in such a guarded way are
obvious in her interiority.

Pamela from *Bright Young Women* becomes similarly cynical when the
police's investigation into the sorority house stabbing stalls. As we saw
in Chapter 6 and will see again in Chapter 11, she once ran excitedly
toward any badge, as it meant she could shield herself from reality.

She doesn't set out to become hardened over the course of the plot, but
here, it's almost like she can't help her new pessimistic outlook. In this
excerpt, "The Defendant" is Pamela's term for the killer (she refuses
him the dignity of a name) and Roger is a false lead:

> I began to envision a life in which the case was never solved, not
> because there weren't any leads but because of pure human
> arrogance. Hopelessness turned to vengeance. I imagined
> ghoulish scenarios where Sheriff Cruso's wife became The
> Defendant's next victim, where he came to me a broken man,
> ruing the day he decided to focus on Roger instead of listening
> to me. My mind had become a bleak and unrecognizable place.[j]

Pamela has probably been socialized against these kinds of thoughts.
It's not "feminine" or acceptable to crave vengeance or wish tragedy
upon someone else, and Pamela is a literal sorority girl. It's risky for
her to travel down these dark mental roads in interiority, but she needs
to believe someone is invested in the case. If she doesn't have the
sheriff to rely on, she'll only have herself, and she's suffering too much
to trust her judgment. She doesn't actually want Sheriff Cruso's wife to
get murdered, but she needs someone else to have skin in the game.

Interiority Insight: Characters and humans sometimes think, say, and do wrong or cruel things. They play devil's advocate. They self-sabotage and act outside of their own best interests. When and why might you add these layers to your characters?

In addition to finding contradictions and inner struggles within your protagonist, you can also play with how aware they are of their turmoil. Pamela, above, doesn't seem to enjoy feeling the way she does. She hates how it reflects on her as a person. This demonstrates self-awareness and a sense of worth. Let's follow her lead along this more enlightened arc toward deeper inner struggle and insight.

Bridging Unconscious and Conscious Inner Conflict

Layers of internal conflict often intersect with the larger theme and premise of the story, especially as characters dump the denial and become more aware of what they're wrestling with and why. This type of inner struggle allows protagonists to examine their needs, flaws, misbeliefs, and worldviews, and also potentially move forward along their growth arcs.

Not all characters are created equal in terms of their potential for self-actualization, so not every protagonist is capable of a huge transformation. But almost all of them will progress, so let's see some examples of conscious inner struggle, which can usually be found from the midpoint on.

August from *One Last Stop* is in an impossible situation—literally. She has fallen for June, who's from the 1970s and stuck in a time loop. August is the type of character who has sworn off most human relationships, as we saw in Chapter 7, because she believes she'll only get hurt. At first, as is common in romantic comedies, August is in complete denial:

> [August is] certainly not the type of person to sit on a train with someone whose name she doesn't even know and imagine her

assembling an Ikea bed frame. Everything is completely under control.[k]

I'll quote Shakespeare and say: "the lady doth protest too much, methinks."[5] August's interiority clearly spells out an advanced fantasy about Subway Girl (bed frames, etc.). This suggests that August has *absolutely* been considering making a move, and that everything is far from "under control."

Next, let's see August wrestling with the same issue about 100 pages later:

Jane's not exactly here permanently. She's not exactly *here* at all. And, well, August has never truly had her heart broken before, but she's pretty sure that falling in love with someone only to send them back to the 1970s would, as first heartbreaks go, win the Fuck You Up Olympics.... This crush, she decides, is just *not* going to work for her.[1]

We still have denial but August is now somewhat willing to admit that *pain avoidance* is her primary reason for guarding her heart. In this interiority, August is intentionally thinking about what she's willing to risk.

A similar conflict plays out with Josiah and Yasmen in *Before I Let Go*, a second-chance romance. In this midpoint-adjacent sequence, both characters struggle to keep their walls up. Here's Josiah's take as he tries to integrate two truths. First, that he still has feelings for Yasmen, and second, that he has an opportunity to move on with a restaurant colleague named Vashti:

I stopped thinking Yasmen and I would reconcile long ago. I stopped wanting it. I could never trust her with my heart, with my happiness, again, but maybe some renegade, obstinate sliver of my soul still felt tethered to her. Even though we're divorced,

---

5. This quote comes from *Hamlet* and is colloquially used to throw someone's sincerity into question, especially when they issue a strong denial.

that small, stupid part of me felt like I betrayed Yasmen when I slept with Vashti.[m]

When you hear characters say they "stopped wanting" something, or that they "could never," especially in a romantic context, these are obvious clues that their denials and needs are grating against one another, like two land masses beneath a fault line.

Here's Yasmen's attempt at the same sentiment, except she's more honest that she's lying to herself (and her therapist). This happens later in the story, after Yasmen and Josiah go on a business trip and hook up "just once":

I know it's for the best.

You can pretend it never happened.

You can be his friend, business partner, co-parent without having more.

You can stop wanting him.

Dr. Abrams says honesty is medicine to the soul. I'll have to ask her the remedy for a lie.[n]

It's important to note that this kind of inner conflict isn't meant to *truly* mislead the reader. Romance and romcom audiences, especially, aren't taking these declarations at face value, or at least they shouldn't. Not every protagonist who contradicts themselves is a liar or unreliable narrator. These conflicted characters represent fallible humans who are often trying their best to figure things out. Interiority is perfectly suited to exploring this kind of internal tension.

In the above examples, the inner struggle is central to the plot and the journey showcases *how* the protagonists finally decide that they're open to love.

> **Interiority Insight:** Sometimes characters play games with others, and sometimes they play games with themselves. Readers are invited to watch ... and keep score, engaging in their own interpretations.

The consequences of self-imposed denial in a romantic context don't always have to be serious. Here's Andi, in *Within These Wicked Walls*, who finds herself falling for her patron, Magnus. When he figures out her feelings and says as much, she becomes defensive:

> "I think you're cross ... because you want to be the one I'm kissing."
>
> I slapped him across the face, so hard I turned his head. I held my breath for an instant, as if my mind had just rejoined my body. It was as if ... he had heard my thoughts.°

This cheeky comment strikes Andi (figuratively) as an intrusion into her mind, so she strikes Magnus (literally). She's upset because he saw right through her façade. Now that a version of the truth has surfaced, they both have to deal with it.

> **Interiority Insight:** It's fun to pair a big action with a vulnerable thought. Without the interiority in the above example, readers would see the slap without the rationale, and this deeper insight into Andi's character would be lost.

Next, I'll reference this excerpt from *Gearbreakers*, which we first saw in the context of Sona's backstory in Chapter 5. As a reminder, she's just realized that her transformation into a Windup doesn't sit right with her sense of self, especially once she realizes she's been misled about the war:

> For weeks I have known I can do damage ... and for weeks, I

have known that I cannot do enough. I am just one girl. I have just one Windup. And I was so drunk on the mere *thought* of having power that I allowed myself to be made into this.[p]

This is a very sober and mature reflection, especially for a teenager. Sona sits at the crux of feeling both powerful and powerless, and this uncomfortable paradox generates inner struggle. Around this time, she decides to join the rebels, perhaps because of her pervasive sense that she "cannot do enough." She wants to matter, just not in the way she originally thought.

As we saw earlier in this chapter, Pamela from *Bright Young Women* is also awakening to her strength while battling serious internal tension. We see her coming online in terms of self-awareness but only after she first expresses major denial. For comparison, let's see her delirious with magical thinking as she pretends Denise is still alive:

[Denise] had fallen back asleep, but when she woke again, I would tell her that the man who'd saved her was handsome and not wearing a wedding ring.... Denise was the type to wind up with a doctor. Maybe this would be the story of how she met her husband, and someday soon I'd be telling it at her wedding.[q]

This is a beautiful fantasy but entirely self-protective. Denise is dead. There will be no wedding. The doctor isn't going to revive her, Sleeping Beauty-style. But Pamela can't admit that to herself yet because she's in shock. She has a long way to go before she's able to subsume the truth ... and her desperate, messy feelings. Later, she's finally able to speak out:

"We have more dignity than that," I said, lifting my head with enormous effort. *Never let them see you sweat*, I was always saying, except I could see the filmy residue my glands had deposited on the window.[r]

In a big personal leap, Pamela actively rejects the requirement to be "socially acceptable" and "proper," even if it means letting 'em see her sweat, literally. This is major for a rule-follower like her, and the interiority, contrasted with her dialogue, makes this clear.

Throughout *Ripe*, Cassie can't articulate her needs, which makes her a tragic character. Though she is positively brimming with inner tension, she's unable to make the leap and voice it. For example, she desperately wants to tell the chef her true feelings but churns with discomfort instead:

> I was choking on what I wanted, on how to tell him. And beyond what I knew I wanted was another desperate desire, one deeply ingrained in me, a need encoded in every single one of my cells: I didn't want him to leave.
>
> There are moments in which a certain level of pain is chosen in order to avoid another, deeper pain.[s]

Unfortunately, she ends up choosing certain pain over potential loss. She comes no closer to revealing her inner self to him, even after she suspects she might be pregnant with his baby. She's completely unable to be vulnerable, not even with an Uber driver who she'll likely never see again:

> His eyes are so kind that the words rise up in my throat and I almost tell him: *I'm terrified, I might be pregnant, I'm floundering here, I'm so lonely.* But I don't know who I can trust. "I'm just fine," I say with a weak smile.[t]

This is how powerful and precarious character inner struggle can be, and how it can hold a protagonist hostage until they either resolve or relieve it. Characters who never address theirs, like Cassie, will keep suffering.

Interiority Insight: Delusions often arise when a protagonist's needs aren't being met, or they're driven to protect their vulnerable inner selves by pretending they're "fine" or happy. What is your character pretending about? What's quivering behind that shield?

As we transition to conscious and evolved characters and their inner struggles, decisions, actions, and subsumations, I'll start to draw the connection between internal struggle and identity in earnest.

Conscious Inner Struggle

Perhaps the best and simplest expression of conscious internal conflict comes from our unnamed narrator in *Death Valley*:

> [Reality] penetrates the veil of acceptance (or feigned acceptance) I have constructed. It touches new feelings (or old feelings I wish not to feel).[11]

Isn't that the rub of it? When a character constructs denials and false realities, all they're doing is keeping the truth at bay. This can be due to fear of failure, or even fear of success. Because if a character excels, they might be asked to do it again, except with higher stakes. Better not to start! Sometimes a character is fully aware of their maladaptive behaviors, but they're not ready to act any other way. What eventually defines them as protagonists is whether they'll take additional risk.

Interiority Insight: Sometimes internal tension leads to realization, which can lead to action, but not always. It's unreasonable to expect a character to act immediately after a new idea strikes or an old paradigm shifts. Sometimes they have to sit with their feelings for a while.

Next we'll see a lovely and slightly mysterious way of talking about conscious delusions. *The Glass Hotel*'s Jonathan Alkaitis sits in prison, enjoying a vibrant inner existence he calls "the counterlife":

> But no, that's memory, not the counterlife. Vincent isn't in the counterlife. He feels it's important to keep the two separate, memory vs. counterlife, but he's been finding the separation increasingly difficult. It's a permeable border. In memory, the air-conditioning was so aggressive that she had trouble keeping

warm, which was why she was always in the hot tub, whereas in the counterlife she's not there at all.[v]

It takes a deep level of insight for Jonathan to realize that he is self-soothing by splitting his consciousness into three distinct dimensions: memories, present reality, and "the counterlife."

Let's see how another character relates to her own denial and inner tension. This is Millie, the calculating surgeon from *The New House*, who sees no problem with compartmentalizing, especially early on:

My ability to put my personal feelings aside is one of the things that makes me so good at my job.[w]

Of course, characters are fallible, even if they want to believe otherwise. She's not always able to smother her feelings, and, unfortunately, makes a critical error later. She decides Stacey is in danger from her son Peter, but it's actually the other way around:

Some instinct is warning me: danger! danger! Predators can always scent blood in the water. Stacey is vulnerable. And Peter's not a normal ten-year-old … [but] I tell myself Stacey will be fine.[x]

Sometimes self-aware protagonists know the right course of action but struggle to take it. Aislyn from *The City We Became* has been living a stunted life on Staten Island and doesn't immediately bond with the other borough characters. The antagonist of this fantasy story, now called "the Woman in White," has realized this, too. Aislyn must decide whether she'd rather save her own ego or New York City itself:

The alternative is to challenge her own belief that the Woman in White isn't so bad. This would force her to question her own judgment and biases and find them wanting. And given how hard she has fought lately to feel *some* kind of belief in herself, she is not ready to doubt again. So it's fine. Everything is fine.[y]

Imagine being so fragile that you'd consider befriending your enemy for some glimmer of attention. That's a heck of an internal conflict, and Aislyn's awareness of the stakes makes this interiority even heavier.

A similarly morally gray character, June from *Yellowface*, pretends to struggle in interiority, a ploy to get readers on her side. She seems to be aware that she has an audience (first mentioned when we discussed breaking the fourth wall in Chapter 4). She also seems to understand that the decision to steal Athena's manuscript *should have* involved shame and guilt.

In reality, she comes to this choice easily, but to beef up her argument, she makes a scholarly justification. While she's unable to actually summon socially acceptable convictions, she wants readers to hear her talk the talk:

> So perhaps we can view this as Athena's great literary prank, as my complicating the reader-author relationship in a way that will provide juicy fodder for scholars for decades to come.
>
> Okay—perhaps that last one is a bit of a stretch. And if this sounds like me assuaging my own conscience—fine. I'm sure you'd rather believe I spent those few weeks tortured, that I struggled constantly with my guilt.[z]

June's ability to admit that she's perfectly fine doing the wrong thing is, after all, a kind of self-knowledge. Readers may even appreciate that she allows her mask to drop and admits to bullshitting them.

In this case, audience engagement with June may be less driven by empathy, and more by wanting to see how the train wreck unfolds. The intersection between fantasy, appearance, reality, and how these notions inform the self is an especially juicy backdrop for character inner tension.

Interiority Insight: Readers may get a kick out of comparing themselves to characters like June and Joe from *You* for a quick ego boost.

Here's another example from *Everyone Here Is Lying*, a story with a large ensemble cast of point of view characters and a presumed kidnapping plot. This POV, Marion, *is* actually the person sheltering Avery, the "missing" girl. However, Avery is manipulating Marion for her own purposes, and Marion is vulnerable to this ploy because she's in love with Avery's father, William.

Another wrinkle is that William has indeed chosen to cheat on his wife, but not with Marion, which makes her furious. Here's the moment she realizes that William loves a woman named Nora, leaving Marion's fantasy shattered:

> Seeing Nora always made Marion feel plain, but now she was filled with self-loathing. She couldn't compete with that, and it made her miserable.... [William and Nora] were obviously having an ongoing affair. They were clearly in love; there was so much passion there, passion that she'd imagined for herself. Now she imagined him leaving his wife, leaving his family, but not for her, for Nora Blanchard.[aa]

The death of Marion's dream hits hard, especially since her fantasy is coming true ... for someone else. Coping with this bitter loss of desire and expectation creates a lot of internal tension. Marion also subsumes the idea that she's simply not good enough.

Interiority Insight: Not all losses and conflicts have an external component. Some are purely internal. For example, when a child dies or goes missing, there's the loss of the child, parenting role, and current lifestyle. However, the purely internal conflict involves the destruction of a parent's intangible dreams and expectations for the future. These only existed in the parent's mind and heart, so they're an "ambiguous loss."[6] Marion's loss of a desired affair partner is similar, as it wouldn't be socially acceptable to share her feelings. She's left alone with her grief as a result. Having your

---

6. This idea was developed in the 1970s by psychologist Dr. Pauline Boss.

character engage in magical thinking, fantasy, and what-ifs in interiority can make these more ephemeral concepts concrete.

Here's another dying fantasy, revealed in witty and cynical interiority by Leila, one of the narrators in *Brutes*, on her wedding day:

> [My fiancé] doesn't say anything, but he looks at me, and the more he looks, the more alarmed he seems, as though only realizing now that I am not a mystery he will never have to solve, but a person, full and humming with shitty life. I am realizing the same thing about him, and it is not a comfortable sensation. I know his name but in my head he is really only a man in a suit. I could leave him now. I could go downstairs and drink wine with the girls. I can already hear their voices, comforting me, concocting plans that will never be realized, until we approach what lies unsaid between us. And then we will finish our glasses, the bottles, and run back to our dusty lives and the dumb men we have chosen to decorate them. We'll spend our days pretending to be happy and sometimes succeeding.[bb]

She feels disillusioned here as she considers "what lies unsaid" between her and her future husband. They are strangers to one another on the level that counts, and the assumed drudgery of the rest of Leila's life unspools in her head. She doesn't have nice things to say about herself, either (she's "full and humming with shitty life"). This demonstrates the cynical worldview that she'll likely "spend [her] days pretending to be happy and sometimes succeeding." Many questions are implied by this self-aware inner struggle. Having imagined this version of the future, will Leila accept it? If she believes that happiness is impossible, is she released from trying to achieve it? Is she settling, or is she allowing the scales to fall from her eyes in order to accept reality? This is high self-awareness and low self-esteem in action, as well as a character with a fixed mindset and extrinsic motivations.

Interiority Insight: The notion of reality is, of course, inherently biased. A protagonist's perceived sense of the world comes from a collection of inputs, ideas, and beliefs. Outside of fixed scientific and mathematical rules, the agreed-upon visual appearance of physical objects, or codified guidelines, like traffic laws, much of what we term "reality" is open to interpretation and the result of subjective experience.

When it comes to putting inner tension on the page, we've been doing a lot of straight interiority. Let's take a look at what some action-based inner conflict looks like, with two instances of characters literally arguing with themselves (imagine the angel on one shoulder, and the devil on another).

The first comes from *Guy's Girl*, as Ginny tries to decide how she feels about Adrian. In this case, she's self-aware enough to realize that her anxiety and lack of self-worth might be interfering with her judgement:

At the back of her mind, Ginny had doubts. Sometimes, when they were kissing ... she would become suddenly, terrifyingly certain that she needed to break up with him. Right then, right at that moment.

He isn't the one, her brain would whisper.

But I like him, she would whisper back.

But do you? Do you really? ... She will examine her life from every angle. Look for cracks, abrasions, weak spots, doubts. And when she finds one, she will pick it apart, bone by bone, worry by worry, until you can no longer tell the truth from fiction.[cc]

Interiority Insight: If you really want to throw your character for a loop, add a new or existing mental illness like anxiety or ADHD to their internal process. This can affect them in moments big and small, and color their perception of events. Of course, mental illness is not just a "fun" or "edgy" character winkle, and should be treated with respect and dignity, if you choose to go down this avenue. It also makes your writing more credible if you have lived experience with the condition in question, as we'll discuss in Chapter 21.

Similarly, Vasya from *The Bear and the Nightingale* argues with herself in a last-ditch effort to come off as "normal," which is ironic. She insists that the spirits she hears and sees are natural, or "sensible," as she calls it. Here, she's torn between what she knows is real (to her and in this world) and what she *should* be seeing and feeling in order to demonstrate that she's "cured" of her "fantasies":

Suddenly Vasya stumbled to a halt. She thought she'd heard a voice. Slowing her breath, she listened. No—only the wind.

But what was that there? It looked like a great tree: one she half-remembered, with an odd sly memory, that slid in and out of her mind. No—it was only a shadow, cast by the moon.

A bone-chilling wind played in the branches high above.

Out of the hiss and clatter, Vasya suddenly thought she heard words. *Are you warm, child?* said the wind, half-laughing.... "Who are you? Are you sending the frost?"

There was a very long silence. Vasya wondered if she had imagined the voice. Then it seemed she heard, mockingly, *And why not? I, too, am angry.* The voice seemed to throw echoes, so that the whole world took up the cry.

"That is no answer," retorted the girl. The sensible part of her pointed out that perhaps a little meekness was in order when dealing with half-heard voices in the dead of night.[dd]

Earlier in the story, Vasya was able to exist in harmony with these magical elements. Now that she's older and the village elders, including her father, are trying to eradicate folk beliefs, she's beaten and threatened. As a result, she doesn't know how to be herself anymore. This inner tension interiority represents her need to decide who she is and what she believes. To break from what's acceptable takes tremendous courage, especially for a young girl in a historical, patriarchal, and religious society. Here, Vasya isn't sure she has it in her yet.

Next, we'll look at the inner conflict that springs up when a character gets what she wants. But wait … isn't that good news? Not always. Sometimes internal tension emerges as protagonists are teased with a perceived victory, only to suspect there's a catch.[7] Miryem, from *Spinning Silver*, has made a bargain to magically pay off the Staryk so he'll keep winter at bay. After years of struggle, her family is flush with resources. But this "success" comes at a price and Miryem cannot enjoy it:

> That night there was a brown roast chicken on the table and carrots glazed with fat, and for once my mother dished out the good food without looking as though every bite would poison her. We ate, and afterwards Wanda went home and we settled in together around the fire. My father was reading to himself, his lips moving silently, from the new Bible I had bought him … my mother was crocheting lace from some fine silk thread, a piece that could someday go into a wedding dress, maybe. The golden light shone in their faces … and for a moment I felt the whole world suspended in happiness, in peace, as though I had reached a place I had never been able even to imagine before.
>
> Then a knocking came on the door, heavy and vigorous … and the Staryk was on the stoop with all of the winter behind him, a whirling cloud of snow that wasn't falling past the windows.[ee]

This interiority goes from narration to interpretation of what this happy scene might mean, to extrapolation once the Staryk reminds Miryem that this precious peace is fleeting.

Both perceived negative *and* perceived positive developments can create inner tension for characters. In *The Bodyguard*, Hannah finally

---

7. I'll talk about the concept of "foreboding joy" in Chapter 16.

has a romantic and vulnerable moment with Jake, her sickeningly handsome (not to mention rich and famous) love interest. Is she happy, though? Of course not. Because this moment of "weakness" challenges her core sense of self:

> It's hard to describe the maelstrom of emotions churning around inside me as I made my way out to the driveway with the singular goal of getting to my car and heading home. Shock, agony, humiliation—all there, sure. But add to that: a sense of deep disappointment at letting myself get caught by a client in a real moment of emotion.[ff]

It also challenges her fixed belief system, which is hilariously summarized here:

> Feeling humiliated was one thing. *Admitting* to feeling humiliated was another.[gg]

For Hannah, the chance at a swoon-worthy romance is a direct affront to everything she holds dear about herself and her personal rules for living. When protagonists are in alignment with their sense of self and worldview, and reality cooperates, all is gravy. But when an element falls out of its usual orbit? More delicious conflict for your character and plot arcs!

This is a great segue[8] to the next chapter, which is all about worldview and how characters relate to theirs over the course of their stories.

---

8. If I don't say so myself!

10

WORLDVIEW

Worldview comes in many different flavors of tone and voice, and encompasses a wide array of ideas and beliefs. A character's expression of worldview contains a range of biases, privileges, prejudices, blind spots, sensitivities to power dynamics, perceptions of hierarchy and standing, and so much more. Worldview can also be expressed through action, dialogue, and, of course, interiority.

Worldview: All protagonists have systems which govern their actions, reactions, and decisions. Worldviews encompass a character's collection of moral and personal beliefs, both important and trivial, which contribute to their personality and sense of self. These ideas can originate in any number of ways, from internal convictions to those planted by family, society, culture, and experience. Worldviews can be rather fixed or change over time as a result of plot and character turning points.

How might you convey who a character is, at their core, and what they believe? We've already considered a protagonist's backstory, sense of self, objective, motivation, need, and inner struggle, but these characterizing details don't exist in a vacuum.

In this chapter, we'll see many examples of character worldview expressed in interiority. First, let's consider how these opinions, beliefs, and philosophies are established. After our discussion of backstory and wound in Chapter 5, you already know protagonists have past experiences which shape who they've become.[1] A worldview can certainly be influenced by one or two foundational events, but it's more likely to result from countless experiences and impressions.

A character's family of origin informs their worldview (whether the protagonist hews to these ideas or rejects them). Friends and social circles also contribute, especially once a character begins to individuate and socialize outside of the home in adolescence. The larger society of the story world influences a protagonist's worldview, too, though characters can similarly accept or reject the many explicit and implicit messages they receive on a daily basis.

These external elements can play a major role in a character's life, but they also fall under the "nurture" theory of personality development. "Nature," which encompasses someone's innate qualities, attitudes, temperaments, and proclivities, contributes, too. A family can do everything in their power to raise a character a certain way—like upper-crust Roman, who is being groomed for an arranged marriage and life of privilege in *Divine Rivals*—but the protagonist might still come out with their own ideas, values, and morals. In fact, this is where a lot of interpersonal conflicts develop, especially if a character rebels against their upbringing because of who they are, or who they become as they grow.

Complicating matters further is the notion that worldview is a moving target, constantly changing, often subtly, but sometimes suddenly, especially following plot turning points. Other characters might inspire the protagonist to do some self-inquiry, like Eris influences Sona in *Gearbreakers*, or external events can shift the character's existing belief system or sense of self, like Eleanor's disappointments in *Eleanor Oliphant Is Completely Fine*.

Worldview shifts often parallel a character's growth arc. To play with

---

1. I avoid saying "are" here because this connotes a fixed state. Change is a crucial component in many character arcs, as we'll see in Chapter 11.

this element, you'll have to create a baseline belief system, challenge it, test it, and maybe even change it. How might worldview transform as a result? When and why could this happen? How might a value system intersect with the plot for maximum impact? Worldview is a barometer of how protagonists feel about themselves, their efforts, and their society or culture at large.

The Worldview-Personality Feedback Loop

If a character has low self-awareness, a fixed mindset, or an especially solidified set of worldviews, they are less likely to examine or change what they think and feel, and why. The downside is a protagonist who's potentially stuck in their ways and not looking to grow. The upside, however, can be someone who holds fast to their integrity or identity. (This is more virtuous when the worldviews in question are positive and productive.) This personality type may not be perceived as the most intelligent or dynamic, but sometimes "still waters run deep," as they say. A "simple" or "straightforward" character can also be seen as consistent and solid, which can anchor a reader.

If a protagonist has high self-awareness, a growth mindset, or worldviews that are still in flux, they can be more likely to change, indulge in self-inquiry, and intentionally choose which beliefs serve them. The upside of such a character is that they're more likely to experience revelations and think deeply. This results in meaningful reader connection, especially if the worldviews shift for the better. But this type of protagonist, who sounds quite desirable at face value, has downsides, too.

The character described above might be too fluid in their sense of self, as if they're trying on various ideas, attitudes, and personalities. This might also mean they can't commit or decide, which makes them tough to pin down or rely on. They could also apply their morality and integrity unevenly, or only when it benefits them. This can allow them to manipulate people and situations, picking and choosing self-serving worldviews and positions as occasions arise.

Characters with dynamic worldviews can be seen as more intelligent or interesting, but it's important to note that smart and self-aware protagonists can have biases, blind spots, and misbeliefs, too. In fact, they might be more vulnerable to being misled because they *know* they're smart, so their confidence can prevent them from doubting themselves or doing due diligence. Characters who believe they have all the angles figured out are less likely to admit they've misunderstood something or gotten it wrong, which may make them seem stubborn or antisocial.

It's one thing for a writer to develop a set of worldviews for a protagonist, express them on the page, and track them over time. It's another to imagine how this element of character development affects reader engagement. When I say this, I don't mean that your reader should *agree* with your protagonist's attitudes or ways of seeing the world. In fact, compelling a reader who disagrees with your character on a fundamental level can be an exquisite writing challenge. When we create an antagonist, after all, we want audiences to be able to relate to them, almost despite themselves.

More important than agreement is *understanding*, as far as the reader-character relationship is concerned. You should portray your protagonist and their static or shifting worldviews in such a way that audiences find the character and their belief systems cohesive. Your goal is to help outsiders understand how a protagonist's worldview makes logical and emotional sense, whether or not they agree with the character's ideas.

Let's go to the shelves. This was a difficult set of excerpts to organize because I was working with several different metrics. As with objective and motivation, a character's worldview can be productive or self-defeating, and it can either elevate them or hold them back. I've decided to showcase some "negative" and fixed worldviews first, even though these are incredibly broad labels, and extrapolate what they might mean for a protagonist's identity.

Negative and Fixed Worldviews

As mentioned in the introduction to this chapter, some worldviews (especially negative ones) come from families of origin. Inner struggles can arise if a character feels they don't belong within the established system or are born an outcast. This is the case for Felicity from *The Fair Folk*, who we already know chose double-edged fairy "friendship" over hanging out at home with her parents. This is her worldview near the beginning of the story, and it's a sobering expression of how she sees herself and her life:

> What else did I have, apart from books? It seemed to me that all [my family] wanted was to make me smaller, closing me into a box like a cow in the crush. They'd take the books, too, if they could. You have no choice, as a child; you're born into a family and there you must stay until you're old enough to run.[a]

This attitude is complicated by the fact that Felicity is an actual child at this point, so family—and her conception of it—deeply affects her life. Even though she's rather sheltered, she expresses some strong ideas in interiority. She believes that books are her only companions and that the objective of growing up is to become "old enough to run," which is revelatory in and of itself. She even compares herself to "a cow in the crush." No wonder she's vulnerable to enchantment. Notice how Felicity seems to accept this grim view of the world as reality without wondering whether change is possible.

Interiority Insight: A fixed mindset can either engender action (the defense of deeply held beliefs) or interfere with it (the character must first imagine new possibilities before pursuing them).

Red Queen's Mare is also unhappy with the worldview espoused by her family of origin. In a society where Reds are shipped off to the army unless they develop a valuable talent, she's taught that she should deal with all of her complicated, rebellious feelings by shoving them down. Unfortunately, Mare isn't exactly good at taking advice, especially if she believes it's misguided:

> *Don't think about it.* That's what Mom always says, about the army, about my brothers, about everything. *Great advice, Mom.*[b]

The sarcasm is clear. Mare either can't stop thinking about her situation or doesn't believe denial will fix anything. While Felicity isn't yet aware that she can question her family's worldview, or her own, Mare is an older character, in full rebellious teenage flower. She has no problem rejecting Mom's "wisdom." Contentment isn't in the cards for Mare, who doesn't believe in denial *or* hope, so she gets inner struggle instead:

> It's cruel to give hope where none should be. It only turns into disappointment, resentment, rage—all the things that make this life more difficult than it already is.[c]

Even with this dismal worldview, Mare decides to take action, especially when she gets the opportunity to infiltrate Silver society.

A less extreme reaction to the world, but one that still shows longing and heartbreak, comes from *Ripe*. Cassie has started working at a Silicon Valley start-up, and while she feels that she *should* be impressed, she can't seem to get there. Instead, she dwells on the expectation gap between what she imagined being an adult would entail and her reality. This excerpt expands on a thematic statement you'll recognize from Chapter 3:

> Isn't that always the way adult life begins? You think you'll become something different, something new. At first, you swim violently against the tide, your body straining until your muscles give out … [then you let] the water take you back to shore, where the rest of the world is already at the office, typing on their computers beneath buzzing fluorescent lights, toiling away in the glare of permanent productive daylight.[d]

Just like Mare, Cassie is experiencing a rude awakening, especially since she's unable to take action and make herself matter in the most important of ways—by voicing her needs. As a result, she doesn't really rise above this level of existential disappointment.

Lamentations in *The Vaster Wilds* also takes a dim view of existence but experiences less angst about it. She was born into a colonial world with no opportunities, so while she sees her situation clearly, she's also not necessarily upset about it:

The world, the girl knew, was worse than savage, the world was unmoved.

It did not care, it could not care, what happened to her, not one bit.

She was a mote, a speck, a floating windborne fleck of dust.[e]

While many characters—and real humans—want to be exceptional, heroic, and significant, Lamentations's interiority suggests that she's made peace with being merely "a mote, a speck." There is, perhaps, a bit of freedom in this worldview, which can allow her to abandon her hopes and worries and live in the present.[2]

For an especially fatalistic worldview, let's go to Eleanor in *Eleanor Oliphant Is Completely Fine*. She doesn't just take a cynical perspective on herself, she also seems to believe that her options for future happiness are limited:

This was my soul curling into whiteness, an existential blank where a person had once been. Why did I start to allow myself to think I could live a normal life, a happy life, the kind other people had?[f]

It seems she literally can't conceive of a reality where she "could live a normal life, a happy life, the kind other people had." Remember how characters often define themselves in relation to others, which we first saw in Chapter 6? This kind of upward or downward comparison usually has a fatal logic flaw. Protagonists often believe that other people have it easier, or better, and that good things come to everyone else without issue. At this very low point, Eleanor sees herself as "other," especially when it comes to achieving "normal" happiness. Obviously, hers is a simplified generalization about other people—and herself—but that's how false beliefs usually operate. If a protagonist

---

2. A useful mindset for someone who could be killed or eaten in the wilderness at any given moment.

could untangle their layers of bias and misbelief, they might see things differently.

Interiority Insight: Sometimes we realize that our position is wrong. Sometimes not. It takes tremendous growth to get to this epiphany, and extreme courage to adopt a new worldview. The evolution after this, if a character reaches that point, is to actively help others achieve the new revelation for themselves, or to challenge the conditions that created the worldview in the first place.

Lynette is a "final girl," slang for someone who survived a mass murder or stalker encounter, in adult horror novel *The Final Girl Support Group* by Grady Hendrix. Similar to Hannah in *The Bodyguard*, who works in private security, Lynette has become obsessed with shoring up her home and defending herself against her would-be murderers, who she fully believes will return to finish the job.

She has prepared masterfully—building a panic room in her apartment, ensuring that everywhere she goes has two exists, and having an escape plan (including a second car stocked with a bug-out bag)—but has also made a critical error. She's been writing a memoir about her case, feelings, and the other final girls she knows. Unfortunately, her computer security is not as advanced, and someone steals the file, endangering them all:

> I was so arrogant to think I was safe.... The world has gotten more sophisticated, and I haven't kept up. While I was guarding my door they snuck in through my computer windows.[g]

This is a negative and paranoid worldview taken to the extreme, but Lynette has our empathy and understanding. Someone *has* tried to kill her and she's convinced they'll try again. (Spoiler alert: They do.) Lynette has also internalized and subsumed this turn of events as a personal failure, thinking she's "arrogant" for needing to stay safe. She doesn't offer herself grace, given all she's been through, but readers might.

August from *One Last Stop* has a pretty clear philosophy about engaging with others:

> A warning light flashes somewhere in August's brain. Her
> mental field guide to making friends is a two-page pamphlet
> that just says: *DON'T*.[h]

If this is her attitude about friends, imagine how she feels about the messy, vulnerable act of falling in love. Because the author, Casey McQuiston, is very good at voice and banter, August has a neatly packaged worldview statement about *that*, too:

> The older she's gotten, the more she prefers thinking of love as a
> hobby for other people, like rock climbing or knitting. Fine,
> enviable even, but she doesn't feel like investing in the
> equipment.[i]

Despite this very unpromising start, August has a triumphant growth arc, which we'll see in Chapter 11. These exact perspectives are challenged by impossible love interest Jane. Romances and romcoms are wonderful at finding a character's most self-destructive, negative, and deeply held worldviews and misbeliefs, and pushing on them, like they're bruises, until the protagonist can't take it anymore and changes their mindset.

Interiority Insight: Wound can impact a character's misbelief, need, sense of self, *and* worldview. You don't have to lean hard into each of these elements, but notice how our From the Shelves characters tend to have most of these ingredients operating below the surface in a cohesive configuration.

Negative worldviews aren't always bad or hurtful to the protagonists who possess them. Some beliefs, like August's, can be self-protective, if shortsighted. Others can both express an extremely cynical bias while also reading as empowering. Check out this unhinged take from Millie in *The New House*, which builds on parts of this excerpt that we first saw in Chapter 3:

> Usually I keep my darker angel on a very short tether ... she holds herself in check and agrees not to set my world on fire.... I never lose my temper. But sometimes I choose to unleash it.
>
> When people think of angels, they usually picture cute cherubs with wings floating on clouds.... But that's not all they do.
>
> Angels are capable of pitiless destruction.... Whenever God needs to do something really awful, She sends an angel.[j]

Not only does Millie fully believe that she has a dark angel inside her, she seems convinced that dark angels are actually more capable and powerful than the halo kind. This interiority also expresses her need to keep her temper in check. Millie, as a character, is all about control, as demonstrated by this glimpse into her sense of self. If you liked her slant on angels, you may enjoy her beliefs about female "friendship," which, oddly, align with Stacey's (she similarly rejects female connection, as we saw in Chapter 8):

> The air between us hums. This is what has been missing from our relationship: the dangerous, deadly rivalry that adds fire and blood to the charm of conquest. Our friendship was a fraud, but this, this is real: the merciless struggle for survival, red in tooth and claw, honest and authentic. Strip away the lunches and the yoga and the confessional intimacy of any female friendship and this is what you'll find: savage, brutal, ruthless competition.[k]

Millie's husband, Tom, also holds some incredibly strong and twisted worldviews, but with a smirking, sardonic slant:

> I'd never cheat on Millie. She's the love of my life. And I have a keen urge to hang onto my balls. But just because you're on a diet it doesn't mean you can't look at the menu.[l]

He seems to express loyalty to his wife, a positive quality, but readers quickly realize this is a self-centered stance. He's not loyal for Millie's sake but his own. He also has no problem looking around, fantasizing, and engaging in some very morally gray behavior with Harper, another female character. All the while, he seems to believe he deserves brownie points for sticking to his "diet."

Both Millie and Tom come across as cynical, but they also, oddly, seem to enjoy their dark attitudes. Notice that their interiority demonstrates fixed mindsets, with little room for nuance or change.

Remember, personal worldviews can also be inflected by conditioning, culture, and society. That's not to say the prevailing attitude is good or just, though. Often, society's ills are glossed over with statements like "it is what it is" and "that's the way it's always been" to discourage people from questioning or trying to alter the status quo (especially if the present set-up serves those currently in power). This especially affects historically discriminated-against people, and racism is one of humanity's most pervasive worldview battlegrounds.[3]

In *Lovecraft Country*, the first protagonist we meet, Atticus Freeman, is a Black man about to drive through what's called a "sundown town," as in, "You better not get caught here after the sun goes down." While this is a terrible thing to have to worry about, Atticus accepts it as reality in certain regions. (It helps that his family was involved in writing and publishing a guide to "safe" counties and routes.) His is a negative worldview, but one that's been reinforced by bitter experience:

> The most hateful [white people] rarely bothered to conceal their
> hostility, and when for some reason they did try to hide their
> feelings, they generally exhibited all the guile of five-year-olds,
> who cannot imagine that the world sees them other than as they
> wish to be seen.

---

3. The vast majority of books selected for this guide are set either fully or partially in the United States, which means I've ended up disproportionately discussing U.S. social issues. But this guide is not a cultural study or critique of *one* society. Unfortunately, discrimination is not uniquely American.

235

All of which was to say: He knew right away there was going to be trouble in Simmonsville.[m]

In adopting this belief, Atticus is also protecting himself by going into the situation with his eyes wide open. To ignore the racism in Simmonsville could be lethal. This state of affairs weighs heavily on Atticus's soul, though, and such is the psychic toll of being discriminated against.

The City We Became also deals heavily with American racism. Here, the multi-racial character who embodies the Spirit of New York looks at a policeman and immediately regrets it:

Cold prickles skitter over my side. I know what it is before I react, but I'm careless again because *I turn to look....* Stupid, stupid, I fucking know better; cops down in Baltimore broke a man's spine for making eye contact.[n]

In this story, the various avatars of New York's boroughs are armed with tremendous power. This protagonist should theoretically be immune to fear. But the setting is still contemporary or near-future America, and even in a book with a speculative spin, there are certain things that young Black or Brown men simply shouldn't do.

Just as characters, cultures, and societies have certain worldviews about racial differences, there are also attitudes about gender, which contribute thematically to a lot of novels and memoirs. Feminist ideas loom large in the background of many of these books, including the following excerpt, which calls out toxic masculinity.

We already know Joe, from *You*, isn't a great guy. I personally found myself wondering how he got that way. While he specifically doesn't go into too much personal backstory, maybe because he isn't willing to be vulnerable or admit to his wounds, he keeps letting things slip. After he kidnaps Beck's ex-boyfriend, Benji, to remove any potential distractions, he imagines telling her about it:

You think Benji was a tough dude to date? Well, try having the same conversation over and over while Benji's in the cage trying to dig his way to China. Yeah, you put up with his bullshit,

Beck, but did you ever lock him in a cage and listen to him bellyache 24/7? ... I'm doing the kid a favor. When he gets outta here, he's gonna be pissed about being locked up but he's also gonna thank me for making him into a man.°

Notice the specific worldviews about gender and relationships in this interiority. First of all, there's the implication that a woman's role is to "put up with [a man's] bullshit." Second, that being locked in a cage by a sociopath is going to make Benji "into a man." What kind of ideas about manhood and masculinity does Joe have? Where might he have learned them or seen them modeled? How do these notions affect his relationship to himself? To men? To women? How does this division between male and female roles[4] inform his (self-imposed) role as Beck's avenger and protector? As Benji's instructor?

Threaded throughout this excerpt is Joe's belief that he's superior, doing everyone favors, and deserves gratitude. Joe is a fascinating character study, even if things are grim and yucky inside his head. Notice him speaking with confidence and conveying no room for self-inquiry or the possibility he might be wrong. This is a rigid worldview, one which cannot tolerate internal or external challenges. (He will literally kill any opposition.)

In the next section, I'll discuss whether a character accepts a certain worldview or rejects it. This comes into play as protagonists examine their own belief systems and society's prevailing cultural wisdom. The next step is deciding whether or not they resonate with these established ideas. Sometimes we'll see a negative worldview that the character accepts, or a positive one they reject. There are many available permutations, and this is where you'll start to see protagonist values and social mores in flux. The following section ends on some positive worldview examples as well.

---

4. I also want to acknowledge that some readers, writers, and characters see gender as a spectrum. I specifically discuss only male and female here because we're exploring the perspective of a character with a binary worldview.

Evolving and Empowering Worldviews

Let's kick off with an amusing statement of worldview from *Milk Fed*'s Rachel. She's disappointed in her family and love relationships and underwhelmed with herself. To cope, she obsesses with food in a bid to maintain control. Of course, this is taxing. In this interiority, she's indulging in the fantasy that she'd be better off as a robot. This is a funny mix of self-awareness and denial, but it's also incredibly relatable to many readers who might be over-thinkers and over-feelers themselves:

> Expect nothing. The simplicity of that directive, its bare-bones, self-contained power was intoxicating.... It was a phrase you'd associate with a person who didn't need anything from anyone; a closed system, an automaton. I wanted to be that person.[p]

Wouldn't life be easier if we didn't "need anything from anyone"? As a busy working parent of three young children, I absolutely feel this idea in my bones.

While Hannah from *The Bodyguard* spends most of the story running away from her real feelings, she actually has a nuanced perspective on love, specifically when it comes to her mother, whose death sends her into an emotional tailspin at the beginning of the book:

> Despite everything, I loved her.
>
> I didn't *like* her, but I loved her.... It's so much harder to love someone who's difficult than to love someone who's easy.[q]

I really respect the level of curiosity and nuance this worldview suggests. Hannah is putting "liking," "loving," "difficult," and "easy" into a giant tangle, and trying to examine why relationships sometimes feel so turbulent, especially if they involve society's expectations of how we "should" automatically slip into subservient roles to maintain the status quo.

> **Interiority Insight:** The idea that we have to love our families without any deeper inquiry is a social worldview that some characters (and humans) end up challenging. This can invite grief and shame because attitudes of filial piety and "blood is thicker than water" are so pervasive, especially in certain cultures.

When we think about protagonists standing at the intersection of their beliefs, instincts, and internal struggles, I want to go back to *The City We Became* and examine various characters' attitudes about the antagonist, who tempts a vulnerable Aislyn and tries to curry favor with Bronca. These interactions force certain POV protagonists to confront their worldviews, some more successfully than others.

Aislyn has low self-awareness and is primarily driven by her own desires and needs, so let's hear from her first:

> Everything in her life has programmed her to associate evil with specific, easily definable things. Dark skin. Ugly people with scars.... Men. The Woman in White is the visual opposite of everything Aislyn has been taught to fear ... [and her] true form could be anyone or any*thing.*[r]

This is exactly the kind of slippery, ill-formed, and confused worldview that a character might have if they lack integrity and faith in their own inner compass. Bronca, on the other hand, is very aware that she's being played by the antagonist, in the guise of "Dr. White," who asks her to display art that goes against her ethos:

> It sounds reasonable. Slippery slopes always do. Bronca narrows her eyes.... "Their whole shtick is trying to prove they're being discriminated against because they're a bunch of rich white boys—"
>
> "So put up some of their art to prove them wrong." Dr. White looks at Bronca as if this is the obvious solution.[s]

Here, the villain comes off as non-threatening, even somewhat reasonable, in her entreaties. Aislyn and her fragile worldview are poised for a rude awakening, while Bronca is much better equipped to play both defensive and offensive ball with the enemy.

So far, we've dealt entirely with the worldviews of individual characters, as expressed in interiority and first-person or close-third point of view. But I did briefly mention omniscient or authorial point of view in Chapter 4. Sometimes a narrator character has a worldview that reflects the story's theme or belies the author's own position, which, of course, informs the story. These observations can be rendered as relevant reactions in scene or delivered as asides.

Fredrik Backman—or his narrator—has a strong authorial voice in *Anxious People* and commentary appears threaded throughout. Various characters have strong positions and worldviews but the book itself is full of observations which break the fourth wall, such as:

> Children notice people's proportions in a different way from adults, possibly because they always see us from below, and that's our worst angle. That's why they make such good bullies, the quick-witted little monsters. They have access to everything that's most vulnerable in us. Even so, they forgive us, the whole time, for almost everything.[t]

Parent-child relationships are part of the plot but the story doesn't really feature many young children, so this seems tangential. Perhaps Mr. Backman's level of literary stardom means he's confident that his audience will follow his digressions. Here's another one:

> The truth of course is that if people really were as happy as they look on the Internet, they wouldn't spend so much damn time on the Internet, because no one who's having a really good day spends half of it taking pictures of themselves. Anyone can nurture a myth about their life if they have enough manure, so if the grass looks greener on the other side of the fence, that's probably because it's full of shit. Not that that really makes much difference, because now we've learned that every day needs to be special. *Every* day.[u]

This seems more like current social commentary than fictional narrative. That said, readers might find it easy to agree. Perhaps by offering these softball opinions alongside the story, the author wants to get audiences aligned as an additional engagement strategy. That's certainly one technique that you can use to foster reader connection, as long as you do it consistently, it feels cohesive, and the asides work within the scene's context or a story's overall tone.

The last few excerpts in this chapter represent either a positive worldview or an empowering one. As I keep saying, there's a bias toward damaged characters, conflict and tension, and tragic situations in fiction and memoir. Sunny, warm days simply aren't as interesting as stormy nights or solar eclipses. As such, breathlessly positive worldviews are harder to come by. If a character demonstrates one, it might be done ironically or invite mockery from a character with a more negative or jaded perspective.

Snow, a fox spirit in *The Fox Wife*, has very clear ideas and biases, which guide how she exists in her world. She's been around long enough that she feels confident in her positions. After years of planning, she misses her chance to exact revenge on the character she believes is responsible for her daughter's death. Snow is gutted (a moment we'll see in Chapter 14) because the cold-blooded errand of killing him must happen according to certain moral imperatives. Now, vengeance seems out of reach:

> I considered my options. I could hire someone to slit Bektu's
> throat, but that wasn't the way debts were paid, at least not in
> the old days. A proper blood debt was repaid face-to-face,
> ideally with a recounting of sins—I'm a stickler for old
> traditions.[v]

Snow is so committed to her worldview of "the way debts were paid … in the old days" that she would rather let this grievous insult go unanswered than to respond in the wrong way, or without her own specific brand of valor. Her integrity and worldview are fixed but, in this case, they lend her character a measure of old-world nobility. Readers are likely to empathize with her, despite her murderous intentions, because she wears the mantle of the grieving mother and is seeking justice but not dishonor.

She also has some empowering ideas about fear and what it means to be a fox. Her strong, certain, and specific worldviews make her a delightful point-of-view protagonist:

> *Fear is whatever you make of it,* I wanted to shout. The mark of a fox is to disrupt order.[w]

There's no doubt in Snow's head that her worldview is correct, even if it complicates matters for her. She absolutely has the courage of her convictions and, to be honest, makes being an ancient fox spirit sound fun, blood debts and all.

Interiority Insight: Who is more impressive to you: The character who has it mostly figured out, or the one who's coming awake for the first time? The answer depends on your personal sensibilities as a writer and reader, and on your story's protagonist, plot, and theme.

You can start with a character who's completely confident in her worldview, like Snow, or you can build a conflicting and sometimes confusing moral landscape for your protagonist to navigate as they decide what to believe. As long as they grapple to subsume their ideals, they have the power to engage audiences.

For an example of the latter, let's look at Leonie, from *Sing, Unburied, Sing,* as she wrings out some hard-won insights. She's mostly a low self-esteem, low self-awareness character who, in her brokenness, has abused her own children. But she occasionally approaches a break-through, which can keep readers from completely throwing up their hands in frustration. Here's a peek into her thoughts during a moment of clarity:

> *Ain't no good in using anger just to lash. You pray for it to blow up a storm that's going to flush out the truth.*[x]

While this interiority shows she's being somewhat delusional by believing that something external—a figurative storm—is going to come and help her find the truth of her situation, she's also demonstrating awareness that "ain't no good in using anger just to lash." This kind of character (or person) can be an energy vampire to those around them, but readers might cheer from a distance to see her recognize her copious biases and blind spots.

I'll end on an incredibly mature take from twelve-year-old Corazon in *The Spirit Glass*, who's on a coming-of-age journey through her mythology-inflected fantasy world. In this excerpt, she demonstrates deep insight into the nature of knowledge:

> People say knowledge is the one thing no one can steal from
> you. Corazon had always thought that was because knowledge
> is invisible. Weightless. Now she knew that was wrong. Knowl-
> edge lives inside you, woven tightly through the pillars of your
> thoughts. Knowledge has a heft and a hue, a sound and a sway.
> What Corazon now knew made her body feel heavy but
> hastened her steps.[y]

This interiority goes back to a core question that's thematically embedded into many character worldviews: Is it better to know or to stay ignorant? Corazon would probably feel better if she hadn't gone in search of her dead parents' spirits, but then her eyes wouldn't have become open to what it means to be older, and to have truth "[live] inside you, woven tightly through the pillars of your thoughts."

Worldview pulls together your character, their sense of self, and their position regarding various issues in your world and plot. In the following chapter, which will close out Part 2, I'll offer several deep protagonist studies to really nail down the idea of character arc, especially as it's supported by interiority.

11

_____

CHARACTER ARC

Character growth and change are crucial for fostering reader engagement and expressing premise and theme. While the plot can entertain audiences and provide tension, conflict, and stakes, the protagonist's transformation over the course of events—relayed using action and interiority—has the power to truly reach inside the beating hearts of your readership.

This chapter will focus on character growth arcs from beginning to end. It will dovetail with our earlier discussion of tentpoles in Chapter 4, including the midpoint, dark night of the soul, synthesis, and ending. Of course, not all protagonists change, and some remain in a relatively unenlightened state for most of the story. But many will have some opportunity for emotional development and showing this can be a great way to inspire readers to care.

_____

Character Arc: A character's emotional evolution over the course of a plot. While the structure takes the protagonist through a largely external story, they are also growing (or, less commonly, regressing) in terms of identity, beliefs, values, objectives, and needs. A character arc often sees the protagonist recontextualize the past, subsume a new understanding of themselves in the present, and become more able to achieve a satisfying future.

_____

Character growth is the figurative "journey" in the Hero's Journey and adds dimension to any literal adventure. There are some tropes and forms, like that of the anti-hero, which normalize protagonist stasis or devolution, but these exceptions are generally rare and reserved for specific categories.

Pacing a Character Growth Arc

If you, like most writers, intend to give your protagonist a growth arc, pacing this progress is important. Ideally, you'll offer incremental benchmarks of transformation throughout. I'd strongly discourage you from writing a character who's suppressed from having any realizations until the 80% or 90% mark of the story, at which point they're struck by an epiphany. A lot of manuscripts that I see in my editorial practice attempt this structure but it generally isn't satisfying.

Some realizations can be woven in early to activate a character around the inciting incident, then more should be offered consistently throughout a plot. Reader interest ramps up when your audience sees a character self-actualize and struggle with their newfound wisdom. If the protagonist is static for the duration of the story, then thunderstruck by self-awareness at the end, readers are only rewarded for a few chapters. They don't get to enjoy the payoff of the growth they've just become emotionally invested in, and they miss out on seeing an entirely new side of the protagonist.

The sudden realization is also an unrealistic approach to character development. The story *is* the struggle. A protagonist's life won't magically become problem-free once a new understanding hits. It's naïve to believe—or to convey—that a character's existence will be smooth sailing once they have their "Eureka!" moment. Even picture book audiences seem capable of understanding this nuance. Life isn't all sunshine and rainbows at the end of a story, even if the present conflict resolves relatively successfully.

When it comes to character arc, writers tend to have a lot of questions. How do they convey protagonist change in a realistic and relatable way? Is the transformation too nicely wrapped up in a neat little bow at the end? Is the resolution too messy? Has the character changed too much, too little, or just enough? Is the change consistent or "out of character," and how can a writer know? Are difficult decisions made in a straightforward way or is there inner struggle? Is the growth process linear, or do characters backslide and regress before new identities, worldviews, and behaviors "stick"?

The answers to many of these questions depend on the kind of story you're writing and your characters themselves. Some genres and categories expect profound development arcs, with memoir being perhaps the most prominent, followed by literary, women's, upmarket, cozy mystery, romance, romantic comedy, and a lot of MG and YA, in no particular order. Others are marked by flatter character arcs and less overt growth, like hardboiled mystery, thriller, suspense, horror, sci-fi, military, and action/adventure. Fantasy and speculative are broad enough labels that you can encounter all kinds of character trajectories within these stories and their various sub-genres.

A thorough exploration of character arc means we'll have to track protagonist development over time. First, I'll present a whole-novel character study of Eleanor from *Eleanor Oliphant Is Completely Fine*, which is basically an interiority-driven exploration of one woman's psyche. We'll also look at Felicity's growth arc in *The Fair Folk*. Finally, our deep dive series concludes with Alex from *The Guest*, which is an interesting counterpoint to the first two positive growth trajectories.

The only constant—in life and story—is change, and that's exactly what we'll explore here.

Eleanor Oliphant Is Completely Fine Deep Dive

Eleanor Oliphant Is Completely Fine happened to be the first book I picked up as I was preparing to write this guide and spend about a year reading exclusively for examples of interiority.[1] I didn't know much about the novel, even though it'd been around for a while and had received a lot of acclaim. Imagine my reaction when I realized it was a superlative character study.

Eleanor is a singular protagonist with an inimitable voice. She prefers

---

1. And professional and personal pleasure, obviously!

an orderly life, but only because she has suffered an unthinkable tragedy, the effects of which she holds at arm's length.

She goes from being willfully in denial to epitomizing "trying to fix the problem the wrong way." After some kindness from a true friend, and therapy, she unburdens herself and is able to believe in a brighter future for perhaps the first time. To be clear, her self-esteem is so low to start that she reaches what others might call "baseline" by the end. But for Eleanor, this modest leveling out is a shot into the stratosphere.

For this deep dive into character arc, I was careful to order the excerpts chronologically. While this novel does offer up some flashbacks, building to an anachronistic reveal of the wound near the end, the majority of the action is linear and takes place in the story's present day.

We'll start with Eleanor's self-reported sense of identity at the beginning. Notice that she comes across as self-possessed and under control, which doesn't square with the analysis I just presented. It's important to realize this is a front and she's desperately pretending:

> I have always taken great pride in managing my life along. I'm a sole survivor—I'm Eleanor Oliphant. I don't need anyone else—there's no big hole in my life, no missing part of my own particular puzzle. I am a self-contained entity. That's what I've always told myself, at any rate.[a]

This is Eleanor before any growth, insisting nothing is wrong and she doesn't "need anyone else." The language suggests she's lying and knows it ("that's what I've always told myself, at any rate"), but readers get no hint that she intends to change this status quo. Audiences don't generally go for a character in *total* denial but they're more willing to engage if some intrigue is teased. To keep those loops open, Eleanor lets a tiny bit more information leak out about twenty pages later. You'll recognize this excerpt from Chapter 5:[2]

---

2. As we progress through this guide, you will start to see some excerpts repeated, but with a different focus, or recut to emphasize a new craft topic.

At home that evening, I looked into the mirror above the wash-
basin while I washed my damaged hands. There I was: Eleanor
Oliphant. Long, straight, light brown hair that runs all the way
down to my waist, pale skin, my face a scarred palimpsest of
fire…. I've been the focus of far too much attention in my time.
Pass me over, move along please, nothing to see here.[b]

Now readers know there was a fire. Eleanor also teases the notion that
people have previously paid attention to her. Sure, she does her whole
"I'm Eleanor Oliphant, this is me, and here's the deal" shtick, but now,
the lid has cracked open on her past, providing dramatic tension. What
happened? Is that why she's in this self-imposed hermitage?

Very few protagonists are true islands unto themselves, even those
who profess to be, and fractures show in her façade before long. 130
pages later, she attempts a misguided solution to the problems she
claims not to have. You already know from Chapter 7 that she falls
head over heels in "love" with a musician who, at face value, seems
totally wrong for her.

Eleanor believes he will legitimize her, please her critical Mummy,
whose toxic voice plays on an endless loop in her head, and usher her
into a new life. By admitting that she *has* wants, of course, she puts the
lie to the idea that "there's no big hole in my life, no missing part of my
own particular puzzle. I am a self-contained entity," expressed above.

To charm the musician, she allows herself a make-over. This decision—
and the resulting interiority and dialogue—shows obvious signs of
trouble and doubt. If she really believed the musician would fall for
her, why would she completely change herself? An interaction with
Laura, her stylist, gives readers a peek into Eleanor's inner vulnerability:

My reflection showed a much younger woman, a confident
woman with glossy hair that brushed her shoulders and a fringe
that swept across her face and sat just over her scarred cheek.
Me? … I swallowed hard.

"You've made me shiny, Laura," I said. I tried to stop it, but a

little tear ran down the side of my nose…. "Thank you for
making me shiny."[c]

Many early-arc characters resist crying (just look at Hannah from *The
Bodyguard*). This is a good way to show internal tension, as the body is
doing one thing, and the mind, another. Only interiority can expose
this kind of nuanced inner struggle. Here, it's heartbreaking to realize
that Eleanor wants to feel and look "shiny," and readers can infer that
she's either stopped herself from trying to be shiny before, or kept this
deep need a secret until this moment.

Then the inevitable—yet still heartbreaking—thing happens. Eleanor
goes to see the musician at a gig and he looks right past her. The meet-
cute she anticipated fails to materialize and she immediately subsumes
this as a personal failure. Worse, she realizes how delusional she was,
and that only adds to her negative self-talk:

> He spoke to the crowd but he did not speak to me. I stood and
> waited…. But still he didn't see me. And gradually, as I stood
> there beyond the lights, the music beating off my body … I
> began to realize the truth…. I was a thirty-year-old woman with
> a juvenile crush on a man whom I didn't know, and would
> never know. I had convinced myself that he was the one, that he
> would help make me normal, fix the things that were wrong
> with my life. Someone to help me deal with Mummy, block out
> her voice when she whispered in my ear, telling me I was bad, I
> was wrong, I wasn't good enough. Why had I thought that?[d]

Eleanor's despair deepens and she experiences some poignant self-
loathing in interiority:

> I didn't know the man onstage before me, didn't know the first
> thing about him. It was all just fantasy. Could anything be more
> pathetic—me, a grown woman? I'd told myself a sad little fairy
> tale, thinking that I could fix everything, undo the past, that he
> and I would live happily ever after and Mummy wouldn't be
> angry anymore. I was Eleanor, sad little Eleanor Oliphant, with
> my pathetic job, my vodka and my dinners for one, and I always

would be…. There was no hope, things couldn't be put right. I couldn't be put right. The past could neither be escaped nor undone. After all these weeks of delusion, I recognized, breathless, the pure, brutal truth of it. I felt despair and nausea mingled inside me, and then that familiar black, black mood came down fast.[e]

Eleanor has alluded to her vodka several times already. It's how she "deals" with life, especially as things get bleak. When Eleanor hits emotional rock bottom, she uses interiority to extrapolate what this disappointment might mean for her future. We first saw part of this excerpt in Chapter 10:

I drank [the vodka] with the focused, single-minded determination of a murderer, but my thoughts just could not, would not be drowned—like ugly, bloated corpses, they continued to float to the surface in all their pale, gas-filled ugliness…. I curled myself into a ball, tried to make myself occupy as small a space in the bed as possible. Despicable. I had made a fool of myself. I was an embarrassment, like Mummy had always told me. A sound escaped into the pillow, an animal whine. I couldn't open my eyes. I did not want to see even a centimeter of my own skin…. This was my soul curling into whiteness, an existential blank where a person had once been. Why did I start to allow myself to think I could live a normal life, a happy life, the kind other people had?[f]

Eleanor's objective wasn't about the musician at all. In fact, it never had been. This was about defeating Mummy and earning a sense of self-worth. Now, as Eleanor churns with self-hatred, she's never been further away from realizing her own value. Once she's scraped off the floor—literally—by her only real friend, Raymond, she decides to try therapy. But this isn't a triumphant upward swing in her character arc. Far from it. She's still holding on to her defenses, perhaps even clutching them more tightly because she was just so spectacularly wounded. We saw some of Eleanor's guardedness about therapy in Chapter 7. After a few false starts, she takes a risk and opens up, surprising herself during a session with Dr. Temple:

Here we were, talking about Mummy, after I'd expressly forbidden it. However, I found, much to my surprise, that I was actually enjoying holding court like this, having Dr. Temple's undivided attention.[g]

Interiority Insight: Interiority can show the walls a character has built—and the reaction when they come down.

After having this breakthrough, Eleanor reaches an unexpected emotional high:

I realized that I felt … happy. It was such a strange, unusual feeling—light, calm, as though I'd swallowed sunshine. Only this morning, I'd been furious, and now I was calm and happy. I was gradually getting used to feeling the range of available human emotions, their intensity, the rapidity with which they could change. Until now, anytime that emotions, feelings, had threatened to unsettle me, I'd drink them down fast, drown them. That had allowed me to exist, but I was starting to understand that I needed, wanted, something more than that now.[h]

Eleanor needs to feel her feelings. She also needs to integrate her past, present, and future. After decades of self-denial and self-judgment, she's now able to consider what freedom might feel like. She even agrees to explore the topic of Mummy in therapy, which she'd taken off the table only twenty pages before:

I'd been feeling so light and free earlier, so centered in myself, that I hadn't had a chance to prepare myself properly for this. As I closed my eyes and exhaled to Maria's count, I had the worrying realization that, before I was even properly aware of it, my brain was off accessing memories in places I didn't want it to go, scurrying into rooms before I'd had a chance to block them off…. Now that it was happening, though, I accepted it with equanimity. There was a certain pleasure in ceding control.[i]

> **Interiority Insight:** Wants and needs can be diametrically opposed. For example, Eleanor needs to lose control to find herself, yet control is what she claims to want most.

And finally, to round out this incredible growth and self-actualization journey, here is Eleanor Oliphant describing herself once more. Compare this excerpt to the first one featured in this section. The difference is stunning:

> The voice in my own head—my own voice—was actually quite sensible, and rational, I'd begun to realize. It was Mummy's voice that had done all the judging, and encouraged me to do so too. I was getting to quite like my own voice, my own thoughts. I wanted more of them. They made me feel good, calm even. They made me feel like *me*.[j]

The lovely thing about *Eleanor Oliphant Is Completely Fine* is all the interiority access to Eleanor's frame of mind in pivotal moments. Sometimes she's evasive, sure, but she eventually overcomes incredible odds to see the world—and her place in it—much more clearly. Things won't always be easy for her, but readers are left with the distinct sense that Eleanor will be "completely fine" ... for real, this time.

> **Interiority Insight:** Notice how victories and defeats play out on a book-length scale. The overall trajectory is positive, but it's not entirely linear. Even though Eleanor is uplifted by the end, she still hits some dire emotional lows and "polarity shifts" (see Chapter 4).

Let's move on to *The Fair Folk*, which tracks Felicity from childhood to young adulthood, a chronological growth arc that supports her character development.

The Fair Folk Deep Dive

As a child, Felicity discovers fairies in the woods behind her parents' farm. She would love to join Them[3] but feels too plain, stupid, and undeserving of their attention, especially when she compares herself to their queen, Elfrida, as we first saw in Chapter 7. Regardless, she tries to give them an offering in a desperate bid for acceptance:

> "I've brought you apricots," I say, and my voice sounds small and shaky. Stupid. Stupid kid. Why would they be interested in you?[k]

Look how she lashes herself. This is very similar to "Mummy's"[4] voice in *Eleanor Oliphant Is Completely Fine.*

As we've already seen in other books with similar mythology, a fairy's offer is a double-edged sword—a bargain with the devil. Their language is intentionally misleading and never reveals the full implications of their generosity. Here, Elfrida seems to know exactly how to snare Felicity with a compliment and, unfortunately, the hook catches:

> I am looking at her now, drinking in her words, and the tears are falling freely. "Rare and special," she called me. In all my life, no one has ever said anything like that to me before. In that moment, I would give her anything she asked.[l]

Almost as soon as Felicity pledges herself to Elfrida, her loyalty is tested. We don't have access to the fairies' perspectives, but my interpretation is that they need to confirm her commitment. (It emerges eventually that the fairies were damaged themselves, which somewhat explains their manipulative and capricious natures. They act like abusers—testing a victim's boundaries to explore how far they can go. We'll see this in Chapter 18.) Shaking off her initial warmth, Elfrida rebuffs Felicity, who doesn't take this rejection well. She's still very

---

3. Felicity's name for the fairies is often capitalized in this work.
4. The dialogue attributed to Mummy is revealed as Eleanor's internalized self-loathing. When Eleanor is speaking to "Mummy," or hearing "Mummy's voice," she's just wrestling with herself. More on this in Chapter 14.

much subsuming the fairies' acceptance (or lack thereof) as a measure of her value:

> None of it makes sense, or no sense I want to hear.... I'm not beautiful, not magic; I'm just Felicity, ten years old and in far too deep.[m]

Felicity would be a major downer to read if she wasn't also simultaneously becoming aware of the danger she's in, which adds tension and triggers audience empathy. She's being played and fears she's in "far too deep." These doubts first emerge on the edges of her consciousness, but she pushes them away—a familiar self-protective gambit. Her lack of self-worth is still blinding her as she continues to pursue external validation.

Interiority Insight: Sometimes you'll want to write a protagonist who is, for lack of a better term, a bummer. They don't like their life situation, they're miserable about not having met their objectives, and they don't see any light at the end of their specific tunnel. This is realistic and can be relatable but tread carefully here. A reader who gets plunged right into a protagonist's doldrums, with no chance of a reprieve, may not want to devote their weekend to hanging out in this mindset. Even the most despairing or discouraged character should have some kind of redeeming spark, measure of self-worth, goodness, or talent. Otherwise, audiences might not be up for 300 pages of whining and complaining. They have their own problems, which is why they're reading in the first place!

The Fair Folk is a long novel, so it's impossible to track every moment of character development. Around the midpoint, Felicity develops more of a backbone and stands up to the fairies after they run roughshod over her home and swap her niece out for a changeling. (We'll see the exact moment Felicity makes a fateful choice to confront them in Chapter 16.)

At this inflection point, a natural distance develops between her and Elfrida when she heads off to Cambridge. While Felicity worries that her new life won't live up to the splendor of the fairy revels, she's pleasantly surprised to realize the real world has its own magic:

> Her inner life was vivid and filled with marvels.... *I've seen the real thing*, she thought, not for the first time, and wondered whether They had killed her appetite for what the world could provide. But she didn't wonder for long. She felt rich and full of blessings, cradled by love and wide open to all that Cambridge could offer.[11]

Felicity's growth arc here hinges on her evolving sense of independence and agency. She has always relied on others to inform her identity. As we saw in Chapter 10, she believes her destiny is to run away from her family and childhood, which is exactly what she does. Achieving this goal helps her feel uncharacteristically optimistic, at least for a moment.

Perhaps the fairies miss their plaything because they quickly encroach on her college life. Even after working so very hard to separate from Them, Felicity is devastated to learn she's bound, after all. Elfrida finally demands repayment for their "gifts": She wants to trade lives with Felicity, entering her body as a changeling and banishing her soul to a mysterious fairy limbo, called Onward. (We'll see this excerpted in Chapter 16 as well.)

Felicity's misbelief, which lasts for a while, is that she's entirely helpless against fairy magic. But the bargain that binds her, originally made by her father, has loopholes. Once she figures out how to separate from Elfrida and truly free herself, she's able confront her dad about his own time with the fairies as a lonely little boy in the woods. While closure about the past won't unite father and daughter after decades of distance, it does change how Felicity feels about her family:

> A part of her longed to tell him everything, to be heard and understood and forgiven. To go up to the house and be made a fuss of by her mother, and to lie in her own bed tonight, free of

responsibilities. But that was a fantasy. It had never been like that, and it never could be, not now.°

Felicity is disappointed her father never revealed this side of himself to her, but she takes this full-circle moment of maturity and understanding in stride. She needs so deeply to be taken care of by someone who cares about her, but now she knows for certain that this love won't come from her family *or* the fairies. Ultimately, her depressing self-assumed identity as an outcast at home, which we saw in the previous chapter, proves true. But there's a glimmer of redemption here, too.

Felicity can only rely on herself and she's no longer going to be dazzled by fantasy. After going to the fairy kingdom and back to escape her reality, she makes peace with what it means to live in the real world, even if that experience will always be somewhat diminished.

While this is a bittersweet emotional payoff, it's a real one. Especially in a novel for adult readers, who have the perspective and context to appreciate this somewhat cynical ending. (If this was, indeed, a middle grade novel, since many of Felicity's experiences align with that category's target audience, it would probably land on a lighter and more uplifting note.)

Many readers might relate to realizing that their expectations and false beliefs—rather than external circumstances—are actually making them miserable. Characters can either change their mindsets or continue in the pursuit of their unrealistic desires. For someone like Felicity, who has struggled to turn her back on childish things, this maturity is a major, if understated, victory.

Finally, we'll track Alex from *The Guest* along her reverse growth arc, as she becomes more and more lost in the limbo between fantasy and reality. I bet Felicity would have some advice for her.

The Guest Deep Dive

The Guest is a polarizing novel because it has no resolution. In fact, it ends mid-scene, right after the final excerpt I'll discuss in this section. As a quick reminder, Alex has alienated her Hamptons sugar daddy, Simon, after believing she's more permanent in his life than she really is (see Chapter 8 for the interiority of this moment). Simon's assistant gives her a ride to the train station, but she doesn't leave.

In fact, she sleeps outside, hooks up with a teenager just to get access to his friend's pool house, and bides her time until Simon's annual Labor Day party, where she believes she'll slip right back into his life. Throughout, it's suggested that she got into some trouble back in New York City and that someone named Dom—maybe a drug dealer, maybe a sex trafficker—is looking for her. But Alex doesn't let reality get in the way of a good fantasy.

From the very beginning, readers get a strong sense that this protagonist will be an unreliable narrator. All the emotionally difficult things she recounts seem fuzzy, like this explanation she gives for getting kicked out of her last apartment:

> Had Alex broken the window unit? She had no memory of it, but it was possible. Things she touched started to seem doomed.[p]

In a traditional character arc, this sounds a lot like rock bottom. The only possible direction to go is up … right? Well, things do look up, actually. But not because Alex is able to be honest or vulnerable. It's because she manages to cloak herself in delusion. When she falls asleep on the beach and avoids a sunburn, she's able to spin it into a benediction:

> She had somehow avoided getting sunburnt. That was lucky. Wasn't she a lucky girl? … The book was splayed open on the ground—she had read almost twenty pages, but couldn't quite recall what the book was about. A memoir by a woman whose mother had loved her too much. Whose brothers had loved her even more. A problem of emotional excess, psychological gout.[q]

Here, readers are offered a rare glimpse of what her upbringing might've been like, but they have to interpret it from a casual aside. This is pretty much the closest we'll come to a sense of her backstory or wound. Perhaps she lacked love in childhood, as she seems to think "too much" love equals "psychological gout," with the negative connotation of illness.

Alex might as well have "nothing to see here" tattooed on her forehead, except it'd clash with the gown she needs for Simon's party. Also notice that Alex fully defines herself by what happens externally. The air conditioner broke? Doomed. Avoided a sunburn? Lucky! Around the midpoint, readers are treated to glimmers of self-awareness, or at least some inward-facing interpretation and extrapolation in interiority:

> Alex had the sick sense that she was a ghost. Wandering the
> land of the living. But that was dumb, a dumb thought. It was
> just when the day was hot like this, hot and gray, anxiety moved
> closer to the surface.[r]

Almost as soon as doubt bubbles up, Alex chases away the "dumb, dumb thoughts" and quickly works to submerge the anxiety once more. She's then able to con a lovestruck teenage boy into giving her shelter in the last days before the party (talk about low-hanging fruit). After entertaining Jack's[5] advances and playing manic pixie dream girl, she tires of the charade because it feels beneath her:

> Was it obvious, how little energy she had for him anymore?
> Even one more night felt interminable. She was too impatient
> for her new life to begin.
>
> When he reached out to hug her, did he notice that she stiffened? He didn't deserve her sudden coolness toward him—it
> wasn't his fault.[s]

By this point, Alex is in a fugue state and completely believes that her new life is just around the corner. And that's exactly what happens

---

5. I had to double-check all the names because it feels like every other male character referenced in this guide is named Jack. For those playing along at home, there are four (from *The Guest, Wellness, Family Meal,* and *The Bodyguard*). There are also two Hannahs (*The Bodyguard* and *The It Girl*).

when she arrives at Simon's party. At least according to Alex's interiority:

> Did she expect some resistance? There was none. The big wooden door was wide open. As if everything was working in concert to allow for Alex's arrival. To urge her forward. Already she had forgotten the walk there: couldn't say how long it had taken, what roads she'd passed. The slate was wiped clean.[t]

The novel ends as Simon sees her from across the room and opens his mouth. That's it. Readers get no satisfaction—no response from the invited guests or host, no harsh wake-up call for Alex. But given her incredibly biased worldview and slippery sense of identity—typified by her confident assertion that "the slate was wiped clean," which, it seems, is all she ever wanted—what do you think happens?

Whether you believe she reclaims easy luxury or leaves in handcuffs (or a straitjacket), you're probably imagining Alex's life beyond the final page. A good ending inspires readers to extrapolate, especially in this kind of trippy, unreliable narrative.

Next let's explore some other character arcs. In most of the following examples, I'll do one or two excerpts per protagonist, and sample various moments along their respective growth arcs. This way, we can connect character development to plot tentpoles. I'll also follow my favorite "low to high" pattern to check in with From the Scenes protagonists who are displaying less self-awareness, then those who are proactively and consciously evolving.

Early Character Arc Examples

It's a bit unfair to talk about Joe's character journey in *You* because he's not living in the same universe as most of us, despite this being a contemporary realistic novel. He sees himself as a knight in shining armor instead of Beck's stalker and eventual murderer. But since I'm starting with examples of stunted characters at the beginning of their trajectories, let's see Joe immediately fixate on Beck after meeting her at the bookstore. Joe notices cash in her wallet but Beck pays with a card, which he takes as a sure sign that she wants him to know her name.

Once he has it, he looks her up online and is shocked she hasn't told Twitter all about their meet-cute (at least that's his perception of their encounter):

> And let me tell you, for a moment there, I was concerned. Maybe I wasn't special. You didn't even mention me, our conversation. Also: *I talk to strangers* is a line in your Twitter bio.... Is our conversation nothing to you? Am I just another *stranger? ... Fuck*, I thought, *maybe I was wrong*. Maybe we had nothing. But then I started to explore you and you don't write about what really matters. You wouldn't share me with your *followers*. Your online life is a variety show, so if anything, the fact that you didn't put me in your stand-up act means that you covet me. Maybe even more than I realize.[u]

Joe murders several people over the course of the story, so it's fair to assume he suffers from some kind of sociopathy or psychopathy (despite my earlier criticism of this characterizing choice). That said, notice how he draws self-esteem from his interpretation of Beck's reaction to him. Characters (and people) dealing with pathological mental illness tend to have very fragile psyches, even if they present as confident to the outside world. Their inner selves become walled off by all kinds of delusions and coping mechanisms to avoid their feelings and traumas. Joe acts cocky, yet this behavior might be hiding an insecure and vulnerable inner self.

This interpretation doesn't excuse his actions but tries to understand why he positions himself at the center of Beck's life, despite having spent ten minutes with her, maximum. It's to explore how he justifies stalking her—first virtually, then in person—and enmeshing with her. People with low or no self-worth will do anything to fill the void ... except look directly into it. Joe lashes out at the world, asserting himself by projecting dominance.

While Joe dives into the center of everything, other characters detach from existence, like the down-on-her-luck unnamed narrator who's facing a few dead ends in *Death Valley*. She shows up to the desert to "research a novel," but, really, like Alex from *The Guest*, she's running away from her feelings about her comatose father and chronically ill husband. Unlike Alex, at least she's honest about her penchant for magical thinking:

> It had taken me years to see clearly that I was not the cause of
> my father's depression. Still, I never stopped hoping that I could
> be an exception to it … and I wanted to be the magic daughter.
> I'd live in that garden once more.[v]

She seems committed to seeing her life clearly but also can't help indulging in delusion. In fact, she'll later go on a fever-dream-like vision quest into an alternate world within a cactus. (You read that correctly. Readers are left to decide whether it's real or imagined.) Meanwhile, she's also wrestling with loneliness:

> I cannot remember why I am here…. It's a loneliness, dark blue.
> I came to the desert because I wanted to be alone. Now that I'm
> alone, it's not what I want.[w]

These very early passages suggest that she's self-aware and on a healing journey but has no idea what shape it will take. This is a perfectly valid place for a character at the beginning of their arc.

Interiority Insight: Even in first person, you'll see more of a crafted narrative distance here, to achieve the effect of loneliness and isolation.

Fully self-aware denial can be fun to explore in interiority. In this next excerpt, Ginny from *Guy's Girl* offers a seemingly contradictory early growth arc self-description that's painful to read:

> Ginny doesn't think of herself as cute. She doesn't think of
> herself as quirky or bubbly or creative or any of the other words
> people often use to describe her. In fact, she thinks of herself as
> little as possible—and only ever in terms of whether her waist-
> line is expanding or not. To be frank, she would prefer that she
> not exist at all.[x]

It's important to note that Ginny has spent years suffering from anorexia, which can be seen as a very real attempt at self-erasure. She has previously whittled herself down into as small a physical presence as possible, and now she's starving herself emotionally.

We'll cap off our peek at early growth arc examples with Sally from *Romantic Comedy*. Unlike some of our deeply unaware or actively in-denial characters, she is incredibly clued into her inner processes. For the most part, she seems to accept her flaws and foibles. She's a comedy writer for The Night Owls, or TNO, a blatant SNL analogue. This is a dream job by any standard. But Sally can also be insecure about her ideas and self-conscious about her position in the male-dominated comedy world. After many years on the show without a breakout sketch, she's also wondering whether there's more to life. She turns this unease into a theoretical question about selfhood:

> Even I wasn't sure if my in-person self (a mild-mannered
> woman of average intelligence and attractiveness) or my scripts
> (willfully raging sketches about sexism and bodily functions)
> reflected my real self—or if I had a real self, or if anyone did. But
> I suspected that much of my writing emerged from this tension
> or lack of integration; I believed the perceptions undergirding
> my sketches arose from my being invisible or at least underesti-
> mated, including being mistaken for someone nicer than I was.[y]

Readers hoping to unearth the character arc implied here will need to read between the lines. While Sally does outright call herself "invisible," and talk about a "lack of integration" in her life, she might also be using her intelligence and keen talent for observation as defense mechanisms. By analyzing everything, she can hang on the periphery without engaging. By critiquing life in her sketches, she can avoid participating directly while retaining the illusion of control.

Interiority Insight: Many stories are about character relationships to control. Protagonists must either let go when grasping starts to hurt, or wrestle with building up their sense of proactive agency to gain power over their circumstances.

Now that we've taken a look at some early growth arc positions, let's check in with From the Shelves protagonist development around the midpoint, which is a crucial character milestone. Some of the following examples aren't going to fall right in the middle of their respective stories, but the excerpts will demonstrate the kind of realizations that protagonist usually have around this pivotal tentpole. For some of these characters, especially those we haven't already tracked, I'll also pull in early growth arc examples for the sake of contrast, so we can see where they started, and where they're going.

Midpoint(ish) Character Arc Examples

The previous section featured instances of protagonists dissociating from themselves and/or their lives. What does it look like to suddenly be plunged back into the world, and all of its horrors and feelings?

Let's go to *Family Meal* and Cam, the self-sabotaging, grieving character who's alienated everyone in his life with a seemingly constant string of bad decisions. Once those who still care about him confront him and attempt to pin him to himself, this happens:

> [TJ] smiles and asks how we're doing.
>
> I try to answer. I can taste the syllables in my mouth. But I can't get them out because I'm too busy trying to breathe.
>
> Cam, says Minh.
>
> Cam, says Fern.
>
> But I can't and don't respond.
>
> I can't really hear anything.
>
> And then, out of nowhere, I hear everything all at once.[z]

This interiority is a wonderful illustration of how it might feel to suddenly break that dam of denial and dissociation. Will Cam fully engage with himself and start to sift through his complex grief now?

No, of course not. But this is a watershed moment for a character who has categorically refused to shed his blinders.

Interiority Insight: The midpoint often involves a process of internal character give and take—approaching the realization, backing away, working up the courage, then meeting the situation with more resolve.

We already know that Hannah from *The Bodyguard* is amazing at compartmentalizing. She's smart, savvy, and knows exactly what she's doing, but she also has fixed worldviews. Then, ironically, a fake dating scheme opens her heart in very real ways. She's still trying to run away in the following excerpt, but this sounds, to me, like more of that lady protesting too much:

I'd fallen for our fake relationship, like the dumbest of dumb dummies, and I'd done a complete one-eighty.

Now all I wanted to do was *stay*.

But of course, I couldn't stay…. It was time to get back to my real life. And my real life—the way I'd set it up, the way I'd always preferred it—was always about *going*, not staying. I was good at it…. In less than two weeks, I'd … start fresh in Seoul— a new job, new clients, and nothing at all to remind me of Jack Stapleton.[aa]

Hannah might fully intend to flee to another assignment in Seoul, but this is an extinction burst of denial. Romcom readers are primed to wonder when and why she'll finally stop running, and this suspense keeps them engaged.

Interiority Insight: An "extinction burst" refers to a behavior pattern where a maladaptive tendency flares up as a character or person realizes they can't or shouldn't continue using their current coping mechanisms. Rather than change, they up the ante on their resistance and temporarily backslide.

Hannah's self-deprecating humor has something in common with how Sally from *Romantic Comedy* hides from her true feelings. "The dumbest of dumb dummies" is great voice, and will get a laugh, but it's also Hannah's last-ditch effort to avoid vulnerability. Humor can be great for showing character coping mechanisms in dialogue or interiority, but tread lightly here. Too much humor, or at the wrong moment, can prevent important realizations and turning points from fully resonating.

Let's compare the above to our rule-following sorority president's growth arc at the beginning and midpoint of *Bright Young Women*. Pamela's first reaction after the slashing is to hand the problem to literally anyone else, including campus security. Rent-a-cops aren't usually considered paragons of authority, but Pamela doesn't care:

> I found myself wanting to crawl across the table and into his arms out of sheer gratitude. Here was a person with an impressive title and no doubt a plan who could tell us what the hell was going on, who could lay out what would happen next. My relief bordered on giddy.[bb]

At first, she abdicates power and passes the responsibility baton. But as Pamela starts coming to terms with what happened, she develops opinions. She even starts to criticize the sheriff because she doesn't feel he's doing enough, which we saw in Chapter 6.

In fact, she launches her own investigation, and, in the process, finally admits to having needs. Hers is a family that doesn't demonstrate feelings, so she struggles with this quite a bit:

> For weeks, I'd been a wave cresting, searching for a shore on which to break. I immediately dissolved into my mother's arms. It had been so long since she'd let me hold her that I'd forgotten her smell.[cc]

At face value, Pamela asking her mother for a hug doesn't seem like a huge breakthrough, but this moment represents tremendous midpoint growth.

Notice that Pamela's still hoping for an external rescue, but progress is progress. I love the image of "a wave cresting, searching for a shore on which to break," too, because it's so full of tension. Imagine all that pent-up energy. This evolution took about 175 pages, so her internal transformation isn't speedy, by any means. But it's extremely satisfying for readers who have been rooting for her to declare something messy and real about herself.

Interiority Insight: A personal development victory doesn't have to be mind-blowing, but it *should* be hard-won. An emotional milestone rendered in interiority has the potential to capture readers. Character change is about the process and progress, not just product.[6]

Anna, the protagonist in *Aesthetica*, comes across as self-aware yet less evolved. But even characters like her deserve to have their trajectories marked and celebrated. This is the former influencer who lost herself in plastic surgery. Now she's preparing for a procedure that will reverse everything and this interiority appears during a preoperative meeting with the surgeon, Dr. Perrault:

> "Expect to be shocked," he said, which was what I wanted. I wanted drastic transformation, wanted to watch myself come back slowly in the bathroom mirror, reborn from blood and bruises, all that violence. The in-between time, before results are final, is my favorite of any procedure, a time when I can be sick, but not truly, just stationed in bed, popping painkillers, my body working to heal, my brain acclimating to the bruises and swelling until one day they're gone and the transformation is

---

6. This is what I always tell writers, too. The creative journey is all about the process. If you're only focusing on the product (the published book), you might have a tough time staying motivated across the never-ending learning curve.

complete. I'm old enough to know that this is how true transformation works, in increments so small you don't notice until one day you wake up and realize you've changed.[dd]

Anna's personal brand of beauty and confidence—being "reborn from blood and bruises, all that violence"—is a little unnerving, but at least she's aware that "true transformation" is incremental. She may have expected miracles once upon a time, but now she knows and trusts the process. This shows maturity, even though she's expecting her next evolution as a person to come from yet another surgical procedure.

Interiority Insight: Certain characters have growth plateaus and upper thresholds. A minor evolution for some protagonists may be life-changing for others, as not everyone has the same capacity for transformation. Fixed-mindset characters also tend to evolve more gradually, with a less pronounced arc, than their flexible-mindset counterparts.

Ifemelu from *Americanah* is an interesting character study because she seems smart and willing to learn, but makes a lot of self-destructive decisions. She's still flailing at the end of the story, as she rekindles her relationship with her on-again, off-again love, Obinze, who is now married. One would look at this choice and wonder how much she has actually changed, even though she's had many profound and vulnerable moments along the way. She often seems confused about her capacity for true transformation as well, so at least the reader isn't alone.

Ifemelu's growth arc starts off hopeful, with a pinch of delusion. As a young immigrant, she seems to believe that simply moving to America will solve all her problems. She doesn't yet realize that she's not automatically owed anything, and that she still has to make her own way:

The real America, she felt, was just around the next corner she would turn.... There was a stripped-down quality to her life, a kindling starkness, without parents and friends and home, the familiar landmarks that made her who she was.[ee]

What does she mean by "real America"? And why keep herself in a state of "kindling starkness," with no significant identity, while waiting for her future to materialize? Ifemelu's interiority suggests she's expecting transformation and success to land in her lap courtesy of external "familiar landmarks." Though she doesn't realize it yet, she has a long way to go in figuring herself out and letting some of these naïve ideas go.

Interiority Insight: A story's prevailing culture and world-building (explored in Chapter 18) can inform a character's growth arc, too. Many "moving to America" narratives exist worldwide, and these contribute to an immigrant, refugee, or migrant character's expectations. Ifemelu's high hopes may have been shaped by myths she consumed in her country of origin. (That said, national and international attitudes about American immigration have shifted drastically in the last several decades, falling a long way from the once-proud notion of the "melting pot.")

When the American dream doesn't come to fruition easily, Ifemelu becomes discouraged. She internalizes and subsumes the heavy burdens of creating an adult life without a meaningful support network and allows her failures to impact her sense of self:

> She felt like a small ball, adrift and alone. The world was a big, big place and she was so tiny, so insignificant, rattling around emptily.... She imagined packing her things, somehow buying a ticket, and going back to Lagos.[ff]

She doesn't state outright that she's disheartened by her circumstances. Instead, she takes them personally and allows them to diminish her and make her feel "insignificant." The wish to "[pack] her things … and [go] back to Lagos" is a simple statement at face value and conveys her despair that things haven't worked out as intended. Not every character would draw this conclusion from a series of difficult setbacks, but Ifemelu, specifically, reels after each disappointment.

> **Interiority Insight:** What are the stories your protagonist is telling themselves about their situation? What are the conclusions and inferences they draw, if any, about whether their current fortunes define who they are? Will they be galvanized to solve their conflicts? Or will they await deliverance?

Ifemelu gets involved with a few men, but each relationship feels like a bust once the spark wears off. In response, she either alienates her partners or cheats. We're past the midpoint in the next excerpt, yet Ifemelu's struggles to understand herself and her motivations are just beginning:

> She imagined her mother saying it was the devil. She wished she believed in the devil, in a being outside of yourself that invaded your mind and caused you to destroy that which you cared about.... She did not know what it was but there was something wrong with her. A hunger, a restlessness. An incomplete knowledge of herself.[gg]

Notice that Ifemelu, again, wishes external forces could explain her floundering. It's easier to blame the devil than to take accountability. At least now she's more self-aware of her propensity for magical thinking. She has "an incomplete knowledge of herself," and correctly identifies this as an issue.

Subconsciously, there seem to be other struggles at work, too. Ifemelu likely wasn't ready to settle down and pledge herself to another person because of this ill-formed sense of self. Sure, plenty of people figure out how to grow and change within the context of a long-term relationship or marriage, but Ifemelu's deep uncertainty would have sabotaged her efforts. It took 350 pages, but she's now working to make the unconscious conscious.

In a similar vein, the two love interest protagonists in *Divine Rivals*, Roman and Iris, are experiencing their own coming-of-age arcs, individually and together. *Americanah* is not primarily a romance, so Ifemelu's relationships are only one facet of her arc. For Roman and

Iris, their relationship takes center stage as part of a romantic premise. At first, both characters feel defined by their circumstances. As their self-confidence grows, they gear up to declare not only their authentic selves, but their feelings for one another. We saw Roman shake off his misbeliefs in Chapter 3. Now here's Iris, honestly admitting her most vulnerable truth:

> Sometimes I'm afraid to love other people.
>
> Everyone I care about eventually leaves me, whether it's death or war or simply because they don't want me.... And I'm not afraid to be alone, but I'm tired of being the one left behind. I'm tired of having to rearrange my life after the people within it depart, as if I'm a puzzle and I'm now missing pieces and I will never feel that pure sense of completion again.[hh]

Roman and Iris seem perfectly suited for a love match, right? Unfortunately, there's a big catch, as there often is in romance, romcom, and romantasy. They've each been revealing themselves in letters to an "anonymous" pen pal via a magical portal, completely unaware that they're actually writing to one another. As we saw in Chapter 7, they started as enemies. Uh-oh! Around the midpoint, their identities are revealed (we'll see that moment in Chapter 14). After reacting poorly, then realizing they can't live without one another—frenemy status be damned—they get married. This story has romance genre obligations to fulfill, after all!

Interiority Insight: The conflicts that keep lovers apart in romance and romantic comedy can often seem contrived. It becomes interiority's job to sell readers on the logic.

Another character growth arc featuring vulnerability and openness to love appears in *Within These Wicked Walls*. Andi has nobody and nothing at first—she's an orphan whose father figure, Jember, disowned her. She acts like she doesn't mind, which is, of course, a defense mechanism:

> I didn't know if it was the woman who bore me or Jember
> who'd given me the name, but it didn't matter—it was only a
> name. I could move to another town tomorrow and change it,
> and no one would care.[ii]

Then she meets Magnus, the rakish and charming owner of a very
haunted house. He's in need of her exorcism services, and she works
hard to keep their relationship professional. But the way she interprets
him in interiority sets off my "lady doth protest too much" alarms:

> I didn't want to talk about my lack of basic human skills, or why
> I didn't possess them. I wasn't sure why it suddenly mattered,
> but for whatever reason, I didn't want him to find me strange.
>
> And I certainly didn't want any pity.[jj]

Andi clearly still thinks of herself as flawed and unworthy, while
conversely insisting that she doesn't want to dwell on her tragic past.
She also wants Magnus to like her "for whatever reason," which is
flimsy. This kind of blatant denial is often found in stories with a
romantic plot or subplot, because the two characters need to remain
apart until their feelings are ready to boil over. Otherwise, they'd get
together at the first blush of a crush, and we'd have no plot.

Interiority Insight: While denial is sometimes necessary to execute
certain plot points in a specific order, don't dwell here. You can buy
time by making the character somewhat aware of their inner
conflict or avoidance, but not much.

Andi's worldview that good things don't happen to her—because few
good things ever have—is expressed when she allows herself a
romantic moment with Magnus:

> I laughed, but it was quickly stifled by the gentle press of his
> lips to my forehead. "I'm waiting for the ax to drop…. I never
> get what I want so easily."[kk]

While this is dialogue, not interiority, it's also attached to an under-lying need that goes unsaid: She wants Magnus to reassure her, to prove her wrong. She's angling. Admitting a fraction of her feelings aloud is also a step forward along her growth arc. Though I hate *what* she's saying, because she should want better for herself, I love her newfound ability to speak it aloud.

Unfortunately, the ax does drop.[7] Magnus is actually engaged to Kekela, a detail he conveniently withheld. What a cad! While readers will resent this betrayal, it triggers some amazing and very gratifying growth for Andi. Earlier, she said she was fine to cut bait and leave. This implied that she felt disposable—a girl without a place or a name. Now, she has a sense of self, has staked a claim, and even demonstrates self-worth:

> Magnus had led me on, knowing full well he was engaged and
> not thinking anything of it. Then, he'd had no intention of
> breaking it off with Kekela except that I'd given him no other
> choice. If I'd valued my dignity less, how long would he have
> kept us both?[11]

Instead of turning Magnus's duplicity into an indictment of herself—"Of course he'd use me as a side piece, I have no value"—Andi realizes that *he* is flawed, and his cheating has nothing to do with her. She's righteous with anger and admits something incredible: she values her dignity; she has worth. We're on the other side of the midpoint here, and her growth arc kicks into a satisfying high gear.

Interiority Insight: MG and YA novels generally demonstrate bigger and more profoundly empowered trajectories, unless the overall tone of the project is dark or tragic.

Whether a character's transformation is modest or hits full throttle, it's

---

7. This is why people who are sometimes called "pessimists" will insist that they're "realists" whenever their dim worldview is confirmed!

fascinating to check in with protagonists as they progress. How can you engineer significant moments of change for your character, and how might interiority underscore their development? We'll end this chapter by studying some more advanced and fulfilling (though not always) growth arcs.

Late-Stage Character Arc Examples

As you read the following excerpts, keep in mind that they come from the climaxes and endings of their respective stories. As we saw with Alex in *The Guest*, not all growth is positive or healing, and there isn't a triumphant redemption at the end of every plot rainbow. Unfortunately, this happens to Cassie in *Ripe*. I'm talking about her here because it's important to track our tragic heroes, too, no matter how disheartened readers might feel about their arcs.

Around the midpoint, we see Cassie feeling good about her career at a glitzy Silicon Valley start-up, even if she's still measuring her success externally:

> A wild, bright pride filled my heart. I wasn't a doctor or a
> lawyer, but I was still someone to be proud of, a child grown
> into a capable adult with a fancy job title and a new life in Cali-
> fornia, a daughter who had gone west in search of gold—and
> found it.[mm]

On the surface, this seems promising. She found gold! But there's also something rotten around the edges. "I was still someone to be proud of" sounds like an expression of defensiveness and desperation, rather than a declaration of self-worth. Only seven pages later, she admits what she's had to do to get and, more importantly, keep her status. This interiority takes place in a moment of existential crisis before she must lead a work meeting:

> You wake up one day and realize what you've become, what
> you allow, and you have to stare down into the pit at yourself, at
> your own choices, at the ways in which you have been cunning
> and stupid and false and wretched to keep up with the world
> around you.

How does anyone bear themselves? How can anyone stare into the darkest corners of humanity and return to the office, enter the meeting room, and deliver the presentation? How do we all just keep working? The CEO nods at me. My fake self opens her mouth and begins.[nn]

Cassie often refers to her "fake self." On one level, this is a self-protective gambit. If she cleaves her identity into a real self and a fake self, she can distance herself from disappointment, since the bad stuff can be deflected as happening to the fake self. This is how she insulates her deep psyche from failure. If something doesn't pan out, she can always assign the shortcoming or desire to the "other" Cassie.

Her real self isn't choosing to sell out for this job, her fake self is. Her real self isn't in love with a chef who has no intention of leaving his girlfriend, her fake self is. Unfortunately, Cassie's real self can't get away from the choices her fake self makes, and her inner sense of worth and value is collateral damage when consequences arise.

Interiority Insight: Once a character identifies their core issue, they've taken an important step. But the truth is, not all characters will have the guts or self-awareness to improve or resolve the problem at hand. Clarifying the wound or deeper source of conflict is an even bigger task, and success becomes less likely. Alas, it's not the destiny of every protagonist to reach self-actualization.

Cassie, for all of her insight and longing, ends up pregnant with the chef's baby, doesn't tell him, and gets an abortion. While it ultimately seems like the right decision for her under the circumstances, this turning point pushes her to an even more fractured and empty sense of self. Here's her interiority on the way home from the procedure:

A woman shouldn't be seen like this, all ruined. Or maybe everyone should have to see me, all of them, especially the men, the aftermath, the knives in their hearts for once.

I open my eyes and I am on an almost empty train: unshowered,

> same clothes from the clinic, a headache, a scathing fire in my
> empty womb. I can smell my own bad breath behind my mask. I
> can't remember how I got here.
>
> Through the fog of pain, a new development: the black hole
> floats above my head now. At first I can't find it, but when I look
> up, it expands, a new dark halo.[oo]

She now perceives herself as "ruined" and decides to cast blame on "everyone … especially the men" who have let her down and broken her heart. She subsumes her circumstances and pictures herself wearing a "new dark halo." This isn't the character arc outcome that readers might've hoped for, but it's honest. Cassie has succumbed to despair because she pinned her love and hopes on the wrong person rather than figuring out how to live with and as herself. This is a modern cautionary tale.[8]

There is a different kind of brutality woven throughout *The Nightingale*, the saga of two sisters in World War II-era France: Vianne, a traditional wife and mother, and Isabel, an untamable resistance fighter. Unsurprisingly, they don't get along. The novel is told as a frame narrative, starting and ending in the present day, with an older Vianne who resolves to finally relive her (and her sister's) wartime experiences.

It's only after the current Vianne realizes that her son doesn't really know her that she endeavors to tell her story. This is her reasoning in interiority, and it appears within the first few pages:

> If I had told him the truth long ago, or had danced and drunk
> and sung more, maybe he would have seen me instead of a
> dependable, ordinary mother. He loves a version of me that is
> incomplete. I always thought it was what I wanted: to be loved
> and admired. Now I think perhaps I'd like to be known.[pp]

---

8. Politics aside, this statement does not refer to the fact that she got an abortion. Like, at all. My disappointment with Cassie's lack of growth as a character has everything to do with how badly she treats herself, and how poorly she allows herself to be treated by others.

This story's structure begins at the end of Vianne's life, offering a snap-shot of who she ends up becoming and what that woman values: "to be known." Then readers meet Vianne's earlier incarnation. Isabel comes and goes as the war ramps up. When Isabel is there, Vianne is miserable. When Isabel leaves, Vianne surprises herself by longing for her:

> Vianne had to admit that life at Le Jardin was easier without Isabelle. No more outbursts, no more veiled comments.... Still, sometimes without Isabelle, the house was too quiet, and in the silence, Vianne found herself thinking too loudly.[qq]

Isabel has a similarly complicated relationship with their father. It's only after the war has stripped her of almost everything that she's able to come to terms with love and loss. This is Isabel's final scene with Papa, and she might as well be thinking about her relationship with Vianne as well:

> "I love you, Papa," she said quietly, realizing how true it was, how true it had always been. Love had turned into loss and she'd pushed it away, but somehow, impossibly, a bit of that love had remained. A girl's love for her father. Immutable. Unbearable but unbreakable.[rr]

These ideas that war, love, grief, and survival are "unbearable but unbreakable" translate into a thematic statement that typifies this novel, which is why we first saw this excerpt sampled in Chapter 3. This rhetoric offers echoes of Josiah's meditation about the love/loss paradox from *Before I Let Go*, featured in that same chapter.

Interiority Insight: Consider tying your character's growth and development to your theme. But tread lightly: Nobody wants an overt explanation or moral, especially in a novel. (Memoirs can be a bit more prescriptive, since readers expect that the author has overcome something and is exploring how they did it and what they learned.) For fiction, you can study some of the thematic state-ments in Chapter 3 and see how these ideas are more subtly transmitted via interiority, especially at moments that cement character growth and change.

Sing, Unburied, Sing is another novel of painful family dynamics that eventually mellow (somewhat) into grace and understanding. Leonie, who we've studied several times, certainly has moments of growth, but her arc pales in comparison to her son, Jojo's. While Leonie believes she is irreparably broken, readers might hold out hope for the next generation, especially since part of Jojo's trajectory involves trying to understand his mother.

In order for his evolution to pay off emotionally, we first have to see how dysfunctional the family is. This first excerpt appears in Leonie's POV around the 150-page mark, as she hurts Jojo, who she believes is disappointed in her (and she's right):

> It feels good to be mean ... and let that anger touch another. The one I'm never good enough for.[ss]

Leonie is in pain and needs to let her rotten parts leak out somehow. Unfortunately, she can't quite advocate for herself or manage her own feelings, so she showers her child with abuse, even though she's already had the realization about "using anger just to lash," which we saw in the previous chapter. Jojo's aware of his mother's limitations, but that doesn't help him much, since he's a thirteen-year-old child in a hopeless situation, lacking agency and control.

Once Leonie's mother dies of cancer, she finally admits that she can't parent anymore. She's so overwhelmed that she can hardly be a person, let alone take responsibility for others. Readers, of course, might wish she'd reached a different epiphany for the sake of her kids:

> "I can't," I say, and there are so many other words behind that. *I can't be a mother right now. I can't be a daughter. I can't remember. I can't see. I can't breathe....* [Michael] puts me in the passenger seat, closes the door, and climbs behind the wheel. The car shrinks the world to this: me and him in this dome of glass.[tt]

Though Leonie is very codependent with her partner, Michael, she demonstrates a tiny bit of growth by expressing her feelings. This is, of course, cold comfort for Jojo, who tries to come to terms with his mother leaving. He manages to display incredible self-awareness and empathy, even after she deserts him:

> Sometimes, late at night … I think I understand Leonie. I think I know something about what she feels. That maybe I know a little bit about why she left after Mama died, why she slapped me, why she ran. I feel it in me, too. An itching in my hands. A kicking in my feet. A fluttering in the middle of my chest. An unsettling.[uu]

This interiority shows that Jojo needs to make sense of Leonie and her choices. Beneath that is the desire to know himself, too. Is Jojo's essence shaped by nature or nurture? Which parts of his mother exist within him? And will understanding Leonie help heal his pain, soothe his loss, and perhaps even set him up for future insight and development? While readers may not have a lot of hope for Leonie, Jojo is on a different trajectory.

Interiority Insight: If you're working with more than one point of view (or one POV protagonist paired with a significant secondary character), you can build several growth arcs into the same story. Readers may not experience deep insight into a secondary character's transformation without inhabiting their POV, but multiple character trajectories can be used to explore your theme or provide counterpoint to your protagonist's evolution. See Chapter 12 for more on the roles secondary characters play.

We've seen several tragic yet profound arcs in this chapter, as deep emotions often accompany major turning points and transformations, so let's end on a joyful note. August from *One Last Stop* certainly doesn't start her story in a promising way. In fact, she is almost fully committed to avoiding human relationships, as we first saw in the previous chapter:

There's this feeling August has had everywhere she's ever lived, like she's not really there. Like it's all happening in a dream. She walks down the street, and it's like she's floating a few inches off the pavement, never rooted down.[vv]

This demonstrates a common self-preservation mindset. By not really engaging, August might miss out on the richness of life, but she can also guard her heart. She acknowledges that falling for Jane, the mysterious time-traveling woman on the train, would mean a nightmare of emotion:

There's always been a schematic in August's head of how things are supposed to be. Her whole life, she managed the noise and buzz and creeping dread in her brain by mapping things out, telling herself that if she looked hard enough, she'd find an explanation for everything. But here [she and Jane are], looking at each other across the steady delineation of things August understands, watching the line blur.[ww]

August must conceptualize things in order to feel safe, and this need is exacerbated by her wound, anxiety, and general dread (which invokes her backstory). Jane doesn't make sense, which pushes August right out of her comfort zone. At long last, August takes a joyous upswing as she painfully but productively removes the limits she's set on herself and her heart:

The only thought in her head is that she's twenty-three years old. She's twenty-three years old, and she's doing something absolutely stupid, and she's allowed to do absolutely stupid things whenever she wants, and the rest doesn't have to matter right now. How had she not realized it sooner?

As it turns out, letting herself have fun is *fun*.[xx]

What a realization! What freedom! Sure, this seems like a small thing—for some people, having fun is second nature. But for a character as wary and closed-off as August, this is a huge breakthrough.

Interiority Insight: When you do a good job of expressing who your character is, whether through their backstory (see Chapter 5) or their worldview (see Chapter 10), you can make stakes and meaning out of events and epiphanies both large and small.

Once all of your characterizing pieces are assembled, you can frame your protagonist within a larger context. Let's transition to Part 3 and discover how to intentionally craft secondary characters, information reveals, reactions, decisions, stakes, and story worlds.

PART 3

SUPPORTING STORYTELLING ELEMENTS

12

SECONDARY CHARACTERS

One of the most popular questions I'm asked about non-point-of-view secondary characters is: Do I have to do the same amount of work to develop them as I do to develop my protagonist? Absolutely not. But you will want to do *some* thinking about their backstory, wound, objective, motivation, need, major inner struggle, worldview, and growth arc. Most secondary characters will have these pieces in play, but at somewhat superficial levels.

Which characters you develop to this extent is a choice that obviously depends on the kind of story you're telling and your target audience. A thriller reader will expect a nuanced antagonist—so they can really get into the villain's headspace—because that's part of the fun. (You are also likely to have multiple POVs in this genre to begin with.) In an intergenerational literary fiction piece, you'll want dynamic dimension throughout the family tree.

On the completely opposite end of the spectrum, you wouldn't do comprehensive development for adult characters in a middle grade novel that's almost entirely focused on the tween hero. Stories for younger readers don't often tolerate extensive insight into adult mindsets (meaning no perspectives or interiority), and instead showcase the protagonist's experience almost myopically.[1]

The next most popular question is usually: What kinds of secondary characters do I need, and how many? This, too, depends. You'll have to decide who to develop and to which degree based on your plot, genre, and target audience. Generally, humans can only sustain a handful of deep relationships at one time, so a domestic thriller or women's fiction story shouldn't spread itself too thin with a large cast. Everyone must be connected, the closer, the better. Instead of the victim being some random person, they can be a protagonist's sibling or child, for example.

To be clear, I'm not talking about random tertiary characters who add texture to the story here. We need cute guys at the dog park, flirty bartenders, snarky baristas, and office friends and enemies to flesh out a world, but they aren't getting the full protagonist treatment. In terms of the characters whose names and stories readers know, you should be more selective, and err on the side of depth instead of breadth.

You're also aiming for characters, not caricatures or stereotypes, even with your secondary cast members. If you find yourself being too broad or reductive, combine two characters, develop them more deeply, or get rid of them altogether.

Caricature: A one-dimensional or stereotypical character who has no layers, or relies too much on archetype (overbearing parent, rebellious teen, power-hungry villain, etc.). Even secondary characters need a few elements that make them interesting and nuanced, like contradictions, needs, and choices that don't seem to fit their "type." Secondary characters can and should have their own evolution or devolution arcs, which can, in turn, help or hinder your protagonist. If you aren't putting much effort into developing secondary non-point-of-view characters, you run the risk of negatively impacting reader engagement.

---

1. I'm not criticizing kid readers and characters for being self-centered. This is considered developmentally appropriate across all six children's book categories.

You can think about secondary characters and make them dynamic by slotting them into the various roles they can play in relationship to your protagonist. There should be a sense of intention and cohesiveness, so design your larger cast with the following ideas in mind.

Character Relationships and Roles

An amazing exploration of character archetypes, among many other craft topics, is Christopher Vogler's *The Writer's Journey*. This guide analyzes and applies Joseph Campbell's Hero's Journey cycle to fiction, memoir, and screenwriting. The author unpacks how secondary characters affect the plot and protagonist, as well as the idea of character roles. While some of the insights are prescriptive, this framework leaves a lot of room for individual interpretation.

All characters have the potential to get your protagonist closer to or further from their goals and needs. They also add stakes to your story, which we'll talk about in Chapter 17. If a protagonist is invested in any relationship, whether positive or negative, they care. Once they're committed to something or, in this case, someone, everything feels elevated, each interaction seems more significant, and the outcome of scenes with that particular character matters more. Readers will start to care, too, and once a reader cares, they're hooked.

Ideally, you'll design your secondary characters to lure the protagonist into backsliding, support their growth, catapult them forward, or push them backward. You should always be thinking about how a secondary character acts upon your POV character and vice versa. (Though the protagonist should also affect other cast members, this dynamic is less important, unless it points back to the main character and changes their trajectory.)

Inter-character relationships offer opportunities to explore your protagonist, theme, and premise. You can also play around with your POV character's larger needs, wants, and sense of self as they perceive themselves in the context of people they know.

I like Vogler's discussion of character roles because that's how I think of secondary characters, too. They should never duplicate your protagonist, unless it's done with a specific purpose. For example, June, from

Yellowface, attempts to slip easily into Athena's life. This premise offers a unique and interesting parallel between the POV and a secondary character, and this comparison forms the backbone of that novel. But if you have a protagonist and secondary character who are overwhelmingly similar for no solid reason, I suggest you examine this choice.

In most cases, you'll want your secondary characters to differ from your protagonist in ways that challenge the POV, inform their sense of self or worldview, meet or subvert their needs, and otherwise create opportunities for conflict and tension. Even in a positive relationship. *Especially* in a positive relationship! Significant conflict tends to arise when characters (and humans) care about someone *more*, not less.

Theme can help dictate how these dynamics connect. For example, a protagonist who's cautious about love may be paired with a best friend who gives love freely and acts as a foil. They might also have another friend who's nursing a broken heart and providing the cautionary tale contrast. These secondary characters can change over the course of the story, but their thematically relevant and clashing individual worldviews will allow your protagonist to explore the broad idea of love with more nuance.

Three major roles that many secondary characters fall into are:

1. Supporters
2. Antagonists
3. Shapeshifters

Your protagonist will probably have plenty of supporters, including long-term ones like best friends or nice parents, and potential short-term ones like mentors, who come and go. Most notably, mentors and guides usually die or vanish before the climax of a more traditional Hero's Journey plot, leaving the protagonist to their own devices in a critical moment. If help is available throughout, your main character might struggle to be or seem proactive.

The antagonist is a crucial character in many stories and deserves lavish development. Sometimes a villain will have henchmen, but they tend to be more anonymous. The exception is anyone who flips on their boss, which would be notable, and readers might want more insight into that character's background and perspective to gauge their trustworthiness. A question I hear all the time is: Does my story *need* an antagonist? Well, you're probably sick of hearing this non-answer but … it depends.

A thriller? Absolutely. That antagonist may even get some point-of-view chapters. A domestic thriller? Absolutely, but in this case, the antagonist is usually coming from inside the house … or at least across the street. Intergenerational literary fiction may have a more nuanced antagonist, too. It could be the family's matriarch who rules with an iron fist, but the children still love her due to a confusing blend of filial piety, cultural conditioning, and those rare golden afternoons when she seems to "snap out of it" and see beyond her disappointments, unmet needs, and impossible expectations.

Contemporary coming-of-age middle grade and young adult largely concern themselves with bullies, siblings, former friends, and other people who can hurt protagonists the most because of the close bonds involved. Of course, in speculative young adult novels, which can be as far-reaching and complex as any adult project, antagonists can be murderous, sexy, or both. (Paging *The Cruel Prince* and *Red Queen*.)

It's important to note that most antagonists don't think of themselves as "the bad guy," which I first mentioned in Chapter 9. Only a disappointing and flat character gets out of bed and says, "I like power, so I'm going to do evil for the sake of evil today." This villain will be a blunt instrument, and while they might cause havoc, they won't truly play on the protagonist's or reader's psyche in any lasting or intriguing way. Most antagonists believe they are the misunderstood heroes of their own stories, at least according to their complicated worldviews, objectives, needs, or all of the above.

In fact, a common piece of storytelling advice about antagonists suggests they should have the same objective as the hero—so these individuals are gunning for one another throughout the plot—but with vastly different motivations. The hero's objective and need are obviously going to be more virtuous, and readers will align with them, but the antagonist's reasoning and drive should also make a twisted kind of sense. This will have audiences conflicted because they've developed a measure of empathy for the "bad guy."

Another question I get: What if I don't have an antagonist? All together now: It depends. But seriously, it depends on the kind of story you're writing, because not all stories have an overt villain. Tread carefully here, though. Your plot does need a reliable and escalating source of tension, conflict, and antagonism, so if you're not going to boil those down into a focal-point character, how are you going to move the narrative forward, menace your protagonist, and raise stakes?

The villain could be society itself, or a major project or undertaking. The antagonizing force could also be represented by something that exists inside the protagonist, like a dark wound or secret that's threatening to take them down from within. The main point here is that you need conflict in the story, one way or another, but it doesn't always come from a single character (or a group of characters, led by one Big Bad).

The final broad secondary character type—shapeshifter—doesn't refer to a paranormal creature. Instead, a shape-shifting character is a combination of supporter and antagonist, someone who changes roles over the course of a story, either suddenly or along a gradual growth arc. A best friend betrays the protagonist. The antagonist saves the hero's life rather than completing the contract kill, belying their true goodness. (If you dig deeper into character archetypes, you'll learn about other potential roles, like the trickster, who can be used to seed havoc and confusion.) The shapeshifter is a character whose polarity flip happens at crucial moments that coincide with plot reveals, escalations, or twists.

In romance and romantic comedy, the love interest almost always plays a shapeshifter role—they start out as a wonderful supporter and potential partner, then, when vulnerable feelings threaten, they can be perceived as an antagonist. Once the lovers gain a new understanding of themselves and one another, they finally reconcile and the beloved flips into a supportive role once more.

This is just a taste of the types of secondary characters you can create and how they can be used over the course of a story to drive plot and add thematic layers. While there are some brilliant secondary characters in shows, movies, books, and memoirs, they all have one thing in common—without the protagonist, they would be incomplete. Especially since the POV character is the lens through which audiences meet and interpret everyone else. That's what we'll talk about next.

Rendering Secondary Characters Without Point of View Access

As we learned in Chapter 4, it's impossible to offer interiority without point-of-view access. If you can't use POV to explore someone's inner life, dialogue and action become your only available methods for conveying what a secondary character might be experiencing.

There's a pretty big issue with these superficial approaches, though. We now know that all kinds of deep and unexpected stuff happens below the surface of every character. Pure showing, the domain of action and dialogue, offers readers only part of the picture. Most importantly, what's narrated, interpreted, and extrapolated about secondary characters is filtered through a protagonist's biased lens. How do writers, then, scratch at any of that complexity without interiority and point-of-view access?

First, the secondary character can drop their mask and level with the protagonist, honestly expressing their experience. But as we've seen throughout this guide, total authenticity and honesty prove difficult for most characters—even the self-aware ones. Also, things like worldview can shift over the course of the story, so a secondary character's earnest assessment of their feelings might be true early on but could change after a turning point.

Second, you can have non-POV characters self-express via other means. Journals and letters are always popular as a shortcut to getting someone's "true" thoughts and feelings, but as we know from best-selling thrillers like *Verity* by Colleen Hoover, journals and letters can be manipulated. You can also have a point-of-view protagonist eavesdrop on a conversation that excludes them, though the same problem applies. The secondary character could just as easily be lying to their scene partner or omitting data, especially if they have to be careful with their information. Readers know not to take everything a non-point-of-view character—or even a POV character!—does and says at face value.

Third, audiences can get a more nuanced—but still biased—awareness of what secondary characters are experiencing, thinking, feeling, or planning by seeing the protagonist's interpretation of these elements in interiority. As your hero goes through the story, they will be attempting to "read" other characters, just as your audience is judging and making assumptions about your protagonist. You absolutely can and should offer up your POV's interpretations and extrapolations about those around them. This information is obviously filtered through your protagonist's biases, perspectives, blind spots, and experiences. It is by no means neutral, but can be helpful in analyzing a secondary character or misleading the reader into thinking or feeling a certain way. (For example, if you're writing thriller or mystery and looking to add some misdirection, as we'll discuss in Chapter 14.)

A character's reactions to others are inherently subjective and tend to change along with the general state of the relationship. Some marriages ride that razor's edge between love and hatred, sometimes over the course of the same dinner conversation. Deep friendships end in betrayal, leaving protagonists second-guessing everything. If we consider the old saying, "there's a lid for every pot," which means that there's someone out there for everyone, conversely, we can also extrapolate that no one person is universally appealing. This means that two point-of-view protagonists can feel very differently about the same secondary character, and various secondary characters can have wildly different opinions about your protagonist.

It's from this colorful web of relationships, thoughts, feelings, interpretations, reactions, expectations, and inner struggles that we create external conflict and tension between characters. If it sounds complicated, it is. But remember: You're the one who wants to write a book. Nobody's forcing you to do it (unless you already have a publishing contract). If you're like me, though, you find the agony of writing to be only slightly more bearable than the agony of not writing, so buckle in. If you're going to do it, you might as well do it right.

Without point-of-view access, we can never truly know a non-POV character's deepest self, but rest easy, because we don't need this level of nuance. And if you find that you do want to develop a secondary character—and your story would be better and richer if readers could also intimately track their experience with interiority—consider giving them a perspective by transitioning to a multiple narrator structure.

In the following section, I'll quickly discuss scene and dialogue, as these are a writer's available vehicles for expressing inter-character relationships. This is an interiority guide though, so I'm not about to do a deep dive into scene-craft. I'd like to, but this book is long enough already! Supplement your learning with the excellent *Make a Scene* by Jordan Rosenfeld and *Dialogue* by Robert McKee.

The Mechanics of Scene

Scene is your opportunity to show off what your secondary characters want and why. It's also a great chance to stymie your protagonist, throw obstacles in their way, and make them dig deep to attempt various actions and strategies, as we saw in our discussion of Stanislavsky and *A Streetcar Named Desire* in Chapter 7.

Protagonists should have an objective, motivation, and expectation at the beginning of every scene. Then they'll play actions to (ideally) achieve the goal, and react in the moment as the objective is frustrated, obstacles arise, or secondary characters introduce conflict and tension. External struggle can also come from the story world, applying pressure to the proceedings.

Interiority is very useful for rendering character reactions as protagonists seek to understand what their scene partner is doing, think about what lies beneath their façade, and otherwise gear up for their next gambit or decision. New information is interpreted, meaning is extrapolated and maybe even subsumed, and the scene puts your protagonist's sense of self into action. The POV character can be honest with others, or they can intentionally mislead, pretend, or play on their scene partner's perceived vulnerabilities and misbeliefs. What's said and done in scene shouldn't be purely literal. Consider how you might introduce subtext and nuance to everyone's behavior.

After a scene is over, the protagonist can also unpack what happened, choose a different plan of attack (literal or figurative) going forward, and decide what this means for their objective or need. A polarity shift is also welcome as the POV character goes from excitement to defeat, or vice versa. This pattern reinforces the cause-and-effect logic I first mentioned in Chapter 4, because one scene should ideally lead to another, taking previous events into consideration, and so on, and so forth.

To kick off our From the Shelves excerpts for this chapter, I'll show how our point-of-view protagonists analyze secondary characters in interiority.

Secondary Character Interpretation in Interiority

When a protagonist thinks about or interprets another character, it's important to note that their interiority should reveal something about them, too. Remember, secondary characters are often defined by who they are in relationship to the point of view narrator. I'll start this section with a few secondary character portraits rendered in protagonist interiority. Then I'll show how secondary character depiction reveals the POV protagonist's biased sense of self, need, or worldview. We'll also explore some antagonists.

These first character interpretations are just delightful, like this one, from *The Nickel Boys*, where young protagonist Elwood describes his grandmother:

> Harriet Johnson was a slight hummingbird of a woman who conducted herself in everything with furious purpose. If something was worth doing—working, eating, talking to another person—it was worth doing seriously or not at all. She kept a sugarcane machete under her pillow for intruders, and it was difficult for Elwood to think that the old woman was afraid of anything. But fear was her fuel.[a]

I absolutely love this writing style and Elwood's inference that "fear was her fuel" as an explanation for her "furious purpose." It's a small moment of deep interpretation, as fear—on a personal, social, and institutional level—is a thematic element in this novel. This interiority also illuminates the worldview passed on by Elwood's family of origin.

A similarly lively character sketch comes from Louise, who's thinking about her late mother, in *How to Sell a Haunted House*:

Their mom didn't have a feel for food. She approached her kitchen the way a bomb squad approached a ticking paper bag. She needed a timer to cook pasta, her rice was always mushy or burned, sometimes both at the same time, and her casseroles never came together, but the cult of Southern motherhood insisted she provide meals for her family, so she distracted everyone from her shortcomings by embracing exotic recipes she tore out of magazines.[b]

While we don't meet this woman in the present action because she's dead, there are so many characterizing details in this interpretation that she emerges very clearly. (This is not technically a flashback since it's compressed narration, not scene, but it does a similarly thorough job of putting character on the page.) I especially love to imagine Mom walking into "her kitchen the way a bomb squad approached a ticking paper bag," and extrapolating how this clashes with "the cult of Southern motherhood." I am not a cook myself, hence the chef I married, so I deeply relate to this woman. Even if I was fabulous in the kitchen, I'd still be able to align with this harried homemaker because her rendering is so specific.

Interiority Insight: General telling is vague. Interiority has the potential to be specific.

Another type of interiority used to interpret secondary characters involves the protagonist assuming what someone else might be going through. An incisive insight is delivered by Isabel, one of the *Brutes* narrators, as she looks at her two young children:

I prefer my son. He is simpler. He likes to run into things at a very high speed and then cling to me until the pain fades. He could do this all day long, it never bores him, the pain followed by the love. I wonder if he is onto something. He wants to experience the two extremes of life constantly. My daughter is doomed. She wants to understand them.[c]

While the binary gender generalization is a bit reductive, Isabel reflects on the theme of experience versus understanding in a way that both reveals what the children might be feeling and characterizes her own worldview.

Interiority Insight: A protagonist trying to comprehend what drives a secondary character shows how various personalities and relationships illuminate a story's theme.

The following two excerpts come from *Sing, Unburied, Sing*, and both are in Leonie's point of view as she considers those closest to her. While she has significant blind spots and issues, she can also be quite intuitive and perceptive. As Mama lies on her deathbed, Leonie watches Pop and worries for him:

> Pop has slid down the wall, all the upright parts of him crumbling as he looks at Mama, makes himself look at Mama, for once. He's been orbiting her like a moon, sleeping on the sofa with his back to the door, searching the yard and woods for pens and bins and machines to fix so he can repair in the face of what he cannot.[d]

This is a beautiful portrait of powerlessness. Now that his wife, the center of his orbit, is about to die, Pop is forced to "look at Mama, for once," which is a thinly veiled way of saying that he needs to confront reality. For Leonie, that's a bit of the pot calling the kettle black, of course.

Leonie's relationship with Jojo is much more complicated. She doesn't like motherhood, and, by extension, projects her sense of dread and inadequacy onto her children, especially her firstborn. When the family is pulled over by police, she watches, frozen in fear, as an officer brandishes a gun at him:

> It's easy to forget how young Jojo is until I see him standing next to the police officer. It's easy to look at him, his weedy height, the thick spread of his belly, and think he's grown. But he's just

a baby. And when he starts reaching in his pocket and the officer draws his gun on him, points it at his face, Jojo ain't nothing but a fat-kneed, bowlegged toddler. I should scream, but I can't.[e]

Imagine standing there while your child has a firearm trained on him. Ancestral wounds about police brutality against Black bodies are operating under the surface here, but Leonie's inability to act, even as she sees Jojo in this high-stakes situation, only contributes to her sense of failure as a mother.

Vincent from *The Glass Hotel* is painted as a savvy operator, deciding to be okay with transactional relationships so she can live a "carefree" monied existence. Of course, reality ends up being much more complicated. Here, she's evaluating the character of Olivia, who we heard from in Chapter 6. If readers dig deeper, they'll see that she might as well be spelling out her own worldview:

> Vincent was charmed by Olivia, as she knew Jonathan was, but something about Olivia made Vincent a little sad. Olivia's dress was too formal, her lipstick was too bright, her hair was freshly trimmed, she was slightly too attentive in the way she looked at Jonathan, and the combined effect was overeager. *You're showing your hand*, Vincent wanted to tell her, *you can't let anyone see how hard you're trying*, but of course there was no way to give advice to a woman two or three times her age.[f]

In this culture, "showing your hand" and trying too hard are cardinal sins. And while Olivia *is* acting desperate, Vincent's own insecurities might be tainting her perspective.

Joey from *Tell Me I'm an Artist* is at least more self-aware about a relationship that she keeps idealizing:

> I was nostalgic for a friendship that made me feel like shit. I missed the consistency of feeling like shit in the same specific way all the time.[g]

Sometimes, characters maintain a bond because at least they know who they are in that role. It's safe, familiar, and doesn't ask much of them.

Rejecting or transforming the status quo takes energy and guts. This is why some humans and characters slip into old dynamics when they encounter people from their pasts. While this might not feel good, it also represents the known versus the unknown. Joey is away at college, drowning in uncertainty. Even disappointing familiarity tempts her because she knows where she stands and who she "is"[2] in that role.

Eleanor from *Eleanor Oliphant Is Completely Fine* makes a friend, Raymond, over the course of her growth journey. He steps in after she drinks herself to the edge of extinction. He also seems to be truly interested in a platonic friendship with her, as seen in Eleanor's evaluation of his motives:

> It was surprising that he should bother with me.... Whenever
> I'd been sad or upset before, the relevant people in my life
> would simply call my social worker.... Raymond hadn't phoned
> anyone or asked an outside agency to intervene. He'd elected to
> look after me himself. I'd been pondering this, and concluded
> that there must be some people for whom difficult behavior
> wasn't a reason to end their relationship with you.[h]

She interrogates his objectives and motivations, finds them authentic, and decides to let him into her innermost world around the midpoint, which is a big development. Eleanor has gotten used to being a curiosity and her "closest" associates are case workers. It's a big deal that someone in her life seems to actually care about her current incarnation.

Rachel from *Milk Fed* has a similar experience when she starts to date Miriam and realizes that her new girlfriend's affection, unlike her mother's, is genuine:

> This kind of love seemed strange to me. It was not out of love
> that I'd obeyed my mother, not really. It was out of fear, the way
> a person might placate a punishing god. Ultimately, I'd always
> been terrified that if I didn't please my mother, she would smite

---

2. I put this in quotes because the self is never entirely fixed, especially in relationships.

me. But I believed Miriam when she said that she cared out of love.[i]

Interiority Insight: Protagonists who struggle with self-worth on the heels of a traumatic backstory might find that secondary characters can help them develop a more evolved worldview—if the protagonist can manage to trust another's motives, of course.

When Sona in *Gearbreakers* sees Eris unmasked for the first time, she's not only taken with her power and essence, but also her beauty:

I am not sure if it is just the fact that she had the ability to obliterate a Valkyrie singlehandedly ... or that she is the first Gearbreaker I have ever laid eyes on and therefore represents every particle of destruction that I wish to embody—but she is the most beautiful girl I have ever seen.[j]

We'll talk about romantic relationships in the following chapter, but notice how each protagonist perspective on a secondary character is inflected with their own feelings, biases, and, in this case, desires. While allies are great, and we'll see more of them later, protagonist characterization of antagonists is also important to explore.

Perceiving the Antagonist

Lily in *Bad Fruit* is an observer who's always taking the temperature of her household to see how she can pacify Mama—and keep herself safe. This is how she "explains" her mother to readers at the beginning of the story:

At work, they call her "The Pink Bitch," because she's impossible, combative, a calculating careerist; she's exactly the same at home. But rarely, perhaps only with me, she cracks open and someone very different peers through: an aging woman on the edge of self-sabotage, waiting for someone to pull her back.[k]

Lily internalizes and subsumes her role in the family—she is the "someone to pull [Mama] back"—and this is constantly at the forefront of her mind.

If you recall our discussion of allies and shapeshifters at the beginning of this chapter, you'll understand how Lily views her relationships with her nuclear family members. If Mama plays more of an antagonist role, Daddy is ... well, Lily doesn't know yet:

> This is interesting. Daddy has never acknowledged that there's anything wrong between him and Mama. For a second, I consider ... talking to him, just to feel what it would be like to be on another side, for there to be another side. I would say I understand. I would tell him to leave her. But Mama's timing is impeccable.... I shake my head. It's too late for new allegiances, and he is too fledgling an ally.[1]

In evaluating him, Lily is trying to determine whether Daddy's an ally or Mama's loyal enabler. Until she knows for sure, she decides to keep her cards close to the vest and not depend on him too much. This is a very lonely proposition for a young woman whose entire life is seemingly bound up in her relationships.

Interiority Insight: Secondary characters all have roles to play, but the protagonist does, too. How and where do they fit within the web of their world?

I alluded to this moment from *You* in the previous chapter, now here's Joe's first encounter with Beck and how he interprets her "decision" to flash her credit card and reveal her name:

> You reach into your Zuckerman's pink-pig wallet and hand me your credit card even though you have enough cash in there to cover it. You want me to know your name and I'm no nut job and I swipe your card and the quiet between us is getting louder and why didn't I put on music today and I can't think of anything to say.[m]

Of course, this is a wild, reaching interpretation of a simple transaction, but for Joe, it's enough to plunge him headlong into obsession. What role is Beck playing here? And Joe?

In the historical portion of *The Villa*, Mari evaluates her stepsister and rival, Lara, who's sleeping with Noel, the famous "mentor" who invited everyone to Italy for drugs, booze, and sexual experimentation.[3] Not only does Mari interpret Lara's motives (and not generously), she allows this tryst to diminish her own self-esteem:

> [Mari] hates that she's a little impressed. "You're shagging him."
>
> "You can't tell anyone," Lara says immediately, but Mari knows she's only saying it because she thinks it's the thing to say when you're having sex with a very famous married man. Knowing Lara, Mari is sure her stepsister would love nothing more than to march through Piccadilly with a sandwich board announcing the fact.[n]

These women are in a complicated competition, fighting for attention, first within their blended family, then from the men in their lives. Mari, who is of a naturally darker and more tortured disposition, subsumes that she's the loser.

Interiority Insight: Even antagonistic characters can be mirrors, cluing readers into the protagonist's state of mind.

In *Red Queen*, Mare analyzes Evangeline, her soon-to-be sister-in-law, and Elara, her soon-to-be mother-in-law. Two antagonists for the price of one! This interiority is technically *about* Evangeline and Elara, but as with so many other excerpts featured in this chapter, it also showcases Mare's inner tension:

> As usual, I'm seated next to Evangeline. I'm painfully aware of

---

3. My invitation must've gotten lost in the mail!

the many metal utensils on the table, all lethal weapons in Evangeline's cruel hand. Every time she lifts her knife to cut her food, my body tenses, waiting for the blow. Elara knows what I'm thinking, as usual, but carries on through her meal with a smile. That might be worse than Evangeline's torture, to know she takes pleasure in watching our silent war.°

One thing to note here is that Mare can't technically read Elara's mind, so "Elara knows what I'm thinking, as usual" is a projection. To keep the points of view distinct, I would've phrased it "Elara *seems to know* what I'm thinking, as usual" (emphasis mine).

Interiority Insight: When you want your protagonist to hedge, assume, or guess what a secondary character is thinking, use "seems" or "as if" language, e.g., "She scowls at me ruefully, as if she knows the malice hiding in my heart."

In the following chapter, which is an extension of this one, I'll continue to unpack how protagonists think about the state of their relationships with others and how these impressions reflect their sense of self and development arc position.

13

THE INTERIORITY OF RELATIONSHIPS

Protagonists evaluate secondary characters in ways that are directly tied to how they feel about themselves and their social lives overall. Sometimes a connection with a secondary character is static, which causes angst for a protagonist who might wish things were different. Alternately, they might appreciate an anchor in the storm of their lives and prioritize their steady connections, for better or worse.

This chapter is in a relationship[1] with the previous one, so let's skip the introduction and plunge right into our From the Shelves excerpts, this time, with POV character perspectives on their social bonds.

Let's look at Pamela from *Bright Young Women* and her unlikely ally, Tina, who believes the sorority house slasher is also responsible for killing her partner, Ruth. Pamela doesn't fully trust Tina at first, only to realize that maybe her former reliance on her sorority sisters was unfulfilling and shallow compared to this surprising new friendship:

> [My relationship with Tina] was more like sisterhood, I realized, than anything I'd experienced under this roof. Because I hadn't chosen Tina, hadn't vetted her like I had members of this chapter, and yet we were fated to go through life together connected by spilled blood.[a]

---

1. I'm starting to think I need a hobby other than cheeky footnotes.

What makes a friend? What makes a relationship feel *real*? Pamela once believed in sorority-sanctioned sisterhood, but now she's realizing that certain bonds are more authentic and consequential than others. As it happens, a person she *didn't* choose has the most impact. Especially for someone like Pamela, who needs to be in control, this is a surprising paradoxical insight.

Jude from *The Cruel Prince* is also stunned to realize that once you kiss an evil fairy royal, you can't really take it back. This subtle status shift informs the rest of the plot:

> It turns out that having kissed someone, the possibility of kissing hangs over everything, no matter how terrible an idea it was the first time. The memory of his mouth of mine shimmers in the air between us.[b]

Interiority Insight: Some character choices, realizations, and developments are one-way doors. Once protagonists know, they can't unknow. (Though they *can* go into denial!) It's up to your POV character to determine where these lines lie for them, and whether their boundaries vary from relationship to relationship.

Let's look at Jojo from *Sing, Unburied, Sing*. We saw his mother's perspective about him in the previous chapter, now let's explore whether he's aware of Leonie's occasional concern:

> All's quiet in the house, and for a stupid second I wonder why Leonie and Michael ain't arguin' about him hitting Kayla. And then I remember. They don't care.[c]

Nope. Not even a little bit. While Leonie might finally be able to admit that she doesn't always do right by her son, it's too little, too late, according to Jojo. The complicated thing is that characters (and people!) often want their parents' love and devotion, even when their elders show no capacity for it. Children keep hoping for the best, as we saw in an aside from *Anxious People* in Chapter 10, but sometimes this desire only generates sadness, longing, and inner struggle, because they're barking up the wrong tree.

Interiority Insight: Sometimes characters react to what is, and sometimes they react to what they wish was true.

The human propensity for wishful thinking allows writers and readers to explore idealized or denial-based protagonist perspectives on relationships. Let's stick with interiority about the family unit for moment. Melissa Broder tends to use consistent themes across her body of work, and a strikingly similar idealization appears in both *Milk Fed* and *Death Valley*. Both protagonists arrive at the notion that it's easier to love the *idea* of a person, rather than the actual person themselves. (This reminds me of Hannah's distinction between "liking" and "loving" her mother in *The Bodyguard*.) Here's the narrator of *Death Valley* considering the upsides of having a "relationship" with her comatose father:

> It is easier to have an intimate relationship with the unconscious than the conscious, the dead than the living. As my father slumbered, I created a fantasy version of him—resurrecting the man from my youth, before his depression set in. I re-entered a world of home-cooked stews, tobacco smells, cozy sweatshirts, plants, and birds; a realm of warmth and worldly cynicism, where I was always on the inside of his sarcasm.[d]

Compare this to Rachel, from *Milk Fed*, and her reflections about her mother:

> I thought about how I used to watch my mother sleep sometimes, how innocent she looked with her hands tucked under the pillow. In those moments, I saw her as a little girl, and I felt that nothing was her fault—just a chain of fears and feelings passed down from generation to generation. In those moments I thought, *You can show her how to love you better by being loving to her*. But it was easier to be loving when the person was asleep.[e]

Notice how both characters subsume their distant parental relation-ships as reflections on their senses of self. The first example shows nostalgia for a revised past, where things are warm and cozy, just the narrator and Dad against the world. Her longing for belonging is clear. The second excerpt involves the realization that Rachel might be able to improve the relationship "by being loving to [Mom]," but she can't seem to gather the wherewithal to actually do it. Since these relation-ships are so unfulfilling for both protagonists, it doesn't take long for Rachel, at least, to become cynical about her odds once again:

> What was saddest was that [Mom] didn't seem to want to know me, not as I was on the inside. I wasn't even sure if she could grasp that I had an inside, that I was real. Sometimes it seemed impossible that she had ever given birth to me at all. Other times, it made perfect sense that I had lived inside her for so long. It explained why she could only see me as an extension of herself.[f]

This is a very mature breakthrough, but a disappointing one. Nobody wants to be merely "an extension" of someone else, to worry that they're not "real." How invalidating for Rachel to feel like her existence and lived experience don't register with the character whose love she craves the most.

Interiority Insight: A deep, thematic need for many characters and humans alike is to be recognized and seen for who they really are.

In the colonial-era African family systems depicted in *Homegoing*, parental favor means the difference between not only happiness and misery, but acceptance and banishment within the larger community.[2] Here, Effia, a pubescent girl, is being presented to an undesirable and much older suitor for the first time. She desperately wants to under-stand what she can do to win her mother's love and approval, instead

---

2. Certain cultures see life through a communal lens which contrasts with Western indi-vidualism.

of the strange man's. Unfortunately, Baaba has seemingly done little to prepare her daughter for this distressing moment:

> Effia ... wasn't exactly sure what this meant, but she could tell from her parents' looks that it was best to keep her mouth shut. Abeeku Badu was the first man they had brought to meet her. Effia wanted desperately for him to want her, but she did not yet know what kind of man he was, what kind of woman he required.... It was only when Effia didn't speak or question, when she made herself small, that she could feel Baaba's love, or something like it. Maybe this was what Abeeku wanted too.[g]

Not only does Effia wish that her mother would guide her, she actively tries to mold herself to what she imagines Baaba wants in this situation, even though it clashes with her own needs. In this society and time period, Effia doesn't have much of a voice, so we see her actively subverting her own reactions and desires and "[making] herself small." If the two characters were more engaged and open with one another, Effia might not feel so lost or desperate for a scrap of "love, or something like it."

A more zoomed-out rendering of a parental relationship appears in *The City We Became*, as Aislyn realizes, with a little perspective and maturity, that she might have something in common with her mother, after all:

> When Aislyn was a teenager, she often thought of her mother as dull. Since then Aislyn has come to understand that women sometimes have to pretend to be dull so that the men around them can feel sharper. Adult Aislyn has had to do the same thing, with increasing frequency as she's grown older. So she and her mother are finally beginning to become friends ... but it's fragile, like any friendship formed amid stress.[h]

This is a great example of interiority that summarizes a relationship's backstory in compressed narration. It's done quickly and gives readers everything they need to understand the characters involved. This is appropriate for a tertiary character like Aislyn's mother, who we only meet a few times in a much larger and more far-reaching story.

Interiority Insight: Sometimes you should use showing and scene, and sometimes you should use telling and summary. It all depends on how important the element in question is to the whole.

Similarly, Felicity in *The Fair Folk* has many ups and downs with Elfrida and the rest of the fairies. First, she feels she needs Them, then she escapes Them by going to college, and, finally, she ends up back in Their clutches (until she finds a way to sever ties for good). In the middle of her college experience, as she gains distance and perspective, she thinks back on her childhood and wonders about Their true intentions:

> I thought about Them, my beautiful friends. I loved the magic
> and the glamour, and their gleeful enjoyment of the tricks they
> played. Sometimes, though, it wasn't so different from the
> bullying that went on at school, and sometimes it was down-
> right cruel.... Were they really my friends, after all?[i]

This transitions us nicely toward relationship growth and change—for better and worse—and how it can parallel a protagonist's own development.

Let's revisit *Bright Young Women* but explore a different point of view. We already got a glimpse of Ruth's self-loathing in Chapter 6. When she first meets Tina in a support group, Ruth can't understand how anyone could be interested in her. Ruth's first reaction to Tina's kindness is driven by suspicion and self-doubt, which reveals her worldview and dismal self-esteem. Tina is an aspiring therapist, and Ruth assumes her only usefulness is as a test subject:

> The implication was a blazing backhand across the face. I
> thought about what Tina had said at the meeting—how helping
> other women was her true purpose in life, what fulfilled her.
> What a fool I was. Tina didn't want to be my friend; she wanted
> to shrink me.[j]

Notice that Ruth reacts to an implication she's constructed in her own mind. This isn't Tina's motive, it's what Ruth *projects*. With work and growth, Ruth ends up overcoming this suspicion and Tina becomes a lover and significant presence in her life. Even after Ruth is murdered, Tina shows her profound commitment by campaigning to bring Ruth's killer to justice. As a reader, I find myself wishing Ruth allowed herself to accept love more freely while she was still alive.

We'll explore romantic relationships in a moment, but here's some interesting interiority about a specifically *un*romantic friendship. Montserrat, from adult paranormal thriller *Silver Nitrate* by Silvia Moreno-Garcia, has been best friends with Tristán, a playboy and fading actor, for years. A casual remark from Tristán triggers a reveal of her true, unexpressed, and unrequited feelings:

> "Oh, Montserrat is not my girlfriend," Tristán said with a careless chuckle. How annoying, his nonchalance, and how annoying, too, the little jab of pain that accompanied it.
>
> It shouldn't have bothered her, because he had spoken a true fact, and yet for a second there was the uncomfortable snagging of her heart before she shook her head and brushed the feeling away.[k]

The problem isn't what Tristán says about the reality of the situation, it's Montserrat's own longing and resentment at being friend-zoned. Even though she knows better, she can't seem to help herself. (I'd argue that Tristán is at least somewhat aware that he's stringing her along but continues to do so because it benefits him.)

Interiority Insight: Complex relationships, especially those where the protagonist isn't getting their needs met, can generate a lot of internal and interpersonal tension.

Even if you're not writing a romance, romantasy, or romantic comedy, you might still want to consider how protagonists can act in—and out

—of love, since these relationships can add both tension *and* growth to story. That's what we'll cover in the following section.

Romantic Relationships in Interiority

Romantic relationships deserve their own focus because a character's chosen intimate partners tend to not only affect their day-to-day existence but provide incredibly high-stakes conflict.

Love bonds also illuminate the protagonist, their worldview, value system, and foundational thematic stance on ideas like trust and vulnerability. If you want a great exploration of romance genre beats and character arcs, check out Gwen Beal's *Romancing the Beat*. A central idea in that guide suggests that characters go from being "hole-hearted," where a piece of them is either missing or they're hamstrung by a misbelief or flaw, to "whole-hearted" after overcoming what holds them back and engaging in a romance.

If you're writing any kind of story with a romantic plot or subplot, pay attention to how the following From the Shelves protagonists view their romantic relationships and partners, how the ups and downs are subsumed to reflect their sense of self, and how high the stakes seem in matters of the heart.

First, let's look at interiority that expresses what it's like to fall in love. I'll go back to Iris's letter from *Divine Rivals*, another part of which was originally excerpted in Chapter 11, because it beautifully encapsulates how she feels as she opens up. This demonstrates that trust and vulnerability are often necessary prerequisites to love:

> I'm not sure who you are, where you are.... I don't know what is connecting us—if it's magical thresholds or conquered god bones or something else we've yet to discover. Most of all, I don't know why I'm writing to you now. But here I am, reaching out to you. A stranger and yet a friend.[1]

Roman's character arc involves overcoming the misbeliefs he was raised with and realizing that his feelings aren't a liability. Here, he seems to break open the emotions he's bottled up since his sibling, Del, died:

He hadn't cried in years. He hadn't cried since Del. He had kept his feelings tightly locked away since then, as if it were wrong to set them free. As if they were a weakness, bound to ruin him.... He wanted to let them go; he didn't want to bring all this baggage into his marriage with Iris. But he didn't know how to be free of it, and he realized she would simply have to take him as he was.[m]

Iris and Roman are both wounded in complimentary ways, and that's what sets them up for a satisfying relationship.

Sometimes love and desperation are so entwined that a character's own need is indistinguishable from their desire for another. It should come as no surprise that Leonie from *Sing, Unburied, Sing* falls into this category, as she remembers how she fell for Michael:

He was just tall enough that when he hugged me, his chin rested on my head, and I was cupped under him. Like I belonged. Because I wanted Michael's mouth on me, because from the first moment I saw him … he saw me. Saw past skin the color of unmilked coffee, eyes black, lips the color of plums, he saw me. Saw the walking would I was, and came to be my balm.[n]

This experience seems to be less about Michael as a person and more about how Leonie needs to be seen, craves comfort, and feels like she doesn't belong. She mistakenly holds Michael responsible for making her whole because she's incapable of doing this for herself. Of course, these unreasonable expectations generate conflict and misunderstanding between them.

Interiority Insight: While love can, indeed, be a "balm," there will be problems in the relationship if a character gives too much power over their own needs and sense of self to a romantic partner.

Hardened and damaged characters are notorious for falling in love, especially those who swear up and down that it's not for them. Here's Hannah from *The Bodyguard*, who has explicitly spent 150 pages asserting that she has no feelings, especially not for Jack. Then, she changes her tune:

> But Jack's face, as he listened, was so open, and so sympathetic, and *so on my side* that in that moment, despite all my rules, that memory just shared itself. I wasn't a sharer. I didn't even share things with non-clients. Especially not painful things. But I suddenly understood why people did it. It felt like relief. It felt like dipping your feet in cool water on a hot day.º

Hannah is a professional compartmentalizer, yet she still falls. Romance and romcom readers specifically enjoy seeing this kind of conquest.[3]

Sometimes, of course, a romance isn't about love at all, and instead reflects a character's own sense of self and worth. Vincent from *The Glass Hotel* might have emotional needs, that's not what she's fulfilling with Jonathan, who comes to the hotel bar when she's bartending. At least her expectations are clear from the get-go once she sees his tip:

> A hundred-dollar bill? Mortifying in retrospect, but she always appreciated the clarity of his intentions. It was always going to be a transactional arrangement. When he beckoned, she would come to him. She would always be well compensated.ᴾ

We already know from Chapter 3 that she continues with this "transactional arrangement," but readers might wonder whether she's short-changing herself, despite her assurances otherwise.

Not all relationships are satisfying, and not all relationships last. While it's rarer to track several different romances over the course of one book because each dynamic requires a lot of development, it's not unusual to build many highs and lows into the trajectory of one love story.

Here's an example of a character falling in love, this time with his

---

3. Saucy double entendre fully intended.

future spouse and co-parent. This section goes into the POV of Ben from *Amazing Grace Adams* as he first meets Grace:

> He isn't sure what this is, what the two of them are doing here, why they have come, but he can feel the pull of her next to him.... And he wonders, Is she feeling it too? ... He wants to lay himself bare, to strip away the veneer and acknowledge how bizarre it is—the fact that they barely know each other and yet they are doing this. He wants to open her up, to gain access to her.[q]

Look at that high-stakes language as he wonders how she feels and describes wanting to merge with her. This is Rachel's romantic fantasy in *Milk Fed*, though Ben manages to make it seem earnest and sweet.

Interiority Insight: Most romances and romcoms offer some access to the romantic interest's POV. Sometimes there's a primary protagonist (*One Last Stop*), and sometimes the narrative is evenly balanced between the lovers (*Before I Let Go*). Non-genre stories with romantic subplots can give some point-of-view sections to characters who are in significant relationships with the protagonist, too, though this is less common.

Unfortunately, Grace and Ben's relationship doesn't end happily, as Grace suffers a breakdown following the death of their second child and disappears, leaving him alone with their surviving daughter. He resents his interpretation that Grace is shirking her responsibilities and escaping reality. Instead of finding empathy for her, he rages. Readers can understand both sides, given the circumstances:

> All of a sudden, he's furious with Grace. The fury is so huge it's like something entirely separate from him, a whole other entity. How? he wants to shout at his wife, wherever the hell she is.... And yes, it is a choice. You. Have. Made. A. Choice. [The situation makes] him want to pick up the chair he's sitting on, hurl it

against the wall. He can hear the smashed-up sound of it, see the wood splintering. *Where are you, Grace?*[r]

Let's check back in with *The Fair Folk*. Early in Felicity and Sebastian's courtship, she makes the mistake of asking the fairies to give him a glamour to help his acting career. Of course, this backfires and Sebastian falls in love, Narcissus-like, with himself (and the attention). For Felicity, love is transformational, and you'll recognize a piece of this excerpt from our thematic exploration in Chapter 3:

That was the most marvellous thing of all.... Just the two of them, curled together in the wide bed, while the rest of the world carried on outside. *Even more marvellous than being with Them?* But the one couldn't be set against the other.... This was grown up magic. This was real.

What if you could have the best of both? What if a night like this could last as long as you wanted? She remembered those fairy feasts that seemed to go on for days, when she'd stumbled out of the woods to find that a single night had passed, and the next morning had yet to dawn. But perhaps that wasn't about magic at all; perhaps it was just about being a child. And her last, fading thought as sleep claimed her: *Perhaps it's the same thing.*[s]

Readers then get to see how transformational it is for Felicity to fall *out* of love with Sebastian, though her feelings are complicated by her guilt over inadvertently "cursing" him. When he comes to visit, he even has the gall to bring his affair partner, Harriet. Felicity is immediately overwhelmed by both of them, can't summon any jealousy, and finds herself actively retreating:

Felicity found it hard to keep up.... By the time they got back to college ... it was a relief to pretend that she had some urgent work to do. Not altogether a lie, but she would certainly have put it off until Sebastian left for London. She didn't care anymore that she would be leaving him in Harriet's company.... She shut her door behind them both, closed her eyes and leaned against it, suddenly exhausted.[t]

> **Interiority Insight:** How does your protagonist deal with inner struggle and confusing feelings in relationships? Do they attack, try to hash it out, or flee?

In the next excerpt, from *Americanah*, Ifemelu wonders why her relationship with Curt failed. At face value, Curt ticked all the boxes, treated her well, and was wealthy, to boot. By all metrics, he was perfect, but Ifemelu couldn't allow herself to be comfortable with him:

> She had not entirely believed herself while with him—happy, handsome Curt, with his ability to twist life into the shapes he wanted. She loved him, and the spirited easy life he gave her, and yet she often fought the urge to create rough edges, to squash his sunniness, even if just a little.[u]

This dynamic goes back to Ifemelu's sense of identity and her belief that she self-sabotages because something is wrong with her. There's also a latent racial dynamic here, since he's white and she's Black. Instead of being honest with Curt about her feelings, she ends the relationship by cheating with a random neighbor in their apartment building. Curt isn't entirely blameless, though. When she comes clean, his reaction seems to validate her choice:

> "Bitch," he said.

> He wielded the word like a knife; it came out of his mouth sharp with loathing. To hear Curt say "bitch" so coldly felt surreal, and tears gathered in her eyes, knowing that she had turned him into a man who could say "bitch" so coldly, and wishing he was a man who would not have said "bitch" no matter what.[v]

Maybe her expectations are unrealistic, as few partners will stand by and let themselves be disrespected. Or maybe Ifemelu's right, and there is a coldness inside of Curt that would've made him a bad long-term match.

Next, Leila, another narrator from *Brutes*, has no problem falling out of love with a bartender she's dating. Though she chose him, she's also clear-eyed about the toxicity of their relationship:

> The bartender was an asshole but he drank a lot and I drank a lot and when we were drunk we were so mean to each other that it seemed like the only honest kind of conversation. All day I indulged in the little kindnesses that kept clocks moving, said, "Have a nice day," "How are you?" "Come again soon." Then over late-night dinners, this boy and I destroyed each other with words so cruel and careful they made a kind of poetry. We sanded each other down until we practically shone. But eventually we were so broken ... but broken men are much more appealing than broken women. Broken men inspire longing. Broken women are just looking to get kicked further down the drain.[w]

She seems to recognize something negative in herself, not just her ex. This is a good reminder that romantic partnerships aren't just reflections of a union between two characters, but deeply related to each protagonist's sense of self and where they are in their specific growth arcs. These layers all tend to influence whether they choose to leave the relationship or stay. Some of our From the Shelves protagonists are in happy relationships (especially at the end of a romance or romcom). Others are unhappy in their love pairings.

Though some protagonists tend to blame their romantic misery on the other partner (attribution bias), compelling characters tend to use relationship conflict as an opportunity for self-inquiry. If a protagonist decides to remain in a relationship after falling out of love, they have their own reckoning to do.

This is exemplified by Mari, from *The Villa*, as she realizes where she stands with her musician partner, Pierce. They're on a dream vacation in Italy at the behest of a famous musician who could offer a career break. But Pierce is more interested in women, drink, and drugs. Here's Mari's interiority as looks at him in a moment of cold clarity:

> He smiles lazily, and she realizes that the haziness in his eyes

isn't inspiration or creation. He's just high, stupidly so, and Mari takes a deep breath. At moments like this, she tries to remember exactly how she felt that day when she walked into her father's house to see Pierce sitting there. How the same smile that now makes her want to scream used to make her feel like she'd swallowed pure sunlight.[x]

Mari is trauma-bonded to Pierce after the death of their infant son and the whole situation is compounded by her desperately low self-esteem. Though she has fallen out of love, she might've stayed in this dysfunctional partnership if death hadn't forced her hand. After Pierce is murdered, Mari decides to stand on her own two feet by channeling her talent into writing a gothic novel inspired by the trip.

In *All the Dangerous Things*, Isabelle's marriage to Ben falls apart after Mason is kidnapped. Ben has moved on with a new girlfriend and has his own secrets. For the sake of the ongoing investigation, Isabelle has to interact with him, but she now sees a very different side of the man she once loved:

> Now, whenever I see him, I taste something metallic. Like sucking on pennies or licking a fresh wound, tasting blood on my tongue. It's like my body is refusing to let me forget how deeply he hurt me. When he looks at me … I don't melt the way I used to. Instead, I harden.[y]

The breakup itself is painful, but this interiority also shows Isabelle growing cynical and incapable of naïve love after her ordeal.

One of my favorite messed-up marriages in our From the Shelves books is Elizabeth and Jack's relationship in *Wellness*. (Remember, this is the couple whose son, Toby, is struggling with a school transition.) Similar to *Anxious People*, this novel also has an omniscient narrator observing the scene and providing commentary.

The insights delivered as asides during this fight sequence between Jack and Elizabeth convey how familiar they are with one another's "combat" styles, and how seamlessly they fall into these hurtful patterns:

They stare at each other for a moment. It's quiet and they're alone and it's dusty and there might as well be little clumps of tumbleweed bouncing between them for how much this suddenly resembles the marital equivalent of a duel: two sharp-shooters sizing each other up. Like most married couples, they have a mostly unspoken set of ground rules about how to fight —specifically, what it means to fight fair or fight dirty, to fight productively or unproductively. And one of the dirtiest and most unproductive ways to fight is, they know, to fight in gener-alities ... to use a small misdemeanor as cause to shoot large holes in the other's personality or character.

... "Do you know how hard this transition has been for Toby? ... Maybe if you were a little more concerned with your son's well-being, maybe if you were a little more involved in his life, then I wouldn't have to do all this alone."... (As an opening volley, it's a pretty deadly one, aiming immediately at Jack's biggest vulnerability, the fact that he himself grew up with a father who was largely emotionally absent, Elizabeth is now implying that Jack is repeating that painful pattern and, by extension, injuring their son in exactly the way Jack was injured; she is not fucking around.... Like most fights, the subtext here ... is, roughly: *You are inconsiderate and selfish, whereas I am generous and kind.* It's the basic ground from which they both start.)[z]

Readers will likely understand that this argument is emotionally cruel and probably doesn't represent each character's best self. Protagonists and people say things they don't mean as they defend their positions in the heat of the moment. These two seem almost locked into old wounds and ruts.

Interiority Insight: If your POV choices and structure allow it, consider using meta-narration to comment on the action as it's happening, either in protagonist interiority or by hovering above the fray.

Cracks appear even in moments when one of them is trying to make a repair. Elizabeth, specifically, seems to feel repelled when Jack appeals for affection:

> She knows what will happen now. He'll come in for a cautious and careful embrace, and if she agrees to it, he'll eventually draw his lips to hers for a light kiss, and if she agrees to it, the kissing will get stronger, deeper, more insistent, and if she agrees to it, he'll be angling for make-up sex tonight … and if she agrees to it, he'll be planning special date nights by tomorrow, and he'll try to engage her in flirty text messaging all throughout the day, and he'll stop her whenever they cross paths in the apartment for lengthy, tender cuddling even though she has work to do, and it will all be so exhausting, so draining. It's like this with Jack: whenever she rises to meet one of his requests, it only creates more requests. The way she experiences it, inside, is that she's already doing the very best she can to attend to everyone's needs while also feeling herself at the extreme outer limits of her own energy and capability, and still it is never enough. She is never enough. He is never satisfied. He always demands more. Every intimacy she gives comes back greatly magnified, and so she finds herself sort of parceling out the intimacies, meanwhile strategically withdrawing from him in a way that won't trigger his disappointment or panic, and, right now, in this moment, in this dusty room, it no longer seems worth it, the emotional gymnastics required to be married to this man.[aa]

Elizabeth, who has nothing left to give, clearly believes that accepting Jack's romantic gestures is yet another emotional and mental load for her to manage. The interiority also casts this as Jack's fault, but readers might not buy it, as Elizabeth seems burned out and tired of trying. For his part, Jack might be experiencing an overwhelming longing for validation, which she interprets as neediness. Both characters are, in essence, broken in their own ways and trying to ineffectively get their individual needs met. Tragically, those needs are in direct conflict with one another.

Romantic relationships can be full of frustrations and conflict. But they can also offer an opportunity to showcase growth, a flexible mindset, and great self-awareness. To that end, here's Sally from *Romantic Comedy*, who doesn't have much luck in the romance department until she gets into a long-distance flirtation with Noah. This is her interiority as she prepares to see him for the first time in months. She's characteristically funny and self-deprecating as she copes with her nerves:

> [I] wished that being aware of my own ridiculousness could somehow decrease my ridiculousness.

> There was nothing left to do except go see Noah. I regarded myself once more in the gas station mirror and thought, as I hadn't for years, of what my mother had said after I'd repeated Elliot's line about confusing the romance of comedy with the romance of romance. First she'd said, "What a pretentious turd." Then she'd said, "I promise that someday you'll find the love you deserve, but it might not be when or how you're expecting it."[bb]

Her hopes are high, but because she's a comedy writer, she calls them her "ridiculousness." However, Sally's flashback to her mother's words in this moment sneaks in some interiority that suggests she does, indeed, care what happens.

Of course, the visit is an overwhelming success, but there are still small moments of turbulence, like the scene where they discuss past partners. Noah, a famous musician living in Los Angeles, admits to dating some beautiful women. This comparison might flatten even a confident person, but Sally is able to take a level-headed approach:

> That I didn't feel completely uninsulted by his admission that I wasn't the most gorgeous woman he'd ever seen meant—what? That I'd nursed some private hope that he thought I was? Either because he had unusual taste or because I'd been holding on to the belief that, as with many a romantic comedy heroine, I was far more beautiful than I realized? At the same time, I didn't feel the impulse to cling to the insult as I might have when I was younger; I appreciated his candor.[cc]

There's a self-referential dig here at the genre of romantic comedy, which extends to this novel's title and suggests the book is being positioned as a category crossover. Sally has waited a long time for this love and is able to enter into it with a low-key confidence that's, honestly, refreshing.

Crossover: There's no hard and fast definition for a crossover book, but this is publishing and marketing speak for a project that transcends its original audience expectations to reach a wider population. An example is *The Book Thief* by Markus Zusak, which was published for both middle grade and adult audiences. Sometimes a separate edition will be issued for each readership, sometimes not. *Romantic Comedy* is technically a romantic comedy, but it upends some typical genre expectations and has more in common with upmarket or women's fiction. This novel strikes a delicate balance and its crossover status can also be attributed, in part, to the author's broad existing fanbase. It's important to note that a crossover book is usually orchestrated because of a publisher's editorial and marketing push, rather than happening organically, or because a writer pitches a project with this desire in mind.

Next, we'll see a surprising example of self-worth and maturity from Elliot in the adult romance *Forget Me Not* by Julie Soto. In a fresh gender reversal of classic dynamics, this male love interest wants to settle down with skittish Ama. Meanwhile, she's busy swearing up and down that she can't deal with commitment:

> I'm going to ask her if we can redefine the rules. She may not believe in relationships, but that's what we're in. She may not care to introduce me as her boyfriend … but to me, forever sounds nice.
>
> If she doesn't want to adjust the rules, I'll be fine with it, I guess. But I need her to know I already think of us as long-term … even if she doesn't want to name it.[dd]

Another male romantic lead who stands by his own self-worth and value system is Josiah from *Before I Let Go*. He becomes pretty seriously involved with his restaurant colleague, Vashti, but realizes he still has deep feelings for his ex-wife, Yasmen. Here's how he nips the potential new relationship in the bud before it can get more serious, and the interiority surrounding his decision:

> "If I waited until I don't have feelings for Yasmen before I
> moved on," I tell Vashti as gently as I can, "I never would." …
> There it is. As much as I don't want it to be the case, getting over
> Yasmen is not a thing I may ever be able to do. That doesn't
> mean I can trust her or even be with her again. I'm not sure I can
> do either of those things, but I can't root these emotions out of
> my heart. They're woven into the fiber of who I am. It's an
> emotional impasse I need to resolve for myself, and until I have,
> I can't involve anyone else.[ee]

Interiority Insight: When a character makes an honest moral decision, reader engagement and admiration goes through the roof.

Romantic relationships are the stage upon which we play out our best and worst moments and display our best and worst qualities. For all of its agony and ecstasy, the foundational human experience of loving and being loved is often central to characters, relationships, and plots. I'll let Isabel from *The Nightingale* remind us all of love's power, especially as it can be leveraged to add meaning to your storytelling:

> How fragile life was, how fragile they were. Love. It was the
> beginning and end of everything, the foundation and the ceiling
> and the air in between. It didn't matter that she was broken and
> ugly and sick. He loved her and she loved him. All her life she
> had waited—longed for—people to love her, but now she saw
> what really mattered. She had known love, been blessed by it.[ff]

Now that we have our protagonist and cast of secondary characters fleshed out and arranged into various roles and relationships, we need to configure the rest of the story. This means introducing information reveals and engineering character reactions which convey how story developments affect your protagonist's sense of self. That's what we'll talk about in the next two chapters as we continue to weave character and plot together.

14

INFORMATION REVEALS

As protagonists begin to interface with the structure, they learn information, react to events, make decisions, and otherwise move through the larger story. How you deploy data affects plot, character, relationships, and how protagonists advance their objectives, needs, and arcs. Before we dive into this chapter on information, I'll offer a cautionary tale about starving your storytelling.

Withholding Information

If you think about it, all stories are crafted from a sequence of data reveals. How you parcel out information depends on the kind of book you're writing. Does your intended project benefit from a slow build to a climactic twist? There are upsides and downsides to this approach. As I mentioned in Chapter 5, you don't want to reserve all of your character development for the final 10% of the story.

If readers are offered too few details to make them engaged throughout the plot, they might not stick around until the very end. Intrigue doesn't develop from the total absence of information, after all. It's created by withholding crucial details. Mysteries and thrillers often present an abundance of clues and red herrings, but it's not until a single new angle or data point is introduced late in the story that everything snaps into place or rearranges into a surprising config-uration.

Red Herring: A misleading piece of information or a misdirect for the audience to follow which distracts from a true clue or suspect.

Even if you're not writing in the mystery, thriller, or suspense genres, you have to decide how much information to present, when, and where. Many aspiring writers like to withhold all the "good stuff" for later, mistakenly thinking that readers will be so tantalized by their own curiosity that they'll keep going indefinitely. Here's the best quote I've found to, I hope, disabuse you of this notion:

"One of the few things I know about writing is this: spend it all, shoot it, play it, lose it, all, right away, every time. Do not hoard what seems good for a later place in the book, or for another book; give it, give it all, give it now. The impulse to save something good for a better place later is the signal to spend it now. Something more will arise for later, something better. These things fill from behind, from beneath, like well water. Similarly, the impulse to keep to yourself what you have learned is not only shameful, it is destructive. Anything you do not give freely and abundantly becomes lost to you. You open your safe and find ashes."[a]

ANNIE DILLARD

In stories where a character has no data after a well-meaning writer decides to stir up some mystery, the protagonist becomes powerless and stymied at every turn, which makes them passive. I'd much rather you reveal plot- and character-relevant information to protagonists and readers at regular intervals. Even if you're planning a mind-blowing twist for the climax, don't wait to flesh out other context. Readers require information to form their interpretations and extrapolations, which is why a reveal is much more powerful once a lot of data has already been established.

If you're working in a genre that hinges on shocking twists, consider this: Instead of presenting 20% and withholding 80%, reverse those figures and hold back only the most incendiary 20%. You might also want to think about using foreshadowing.

Foreshadowing: An image or other subtle hint of a story, character, or plot element that will be important later. This can be used earnestly or to mislead. Foreshadowing is a great way to seed information and bait curiosity hooks for readers. Consider using this tool as you're giving your characters things to think about and react to, regardless of genre.

One exception to this advice is the strategic withholding or teasing that you might want to use at the end of a section or chapter. When a scene concludes, readers might be tempted to put in a bookmark and go to bed. Keep their interest piqued with a reveal, curiosity hook, or character reaction that emphasizes high stakes (much more on this in Chapter 17) to entice audiences past a section or chapter break and over that yawning white space.

You obviously don't want to button every moment on a cliffhanger unless you're writing high-octane thriller or a climactic sequence. Any effect, if overused, quickly wears off.[1] As long as you don't overdo it, strategic withholding is one powerful way to shape reader experience with information and character reaction.

Directing Reader Attention With Information

Your decision to present audiences and characters with information

---

1. The Law of Diminishing Returns is an economic concept, but I apply it to creative writing to express that any technique used too frequently will lose its ability to grip readers. If you take your level of action and danger up to 10 out of 10, readers will soon become numb to this kind of excitement. You'll have to either raise it to an 11 the next time or give audiences a break. Another 10 out of 10 scene right after is going to feel like a 7 or 8. This is why the biggest, most dire action usually comes toward the end of a story. Characters have already run through all of your possible lower-stakes conflicts, including the Act II crisis that comes before the climax. Now they're ready to summit Everest. Everything else will be a molehill by comparison.

throughout your story can be a powerful way to manipulate[2] reader experience, which should be one of your primary goals. For now, let's return to the idea of balancing action and information. As you write, you'll also need data points and fresh revelations because your character requires inputs to react to, interpret, and consider as they make decisions.

If a protagonist has no information to work with, they might be at risk of solving problems or making choices by simply "knowing," which completely alienates the reader. Intuition, insight, and divergent thinking are largely unconscious reactions to stimuli and don't demand any interpretation or extrapolation. Whenever a character realizes something that you can't or don't convey via interiority, readers won't be able to participate in your protagonist's experience. The character's reactions and decisions to act on whatever it is they "know" also risks seeming contrived, especially if their magical knowing-out-of-nowhere leads to the correct guess or course of action. This can feel cheap and easy.

A word of caution here about body language, too. Some writers really try to put a lot of information into a glance or tilt of the head. The protagonist then interprets this through interiority, and arrives at an oddly specific (and, usually, correct) conclusion. That's asking a lot of a gesture or tone of voice, per our discussion of the theatre from Chapter 7. It's also similarly disengaging to readers, just like a character deciding something out of the blue or simply knowing the solution to a problem. Let audiences into this process instead.

As we've seen throughout this guide, especially in the previous chapters on secondary characters and relationships, protagonists are always using interiority to assess and analyze the world around them through their biased points of view. Writing great, proactive character reactions, which in turn lead to decisions—or readers to an intended impression —is a hugely important skill. Information is at the heart of this action and reaction process. Let's see how data can be deployed in the service of story.

---

2. I mean this term positively, even though it often has negative connotations. In this case, you will want to intentionally shape what audiences are going through as a means of keeping them invested in the story.

Reveals and Interiority

Narratives are woven together from information, but not every reveal is created equal. If you still want to give your characters some intuition-based realizations without resorting to magical "knowing," as discussed in the previous section, you can leverage physical sensations and figurative language, which we'll cover in Chapter 19.

Let's start with a few examples of how you might pull this effect off in an engaging way while introducing data. For example, here's how Bronca reacts to some bad antagonist vibes in *The City We Became*:

> A ripple of unease prickles over her skin. Unease and … recognition? If something so atavistic can be called that. When a mouse that has never before seen a cat spots one for the first time, it knows to run because of instinct. Something in the bone knows its enemy.[b]

The instinctual prickle and the cat/mouse image support Bronca's interiority realization that the character she's encountered is an enemy, not a friend.

You can see something similar from Eden in *The Way I Used to Be*, when she senses Kevin, her rapist, in her house months after the assault:

> I hear footsteps creep up behind me. It's Kevin—it's like my body knows before my brain does, my senses heightened, my skin suddenly hot and itchy. Like I'm allergic to him. The proximity of his body to mine causing an actual physical repulsion, like a warning sign, flashing neon lights: DANGER DANGER DANGER. Get away from him, my body tells me. But it's hard to get away from someone like him.[c]

Another kind of reaction, common in certain types of fantasy and science fiction stories, conveys how a protagonist feels when they use magic. The following two excerpts demonstrate a balance of action and information as we get a character's interiority experience of their powers and how this add world-building context. These kinds of passages go a long way toward establishing magical rules and logic, as well, which we'll talk about in Chapter 18.

In the introduction to adult fantasy novel *Jade City* by Fonda Lee, we meet Bero, a hapless street kid who manages to get his hands on jade, which lends its users incredible power. Only members of several notable families are generally chosen to wield it, so Bero's stolen jade is about to get him into massive trouble. Notice how we learn about the importance of jade and the concept of Lightness through action instead of outright telling:

> A sudden surge of heat and energy unlike anything he had ever felt before ripped through him like an electric current.... Bero rushed up the stairs, clearing the entire expanse in a few bounds, his feet barely touching the floor. A gasp ran through the crowd. Bero's surprise burst into ecstasy. He threw his head back to laugh. This must be Lightness.
>
> A film had been lifted from his eyes and ears ... everything was razor sharp. Someone reached out to grab him, but he was so slow, and Bero was so fast.... Without thinking, without pausing, he crashed through the barrier like a charging bull ... with a mad shout of exultation. He felt no pain at all, only a wild, fierce invincibility.
>
> This was the power of jade.[d]

Think back to our discussion of story openings in Chapter 4. This excerpt appears fewer than ten pages into the novel. It's an electrifying introduction to this world, which helps the necessary data about jade powers weave in smoothly.

A similar reaction happens in *Red Queen* when Mare realizes she somehow possesses potent Silver magic, which is unheard of for a Red. Because of her power, she suddenly becomes valuable and dangerous. Here, she lets loose for the first time while working with her new trainer, Julian, before she even realizes what she's capable of:

> *Let go. Let yourself go*, the voice in my head whispers. My eyes

slide closed as I focus, letting my thoughts fall away so that my mind can reach out, feeling for the electricity it craves to touch. The ripple of energy, alive beneath my skin, moves over me again until it sings in every muscle and nerve. That's usually where it stops, just on the edge of feeling, but not this time. Instead of trying to hold on, to push myself into this force, I let go. And I fall into what I can't explain, into a sensation that is everything and nothing, light and dark, hot and cold, alive and dead. Soon the power is the only thing in my head, blotting out all my ghosts and memories. Even Julian and the books cease to exist. My mind is clear, a black void humming with force. Now when I push at the sensation, it doesn't disappear and it moves within me, from my eyes to the tips of my fingers. To my left, Julian gasps aloud.[e]

The incredible elation of accessing this level of power immediately turns to fear because Mare has also exposed herself as unnatural and unusual. The interiority reflects her reaction as she pivots from thrilling at the power to being terrified of it. She doesn't know if she can trust Julian, either, so losing control in front of him makes her vulnerable.

Hannah from *The It Girl* ends up testifying against an innocent man after April, her college roommate, is murdered. Here's how she got to that point in the historical timeline, and how her impression of John Neville, the dorm's security officer, influenced her actions:

She knew she was being slightly ridiculous, but at the same time, there was just something about the thought of him lying in wait, maybe even coming out to ambush her, that set her skin crawling with a mix of fear and revulsion.[f]

What's notable here is how much Hannah *doesn't* know. The gaps in her knowledge are much more telling than the facts themselves. She has a visceral reaction to John and imagines him "lying in wait," but that doesn't automatically mean he's a murderer. In the present timeline, Hannah has to live with the guilt of knowing he went to prison and died there, especially after she figures out that one of her close college friends was responsible for the murder instead.

Information about the past comes into the present in various ways. Backstory and flashback might feature more heavily in the first quarter or third of a story's structure, but some narratives keep teasing past information throughout the narrative, such as the repeated curiosity hooks foreshadowing Eleanor's wound in *Eleanor Oliphant Is Completely Fine*. After she meets her new friend Raymond's family, she reflects on how weird it is that he seems to forget he has a sibling:

> This was puzzling. How on earth could you forget that you had a sister? He hadn't forgotten, I supposed—he'd simply taken his sibling for granted: an unchanging, unremarkable fact of life, not even worthy of mention.[g]

It's not until much later in the story that readers finally learn Eleanor had a younger sister. Alas, she died in a house fire which Mummy deliberately set to try and kill both of her daughters. Once readers reach the end of the story and realize that Eleanor has been willfully suppressing the fact of her *own* sibling, they can go back to this moment of foreshadowing and appreciate the irony.[3]

Here are a few more instances of foreshadowing from *The Fair Folk*. There's a hint of it as Felicity makes this assertion, which you'll recognize from Chapter 7:

> So if I told the truth when they asked me what I wanted to do when I grew up ... it would have been this:
>
> "I don't want to grow up. Ever."[h]

It's not until much later that Felicity realizes the fairies are mostly children who have been enchanted, and their moral code—if it can be called that—is immature and cruel. In other words, the fairies never grew up themselves, which was artfully hinted early on. (We'll see this realization in Chapter 18.) Later, Felicity wonders what she can do to finally break her alliance with Them:

3. As it turns out, Mummy died in the fire, too. This book uses several masterful strokes of foreshadowing because Eleanor Oliphant calls herself a "sole survivor" on page 8 of the novel. It's all right there for audiences who are paying close attention!

What will [Elfrida] ask for? I've read the stories. The power of speech? My eyesight? My firstborn child?[i]

This interiority is revealed to be ironic, in hindsight, when Felicity learns that her entanglement with the fae was fated when her father promised them his firstborn—her—in exchange for acceptance. Sound familiar? Like father, like daughter.

August from *One Last Stop* invokes an offhand image via interiority which actually ends up foreshadowing the solution to setting Jane free from her subway time loop. August eventually realizes that she'll need to orchestrate a power surge, but for eagle-eyed readers or fans doing a reread, this was seeded 200 pages before:

Maybe she's imagining it—maybe it's the fear, the uncertainty, the atmosphere creeping under her skin—but she swears she feels it.... A charge in the air, like someone's dropped a toaster in a bathtub down the block, a surge of power just before the lights go out.[j]

Interiority Insight: Imagery is useful for hinting at information and subtly directing attention. It also adds voice and emotion, which we'll discuss in Chapter 19.

In *Ripe*, before Cassie gets pregnant herself, she deals with some TMI oversharing from her demanding boss, Sasha, who seems to have it all together. Under the surface, though, she's stressed because she's having fertility issues and the treatments aren't working. After this unexpected moment of forced closeness, Cassie considers the encounter:

I picture Sasha's insides, the pink of her womb, the eggs in her ovaries shriveling, already rotten.[k]

While Sasha struggles, it's Cassie who ends up terminating a pregnancy by the end of the novel.

A brilliant bit of foreshadowing, hidden in an amazing characterizing detail, can be found in reference to Vincent in *The Glass Hotel*. As she adapts to her trophy girlfriend lifestyle, she spends her time staying fit, but with an unusual mindset:

> Her relationship with the pool was adversarial. Vincent swam
> every night to strengthen her will because she was desperately
> afraid of drowning.[1]

What a strange notion to relay in interiority. Well, after Jonathan heads to prison and the Kingdom of Money collapses, Vincent decides to live and work on a ship. During a storm, she's accidentally swept overboard and dies. This isn't a shock to readers, though, because the novel begins with a prologue that flashes into the future and shows audiences the moment Vincent plummets into the sea.

In fact, certain genres and structures represent other opportunities to play with information, and a writer's intentional manipulation of data becomes very important to consider.

Mystery, Thriller, and Suspense Reveals

Information can absolutely be used to lead, as it does in the majority of the interiority excerpts throughout this guide. But data can also be used to mislead. Most mystery, thriller, and suspense writers spend copious time and energy crafting red herrings to consciously direct reader attention toward or away from certain characters and details. The interiority used in these genres must not only express a protagonist's perspective, but shape the reader's impression of events and, most importantly, other characters (including false and true suspects). By having various POV protagonists evaluate one another and the action, you can plant curiosity hooks, steer audiences to or away from the antagonist(s), and signal which information matters.

Think about who seems guilty in the following excerpts, and why. Don't be surprised if your impressions are swayed by the biased evaluations offered by the point-of-view characters.

In *The Villa*, our present-day writer protagonist, Emily, used to marvel at how well her (now) ex-husband, Matt, and her best friend, Chess, a successful self-help guru, seemed to get along. Though Emily initially takes a sunny view of the situation, she later realizes its inherent danger:

> It had actually been surprising how quickly Matt and Chess had become friends. A good kind of surprising, like it was something I hadn't even known I could hope for. It was nice seeing two people who were so important to me take an interest in each other. It made me feel ... I don't know, special I guess.... [They] were alike at a molecular level, too. Both ambitious, driven. Sometimes more than a little self-centered. And like Chess, Matt moved through the world like everything was going to fall into place for him—and maybe because of that, it did. Thing is, while that's a great trait in someone you love and who loves you, it's pretty fucking terrifying in someone who is now pitted against you.[m]

Matt, of course, is "pitted against" her in the divorce and trying to take half of her publishing empire. But Chess is also emerging as a problematic, shapeshifting character. While they vacation in an Italian villa where Pierce's murder took place in the historical timeline, Emily becomes paranoid that Chess is going to steal her next book idea.

Later, Chess not only admits that she went behind Emily's back and hooked up with Matt, but she summons him to Italy. Is Chess now "pitted against" Emily? When Matt ends up dead in the pool, readers realize the full implication of this strange threesome, and that Emily and Chess are now bound together by something bigger than friendship or marriage: murder.

The following books have large ensemble casts and multiple points of view, so we'll hear interiority from more than one character in each instance. The interpretations and assumptions made by the various protagonists in *The New House* do a good job of directing and misdirecting audience expectations and impressions. In this excerpt, notice what Tom's trying to make readers think or feel about his wife, Millie:

> My wife is a mass of contradictions. She's cool and forensic;
> she's passionate and hot-tempered. She can be chillingly

335

detached when she assesses our children's flaws, but she wouldn't think twice about killing to protect them. She has absolutely no self-doubt when it comes to her work, but she's so afraid of being hurt she's never learned to make friends. And she'd rather believe herself a sociopath incapable of human connection than admit that particular truth.[n]

While he nails Millie's vulnerabilities, which readers can check against their own interpretations, notice how confident he seems in his own analysis. There's an attempt at some misdirection with "wouldn't think twice about killing." She *is* a surgeon, after all, and knows her way around knives and human bodies. Readers already know that she killed her abusive father. Even her own husband seems unable to fully trust her.

Millie, for her part, seems to sway suspicion to her son, which is surprising, given what Tom has shared about her loyalty:

Peter bounces up the stairs, a shit-eating grin on his face. He's still on an adrenaline high, too buzzed to give a damn about the trouble he's in ... when most children do something that makes their parents sad or angry, they observe that reaction and feel bad about it: it's how they learn to feel guilt. But Peter has zero regard for the feelings of others and is therefore unable to internalise social emotions like shame.

The only thing he'll learn from this is that he can get away with it.[o]

After reading Millie's character evaluation of Peter, a reader might be tempted to think he's the main antagonist. (Peter *does* end up involved, but only as Stacey's accomplice.)

What a difficult situation all around, especially to be a mother seeing these qualities in her own child. Millie also works to plant doubt about Harper, an influencer who's angling to buy her existing house if she succeeds in her bid for Stacey's. Harper is trying to win Tom over behind Millie's back, so they're already in a tension triangle. Here's how Millie evaluates this other woman:

I already regret getting into bed with her on this. The disconnect between her vlog persona and the woman waiting for me in the dark in the car park is disturbing.... Harper's emotions are too close to the surface. She's brittle and impulsive and unpredictable, and that makes her dangerous.[p]

Are you confused yet? Is Harper the villain, or is Millie? Or is it Peter, the creepy child? Could it be Tom, who seems to be watching everyone so carefully?

Our last juicy thriller pairing comes from *Everyone Here Is Lying,* another ensemble-cast multiple-POV novel. First, let's hear from Nora, who's sleeping with William, the married father of the missing girl. He's framed as the prime suspect for large swaths of the novel, for reasons we'll see in Chapter 16. Though Nora calls off the affair before Avery disappears, she's still on edge. If her involvement with William is uncovered, that information could be used to fabricate a motive that implicates her. Here, Nora wonders whether her own husband, Al, knows:

As [Al] looks at her, there's something different in her husband's eye, a gleam of something, something nasty she doesn't like.... Where is it coming from? Her heart suddenly seizes—*Does he know? About her and William? Is he enjoying her suffering?* Maybe he's not as oblivious as she assumed. Had he followed her, seen them together at the motel? She feels the tension, suddenly thick in the room.[q]

What *does* Al know, if anything? Is Nora allowing her sense of guilt and shame to tinge her interpretation? As it happens, we get to hear Al's perception of Nora in a very similar scene about fifteen pages later:

He glances at his wife. She's staring at the television, rigid, her face washed out in the pale light. He almost feels sorry for her. It must be hard, he thinks, realizing you've been sleeping with a murderer. That you're in love with a monster.[r]

Al not only knows, but he's convinced that William is guilty, which makes him see Nora as morally bankrupt. He has lost all respect for her

—"He almost feels sorry for her"—and readers might even suspect, as a red herring, that Al has taken revenge on William's family and killed Avery himself.

Interiority Insight: Character relationships are always complicated, but interpersonal tension is often compounded by interpretations, assumptions, projections, and even an author's efforts to sway the reader's reactions to all of the above.

Of course, novels and memoirs are full of scenes, exchanges, and information reveals, but notice how small interpretations and extrapolations attempt to steer the audience. It's up to you to use character reactions, especially biased ones delivered via interiority, to lead and mislead readers, whether or not your story hinges on a suspense, thriller, or mystery mechanic.

Now that we're planning what to disclose, when, and where, you need to consider how this important information will not only be given, but received. This is where interiority and character reaction come to the forefront.

15
_____

CHARACTER REACTIONS

You have an entire arsenal at your disposal for creating meaning with interiority. How your protagonist interfaces with your plot will, in turn, help readers make meaning from your story. The importance of character reactions cannot be overstated. Whether the input is big or small, you can generate energy around any stimulus. First, you must decide what matters. Then let characters clock this, too. Finally, you can use interiority to show when and how your protagonist reacts to action and information. This is key to enhancing the protagonist-story connection.

A character's reaction to events is the foundation for developing stakes and tension while also juicing as much conflict and emotion as possible from the plot. Nuanced reactions at important moments make the story resonate at a higher frequency and help readers track the cause-and-effect logic of any identity evolution your protagonist might experience. Readers become more engaged in the choices you've made and you stand to get the most out of the irresistible character you've created.

When you put a POV protagonist into action, your job is to show them reflecting on their scene partners, interpreting situations, making assumptions, and extracting meaning from events. This is interiority in a nutshell. Protagonists can then use their insights—whether correct or not—to make progress in the plot and within relationships. Reactions should happen in every scene, but sometimes, you'll want to dig deeply into especially consequential ones, which I call turning points.

Turning Point: The ultimate intersections of character, arc, plot, and relationship. Turning points include the major tentpole moments that we first codified in Chapter 4, but can also refer to scenes where characters address wounds, shift worldviews, abandon superficial objectives, change relationship dynamics, or experience revelations. Compelling turning points can also trigger sublimation and growth. A protagonist's interiority—thoughts, feelings, reactions, expectations, and inner struggles—at important junctures can absolutely make these moments land on both characters and readers with maximum emotional impact.

Your goal is to craft a story that maintains momentum throughout by making and manipulating meaning. When readers see protagonists faced with obstacles and reacting according to where they are in their growth arcs, audiences become and stay invested. Without further ado, let's go right to our excerpts and show the variety of character reactions you can play with.

Rendering Reactions in Interiority

First, let's revisit Snow, from *The Fox Wife*. Remember her desire to avenge her daughter? Well, she finally tracks her nemesis down, only to get overeager and show her hand. He freaks out and the opportunity vanishes. This is her heartbreaking reaction:

> The moment had vanished. My moment, which I'd planned and agonized over. Which I'd waited two years for. I'd told myself I was prepared, but in the end, I'd missed it. I felt like drowning in silent, numb misery.[a]

This is a devastating blow, especially since Snow has thus far prided herself on playing the long game, making deliberate choices, being crafty, and acting with complete self-control. She's embodied the qualities of a fox spirit, yet has now bungled her objective. As a result, she must decide how to proceed, which completely changes both the plot and her character trajectory.

Let's now look at a pivotal moment from *The Fair Folk*. Felicity previously gave the fairies access to her house and extended family. As a result, They identified her baby cousin, Christine, as a kidnapping target. Of course, when fairies take a baby, they usually leave a changeling in its place, glamoured to fool the humans who must now raise it. This is exactly what They do to Christine, and here's Felicity's reaction when she realizes it:

> I don't quite know how to describe what happened next. She *flickered*, the way films do at the cinema when the projectionist gets the speed wrong. There was my little cousin, pink-cheeked and laughing, holding up her sticky hands to show me. And somehow, at the same time, there was that other thing, its eyes gleaming with a kind of dull cunning.[b]

The problem—other than having a creepy changeling for a cousin—is that Felicity feels guilty for making Christine vulnerable to the fairies in the first place. Worse, she also needs to decide whether her allegiance is to Them, or if she's going to rescue Christine and return the changeling to the woods. (We'll track how she comes to this decision in the following chapter.) The fairies might never forgive her. This small reaction shoots the story stakes higher.

Americanah gets off to a rough start for new immigrant Ifemelu, who is broke and answers an ad for sex work. She suspects this is the nature of the job but goes through with it anyway. Afterward, she plunges into a downward emotional spiral:

> She woke up torpid each morning, slowed by sadness, frightened by the endless stretch of day that lay ahead. Everything had thickened. She was swallowed, lost in a viscous haze, shrouded in a soup of nothingness. Between her and what she should feel, there was a gap. She cared about nothing. She wanted to care, but she no longer knew how; it had slipped from her memory, the ability to care.... She knew there was no point

in being here, in being alive, but she had no energy to think concretely of how she could kill herself.[c]

While the desire to die by suicide is there—since she seems to believe death might feel less painful than grieving her dignity—she wavers and can't commit. Ifemelu eventually falls in love with a fellow Nigerian, Obinze, but sabotages that relationship, as she has so many others, by ghosting him.

Obinze doesn't think fondly of her as a result, especially when his life hits its own rough patch. Years later, he illegally immigrates to England and finds work as a janitor. When Ifemelu emails him out of the blue, acting as if they'd never fallen out, he's understandably upset:

> And now here was her e-mail. Her tone the same, as though she had not wounded him, left him bleeding for more than five years. Why was she writing him now? What was there to tell her, that he cleaned toilets and had only just today encountered a curled turd? How did she know he was still alive? He could have died during their silence and she would not have known. An angry sense of betrayal overwhelmed him. He clicked Delete and Empty Trash.[d]

Yes, Ifemelu betrayed him and can be a problematic partner in general, as we saw in Chapter 13. But Obinze's emotional and stubborn reaction reveals he might still have feelings for her, despite everything. Otherwise, he'd be calmer about ignoring her email. He could even read it and respond to the update. Here, readers are invited to extrapolate between the lines of the interiority.

But reactions don't always have to be negative, or to anchor characters in disastrous or consequential moments. They can also underscore exciting or intriguing developments, like this one, from *Romantic Comedy*, as Sally realizes Noah might actually be flirting with her:

> As he continued singing, we continued making intermittent eye contact that turned into sustained eye contact. Was he mocking me? ... Or was he, like, *serenading* me? In the most literal sense,

he was definitely serenading me—he was standing on a stage with a guitar, and I was a few feet away, and he was singing—but what did it mean? Perhaps, as was often the case with human interactions, it meant nothing. Yet instead of the jolt induced by our first eye contact dissipating, some feedback loop was occurring in me, a thrumming awareness of my own physical body.[e]

There's some great humor here, as Sally clarifies that "in the most literal sense, he was definitely serenading me" but suggests she was hoping for the romantic connotation of the word. Later, when she goes to Los Angeles to visit him and they consummate their long-distance flirtation, this reaction captures her soaring happiness (you'll recognize part of it from Chapter 3):

It felt like a relief … like something I'd been waiting for my whole life. And it felt like an astonishing miracle. If this was all I ever got, it would be the best thing that had ever happened to me, and if this was all I ever got, I'd never stop wanting more of it.[f]

Interiority Insight: The tone and voice used to convey a reaction help to underscore the moment's emotional impact on both character and story.

A reaction's timing is also important. In *The Spirit Glass*, Corazon reaches her objective only to experience her dark night of the soul, think back over her adventure in the spirit realm, and tally the toll of what she's been through:

How did she feel? Corazon cast her mind over the past few days. . . Tina had told her that once Flordeliza was laid to rest, Corazon's powers would awaken. She would be able to bring her parents back. Was that why her mom and dad were here now? Were they here for a little bit? Or forever? For some reason, Corazon's heart felt heavier than she'd thought it would when the quest was completed. Corazon was so close to having everything she wanted.[g]

She stands on the brink of apparent triumph, yet there's a bittersweet tone to this interiority, compared to what readers might expect. She still has questions, and it's almost like she's hanging back, uncertain, instead of plunging ahead toward the climax. This is a paradoxical reaction, and Corazon's unexpected shift invites readers to pause and see her perspective in interiority.

Notice how many of these reactions introduce thoughts, feelings, additional context, critical thinking about the situation, and even denial or vacillation. Next, let's dive into some deeper-level reactions and explore how they become subsumed into a character's sense of self.

Character Reactions and Making Meaning

A proactive protagonist's identity is demonstrated externally through action—toward objective, need, relationship progress, and personal growth. But characters can also be defined in moments of reaction, as long as they don't spend the entire plot passively ruminating, of course. Let's see some significant reactions in interiority and dissect how they inform their respective protagonists' senses of self.

I'll start with a pretty morally bankrupt reaction from Leonie in *Sing, Unburied, Sing*. She demonstrates her priorities when she hears about an oil spill at the derrick where Michael works. Though the accident involves environmental damage and significant loss of life, her first impulse is unapologetically selfish:

> I'd spent the days after the accident with Jojo in the house watching CNN, watching the oil gush into the ocean, and feeling guilty because that's not what I wanted to see, guilty because I didn't give a shit about those fucking pelicans, guilty because I just wanted to see Michael's face ... guilty because all I cared about was him. He'd called me not long after the story broke on the news, told me he was safe, but his voice was tiny, corroded by static, unreal. *I knew those men—all eleven of them.*

Lived with them, he said. When he came home, I was happy. He wasn't.[h]

Sometimes a character's reaction is telling, and other times, it's their reaction *to* their reaction that reveals a deeper level of nuance. (Remember Montserrat's resentment over her stubborn crush on Tristàn in Chapter 13?) Here, Leonie feels "guilty because all she cared about was him," but not guilty enough to change her position. She's so consistent in her bad decisions and misplaced loyalties that it's almost impressive. Her saving grace, to some readers, might be her transparency. This keeps her from tipping into full-on villain territory.

As we climb the self-awareness ladder, we find Bronca from *The City We Became*, who's growing in her sense of self and worth, though this process is slow going at times. When she acts rude to Brooklyn, she wonders why and comes up with an interesting insight:

Bronca feels herself getting heated … she's old enough to know that she's only sniping at Brooklyn because this is something she can control, unlike the rest of their whole awful situation. But even knowing all this … well, Bronca's never going to be a very good wise elder, if she even makes it that far.[i]

It must be terrifying to be tasked with saving New York City from a primordial antagonist. Bronca feels completely out of control, so she attempts to be the master of her domain in any way possible, even if she's not exactly nice about it. The dopamine hit she gets from bullying Brooklyn might help her feel momentarily powerful, but she knows it won't last. Like Leonie, she's honest about her uncharitable thoughts and actions, but unlike Leonie, Bronca seems motivated to do better.

Sometimes characters and people turn their reactions into arrows that point outward—like Leonie glossing over the oil spill deaths, and Bronca railing at Brooklyn—and sometimes they turn their reactions inward.

We've already read about Cassie's sad slide into disappointment in *Ripe*. For how heavy this novel is, I really enjoyed the compelling writing and nuanced character development. While nobody's going to call it an inspiring or hopeful take on contemporary culture, it does

345

manage to create a lot of audience empathy and relatability. For example, here's Cassie's reaction to a romantic picnic with the chef, even if she's not sure what to think about the oysters:

> He squirts a slice of lemon onto the gray sludge in the shell, then spoons red sauce on it. He lifts the shell to my mouth. The gesture is so romantic that I almost rear my head back. The scene feels too much like a movie, too much like a life that isn't mine.... The flavor is a wave of brine and seafoam paired with the sensation of swallowing a second tongue.... I'm not sure if I like it, the oyster, but ... I smile for him now.[j]

This subsumation reveals Cassie's sense of self. The moment feels *too nice*, so she rejects it, because it's "too much like a movie, too much like a life that isn't mine." This reminds me of Eleanor Oliphant's belief that she doesn't get to be happy, as seen in Chapter 10. Why doesn't Cassie deserve nice things? That's a question readers might ask, or maybe they'll recognize their own self-defeating thought patterns in this glimpse beneath what could have been a lovely evening.[1]

Sona is good at keeping her emotions bottled up, as we've seen in several other excerpts from *Gearbreakers*. Here, a small moment presents her with the choice to either display emotion or shove it down. Sona's reaction shows readers where she is in her growth arc:

> I want to cry, and just never stop crying. I want to choke on my cake. I have the strange, violent urge to swallow my fork, to feel the metal catch awkwardly in my throat, prongs snagging raw, pillowy flesh.... I do not cry. I cradle the heat behind my eyes until it dissipates.[k]

At least Sona makes breathing room for some of her feelings, even if she's not yet comfortable enough with vulnerability to express them outwardly. Most readers know what it feels like to hold back tears, so this moment is relatable.

---

1. If we're able to look past Cassie's immoral choice to be involved with a committed man.

Rachel from *Milk Fed* is a similar personality type. When she goes to therapy and is startled to learn that she has mommy issues,[2] she turns her back on the whole messy business of self-inquiry altogether:

> I was crying. I felt angry, tricked. This was supposed to be closure, not some psychological art show. I stormed out of the office without even paying my copay.... "Fuck insight," I said.[1]

This is an example of vacillation in action. How many of us—upon first realizing the incredible work involved in reaching our lofty goals—haven't been tempted to run in the opposite direction, back to stasis and "safety"?

Interiority Insight: Of course, once a realization strikes, it can't be snuffed out easily. This new pressure only adds to the character's internal tension and pushes them along their growth arc.

Similar doubt hits Isabelle in *All the Dangerous Things* after she engages Waylon, a podcaster, to help her tell her story on her terms, as we first saw in Chapter 7. Isabelle has performed her spiel many times, yet she's unhappy with how she's vilified by public opinion. Surprisingly, as she sits down to claim her objective, she seems to change her mind and regret putting herself out there again:

> I realize now that no matter how many times I've done this, no matter how many times I've told my story, this time, it's different. This isn't detached, standing on a stage somewhere and reciting the same thing over and over again to strangers at a distance. This time, it's personal. I have no idea what questions he might ask. I have no way to escape.[m]

Isabelle got what she wanted, but her in-the-moment reaction generates some unexpected internal tension, which adds to her depth as a

---

2. Even this early in the novel, readers will wonder how she could possibly be surprised.

character. Alas, Waylon *does* indeed have his own reasons for giving her airtime, so she's not exactly being paranoid when she second-guesses his intentions. Her worldview is a cynical one, given all that's happened, but in this case, her intuition proves correct. Since readers don't yet know Waylon's backstory, they're tasked with deciding whether Isabelle is being unreasonable or if Waylon is, in fact, untrustworthy.

Interiority Insight: An expected reaction is just that … expected. It doesn't give readers much bang for their buck. An unexpected reaction, on the other hand, is very engaging to audiences, inviting them to guess what's really going on beneath the surface.

Reactions can happen in big moments or small. A tiny but engaging paradoxical reaction appears as Joey, from *Tell Me I'm an Artist*, catches herself having a good time at a party. This is the same character who walks around holding two beer bottles so people think she's cool in an excerpt from Chapter 7. Now she's with friends but it's not turning out as she'd hoped:

> I had to excuse myself so I could quietly rage about my wildly lopsided expectations of reality in my bathroom. I stood in front of the mirror. I had scary eyes, I noticed. Eyes that conveyed deadness. The kind of eyes that failed to express emotion. I visualized tearing them out of my skull with my fingers…. Having fun with my friends was giving me spontaneous, hot terror.[n]

Looks like achieving her objective and cultivating some friendships didn't actually fix her low sense of self-worth. She's unable to relax and have fun, even when she's further along in her personal growth arc.

This kind of inner struggle in a seemingly insignificant moment—paired with a paradoxical reaction—can lead to engagement as readers track a character's growth (or regression). In this case, Joey's mom is guilting her for trying to have a life. Meanwhile, her deadbeat, drug-addicted sister is missing. This isn't technically Joey's problem, but it's clear she doesn't feel entitled to anything good, especially coming from a family whose mindset is, "You think you're better than us?"

Here's another stark and unexpected reaction from Hannah in *The Bodyguard*. Her boyfriend, Robby, broke up with her because she wasn't coping well with her mother's death. Ouch. We later learn this was likely an excuse because he's sleeping with her best friend, Taylor. They're all colleagues at the same private security company, which makes me think Robby isn't too smart, or *wants* to be caught. And that's exactly what happens. This is the moment Hannah sees them making out on a closed-circuit surveillance camera:

> Robby … who had dumped me a month ago on the night after my mother's funeral … and Taylor … who had come over right afterward to console me while I cried … [were] kissing.
>
> And worse than that: *on the job.*
>
> … My eyes tried to look away but could only stare, *Clockwork Orange*-style, as the two of them went on and on…. The closest word I have for it is panic. Just an agonizing, urgent feeling that I needed to turn it off, or make it stop, or find some way for it to *not be happening.* Then add some rage. And some humiliation. And disbelief, too—as I tried, and failed, to understand what I was seeing.°

This is a great characterizing reaction because Hannah really show-cases her priorities. It's bad enough her ex is sucking face with her best friend, of course, but Hannah seems most incensed that they have the gall to do it on company time. I'd hate to give this scumbag any credit, but Robby is right about one thing—Hannah *is* as detached from her feelings as humanly possible.

Sometimes characters react unexpectedly to stimuli, and sometimes those reactions reveal a new emotional path or an insight that can't be ignored. The moment denial falls away is always tough for a protago-nist. In this excerpt from *The Bear and the Nightingale*, we see Konstan-tin, the self-involved priest, confronting Vasya, the young girl who believes in folk mythology. He acts impulsively, striking her, and this sends his carefully crafted façade crumbling, revealing more than he intended, especially to himself:

> She was standing too near. His hand shot out; he struck her across the face. She stumbled back, cradling her cheek. He took two quick steps forward, so that he was looking down at her, but she stood her ground. His hand was raised to strike again, but he drew breath and forbore. It was beneath him to strike her. He wanted to seize her, kiss her, hurt her, he did not know what. *Demon*.[p]

Ah, here lies the truth. On the one hand, he wants to do the acceptable thing that his station requires and bring Vasya to God. On the other, he's reeling from the realization that he might be attracted to someone he considers demonic.[3] This interiority shows inner turmoil hitting a flashpoint in an instant.

Let's look at another profound moment of realization, the time from *Eleanor Oliphant Is Completely Fine* (part of this excerpt was previously cited in Chapter 11). This is the instant Eleanor's delusion shatters and she realizes she's been chasing a false belief for about 200 pages:

> I didn't know the man onstage before me, didn't know the first thing about him. It was all just fantasy. Could anything be more pathetic—me, a grown woman? I'd told myself a sad little fairy tale, thinking that I could fix everything, undo the past, that he and I would live happily ever after and Mummy wouldn't be angry anymore.[q]

Of course, this is transformative because Eleanor now knows, in no uncertain terms, that she alone is responsible for her own destiny. That idea is, at first, unbearable, and Eleanor decides to die. Once the vodka wears off and she heals some more, she realizes what a blessing it is to be in charge of her own story. Her upswing is an incredibly gratifying and uplifting character arc.

---

3. In today's society, this interaction would also be problematic because she's a minor. Unfortunately, she's considered old enough to marry according to the standards of this historical period, so his attraction to her isn't as noteworthy as it otherwise be.

Vianne from *The Nightingale* has valiantly kept reality at bay, even as Nazis occupy her corner of rural France. In a small moment, though, she lowers her defenses and thinks about the very real possibility that her husband won't return from the front:

> Vianne felt as if she were breaking apart bit by bit, losing blood and bone as she stood here, contemplating something she had studiously avoided thinking about: a life without him. She started to shiver; her teeth chattered.[r]

It's reasonable to imagine that a little denial helps Vianne keep going in her day-to-day life. But at some point, about 150 pages into the story, she takes a beat to assess. This honest interiority conveys her courage and growth.

Interiority Insight: As we've already seen, denial is self-protective. But once a character evolves, they might outgrow this defense mechanism, since they're now more capable of grappling with reality. This disarming process doesn't have to be shocking or disturbing, it can also be empowering.

As we transition to more and more consequential reactions and realizations, let's look at *Divine Rivals*. First, Roman reacts to learning that his father has arranged a marriage for him:

> Roman exhaled through his teeth. It felt like had fractured a rib as he struggled to fathom what his parents had done. Arranged marriages were still common in the upper class, amongst viscounts and countesses and anyone else still clinging to a dusty title. But the Kitts were not those sorts of people.... It also struck Roman as odd that his father was arranging a marriage with a *professor's* daughter, not the daughter of a lord. He sensed that something else lurked beneath the surface of this conversation, and Roman was simply a pawn in a game.[s]

Readers see the expected resistance, which tracks with Roman wanting to live his own life and get away from his family's machinations. But they also get some critical thinking and extrapolation about what this maneuver really means. As Roman considers why his father chose the bride he did, he's also subtly teaching audiences about how upper-crust society works in this fantasy world. This is a great example of context in telling, and it's done with a light hand while the author keeps an eye on the balance of action and information.

Roman isn't the only character in this novel who responds to big events. When Iris realizes that her mysterious pen pal is actually her former rival, she's rattled on a number of levels:

> Roman Kitt was Carver.
>
> He had been Carver all along, and this realization struck her so hard she had to sit down on the floor. She was overwhelmed by a startling rush of relief. It was him. She had been writing to him, falling for him, all this time.
>
> But then the questions began to swarm, nipping at that solace.
>
> Had he been playing her? Was this a game to him? Why hadn't he told her sooner?
>
> She covered her face, and her palms absorbed the heat of her cheeks.[t]

On the heels of what should be a happy moment—the revelation of her love's identity—Iris is unable to relax. A new internal conflict emerges. She has fallen for the last person she expected, so how can she trust him or believe his soul-baring letters were in earnest? Especially since, once upon a time, he's the one who didn't want to give up his "tactical advantage" over her in the excerpt cited in Chapter 7? Has Roman really changed?

> **Interiority Insight:** When you're playing with paradoxical or consequential character realizations or reactions, be sure to ask: Why did this become clear now and not before? Then ask: Where to from here?

Readers have witnessed Roman's genuine character growth in his POV chapters, but now Iris has to attain buy-in, too. Meanwhile, audiences are invested and rooting for them to see eye to eye and move forward together.

> **Character Buy-In:** The moment a character decides to fully engage with the story, and an internal component of the inciting incident and other major plot turning points. A narrative doesn't truly begin until the protagonist achieves buy-in, whether they believe they've been sucked into a fantasy portal and given magic powers, or they overcome their denial and engage with the reality of their situation. Don't dwell on performative "I must be imagining things" or "Am I dreaming?" sequences. Those initial reactions are reasonable, but they shouldn't last too long. Buy-in is also the antidote to flip-flopping, which we'll talk about in the following chapter.

Another big-deal reveal occurs in *Red Queen*, as Mare realizes that the roguish guy who came to her village and saved her from conscription is actually Prince Cal. Worse, he represents the Silver royal family, which she hates and blames for the denigration of the Reds:

> The other servants make way, letting me shuffle to the back of the line while my head spins. He got me this job, he *saved* me, saved my family—and he is one of them. Worse than one of them. A prince. *The* prince. The person everyone in this spiral stone monstrosity is here to see.[11]

Here, Mare is ensnared in a conflict that appears in many stories where class and status inform identity: If Cal is a prince and was raised as such, does his role define him? Or can he possibly be different? This also invokes the question of nature versus nurture and potentially informs whether Mare decides to trust him, which is her biggest issue in this moment.

So far, we've explored examples of consequential information reveals and character-defining and thought-provoking reactions. In the following chapter, we'll see how information and interiority collide with action and stakes, electrifying the connection between character and plot. Now that we've understood how reactions set characters up to make decisions, we can dissect these pivotal turning points themselves.

16

THE POWER OF DECISIONS

Our goal, as writers, is to make readers care, create meaning, and connect character, plot, and theme. Now that you're comfortable in your understanding of what interiority is and how it's used to convey character experience, let's examine some instances of big decisions and how those showcase a story's stakes.

Once a character makes a choice in the plot or about their sense of self, there may not be an opportunity to reverse it. New decisions and options flow from the previous turning point. What's decided might be celebrated or regretted in hindsight, but it has become woven into the story, either way.

This is especially true of turning points and one-way doors, like the inciting incident, after which there's truly no going back to the character's previous life or frame of mind. Storytelling means you're always applying conflict and tension to your protagonist, and this might push them to jettison their misbeliefs, temporarily doubt themselves, redouble their efforts, or all of the above. Decisions are powerful benchmarks in any novel or memoir.

Character and Choice

The last thing you want to do is craft an entirely linear plot with no opportunities for your character to make mistakes, reckon with their actions, and choose the wrong option. With this chapter's excerpts, I'll explore how and when protagonists use interiority as they make decisions, where their attention goes, and what they consider in the moment.

Characters (and humans) often vacillate, especially when faced with a serious choice or big potential consequences. They weigh various outcomes and sometimes even experience instant regret or the urge to flee, whether or not they act on it. As we discussed in Chapter 1, it's common for characters to revisit memories and imagine how things might've turned out differently. This isn't a sign of weakness, either. In fact, it's a very relatable trait—a mark of self-awareness and humanity. Just don't do it constantly, and let the most important decisions "stick," so you can avoid outright flip-flopping.

Flip-Flopping: The undesirable tendency for characters to go back and forth to opposing extremes rather than committing to any one decision. An example would be a protagonist in an enemies-to-lovers romance claiming to hate their crush, then love them, then hate them again *without* turning point moments in between that help readers track the character's wildly shifting feelings. Every change of heart should be motivated by the plot and contextualized with interiority to express the logic of the protagonist's new position.

There's Always a Choice

Before we proceed, I want to hammer home three very important points about character decisions. First, you should engineer difficult choices into your story. If a decision is simple, there's no emotion or sacrifice involved. The character's next move is predictable and nobody cares. Protagonists show who they are in part with the choices they make. Put characters to the test and don't let them get away too easily, especially when they're at an important turning point or plot tentpole.

Second, you want the character to make intentional decisions rather than acting without thinking. Sure, they might have moments of impulsivity, but at junctures that matter—buying into a conflict with the antagonist, declaring feelings to their crush—don't have them simply blurt things automatically. Make them consider the pros and cons, or imagine the potential ramifications, then choose to do the hard thing. (An exception is if a character gets drunk to work up the courage, which we'll see later in this chapter.) Blurting is storytelling cowardice. It absolves a character of accountability.

It's also important to avoid what is sometimes called "jumping conflict,"[1] or a skip between logical steps. Use interiority to ground readers in why a character makes a specific choice or reacts a certain way. Excluding the audience and simply jumping to a decision or action can feel alienating or, worse, like a plot hole or "out of character" moment. Remember what I said in Chapter 9—they may not always be rational, but they'll each have their own rationale.

Finally, there's always a choice. I cannot tell you how often I pick up a manuscript (and sometimes even a published book) and read some variation of, "He had no choice."

This is false. There is *always* a choice.

The character might not *like* the menu of available options, but there is always something they can do, as long as they are still alive, to try and tilt the odds in their favor or escape a situation.

Dangling off a cliff?

There's still a choice. Jane can let go and risk the fall or try to swing onto a ledge.

Gun to the temple?

There's still a choice. Sam can try to disarm the assailant; humanize himself by sharing personal details from his backstory; try to subtly

---

1. This phrasing comes from *Writing for Emotional Impact: Advanced Dramatic Techniques to Attract, Engage, and Fascinate the Reader From Beginning to End* by Karl Iglesias.

press a button to have his smart watch dial for help; or maybe even charm the antagonist with a well-timed joke.[2]

Someone is about to expose damning blackmail information?

Even though a villain is in control of the leak, there's still a choice. Molly can let it happen and deal with the aftermath, offer a trade, or regain power by revealing the information herself (though she'll still have to deal with the aftermath, she'll now do so while controlling the narrative). As you can see, "He had no choice" is lazy. It makes the protagonist passive and signals a failure of imagination.

In fact, the most interesting choices a character can make are those that go against their established value system or the prevailing world-building culture. Does a decision create inner struggle or represent a forward or backward step on a protagonist's personal growth arc? Choices can be central to demonstrating what's going on with your characters internally *and* externally. Interesting decisions are often buttressed by information, which we explored in Chapter 14, and world context, which we'll cover in Chapter 18. Undergirding it all is interiority, which helps readers understand the emotion and logic involved. Let's now use some From the Shelves excerpts to unpack how instances of choice are supported and explored with interiority.

The Interiority of Decisions

One of the most clear-cut and binding things a character can do in any story is to make a decision, especially if it's irreversible. They might have complex feelings about it, and it may result in unexpected consequences, but the choice itself is usually a line in the sand that demonstrates action, growth, sacrifice, or all of the above.

If you're like me, you've been rooting for Hannah from *The Bodyguard* to get over herself and take the leap—in the form of admitting her feelings for Jack. After more than 200 agonizing pages, she finally breaks, right as it's time to wrap up her assignment as his fake girlfriend:

> The idea of not saying goodbye to Jack made me feel ... panicky

---

2. Anyone wanna guess which one I'd pick?

—even though I never said goodbye to clients. Would saying goodbye even matter? It wouldn't change anything. But I felt like I had a hundred urgent messages for Jack—and all I wanted was to convey them all.[a]

Hannah has waited until the last possible moment to admit her feelings and this leaves her in a tizzy. Unfortunately, she's not able to confess, even after she makes up her mind, because the plot forces the lovers apart. Such decisions to engage or disengage are often the major watershed moments in romances and romantic comedies.

Here's a particularly raunchy choice made by Red, the romantic interest in *Get a Life, Chloe Brown*. After about 100 pages of insisting he doesn't like Chloe, he finally can't suppress his attraction:

He could feel his own good sense flying out the window. The little demon that sat on his shoulder and whispered bright ideas like *Drop out of college*, and *Let your mate tattoo you in his kitchen*, and *Follow your heart*, said slyly that now was … the time to roll her over, push up her skirt, and make her beg.[b]

Notice how we get the good ol' devil-and-angel-on-the-shoulder dynamic in interiority as Red's impulses battle one another.

We see a similar push and pull of desire between divorced exes Yasmen and Josiah in *Before I Let Go*. The plot puts them on a business trip together and, since romance is full of tropes, they "have to" share a hotel room.[3] Here's Yasmen in the moment, vacillating about whether or not to make a move:

Can I do that? Can I live with having him just one more time, knowing I'll probably always want him? With the promise of pleasure we've always found together, my body screams yes. My mind and my heart ask if I'm sure. I hurt him. I know that, but does he have any idea how much he could hurt me? That if I give him my body, my heart can't help but follow? I wish we'd

---

3. There's a conference in town and every other option is booked. Because of course it is!

talked sooner.... Maybe it would have saved us, but none of those things happened and this is all that's left.

His body, tonight and no more.

I'll take it.[c]

Yasmen also faces a profound and emotional moment of decision later in the story. This time, it affects her relationship with her daughter, Deja. Previously, Yasmen shut down in the midst of her grief over a lost pregnancy, which we saw in Chapter 5, and this withdrawal is widely blamed for the divorce. Deja hasn't forgiven her and though Yasmen has suffered the brunt of her daughter's anger and blame for years, she's finally able to see the hurt beneath it. Overcoming her own big feelings, Yasmen decides to lead with empathy:

> *What's really the use of forgiving myself if the people I love most never will?* But looking at my daughter, her face contorted with rage and hurt, I recognize her anger laid out like a rug covering her pain. I used to do that, too, and I know a fight won't fix that hurt. I want peace for her even more than I want it for myself.[d]

By this advanced point in the plot, Yasmen has done enough soul-searching to recognize Deja's pain because this is exactly how Yasmen covered up her grief and pushed Josiah away. The decision to lean in—to both Josiah and Deja—signals a new healing season for the whole family, and tremendous growth for Yasmen.

Interiority Insight: Present a character with two similar choices at different moments in the plot. How—and what—a character decides can show their evolving sense of self and growth arc in action.

Sticking with romance for a moment, let's see August choose to engage with Jane in *One Last Stop*. August makes this difficult decision even as she suspects Jane will blow all of her self-protective walls apart:

She touches things … and it feels like she hasn't touched anything at all, like it's all a place she lives in concept.

… So maybe that's why… she finds herself stepping onto the Q. At least here she knows where she is. Time, place, person.[e]

August takes 100 more pages to admit she wants Jane to stay, if at all possible. She's still gun-shy about her feelings, so she has to get drunk before she allows herself this thought:

She'd promised herself—she'd promised Jane—she was doing this to get Jane back where she belonged. But it's as blazing and unforgiving as the spotlight on the stage, nothing left in August's sloshy drunk brain to hold it back. She wants to keep Jane.[f]

The author even uses a spotlight image (see Chapter 1) to direct reader attention to this important moment.

Interiority Insight: If you have a character who can't quite bring themselves to think what they need to think, say what they need to say, or do what they need to do, get them drunk or high to grease the tracks. Sure, this isn't always an elegant or ethical solution and doesn't work with sober protagonists, but many stories use this conceit. As a bonus, characters will still have to deal with the ramifications of their actions after they dry out.

In *The Guest*, Alex has fled to the Hamptons for the summer. She keeps what she's escaping from purposefully vague. A guy named Dom keeps calling her and it's clear she owes him money. This constant overhanging anxiety bothers her to the point she considers asking her sugar daddy, Simon, for help:

Tense. Alex was tense. She didn't want to see Simon when she was riled up like this, off her game. Making bad choices. Dom knew she was out here. This whole thing would be tricky. She'd talk to Simon later. On the drive home. No more stalling: she'd tell Simon everything, or a version of everything. They'd figure it out together.[g]

"A version of everything" could be considered a thematic statement for this novel, as Alex is full of lies and delusions. Even as she needs help, she won't tell Simon the truth.

After their break-up—which is the direct result of one of her "bad decisions"—Alex makes her final play to redeem herself. Immediately before returning to Simon's mansion, she throws her phone away, a symbolic gesture that signifies a break from her past:

If Jack was calling, she didn't know about it. If Dom was calling, she didn't know about it. So it was the same as if they weren't calling.[h]

Somehow, I doubt this will work out for her, as escape isn't quite that simple. This demonstrative action only reinforces the notion that Alex has completely split from reality.

In *Ripe*, Cassie has a similarly disembodied and disjointed experience as she decides to take a pregnancy test after weeks of avoiding it:

In my bathroom, I pull the horrible box from my canvas shopping bag. The same sensation I experienced in my last presentation to the CEO returns: my fake self takes over and it's as if I've left my body, which continues without me…. She places the stick on the sink. The stick has two small windows…. My mind is floating, safe in a kind and soft space made of sweet white light. From up here, it doesn't matter whether I am pregnant or not. There is only the light of eternity. Here in the light, nothing can touch me.

Until the second line appears, ripping me from the warm light and back into my body.[i]

In order to begin processing the situation—getting pregnant by a guy who's committed elsewhere—Cassie separates herself from her body and cleaves into her real self and her fake self (we previously saw this happen in Chapter 11). She goes so far as to talk about herself in the third person. But the positive test result snaps her back into reality, and eventually she'll have to choose her next course of action.

A similarly deluded character, June from *Yellowface*, makes several fateful decisions. First, she steals Athena's manuscript. Then, she starts rewriting it:

> But then I just kept going. I couldn't stop. They say that editing a bad draft is far easier than composing on a blank page, and that's true—I feel so confident in my writing just then. I keep finding turns of phrase that suit the text far better than Athena's throwaway descriptions. I spot where the pacing sags, and I mercilessly cut out the meandering filler. I draw out the plot's through line like a clear, powerful note. I tidy up; I trim and decorate; I make the text sing.[j]

This obviously gets June invested in the project, helps her justify her involvement, and moves her closer to passing off the book as her own. When the manuscript's provenance is questioned and she gets the chance to come clean, June doubles down instead, digging herself deeper:

> It's not lying. I swear, it was never as psychopathic as it sounds. It's all just stretching reality a bit, putting the right spin on the picture so that the lurking social media outrage mob doesn't get the wrong idea. Besides, the train has left the station—coming clean at this point would tank the book, and I couldn't do that to Athena's legacy.[k]

My favorite part is that June still insists this whole endeavor is about "Athena's legacy," rather than glorifying herself. Luckily, readers are onto her and are instead watching to see how this series of bad choices will play out.

Big decisions can be scary or ill-conceived but also empowering. Here's Sona in *Gearbreakers* as she enters an elite training program, and you'll recognize this thematic statement from Chapter 3. She's full of rage and the desire for revenge, yet Sona claims her power instead of losing her temper:

> "Do not die and embarrass me, child," he spits.
>
> I take a moment to imagine the mark my knuckles would leave across his cheekbone ... but power comes from finishing fights, not starting them. So instead, my fist uncoils at my side. I smile and say, "I will damn well die when I please."[l]

Later, Sona remains true to her word and decides to put her life on the line in battle. Frostbringer is a nickname for Eris, one of the leaders of the resistance, and—inconveniently—Sona's future love interest:

> And suddenly, the Frostrbringer's eyes were resting on mine again, the furious, chilling gaze, as if she was the one on the offensive, as if this was her battlefield and I was the one intruding. The single glance promised destruction and promised hate.... I may die as theirs, but I will damn well take them with me.[m]

Here, Sona's honorable commitment is tested and she remains true to her intentions. Until she decides to join the rebels, that is.

A similar pivotal decision is made in *The Cruel Prince* as Jude chooses to stay in the fairy kingdom—where she's an outcast—and fight the powers that be:

> I think of all the vows I made to Dain, including the one I never spoke out loud: *Instead of being afraid, I will become something to fear.* If Dain isn't going to give me power, then I am going to take it for myself.[n]

Interiority Insight: Decisions can proclaim a character's objective and identity, both to themselves and others. Reinforcing these decisions in interiority adds to a reader's sense of the protagonist's value system.

Andi from *Within These Wicked Walls* is cast out by her mentor and father figure and must secure a patron to support herself as an exorcist. After sleeping in a barn—a low point—she walks into the most haunted house she's ever seen.

Worse, its master, Magnus, is by turns annoying and charming. She doubts she can stay because the job is too dangerous, not to mention emotionally messy. But then she makes her decision:

> *Remember where you were this morning, Andi.*
>
> *You woke up in a stall with a bunch of goats. You chased a sleazebag off with a rock.*
>
> *A slightly irrational employer is nothing.*
>
> I took a third and final soothing breath, and then I went back downstairs to finish my dinner.[o]

Later, after she's fully committed to ridding the house of its various terrifying demons, she experiences a night that almost tempts her to run again:

> My mind was so chaotic I couldn't process anything. All I knew was that I was panicking, a leveled panic full of adrenaline, familiar as the back alleys back home. I had learned to perfect that panic, because my survival depended on it.
>
> … *Fight or flight, Andi?*[p]

Interiority Insight: It's fine to bring a character to the threshold of a commitment, or show them re-evaluating a decision they've already made. Each time they come to that threshold, though, their objective and need should be different or have new context. The stakes must also be higher. Otherwise you run the risk of characters flip-flopping or simply repeating the plot.

Now we'll see a life-changing choice made by Obinze in *Americanah*. When he's caught by British immigration officials and put into a holding cell, he decides he's had enough and won't fight deportation:

> "I'm willing to go back to Nigeria," Obinze said. The last shard of his dignity was like a wrapper slipping off that he was desperate to retie.
>
> The lawyer looked surprised. "Okay, then," he said, and got up a little too hastily, as though grateful that his job had been made easier. Obinze watched him leave. He was going to tick on a form that his client was willing to be removed. "Removed." That word made Obinze feel inanimate. A thing to be removed. A thing without breath and mind. A thing.[q]

This interiority demonstrates Obinze's subsumation of how getting deported defines him. Meanwhile, readers are privy to a once-in-a-lifetime choice.

Let's pivot to a speculative world for even higher stakes for certain character predicaments. Some of the following excerpts will be paired to show protagonist evolution over time when it comes to making big decisions.

Speculative Choices

For reasons too intricate to explain here, Atticus, a Black man, is lured to the mansion of Samuel Braithwhite, a cult leader seeking immortality, in *Lovecraft Country*. Once it's too late to escape, Atticus realizes he's an unwitting blood sacrifice in an arcane ceremony. Luckily, he has a spell hidden in his pocket for scuttling the proceedings. Here's the moment he decides to use it:

> [Atticus] liked who and what he was. He always had. It was God's other creatures he occasionally had problems with.
>
> And so, because he did not seek oblivion, and because he wasn't ready to die, either, he reached into the rolled-up cuff of his left sleeve and pulled out the slip of paper that was hidden there.[r]

> **Interiority Insight:** We've seen many examples of self-loathing, but self-love is always an option, especially if the story threatens that rare and precious confidence with high stakes!

Mare has a different relationship to her sense of self in *Red Queen*, as she must pretend to be a Silver heiress and fit in with a court she despises. Yes, she's in the palace to save her own life, but she experiences inner struggle when the ramifications of her decision hit. She generally likes herself, but that's a person she can no longer be:

> I'll have to leave, and this world I can't understand will become my only reality. I'll never be able to go home. *You knew this*, I tell myself, *you agreed to this*. But it doesn't hurt any less.[s]

> **Interiority Insight:** Decisions can feel bad or bittersweet before, during, or after the fact. Even the right decisions. The more conflicted your protagonist is about an important choice, the better. Easy decisions—which don't require any sacrifice or loss—deprive a story of conflict and tension. Difficult decisions allow a character to demonstrate who they are in action and interiority.

Later, Mare has to stuff down her feelings as she watches a colonel who came to report the real status of the war get called a liar by controlling Queen Elara. The Reds, including Mare's brothers, are on the front lines and know the truth. Mare is incensed to realize the Silvers are being misled, which only stokes support for the conflict. Alas, within the palace walls, she is Mareena. She must play the part and hide her horror:

> A few women at the table clap and nod, agreeing with the queen's sweeping lie. Evangeline joins in, and the action quickly spreads, until only the colonel and I remain silent. I can tell she doesn't believe anything the queen says, but there's no way to call the queen a liar. Not here, not in her arena.

As much as I want to stay still, I know I can't. I'm Mareena, not Mare, and I have to support my queen and her wretched words. My hands come together, clapping for Elara's lie, as the scolded colonel bows her head.[t]

Mare's energies and desires find other outlets, like kissing Cal, the prince who rescued her (and who's betrothed to her nemesis). Mare knows this is a dangerous decision but makes it anyway:

As much as I want to pull away, I just can't do it. Cal is a cliff, and I throw myself over the edge, not bothering to think of what it could do to us both. One day he'll realize I'm his enemy, and all this will be a far-gone memory. But not yet.[u]

Interiority Insight: Sometimes the consequences of a decision surprise a character. Other times, the risks and potential adverse outcomes are clear, yet the protagonist forges ahead anyway.

In *Spinning Silver*, Miryem is starving because her father, a debt collector, has too much empathy for the poor peasants he serves. She decides to take over his job, which is highly unusual for a girl in her world and time. Here, an indebted man doesn't take her demand for repayment well, especially since it comes from someone outside the established power hierarchy:

No one had ever shouted at me in my life: my mother with her quiet voice, my gentle father. But I found something bitter inside myself, something of that winter blown into my heart.... I stayed in their doorways, and I didn't move. My numbers were true, and they and I knew it, and when they'd shouted themselves out, I said, "Do you have the money?"[v]

This is also foreshadowing, as Miryem will soon find herself working for the Staryk, too. Later, when this powerful and terrifying fairy entity demands that she keep changing silver into gold for him, she summons the inner reserves of courage readers have watched her build. We first saw a glimpse from the following excerpt as a thematic statement in Chapter 3. Just as Miryem did with her first customer, she decides to challenge the Staryk, despite infinitely higher stakes:

> He held another purse out to me, clinking like chains.... He wore spurs on his heels and jewels on his fingers like enormous chips of ice, and the voices of all the souls lost in blizzards howled behind him. Of course I was afraid.
>
> But I had learned to fear other things more: being despised, whittled down one small piece of myself at a time, smirked at and taken advantage of. I put my chin up and said, as cold as I could be in answer, "And what will you give me in return?"[w]

Compare this to the moment a naïve Felicity falls for fairy promises of magic, glamour, and acceptance in *The Fair Folk*. We first saw this passage excerpted in Chapter 11:

> I am looking at her now, drinking in her words, and the tears are falling freely. "Rare and special," she called me. In all my life, no one has ever said anything like that to me before. In that moment, I would give her anything she asked.[x]

Two very different decisions from Miryem and Felicity here, one empowering, one diminishing, yet both lead to suffering. Speaking of Felicity, remember Chapter 14, when she realized her cousin had been replaced with a changeling? The fae have made Christine into a toy for the demented Alys. Standing up to Them will be dangerous. It might even get Felicity rejected by her only "friends," who make her feel "rare and special." Felicity really struggles but ultimately becomes willing to risk her own happiness:

> For the first time, it comes home to me. The changeling—*that creature*—used to be human. It used to be a beautiful baby, loved and cherished. Then the fairies came and stole it from its mother, to be a plaything for Alys until it was no longer beautiful, and she grew tired of it.... I know, beyond all doubt now, that I've

made the right choice, whatever the price may be. It's too late for the poppet, but it's not too late for Christine.[y]

This decision takes on a deeper resonance in interiority as Felicity intuits that this moment will become either a stain or a glory on her deepest sense of self, affecting her for the rest of her life:

I had realized along the way that if I didn't do something about the changeling, I myself would be changed. What I hadn't foreseen was that I would be changed anyway. Before that, I think, nothing I had done had made any real difference to anything. When does a child begin to realize that her actions have consequences?[z]

As I summarized in Chapter 14, Felicity fears she's doomed to give her body to Elfrida and become a changeling herself. Here, she feels all is lost and this represents her dark night of the soul:

She felt numb. She kept going, one step after another, but not ready to arrive. *I am going*, she thought, but without any particular emotion, as though all feelings were used up and this was the only thing left to do now. *There's no coming back*. Walking out of the wreckage of her life; going Onward into who knew what, leaving a changeling.[aa]

Fortunately for her, and readers who have developed deep empathy for this protagonist, Felicity figures out a bargain that'll beat the fairies at their own game. Remember, you never want a character to have "no choice." There's always a choice, but it often takes sacrifice and ingenuity.

With each exceedingly difficult decision Felicity makes, readers see her develop as a character. Her final victory is incredibly gratifying because she proves she's a true hero, choice by choice, for over 400 pages.

Climactic Real-World Choices

Let's go back to the realistic world but examine more pivotal decisions that are fraught with stakes and danger. In *Anxious People*, a presumed terrorist ends up trapping a random group of strangers at an apartment open house. Over the course of the story, the characters develop empathy for their captor, who's actually a freaked-out single mom fleeing a botched bank robbery. Jim, the older police officer who needs to be needed, as described in Chapter 8, makes a fateful decision as he purposefully lets her escape:

> "Even if you release the hostages and give up, you'll still end up
> in prison. Even if the pistol isn't real," he said mournfully, and
> of course he'd been a police officer long enough to have seen
> that it was. He knew she wouldn't stand a chance, no matter
> how sympathetic any decent person might feel about her situa-
> tion. You're not allowed to rob banks, you're not allowed to run
> around with firearms, and we can't let criminals like that go
> unpunished if we catch them. So Jim concluded there and then
> that the only way she wouldn't get punished was not to do that.
> Not to catch her.[bb]

He follows his moral code even as he ignores the rule of law, which has defined his entire professional life.

In *The Nightingale*, Vianne is forced to host a series of Nazi officers in her home. Her rebel sister, Isabel, hatches a plan to kill one, even though this is extremely dangerous. Vianne's friends and neighbors have been strung up in the town square for less. Here, she prepares to do the dark deed:

> Vianne slipped a sleeping draught into Sophie's lemonade and
> put the child to bed early. (Not the sort of thing that made one
> feel like a good mother, but neither was it all right to take Sophie
> with them tonight or let her waken alone. Bad choices. That was
> all there were anymore.) While waiting for her daughter to fall
> asleep, Vianne paced. She heard every clatter of wind against
> the shutters, every creaky settling of the timbers of the old
> house. At just past six o'clock, she dressed in her old gardening
> overalls and went downstairs.[cc]

She also puts herself in grave danger by raising a Jewish boy as her own after her neighbor is taken away to the camps. After the war, Ari's relatives in America send word that they want to adopt him. Even though it breaks her heart, Vianne thinks of the massive toll of the Holocaust and decides to send the boy to be with his people:

> Vianne thought of the people she'd seen.… Millions had been killed. A generation lost. How could she keep Ari from his people, his family? She would fight to the death for either of her children, but there was no opponent for her to fight, just loss on both sides.[dd]

The emotional devastation of war is clear from these passages. Who the characters are—as evidenced by their choices—makes them profoundly heroic.

Many decisions can lead to powerful consequences, and nowhere is that more true than in a mystery or thriller story. To finish out this chapter, I'll sample from our suspense novels as we prepare to explore stakes.

Our first excerpt is from *The It Girl*, as Hannah confronts her suspicion that the creepy college security guard she accused of murder, a moment shown in Chapter 14, is actually innocent:

> *You convicted an innocent man.*
>
> And suddenly she cannot do this. She cannot do this anymore—not any of it. Not the memories crowding her head, not the voices in her ears, not the faces in the crowd around her, looking at her curiously as she puts her hands over her face and screams silently, internally, wanting nothing more than for it to all *just stop.*[ee]

Here, Hannah's on the verge of breaking down from doubt and guilt. Against her better judgment, she decides to start digging back into April's murder to figure out what really happened years ago. What she learns unravels her sense of not only her past, but her present and future, too.

Isabelle from *All the Dangerous Things* is convinced for most of the story that, as a child, she led her younger sister, Margaret, into the bayou to drown one night. This misbelief is revealed to be a false memory. Margaret did die, but Isabelle was not responsible, and her parents are hiding a nefarious secret.

Before the truth comes out, Isabelle's guilt drives her choices and objectives. She convinces herself that becoming a parent will bring redemption, so she decides to get pregnant despite her marital problems. Going off of birth control without discussing it with a partner is a form of sexual assault but she does it anyway:

> It would be my chance to take care of someone after I had failed to take care of Margaret. My chance to make up for my past.
>
> … I walked into the bathroom and shut the door behind me, the silent click of the lock making my heartbeat rise to my throat. I can still picture myself standing over that toilet and pushing my birth control pills through their foil casing, one by one, and into the water, like they were some kind of ceremonial sacrifice. The tickle of anticipation in my stomach as I flushed, watching them spin in circles until they disappeared altogether. Ripping Ben's clothes off as soon as he got home and lying in silence together afterward, wondering. Waiting. Trying to somehow feel it happening beneath my skin. And I felt guilt, yes. The shame for lying and even a little twinge of embarrassment at having stooped to something so devious and low—but also the thrill of having some semblance of control over my life again. Of making a decision for myself for once.[ff]

Isabelle knows this is wrong but has a blazing need to feel in control and fill a familial void. The isn't rational, but readers are treated to her rationale.

Interiority Insight: Characters can disclose secrets via interiority and this can engender closeness with readers. But as we saw in Chapter 14, not all revelations should be taken at face value, and not all reflect well on the protagonist.

The next three excerpts in this section come from *Everyone Here Is Lying*, which has a large ensemble cast of POV characters and a missing child plot. We'll hear from William, Avery's father, and Nora, the woman he was recently having an affair with.

Before she disappears, Avery comes home early from school and has a fight with William. This is the inciting incident of the story and the reason he comes under suspicion later:

> "No," Avery says. And it's that defiance in her voice, as if she holds all the cards, as if he's nothing and has no authority over her at all, that sets him off. In three long strides he's across the kitchen, in a blind rage. Something inside him has snapped. It happens so fast, faster than conscious thought. He strikes her across the side of the head, harder than he meant to. She goes down like a stone, the expression of defiance wiped from her face, replaced by shock and then vacancy, and for a fraction of a second, he feels satisfaction.[gg]

This is a jarring moment that's made even more disturbing because William seems to enjoy taking his frustration out on his nine-year-old daughter. Immediately after this, Avery flees, which means William is the last person to see her alive. When the news breaks, Nora reacts in her own POV:

> She can't shake her feelings of guilt, that she and William are being punished for what they've done. She's terrified that the police will find William's secret phone. Of course they will, now, if they're treating the house as a crime scene. Collateral damage, that's what she will be. She and her family, destroyed. And then she's ashamed, because a little girl might be dead and she's thinking about how it will affect her.[hh]

As we learned in Chapter 14, Nora dumped William before Avery's disappearance, but now she fears this technicality won't matter. An even deeper layer of subsumation here shows Nora grappling with how this situation reflects on her character. As her lover's child is missing and could well be dead, Nora's primary concern is her own life and these selfish thoughts make her feel dirty.

Next we zoom to a police interrogation where William is sweating. The detectives ask him if he saw Avery after school, which readers already know he did. The cops have found conclusive evidence that she stopped at home—a jacket on the coat rack—but William doesn't know this and makes a fateful decision to lie:

> William swallows and still says nothing.... He knows that Avery was home today after school. She used the key under the front doormat to get in. He talked to her. He hit her. He's a monster and a liar. He feels sicker by the minute; he's afraid he might throw up. But he must not. He swallows down the bile, clears his throat, and suggests, "Maybe she ran away."[ii]

> **Interiority Insight:** With each major choice, readers should see a protagonist's thought process. Sometimes characters dig themselves deeper into the hole, which is especially engaging when readers know more than the POV protagonist and can anticipate how the decision will lead to disaster.

In *The New House*, Millie makes several pivotal choices over the course of the story. In a stunning and uncanny twist of fate, Harper, a woman who's been sniffing around her husband, Tom, ends up in Millie's OR after a car accident:

> For a moment, I literally hold Harper's heart in my hand. I've just been gifted the perfect opportunity to extinguish any threat this annoying woman might present to my son, my marriage, or my peace of mind. I don't have to do anything: I just have to perform a little less than my best. No one would ever know.
>
> I've never performed at less than my best in my life.[ii]

What a huge declaration of Millie's rigid moral code and value system! Harper is on the brink of death and nobody would blame Millie if the surgery failed. These things happen. Yet Millie cannot sacrifice her professional standards, even if doing so might improve her personal life.

During the climax, Millie is forced to make another decision. She's handcuffed in Stacey's basement and time is running out to save herself and her son, Peter, who's trapped in another room. As we can see, above, Millie's surgical skills are crucial to both her external identity and most foundational sense of self. Now, with no good options available, she sacrifices her hands—cutting off her own thumbs and ending her career—to slip out of her restraints:

> I'm cool and collected as I pick up the rusty Stanley knife....
> Self-pity isn't an option. I can't use brute force to break the
> handcuff: I've tried. My son doesn't have time to wait for an
> unlikely rescue. I've known since the moment Stacey told me
> my son was trapped here with me I only ever had one choice—
> which means it wasn't a choice at all.[kk]

This phrasing isn't exactly true. She *has* a choice—she can wait and hope—but she doesn't make it. Surgeons, particularly highly skilled specialists, insure their precious hands. Very little shocks me in my reading life, but when Millie did this to herself, I gasped. Such is the power of a great moment of character decision. Once you've built these information reveals, reactions, and choices into your story, you can use them all to generate stakes.

17

LEVERAGING STAKES

Once we unlock the power of decisions, it's all about the stakes, baby. The bloodier the better. Actually, that's not true at all, as we'll see in some excerpts that manage to load small moments with major perceived significance. Here's a comprehensive definition to get us started.

Stakes: *Why* a development, reaction, decision, action, or idea matters. Stakes make meaning. Why is this story element important to the protagonist? How might it change their internal or external trajectory? Did they get what they wanted? And? So? Did they fail? And? So? Routinely ask these questions as you use interiority to show how characters interpret, extrapolate, and even subsume your plot's events and define their impact. This is how readers understand the ramifications of various experiences on your character's sense of self, which is where you can explore the most profound stakes of all.

Stakes enhance moments of plot and character intersection. They emerge as a result of need and want, can be positive or negative (more on that in a moment), lead to or result from decisions, anchor a moment or reaction, eliminate or create options for the future, and are often held together with cause-and-effect logic and interiority.

You've already read many examples of stakes in this guide, maybe without realizing it. How much attention writers and characters pay to any story element also shows the reader its importance. By this point, you should have no problem both creating high-stakes moments in your plot and expressing the stakes via character interiority.

My favorite questions of "And? So?" are useful for teasing out stakes. They can help you imagine what the best-case and worst-case scenarios are for any plot or character development. Turning points offer major opportunities to combine growth arc, plot, and character relationships. These events are only impactful if you define their stakes and have protagonists use interiority to anticipate them before, react to them during, interpret them after, or all of the above.

Writers often take it too easy on their characters. This chapter reminds you to make tension ever-present by using interiority as your secret weapon. Information reveals, reactions, decisions, and stakes can also rescue your muddy middle. The writer's job in this long stretch of manuscript is to use protagonist growth, plot action, and relationship development to pick up the slack. There are many opportunities for a book to droop and interiority must be threaded through every event to make sure readers stay engaged.

Interiority Insight: Focusing on stakes in key narrative moments can keep readers turning pages. Don't just think about the scene you want to write, consider when and where it can create maximum impact in your structure.

Stakes exist on a grand, story-wide scale for the character's primary objectives and needs, but also in the small day-to-day moments as protagonists pursue their desires. Let's see how our From the Shelves authors make meaning, starting with minor but impactful events.

Stakes in Small Moments

Each internal and external development you put on the page has to matter. Interiority helps readers understand the deeper implications of any given scene, interaction, realization, and decision, and is key to creating that sense of meaning.

I want to start with the stakes of small moments, whether they come from a passing thought or an innocuous-seeming interaction in scene. This really showcases the power of interiority to enhance stakes, even when the external stimuli doesn't seem too consequential.

One of my favorite small-moment, high-stakes examples comes from *Amazing Grace Adams*, as Grace realizes that she doesn't have to stand there and talk to a neighborhood mom. Instead of saying anything to politely disengage from the conversation, she simply ... leaves. She's obviously having some issues, from the mention of the abandoned car, but the realization inherent in this scene is powerful, no matter the circumstances:

> Freja is still talking but Grace isn't hearing a word. Her mind flashes to the car she's abandoned five hundred meters back down the road, the man up the ladder, the woman in the chemist, her boss on the phone, the crushing heat, and before she knows what she's doing, Grace starts to walk away. She's aware, in some blurred part of her, that Freja is scrutinizing her, frowning, as she leaves ... and doesn't look back. There's a whizzing feeling in her—around her—that seems to stir the dead air in the street. Such potency in a simple act. Quietly, calmly, she has taken the bolt cutters to social convention. She has set herself free.[a]

For a person like Grace, who feels constrained by social mores and her own people-pleasing nature, this small act is both shocking and liberating.

Ruth, Tina's dead partner, gets a POV in the historical timeline of *Bright Young Women*. Here, she's talking to Tina, who tries to tease and flirt with her. While Tina's intentions are good, Ruth is too insecure to tolerate the exchange and reacts with uncharacteristic bluntness:

"I wish you'd knock it off," I said, to my own absolute shock. I never spoke to people like that. I hated to hurt people's feelings, to make anyone feel bad even when they deserved to feel bad. I started to apologize, but ... I was amazed that she'd taken my outburst in stride.[b]

This short interaction takes on big meaning and high personal stakes because of how it makes Ruth feel and what it makes her realize about herself and others. She also seems to gain some respect for Tina here, and this plants the seed for their eventual romantic connection.

While stakes can be used to underscore empowering moments, they often enhance threats and danger. For example, Josiah from *Before I Let Go* has always been wary of therapy. In fact, his resistance to counseling was one of the reasons his marriage to Yasmen failed the first time. When he decides to go in solidarity with his son, Kassim, his worst fears about it are seemingly confirmed:

We stare at each other for a few seconds in a silence that grows tighter the longer it stretches out. I'm determined not to break it. I'm not to give him anything, because why would I? I don't know this motherfucker from Adam, and he wants to dig around in my head? Drag out all the shit I store in neat compartments so I can find some measure of peace? He wants to shake all that up, but he wouldn't have to live with the fallout. I would.[c]

A reader's sense of stakes can flourish in moments of denial and resistance, especially as walls come tumbling down and characters face their true feelings in interiority. Josiah would get along well with Hannah from *The Bodyguard*. But *her* carefully constructed emotion-phobic reality implodes when she must reveal that she's struggling with her mother's death to her boss:

Usually, the antidote to fear was preparation—but I hadn't been prepared for anything about this week.... And right here is where my voice broke.

Right here is where I lost hold of "angry" and my emotions just kind of crumbled … my voice sounded broken, even to me.[d]

This is a teeny moment on the page, but by focusing on interiority, the author is able to tease out depth, feeling, and vulnerability as Hannah subsumes what this perceived brokenness means about her character.

The below excerpt was originally referenced in Chapter 11, but I'll reprint it here because it's such a beautiful example of catastrophic stakes captured in a small moment of interiority. In this excerpt from *Sing, Unburied, Sing*, Leonie basically throws in the towel on her entire life and admits compete defeat to Michael:

> "I can't," I say, and there are so many other words behind that. *I can't be a mother right now. I can't be a daughter. I can't remember. I can't see. I can't breathe....* [Michael] puts me in the passenger seat, closes the door, and climbs behind the wheel. The car shrinks the world to this: me and him in this dome of glass.[e]

Interiority Insight: Stakes rise every time a character is completely cleaved open or laid low.

Let's also re-examine this excerpt from *Gearbreakers* which initially appeared in Chapter 6, as Sona subsumes what her new role as killer might mean. Bluster aside, she is still a child, and she struggles with the thought of actually killing, even if she has trained to do so:

> I am not steadfast; I am not something rigid. I am a child who must kill today, and it makes me scared for myself.[f]

This interiority is a stark example of a character staring down the barrel of devastating personal stakes that threaten to reshape their entire sense of self.

Sometimes stakes come from present-moment action, and other times, they're generated by a character's fear of a hypothetical future. Protagonists often expect failure and suffering, especially after they fail to get what they want. The risks they imagine might be blown out of proportion, or could represent a reasonable possibility.

Ama Torres is the wedding planner love interest in *Forget Me Not*. She recently started her own business, leaving her former boss, Whitney, and booking a gigantic influencer wedding. Whitney is watching her every move because now Ama is a threat. Here, Ama doubts herself:

> If I wasn't already regretting this, I would be now. This is far more exposure than I've ever handled, even under Whitney. And exposure means just as many opportunities for mistakes as there are for successes. Every wedding has its pressures, but not many have the possibility of advancing or ruining your career with one small swing of the pendulum.[g]

Notice how this interiority evokes not only the normal pressures of being a wedding planner, but the additional pain of potential public failure. Ama is terrified, especially now that she's building her reputation as an independent business owner. Ama's pessimistic worldview reflects a fixed mindset. She's so afraid of her moonshot backfiring that she's unwilling to take the risk at this point in her growth arc. This expression of stakes comes from her deep and realistic knowledge of the situation and her industry. Readers are likely to find Ama's hypothetical worries credible.

Other characters go all out in imagining dramatic stakes that have little to do with reality. As Roman falls in love with Iris in *Divine Rivals*, he worries the relationship will end poorly. Why? Vibes, mostly:

> It was that ache again. The one that tasted like salt and smoke. A longing he feared would only grow stronger with each passing year. A regret in the making.[h]

I'd much rather see a more grounded and specific sense of stakes, but I do like Roman's commitment to generating tension and internal conflict with these vaguely dark images of love as "a regret in the making." This rhetoric demonstrates his mindset at this point in time.

Similarly dramatic is June from *Yellowface*. She imagines what might happen if she has to stop writing, or if she doesn't become successful, then reacts to the dismal possibility she's conjured in her head:

> To stop writing would kill me. I'd never be able to walk through a bookstore without fingering the spines with longing, wondering at the lengthy editorial process that got these titles on shelves and reminiscing about my own. And I'd spend the rest of life curdling with jealousy every time someone like Emmy Cho gets a book deal, every time I learn that some young up-and-comer is living the life I should be living.[i]

With this hypothetical outcome looming, June consciously or unconsciously uses these stakes to justify stealing Athena's manuscript because she feels entitled to "the life [she] should be living."

Interiority Insight: Fear and self-preservation are great motivations. Offer your protagonist the opportunity to confront death, or something that *feels* life-or-death.

Eleanor in *Eleanor Oliphant Is Completely Fine* similarly convinces herself the musician is the answer to all her problems, as we first saw in Chapter 7:

> Tonight, I was going to meet the man whose love would change my life.
>
> I was ready to rise from the ashes and be reborn.[j]

Notice how desperation creates stakes in this example of interiority. Eleanor's internalized sense of urgency and danger is at its highest right as she believes she will succeed. The truth is she's chasing the wrong things and her delusions are running rampant. Instead, what's "reborn" is her grasp on reality once she comes to her senses.

Reactions to real events can also trigger bursts of stakes, anxiety about the future, and deep uncertainty. Brené Brown speaks and writes about the concept of "foreboding joy," which refers to a paradoxical feeling of imminent doom that some people get when things go well. Why might a character or human experience foreboding joy? It can be a byproduct of anxiety or pessimism. It can also stem from a wound or worldview that has trained someone to expect that "the other shoe will drop" at any moment, either ending a good streak or cementing a bad one.

Some characters (and people) self-sabotage when they're on a high, effectively creating their own stakes because at least then they have some conscious or unconscious control over that other shoe. It's illogical, but if we think about this from the perspective of feeling vulnerable and not wanting to be surprised, creating our own doom—even in good times—makes a twisted kind of sense.

We already know that Ifemelu, from *Americanah*, has some self-defeating tendencies:

> Sometimes she worried that she was too happy. She would sink into moodiness, and snap at Obinze, or be distant. And her joy would become a restless thing, flapping its wings inside her, as though looking for an opening to fly away.[k]

The same can be said for August from *One Last Stop*, who doesn't have much faith that things will work with Jane. The difference here is that August throws caution to the wind—a big deal for her—and decides to go for it anyway:

> There aren't perfect moments in life, not really, not when shit has gotten as weird as it can get and you're broke in a mean city and the things that hurt feel so big. But there's the wind flying and the weight of months and a girl hanging out an emergency exit, trains roaring all around, tunnel lights flashing, and it feels perfect. It feels insane and impossible and perfect. Jane reels her in by the side of her neck, right there between the subway cars, and kisses her like it's the end of the world.[l]

Notice, once again, the high-stakes language in this interiority, which elicits both character emotion and reader engagement. The action is two people kissing on a train, but during this climactic story development, August feels like it's "the end of the world."

Such voice and language can easily veer into melodramatic territory, but if you've done your story work, you can avoid this pitfall.

Melodrama: A disconnect between context and emotion that doesn't offer enough reason for empathy. For example, if I deny my eight-year-old son access to a screen one afternoon, and he drops to the floor, wailing, this might like melodrama (especially to a tired parent). But if readers already know from previous information— or he shares in interiority or dialogue—that his best friend is competing in a televised chess tournament that afternoon and he promised to watch, the outsized reaction makes more sense.

If you're giving your characters big reactions, or using high-stakes language to make statements like "end of the world" (*One Last Stop*), then you need to offer enough context for the emotion to read as warranted and relatable, rather than overblown.

As you try to balance stakes and emotion without overdoing it, consider playing with paradoxical reactions—a character acting stoic in a grueling scene, or indulging in deep feelings in a relatively calm moment. There are many different ways to achieve emotional depth and nuance without stretching the limits of what readers can logic, understand, and empathize with.

Finally, don't forget that small triumphs should be marked and called out for the high-stakes emotional resonance they represent because these can be few and far between in storytelling. In *The Underground Railroad*, Cora, who has escaped enslavement and reached a free community, observes her new home and marvels:

There were no white visitors this night. Everyone who lived and worked on the farm was in attendance, as well as the families from the neighboring colored farms. Seeing them all in one room, Cora got an idea of how large they were for the first time.... She was surrounded by men and women who'd been born in Africa, or born in chains, who had freed themselves or escaped. Branded, beaten, raped. Now they were here. They were free and black and stewards of their own fates. It made her shiver.[m]

What an incredible reaction as Cora experiences something she never imagined possible, in her day and age: A moment of community, celebration, and solidarity from characters who have suffered and overcome so much, at such great cost. At face value, all she's doing is looking around and noticing, but inside, her heart is brimming.

Now that we've tracked how stakes can be developed in small moments, we need to talk about the kind of stakes most people think of when this term is used in writing theory. Let's see how interiority is used to underscore threatening, dangerous, and even deadly events.

Serious Stakes

This section begins with two excerpts from *Sing, Unburied, Sing*. They show Leonie's point of view and take readers from a small moment with amazing high stakes to the actual worst-case scenario of the story —Mama dying of cancer. The first excerpt appears as Leonie holds a bedside vigil, where Mama's every breath seems like the most significant thing in the world:

> Mama is lying in bed with her face turned to the wall, and her chest is still.... Her arms are all bone.... She swallows, and I feel relief wash through me, and I realize I was watching to see if she was breathing, to see if she was moving, to see if she was still here. It's like a quick rain over hot, dry earth.[n]

While Mama survives that moment, she does end up dying soon after. Leonie's interiority when she realizes Mama's gone is nuanced, full of magical thinking, and even a little bit funny. There's no rending of hair or gnashing of teeth—gestures that stereotypically accompany a death —and this makes the reaction all the more interesting:

> [Mama] couldn't be sleeping. I ain't seen her face this smooth, without tension, in years. I want to slap her awake, for asking me to let her go.... And I want to bring Given back from the dead and make him flesh again just so I can slap him, too, for

leaving. For taking her. There's too much blank sky where a tree once stood. All wrong. The noose tightens.[o]

Notice how this event also triggers Leonie's grief for Given, her brother who preceded Mama in death. Instead of staying in one moment, Leonie tracks her other losses over time.

Interiority Insight: Stakes that add resonance to a plot point don't always come from the present or an imagined future. Sometimes they link back to a past wound as well.

In our next excerpt, from *Guy's Girl*, Ginny is sitting and eating. Externally, this seems low stakes (or maybe steaks?), but the interiority shows she's sliding dangerously back into the arms of an eating disorder:

While she ate, Ginny felt strangely numb. She could almost detach from herself…. All that kept her inside her body was the press of each sugared bite onto her tongue, the feel of it sliding down her throat. It was easy, in the middle of her frenzy, to detach from the reality of what she was doing. What she was putting into herself. What it would do to her…. Ginny is fucking terrified.

The fear rolls over her in long waves. *What did I just do? What did I just do? What did I just do?* Each wave sucks her in, pulls her under, clogs her nose and mouth until she can no longer breathe.[p]

Without the additional context offered in interiority, readers would have no sense of why this moment is so pivotal.

Let's look at another instance of self-inflicted stakes. We've already heard from Joe in *You* about the little secret he's keeping in the bookstore basement: Benji, Beck's ex-boyfriend.

Joe is normally unflappable when it comes to objectively real danger, like, oh, you know, murder. But in this case, it's actually Beck's lack of affection, or her deviations from his expectations, that Joe can't stand. These throw him into (more) high-stakes madness, as shown in interiority:

> It's Thursday morning and our date tonight is my reward for the past three days. Babysitting Benji is no joke, Beck. I don't even know how many times I've locked and unlocked and locked the basement doors as I've come up and down. [The new employee] knows he isn't allowed in the basement and he doesn't have a key. My hand is cramped from gripping the key like it's my lifeline. And it is.[9]

Joe seems nervous about Benji because his new colleague could easily stumble upon him locked in the rare books cage. In an uncharacteristically honest moment, Joe seems to acknowledge his actions as inherently dangerous, even if this whole endeavor was his idea.

He could've feasibly gotten Beck to go out with him without abducting her ex, but Joe's not like other guys, as he'll be the first to tell you. Instead, he's chosen to live on the edge, maybe in a conscious or unconscious bid to hurt Beck, "save" her, or even get himself caught.

If a deranged character feels some measure of unexpressed shame or guilt about their choices, they might "make a mistake" to tie their own hands and forcibly save themselves from their dark urges. They can then be removed from society and play victim without having to face the reality of their actions.

Now let's leave the realistic world for one with stakes and maybe even *stakes*—the wooden weapon kind.[1] Fantasy and adventure stories carry a lot of stakes potential, and these genres offer tons of external conflicts that translate to big emotional ramifications.

---

1. Told you there were bad stakes jokes.

Speculative Stakes

When a frozen, smiling body is found in an alley in *The Fox Wife*, it has all the hallmarks of a fox spirit's victim. Fox spirit Snow, who gets along on her wiles and by keeping a low profile, considers this bad news for her entire species:

> I'd had a bad feeling about that rumor as soon as I heard it. A virtuous fox ought not to prey on people; it's precisely this kind of behavior that gets us hunted down and skinned.[r]

She has seen harm come to others of her kind, so her extrapolation and concern carry real weight.

As we get further into plot-heavy fantasy From the Shelves stories, the stakes rise, and character reactions become bigger. Here, in *The City We Became*, the spirit of New York City attacks the antagonist, now in the form of an amorphous monster:

> *You came to the wrong town.* I curb stomp it with the full might of Queens and something inside the beast breaks and bleeds iridescence all over creation. This is a shock, for it has not been truly hurt in centuries. It lashes back in a fury, faster than I can block, and from a place that most of the city cannot see, a skyscraper-long tentacle curls out of nowhere to smash into New York Harbor.[s]

The far-reaching ramifications of this clash are beautifully expressed here, as is the dynamic energy and courage it took for this protagonist to fight for his city. We also get some world-building context about how long the villain has gone unchallenged, and it's worked in seamlessly.

Sometimes, though, the antagonizing presence is sneakier, more creepy and off-putting. It's less of a fireworks show and more of an icy finger down the spine, as seen when Nahri encounters a zombie-like creature in *The City of Brass*:

> After a few minutes, she stopped, growing disturbed. There was nothing. No beating heart, no surging blood and bile. She could

sense no organs, nothing of the sparks and gurgles of the hundreds of natural processes that kept her and every other person she'd ever met alive. Even his breathing was wrong, the movement of his chest false. It was as though someone had created an image of a person, a man out of clay, but forgotten to give it a final spark of life. He was ... unfinished.[t]

I love the way Nahri thinks about her opponent and how slowly her suspicions dawn as she realizes what she's dealing with. In her world, she must constantly be on edge, because danger and magic lurk everywhere. After Nahri runs into a darkened cemetery to shake a pursuer, she feels incredibly vulnerable, especially since she's unarmed. She grows increasingly worried for her safety and engages in some bargaining behavior, a snippet of which we first saw in Chapter 8:

The cemetery was silent, free of the sounds of pursuing feet or angry threats. Could she have lost him?

She leaned against the cool stone, trying to catch her breath and wishing desperately for her dagger—not that her puny blade would offer much protection against the excessively armed man hunting her.

I can't stay here. But Nahri could see nothing but tombs in front of her and had no idea how to get back to the streets.... *Please, God ... or whoever is listening,* she prayed. *Just get me out of this, and I swear I'll ask Yaqub for a bridegroom tomorrow. And I'll never do another zar.* She took a hesitant step.

An arrow whistled through the air.[u]

The pacing is very well done in her interiority, as she worries, begs, then wonders if she's finally safe ... and *BOOM*! She narrowly misses death and the pursuit starts all over again.

Interiority Insight: Allow your characters to take a breath and lower their guard, even when they're in danger. Manipulate them into complacency or bravado, then reverse their expectations with a reveal or surprise.

I'll end on two excerpts from *Red Queen*, as Mare grapples with what it means to have supposedly impossible magic. First, we get her interiority after she demonstrated her unbridled electricity powers to her trainer Julian for the first time (this moment itself is excerpted in Chapter 14). She doesn't trust anyone in the Silver world and is immediately convinced she'll be jailed or killed for her show of force:

> *He knows. I'm finished. It's all over.* I should beg, plead for him to keep my secret, but the words stick in my throat. The end is coming, and I can't even open my mouth to stop it.[v]

But this worst-case-scenario thinking turns out to be overblown and Julian helps her. Danger lurks elsewhere, though. As she faces off in battle with some other palace Silvers to determine the court's pecking order, she's pitted against Evangeline, her nemesis and future sister-in-law, who was described in Chapter 12. Mare suspects she could very easily defeat Evangeline but keeps her power a secret. The stakes couldn't be higher, as Maven, the prince she must charm, is watching:

> I hear Maven through the shriek of metal and cheering classmates, roaring for me to finish her.... For a brief moment, I feel what it's like to be one of them. To feel strength and power absolutely, to know you can do what millions can't. Evangeline feels like this every day, and now it's my turn. *I'll teach you what it's like to know fear.*[w]

As it turns out, Mare doesn't just hate Evangeline, she covets her power. And now that she's able to wield magic, she may survive this trial by fire in the Silver palace, after all. With this interiority, readers are more likely to root for her because audiences like to track character empowerment.

As we saw in this section, the larger setting of a story world—whether it's a fantasy with different magical rules, or simply a specific contemporary and realistic society or culture—supports and influences premise, protagonist, and plot. Creating a story world isn't the first thing writers think of when it comes to character development, but interiority is useful in this discipline as well. That's what I'll talk about next, in the final chapter of Part 3.

18

STORY WORLD

As I first mentioned in Chapter 2, many fantasy, speculative, sci-fi, and historical novels must do more telling, especially early on, simply because the writer needs to flesh out a time period, location, and set of magical or scientific rules (if applicable). But make no mistake: A contemporary realistic book set in the current time and a recognizable place needs world-building, too. A rural setting differs from an urban one, and nepo babies can have very different perspectives on the same piece of property compared to the landscaper's kids, living in the carriage house.

Interiority is very useful in establishing this kind of context, defining the rules of the world, and, best of all, helping characters reflect on how their environments affect and inform their sense of self.

You don't have to be hindered by "write what you know" when it comes to world-building (more on this specific maxim in Chapter 21). Yes, it's true that your experiences and culture inform your writing on a general level. But you can expand beyond your setting horizons, especially if you're writing a speculative story, by leveraging research and imagination.

Historical is one major genre that requires intense world-building. Sometimes your narrative will stick closely to what you're able to learn from first-person accounts. Other times, a premise will take some liberties by imagining what a well-known historical person's life might have been like behind closed doors, or use a speculative or revisionist approach, as Colson Whitehead does in *The Underground Railroad*.

Intention is important here. Why are you tweaking history? Whose story are you telling? What is your objective in telling *this* story in *this* way? Is it to shine a light on an undiscovered or unexamined historical figure or time period? Is it to find an imaginative way to dramatize a social movement or the ramifications of a prevailing narrative?

Working with historical settings takes a lot of research, planning, and decision-making, especially since you may be asked by a publisher to show your work, clear yourself of any potential liability (for example, if you're demonizing a historical figure who still has an active estate), and answer to academic experts on your chosen figure, location, or time period. You don't have to write *to please* other people, but get ready to hear from strangers with have qualified (and unqualified!) knowledge and opinions about any historical person or event.[1]

Every story world is distinct. For our purposes, I've divided our From the Shelves examples into those with a more realistic setting, including historical projects which take place in an imagined version of our world, and those that showcase more expansive speculative world-building.

Realistic World-building

While fantasy and science fiction stories have alternative universal laws and magic rules, our realistic world has cultures and family systems, and these still need definition. Early in the story, the familial worldview is often the accepted status quo, and nobody is actively rebelling against or trying to change it. This means there's room for a personal growth arc that sees the protagonist separate from their family of origin.

This is demonstrated by Lily from *Bad Fruit*, who's very skilled at taking the temperature of the family weather system, which happens to be dictated by her unpredictable and unreasonable mother. Lily's older sister, Francie, has left home and seems ignorant of the trouble brewing

---

1. Let's be honest, strangers will have all kinds of opinions about every kind of book.

with Mama. In fact, Lily has largely worked to keep her sister in the dark, especially for the sake of her two nephews. Lily observes, which she does a lot, and extrapolates:

> But Francie isn't schooled in forecasting Mama's weather. From the minute their shotgun wedding was announced, we shielded her from how bad Mama could get, inventing excuses for why she can't come to the boys' events, diverting her from seeing the boys when she was in one of her moods. So it is, in part, our fault.... She hasn't realized the threat.[a]

Lily feels responsible for Francie's obliviousness, and questions whether she made the right decision to shield her. These emotions add a layer of shame, since Lily could potentially lighten her own mental and emotional load by involving reinforcements. This scene happens early in the story, before anyone asserts any power or challenges the prevailing norms. Notice the high-stakes language here and how it enhances the interiority.

Domestic culture and world-building also feature in *The New House*, as Millie studies the features of the home she hopes to buy from Stacey and interprets its inhabitants:

> Her sweaters are neatly folded in colour-coded stacks, but his side of the wardrobe is a tangled mess, with ties dribbling down the shelves, and balled-up socks on the floor. In my experience, incompatibility in a wardrobe is a more reliable indicator of divorce than infidelity.[b]

This might seem judgmental and unnecessarily fussy to some, but Millie is actually on to something. Let's go over to Stacey's POV and see how she, the owner of the "colour-coded stacks," characterizes the domestic culture of her marriage:

> Ever since Archie went off to boarding school, things between [Stacey and her husband] have escalated. Their son's absence has allowed them to fight without boundaries. They don't have to wait till he's asleep and keep their voices down as they tear into each other behind closed doors. It's almost as if they've

come to relish the chance to plumb the depths of their sickness together.[c]

Joe from *You* is similarly deranged. Let's expand the lens a little to learn how Joe sees the world. As he imagines what Beck's life is like based on her social media and glimpses through her window, his observations are full of patronizing and creepy (feigned) concern:

Days pass and I grow anxious. You parade too much and it's unsafe and it only takes *one* weirdo to spot you inside and decide to go and get you. A few days later I wear my carpenter costume and I fantasize about putting bars on your windows, protecting this display case you call a *home*. I think of this neighborhood as safe, and it is, but there's deathliness to the quiet here. I could probably strangle some old man in the middle of the street and nobody would come outside to stop me.[d]

Of course, Joe says this with a completely straight face as he's lurking outside Beck's apartment, totally unable to admit to himself that *he* is the "weirdo" he claims to worry about. He also demonstrates a very casual attitude about violence, easily imagining himself strangling "some old man in the middle of the street" to prove a point. This interiority not only offers his biased sense of what Beck's neighborhood is like but showcases his skewed worldview.

Let's continue to explore some very specific worlds and settings as seen through the biased eyes of our various protagonists. *Sing, Unburied, Sing* offers an atmospheric description of Mississippi as Leonie considers running away from her problems while slotting a reluctant Michael into the role of knight in shining armor:

But I know that if I continue to ask, sour the air of the car with *pleases*, he will drive ... for hours into the black-soiled heart of the state, back toward the cage that held him, drive so far the horizon opens up like a shucked oyster shell.... We move forward, and the air from the open windows makes the glass shudder, alive as a bed of mollusks fluttering in the rush of the tide: a shimmer of froth and sand. The tires catch and spit gravel. We hold hands and pretend at forgetting.[e]

Her descriptive language adds a dreamlike quality to this imagined, escapist road trip. The "pretend at forgetting" phrasing also shows some self-awareness that running away won't solve anything. But Leonie might not be able to come up with any better ideas because escape has been her coping mechanism for so long.

While dreams can be romantic, Leonie and Michael's reality is a lot grittier and more depressing, especially when we switch POVs and see it through Jojo's eyes. In this excerpt, they're visiting an "associate" of Michael's:

> There are tables with glass beakers and tubes and five-gallon buckets on the ground and empty cold-drink liter bottles, and I know I've seen this before, know that smell.... The reason [Michael] and Leonie fought, the reason he left, the reason he's in jail. The man is cooking, moves as easy and sure as a chef, but there is nothing to eat here. My stomach burns. I sneak back around to the front of the house.[f]

It's incredibly telling that young Jojo knows what a meth lab smells like and uses accurate terms like "cooking"—though he makes sure to clarify "there is nothing to eat here." He needs normal childhood comforts like sustenance and nurturing, but his desires go unmet. This pointed interiority describes the depravity of this setting and offers a sense of Michael's backstory, too.

Isabelle from *All the Dangerous Things* tour-guides readers through the niche world of true crime conventions, which are depressing in a different way. Her interiority is inflected with judgment because Isabelle is sick of doing these—and tired of the questions, inquisitive stares, and dark fantasies—but feels she can't stop in case an appearance leads to Mason's return:

> That's why events like TrueCrimeCon exist ... a safe space where they can bask in the bloody glow of violence for just a few days, using another person's murder as a means of entertainment.[g]

Here's another skewed depiction of the vibe. This is notable because Isabelle ends up partnering with Waylon for an exclusive interview after this conference leaves her felling more jaded than ever, as we saw in Chapter 3:

> After a while, you start running into the same people over and over again. There are regulars at these things, and they always find me, somehow, introducing themselves again or just assuming I should remember them. Expecting me to engage with their questions and their small talk, as if I am nothing more than an author at their book club.[h]

Interiority Insight: World-building can illuminate norms and social expectations, which are especially relevant as a character considers their place within the established context.

Montserrat from *Silver Nitrate* is similarly suspicious of the faith traditions that are popular in her Mexican culture. Here, she expresses disappointment at how hollow these rituals ring to her:

> Montserrat's faith in such remedies was lukewarm. She'd placed a statue of San Antonio upside down to get a sweetheart and tied ribbons around an aloe vera plant, but it was out of habit more than pure belief. She wished she could believe, though.[i]

While she establishes some cultural world-building with this interiority, Montserrat also judges herself for being unable to muster true belief, which she assumes comes easily to others.

American culture is a pervasive world-building element in many novels and memoirs set in the United States. Let's see how it's depicted in a section from *Brutes*, narrated by Hazel:

> There is a specifically Floridian smell, the stink of America (microwaved plastic, air freshener, hot oil) mixed with mildew and something else, something ancient, rotting, and sweaty,

possibly life.... The smell is so familiar it's like I'm rocking back in the womb.[j]

This novel offers an incisive critique of American culture, especially when it comes to teen and twentysomething ennui. Florida, where the author is from and the story is set, becomes a character in and of itself:

> We are surrounded by dying plants. Through the porch screen, I can see a yard full of rusting toys, a chair frame with no seat, a collapsed clothesline, all leading down to a small, low lake. A screen of insects hums above its surface. A shopping car sticks out of its center, the wheels spinning slowly with the first curls of storm wind.[k]

There are some wonderful word choices and images here. The mall is also a major setting, infused with interpretations of teen culture. (Remember the girls hoping to get discovered by Star Search in Chapter 8?) Though many of us have been to an American (or American-style) shopping mall, this interiority still offers readers a very demographic-specific interpretation, this time from the POV of the young joint narrators:

> [Teenagers] cry about sexy photos sent around school. They cry about being dumped. They cry about death. They cry about their parents getting divorced. No one mentions abortions, though we know some of the girls have held their mom's hands on the way to Planned Parenthood. No one talks about pills, though we know half the boys have baggies of them rattling in the pockets of their cargo shorts.[l]

Anna in *Aesthetica* presents another vision of the mall, but on the opposite coast and end of the socioeconomic spectrum. This interiority offers readers a vicarious peek at Beverly Hills and includes a meditation on the protagonist's privilege as a young, white, and good-looking woman, which allows her to exist in this space without anybody thinking twice about whether she belongs:

> I wandered around the Beverly Center, watching my reflection

in every window, a small, solitary girl projected over shoes, bags, lush swathes of leather and silk. Meaningless objects next to the young, white beauty I wore as a pass, permission to enter and browse. Still, I was aware of the scratched pleather backpack I used as a purse, the silver clutch I carried at night, their cheap sameness in every picture I shared.[m]

Notice the conflict introduced via this world-building interiority because Anna *doesn't* actually belong. She can't afford any of the things she sees, and this is an issue for an aspiring influencer because she intends to build her career on looking good and consuming luxurious material possessions.

Interiority Insight: You're not merely describing a setting when you do world-building. You're also layering in cultural and character considerations. Don't forget about conflict and tension, either. Above, the high of shopping in an exclusive place is immediately undermined when Anna is reminded of her cheap accessories and outsider status.

Now we switch gears to the Pacific Northwest, where the setting takes on a darker atmospheric tone in *The Glass Hotel*. In this excerpt, a character who has accepted a job at the titular hotel first sees its location on a remote island:

Melissa piloted them around the peninsula and the hotel was before them, an improbable place lit up against the darkness of the forest, and for the first time Walter understood what Raphael had meant when he'd talked about an element of surrealism. The building would have been beautiful anywhere, but placed here, it was incongruous, and its incongruity played a part in the enchantment … [Walter] closed the curtain against the darkness and thought about what Raphael had said, about the hotel's existing outside of time and space. There's such happiness in a successful escape.[n]

There's something otherworldly about the place. It feels distinct from the suffocating consumerist blur of Florida. This island is as isolated as you can get, and it's interesting to see the kind of character who enjoys that sort of thing. There's tension introduced in the interiority, as readers know where Walter is heading but are left wondering what he's escaping.

Visitors and immigrants tend to have distinct interpretations of American culture, too. When Ifemelu first emigrates from Nigeria in *Americanah*, which deals with many issues of personal and cultural identity, she interprets her new home via smell, just as Hazel did in the *Brutes* excerpt. Her interiority hits a different note, though:

> Philadelphia had the musty scent of history. New Haven smelled of neglect. Baltimore smelled of brine, and Brooklyn of sun-warmed garbage. But Princeton had no smell. She liked taking deep breaths here.[o]

Interiority Insight: Don't forget sensory details when world-building or plunging your reader into a scene. Sight is easy to access, especially when writing description, but you shouldn't neglect touch, taste, sound, or, yes, smell.

A disillusioned Obinze, who has left England and moved back to Nigeria by the end of the novel, now believes American culture taints a person. As Ifemelu returns, he can't help wondering whether she will be similarly affected:

> There was a manic optimism that he noticed in many of the people who had moved back from America in the past few years, a head-bobbing, ever-smiling, over-enthusiastic kind of manic optimism that bored him, because it was like a cartoon, without texture or depth. He hoped she had not become like that. He could not imagine that she would have.[p]

Obinze shouldn't worry. Ifemelu eventually loses her enthusiasm for her adopted country, especially as she becomes aware of slavery's legacy and how it affects people's perceptions of her, even though she's African, not African-American. She writes the following on her blog:

> Being American means you take the whole shebang, America's assets and America's debts, and Jim Crow is a big-ass debt.... In the hatred of American Blacks, there is no possibility of envy— they are so lazy, these blacks, they are so unintelligent, these blacks.[q]

Ifemelu's specific personal take on the issue of racism suggests she doesn't want to shoulder the repercussions of slavery and deal with the vile ideas that some Americans express about *all* Black people. This attitude is the opposite of the "manic optimism" Obinze expects, which sets them up to reunite in Nigeria.

Let's leave our contemporary time and culture behind and look at how world-building functions in a historical context. While much of *The Underground Railroad* reflects a realistic historical setting, the novel also has fantasy elements. The figurative Underground Railroad network of safe houses that aided enslaved peoples' escape to free states becomes a literal railroad that has its own rules and magical properties, including the ability to disgorge its passengers into alternate realities.

This world and time period are defined by rigid divisions between white and Black, rich and poor, and masculine men and those who don't fit the mold. The following excerpt expresses the prevailing attitudes of the day as the primary antagonist, Arnold Ridgeway, a blacksmith's son and slave catcher, judges the "wealthiest men" of the material world. While readers have no empathy for him or his heinous acts, we're treated to his perspective on society's power dynamics and his interpretation that proper gentlemen are uninspired cogs who add little true value. He's bitter, of course, because he's forced to work an odious, if lucrative, job instead of landing a white collar vocation or inheriting easy wealth:

> He couldn't turn to the anvil because there was no way to surpass his father's talent. In town he scrutinized the faces of men in the same way that his father searched for impurities in metal.... Even the wealthiest men, influencing the far-off

London exchanges and local commerce alike, provided no inspiration. He acknowledged their place in the system, erecting their big houses on a foundation of numbers, but he didn't respect them. If you weren't a little dirty at the end of the day, you weren't much of a man.[r]

This would read very differently if we were getting the interiority of those wealthy Londoners, busy spreading the gospel of capitalism. What might a "proper gentleman" say about a blacksmith? A slave catcher? An enslaved person? One of the book's primary protagonists, Cora, is able to escape Arnold's clutches and the geographical south, but she begins to realize that she can't entirely get away from the time period, racism, or her identity as a formerly enslaved Black woman. A real and present danger is the spread of pro-slavery ideology in one of the places she visits:

Last week a feed store hung a shingle saying WHITES ONLY—a nightmare reaching up from the south to claim them.[s]

This sentence of world-building interiority offers a lot of emotional resonance. Another stop Cora makes on the Underground Railroad provides neatly structured lives to formerly enslaved Black women in an up-and-coming city. They get jobs, a place to live, and the promise of upward mobility. At face value, this package deal sounds good. But Cora's impression changes after she experiences what it's like to sleep in the bunkhouses:

She slept poorly. In the eighty bunks the women snored and shifted under their sheets. They had gone to bed believing themselves free from white people's control and commands about what they should do and be. That they managed their own affairs. But the women were still being herded and domesticated. Not pure merchandise as formerly but livestock: bred, neutered. Penned in dormitories that were like coops or hutches.[t]

This introduces an interesting and nuanced question: What does "freedom" actually mean? Here, Cora is technically free, but she is still "penned" together with many other women into an anonymous "herded and domesticated" existence. Yes, she isn't "pure merchandise as formerly" but she still doesn't feel this stop on the Underground Railroad represents the full extension of what free life could be. She decides to move on and seek her fortune elsewhere.

If we go back further in time to colonial America and Lamentations's trek across the sparsely inhabited forest in *The Vaster Wilds*, we'll see that her world looks very different, even compared to Cora's. This new, unconquered[2] land is dangerous, threatening her with predators, thirst, hunger, and strange men:

> Her breath was ragged and with effort she quieted it. She let the silence seep back into her, into the forest, and it smoothed over the memory of her crashing footsteps, and she wondered if she had been loud enough to have waked the men of the fort or the original men of this forest. The men known, the men unknown. Either could be creeping near to her even now.[u]

Part of this particular world-building interiority emphasizes how vulnerable Lamentations is, and her perspective adds to our understanding of the woods. Next, Lamentations sees the wild through the filter of her culture and understanding of human nature as she imagines what expansion-minded men would do to this unspoiled place:

> And the girl looked upon the vast and stretching canopy of the trees, the birds thick flying branch to branch, the sun in softness falling through the new leaves and shivering with happiness upon the ground, and said with sadness, My people would look upon such places and hate what they saw, would replace it all with cobbled streets and smithies throwing black clouds of smoke into the air.[v]

To her, the sanctity and solitude of the woods is preferable to the crush of human society, which is why she escaped to begin with. Even

---

2. Of course this territory is already populated by indigenous people.

though her life has become much harder, Lamentations seems to prefer it.

Interiority Insight: What would an idealized version of your story world look like to your particular character? Would they ever try to make that world, or something close to it, a reality? Why or why not?

I'll end our exploration of realistic world-building on a similar theme, this time from Jack in *Wellness*. He was raised on a farm in the Midwest and has witnessed the land transform into strip malls and highways, almost as if against its will. Nostalgic for a history he'll never truly experience, he tries to picture the prairie's glory days:

> Jack tries to imagine what America's prairie looked like before the farms came: swells of grass rising above his head, swaying and rocking in the unstoppable summer wind, the same view in every direction, a perfectly straight and uninterrupted horizon. All of it, now gone. He wonders if this is also why travelers through the Flint Hills look around and see nothing, if maybe we call something "nothing" to avoid the knowledge that it's been lost.[w]

Jack's interiority introduces a wonderful meditation point: Humans call "something 'nothing' to avoid the knowledge that it's been lost." He believes we either ascribe meaning to essential places or bury their memory because it hurts too much to grieve them. By adding Jack's worldview to this interiority, the author expresses a complex thematic idea in a very elegant way.

World-building tends to be more overt and rule-based in a fantasy, sci-fi, or speculative context, so let's pivot to showcase some of our other From the Shelves worlds.

Fantasy World-Building

This is not meant to be an exhaustive guide to fantasy and science fiction world-building. For a deeper dive into this topic, check out *Wonderbook* by Jeffrey VanderMeer. Given our purposes, I suggest you create your planned magic system and fantasy or science fiction society by prioritizing its effect on your protagonist. Often, a compelling character is on the outside of prevailing cultural dynamics and power structures. They have to figure out their own way to make a difference, take down those in control, or reconcile their personal moral code with that of their society.

Not all speculative stories feature characters with special abilities—or who can interface with powerful creatures or technology—but many do. These powers can be granted, earned, wielded with a spell or object, or innate, and it's especially interesting to meet a protagonist when their own magic awakens (or doesn't), or a character who represents an exception to an established rule. In fact, there is a familiar archetype that tends to crop up in a lot of fantasy and science fiction stories, called the Chosen One.

The Chosen One: This common plot and character trope usually entails a protagonist who's selected (by external forces, prophecy, or some innate quality) to perform a high-stakes task (i.e. save the world). In order to make this premise compelling to readers, agents, and publishers who are quite jaded with it, you'll need to include logic for why *this* character is charged with such a vital mission. Why would a powerful entity like a monarchy or the FBI need someone who has never wielded magic (or is just a kid, in the case of MG and YA) to do an important job? Why not do it themselves or bring in trained professionals? This is a plot hole that you'll need to overcome with strong reasoning right away. Consider inverting or otherwise playing with expectations about a Chosen One-style character, too. For example, the protagonist might be grossly unfit for the task but has to rise to the occasion anyway, even though this twist is also becoming rather familiar.

Let's explore what a Chosen One story looks like when a protagonist's internal or external identity expectations aren't met, and they have to go on a journey to figure out whether they'll get their promised powers. This is the conflict in *The Spirit Glass*, as Corazon has high hopes but no magic yet:

> All her life she had been told that she would be a great babaylan. She just had to wait. But she'd been waiting for years, and in two days she would be twelve! That's when most babaylans started their official training … and Corazon still had no sign that her magic was anywhere near waking up.[x]

She does end up journeying to the spirit realm but nothing happens how Corazon expects it to. With the support of several relatives and allies, she quests to be reunited with her dead parents. This is the moment she first sees beyond the veil which separates the world she knows from the one she doesn't:

> A slit of darkness opened behind her, as if someone had unzipped the air from the other side. A thing that was not quite a hand reached through.[y]

We get some colorful voice and interpretation from Corazon as she confronts this new world:

> Corazon had seen plenty of manananggal on the Midnight Bridge, though she didn't always recognize them at first. They were very pretty and tended to wear long dresses. If it weren't for their "I like to munch on human organs" tendency, it would be easy to mistake them for a lovely nature spirit like an engkanto maiden.[z]

This is where we get a sense of the fun and promise of the premise (see Chapter 3) for this universe and its mythological cast of characters. World-building offers wonderful opportunities to showcase your writing style, fantasy imagination, and any research you're bringing to the table in order to give even a strange and alien dimension the ring of truth, which is often so important in a fantasy.

Interiority Insight: Sometimes a speculative world is completely different from ours—not even in the same universe. Other times, we're in our world but with a twist.

In *The City We Became*, Aislyn is an outsider who has already aligned with the antagonist. Here, she considers whether she fits within a strange peer group of unlikely heroes:

> Aislyn stares back, understanding at last. Five of them, plus some sixth who is *primary*. She is Staten Island and they are the other boroughs, plus New York itself. And are they like her, these other strangers? Do they feel the needs of thousands, hear the voices of millions in their heads? She wants to meet them. Ask them questions, like *How did you get your borough to shut up? And is it really my friend or am I just that lonely?*[aa]

Remember, she's an outcast, so she finds these dynamics difficult to navigate. But there's also a glimmer of hope in her interiority that she'll be able to relate and find community. Readers also get a peek at the minutiae of having these powers. For example, Staten Island speaks to her, which she finds annoying. This is a specific and unexpected gripe, so it commands attention.

A protagonist must figure out the rules of their magical, fantasy, or science fiction world, and this tends to be a big part of the first act of any speculative plot, as is the case with *Red Queen*. Sometimes, crucial world-building snaps into focus much later, as a character realizes the true meaning and purpose of the fantasy element they've been grappling with, which happens in *The Spirit Glass*.

"The setting both *mirrors our real world* and *deviates from it* in interesting ways."

JEFF VANDERMEER

Speculative world-building can also tie into theme. In *The Fair Folk*, Felicity finally realizes the fairies are just lost children, and this world-view informs how they interface with the human realm, a truth foreshadowed by an excerpt we saw in Chapter 14. Felicity is the perfect character for this story because she wouldn't necessarily have been able to develop this insight or empathy for Them if she wasn't on her own coming-of-age growth arc:

> Damaged or desperate children, who found that whatever they imagined could become real … could create and sustain wonders beyond anything they could have managed on their own. If there was a leader, perhaps a little older or more daring than the rest, they could become a force to be reckoned with. But with the values and judgment of children, of course they would be mischievous, capricious, not to be trusted. And if they sought revenge for the wrongs done to them, they would be capable of great malice and thoughtless cruelty.[bb]

Felicity recalls her childhood bullies and realizes the fairies make her feel a similar way, as we saw in Chapter 13. This helps her understand the fantasy magic she's trapped within and leads to her idea for disentangling from the fae at last. This is an example of world-building logic in action, and hints at another relevant issue to explore in your fantasy, science fiction, and magical realism stories: power dynamics. In most worlds, including the real one, there's generally a faction in power. This sets some characters apart to be outcasts and underdogs. Since readers tend to naturally empathize with and relate to David, not Goliath, our protagonists often find themselves on the outside of the prevailing hierarchy.

Status can be determined by race, creed, gender, magical skill, caste, or any other element which separates characters into groups. This power imbalance is often quite alienating and difficult for the protagonist to navigate, especially if they live in a world where authority is wielded by a corrupt regime. This can create worldview and value system inner struggle.

Every world has power dynamics, as does every scene. In fact, a lot of interpersonal conflict arises from characters chasing objectives and needs or negotiating status imbalances. Someone generally has the upper hand and it's usually not the protagonist. There's inherent tension in any set-up where one person has more knowledge, rank, control, capital, or authority than another.

We can see this dynamic in *Red Queen*, as Mare deeply resents playing along and pretending to be Mareena. To successfully survive the highly imbalanced power dynamic of the Silver court, she must marry a prince, but even this might not guarantee acceptance. Far from it. Not only because she can't stomach pretending and being submissive to people who deeply hate Reds, but because she senses danger will befall her anyway:

> When the maids pinch and pull me into a gown, I feel like a corpse being dressed for her funeral. I know it's not far from the truth. Red girls do not marry Silver princes. I will never wear a crown or sit on a throne. Something will happen, an *accident* maybe. A lie will raise me up, and one day another lie will bring me down.[cc]

Interiority Insight: Remember to find the stakes of any power discrepancy—the higher, the better. Speculative stories often have action-driven plots, so the stakes potential is ever-present.

Conflict can also come from being part of the powerful elite. In *Jade City*, various neighborhoods are ruled by crime families in a strictly regimented social structure. Those with status are able to wield the power of jade, which we saw in action in Chapter 14. Shae is part of a well-known family but is trying to fly under the radar as she attempts to make her own way:

> Shae checked into a hotel room in the city and spent the next three days searching for an apartment … it wasn't as if she could live wherever she wanted. She could take off her jade but not her face or her name; there were parts of the city it would be best for her to avoid. Even confining the search to districts firmly in No Peak control, she spent from dawn until past dusk

taking the malodorously crowded subway from stop to stop, sweating ferociously in the summer heat, visiting one building after another.[dd]

I love the interiority of "she could take off her jade but not her face or her name," which offers readers a stark reminder that Shae has been classified a certain way in this society. It hard to escape when everyone knows who and what she is, especially since she must stick to "friendly" neighborhoods for her own safety.

Let's peek into the perspective of another character who represents the prevailing power structure, Father Konstantin, from *The Bear and the Nightingale*. This is how he evaluates his provincial charges and prepares to bring them out of the darkness of their old ways:

> The place was infested with demons: the chyerti of the old religion. These foolish, wild people worshipped God by day and the old gods in secret; they tried to walk both paths at once and made themselves base in the sight of the Father. No wonder evil had come to work its mischief.
>
> Excitement rolled through his veins. He'd thought to molder here, in the back of beyond. But here was a battle indeed, a battle for mastery of the souls of the men and women, with evil on one side and him as God's messenger on the other.
>
> The people were gathering. He could almost feel their eager curiosity. It was not yet like Moscow, where people snatched hungrily at his words and loved him with their frightened yes. Not yet.
>
> But it would be.[ee]

As discussed in Chapter 9, no antagonist thinks they're evil, deep down. Here, Father Konstantin not only believes he has the moral high ground, but that he'll whip the villagers into spiritual shape. He sees his as a divinely ordained purpose and fully intends to save their souls. How could this be a bad thing? Of course, he's getting into a fight with forces he doesn't understand, but early in the story, he assumes his position at the top of this world's power structure is secure, and extrapolates that he, personally, is blessed.

In many narratives where fantasy, speculative, or science fiction protagonists face an unequal power dynamic, they also get the opportunity to experience "how the other half lives." Even though she hates it, Mare gets the rare chance to inhabit the palace as a Silver heiress, while Father Konstantin is humbled in the woods. Of course, there are problems inherent in any reversal of fortune, as it represents a fragile truce with a new and dangerous world. Stakes rise as the protagonist fears discovery, loses their moral code and value system, or risks being ousted or killed.

Lovecraft Country is a speculative historical novel that imagines a world where magic is very much alive, especially as it pertains to racial dynamics. This power offers Ruby, a Black character, the incomprehensible opportunity to become a white woman whenever she drinks a potion. (You'll remember Ruby's strict moral code from Chapter 6, as she imagines how clean her soul will be on Judgment Day.) Unfortunately, she succumbs to temptation, though the first time she drinks the elixir, she's tricked into it without understanding its power or provenance.

Here's Ruby's interiority as she experiences a power dynamic reversal as her new avatar, Hillary. She's able to shop in a department store and a policeman offers her assistance. This is unheard of when she's Ruby. After making her way through this bizarre new world, Ruby studies her—well, Hillary's—mirror image:

> She ... focused on Hillary's reflection in the glass. Bad girl, Ruby told her, but Hilary just smiled, shameless, and Ruby felt herself smiling too. She thought: Revenge, free lunch, my own police escort if I want.... What else comes with being you?[ff]

The horrible truth soon emerges that the potion is made from the blood of a captive white woman. This human toll is tough to justify, no matter how good the drink and its effects make Ruby feel. This taste of power is intoxicating, but once Ruby realizes the dark side of the magic, she'll have a big decision to make.

A story's world, whether realistic or fantastical, reflects and informs a protagonist's standing in their culture or society, orients them within various power dynamics, and presents them with high-stakes choices about who to be, how to act, where to align themselves, and what they truly value. Done with an eye toward character development, world-building can be a pointed way to add further nuance to your protagonist and plot.

This wraps up our Part 3 discussion of external story elements including secondary characters, relationships, reactions, decisions, stakes, and the story world. Up next is Part 4, which I'll kick off by tackling the final character-specific craft topics that infuse a story with a unique perspective: voice and writing style.

PART 4

PUTTING IT ALL TOGETHER

19

VOICE AND WRITING STYLE

Now that your story's character development and structure are in place, let's explore the all-important topics of voice and writing style. These ideas have been heavily referenced throughout this guide, but this chapter really buckles down and confronts the enigmatic voice questions many writers ask: What is voice? Do I have it? If not, how do I get it? It's almost impossible to separate ideas of interiority from voice and writing style. If we're doing our jobs as writers, every time we inhabit a character point of view, we assume the character's voice and personality, especially in first and close-third POV. If we're using an intrusive narrator, we must also develop their particular brand of authorial voice.

Authorial Voice: This can refer to the author-as-narrator, who's cloaked as a POV character, breaking the fourth wall and speaking directly to the audience. It can also be a broader term for the hall-mark writing style that you use as a creator. While some writers vary their tone and voice from one project to another, this term generally applies to consistent elements across someone's body of work. Think about Melissa Broder's deeply neurotic protagonists, Jesmyn Ward's lyrical and emotionally raw descriptions, and Casey McQuiston's witty banter.

Remember, readers want to care and connect. Access to character is the most direct route to this goal, especially when it offers layers of vulnerability, desire, objective, motivation, need, inner struggle, and growth. Voice can be a great craft tool that adds energy and dimension to these elements.

But what *is* voice? Many literary agents and acquisitions editors simply say, "I know it when I see it."

This answer is a copout, and a bit lazy, too. Of course, voice is incredibly subjective, so there's some truth to this statement. A more accurate brush-off would be, "Voice really depends on the writer, project, genre, and protagonist at hand. As long as the prose and dialogue are intentionally done, you're likely to be writing with voice. Whether it personally appeals to an individual gatekeeper is another question."

But we're not here for the brush-off, so let's dig in. To me, voice is a combination of:

- Word choice
- Syntax
- Imagery
- Emotion
- Character

In the following sections, I'll unpack how these elements tend to function in practical terms. Of course, voice and style can be individual to an author, a book, or a singular character, so it's tough to make broad generalizations about all writers and writing. My goal is to give you enough to think about when it comes to your own work.

Word Choice and Syntax

Word choice simply refers to each building block of your sentences— the individual words you're using. Verbs are a great starting point. If possible, you should try to get away from "is" and "was" and reach for another word that's more active and evocative. "Lumbered" and "flitted" are opposites and pack a punch compared to the more neutral "walked."[1]

Notice how each contributes emotion and informs tone, too. You certainly don't want to overdo it on the verbs, but consider what your individual choices are saying and how they set the tone.

Verbs aren't the only driving force of voice, though. You'll also want to analyze the connotations of your adjectives and nouns as you compose with emotional resonance in mind. When you choose a word (or an image, as we'll see in one of the following sections), you should consider what it suggests about character and tone.

This is not, of course, to say that you need to agonize over every single decision you make, sentence by sentence. As long as you think critically and intentionally about how you're conveying your ideas and having your characters come across, you'll be ahead of the curve.

A common misconception is that adverbs make writing active and exciting. I'd like to steer you away from that notion. In fact, adverbs can ruin prose faster than almost any other part of speech. If you find your characters "promenading leisurely," for example, that's a double strike. "Promenading" is a bit of a formal word with historical connotations, so make sure it's actually relevant to your genre and target audience. "Leisurely" is literally part of the definition of "promenading," so you're saying a lot without conveying much meaning.

Moving on from word choice, let's talk about syntax. This refers to the length and complexity of your sentences. If you're writing a younger character or one who's blunt or nonchalant, you might want to use shorter and more straightforward syntax, including sentence fragments.

On the other hand, an erudite or loquacious character might think in more complex sentences, with several clauses tied together, or even the

---

1. However, the opposite is true of fancy "said" and "asked" synonyms in dialogue tags ("she groused," "he shrieked," etc.), as discussed in Chapter 7. For speech tags, the simpler verbs are strongly preferred because they tend to fade into the background, letting your other scene elements shine. You want the dialogue to speak for itself without scaffolding from verbs or adverbs, especially.

occasional run-on. This may not extend to their speaking voice, per the below, but their interiority is likely to have a specific flow to it.

Voice tends to shift when used in dialogue as opposed to narration, which includes interiority. Our dialogue is hindered by the physical and mechanical constraints of breath. Dialogue sentences tend to be shorter because we're limited in how long we can talk before we need to pause. Avoid overlong sentences in speech because they won't seem organic.

Narrative doesn't have to play by these same rules, of course, but I'd still try to keep your sentences to a reasonable length, even for characters who tend to take their time and use more descriptive language. Simple writing is not stupid writing. In fact, it's actually quite difficult to communicate clearly and effectively in a condensed way.[2]

"I didn't have time to write a short letter, so I wrote a long one instead."

MARK TWAIN

Remember to also consider mimetic writing so your mechanics and style align with your scene's pacing. Choose when to zoom in and slow down, and when to zoom out and focus on action.

Mimetic Writing: When writing style mimics the content. A long, congested sentence isn't good for conveying events that happen quickly. Short sentence bursts don't work for languid, luxurious moments. The style should feel consistent with the substance.

Needlessly complex phrasing doesn't make your writing seem smart or impressive. Quite the opposite. When I run into purple prose or overwrought imagery, I see a writer trying too hard. Paradoxically,

---

2. This guide clocks in at 154k words, so I'm a complete hypocrite.

spending your energy on churning out "impressive writing" can actually communicate insecurity, and this often comes down to word choice and syntax.

Purple Prose: A writing style which overuses description, adjectives, adverbs, imagery, and "reach" words (obscure or overly elaborate vocabulary) and somehow manages to come across as both self-conscious and self-satisfied. Imagery and description are fun to create but can also be a writer's downfall. Is the material serving the story, or is it serving a misguided attempt to be a Writer With a Capital W? Ironically, most beginning writers believe purple prose is the essence of talented writing, but voice should support the story, not the other way around. Purple prose is similar to melodrama, defined in Chapter 16. Histrionic, show-off writing can easily become overwhelming, pull focus, and turn readers and gatekeepers off.

Now that you have a clearer sense of the individual building blocks of voice, let's discuss the components of imagery and emotion.

Imagery and Emotion

Your goal is to use imagery and emotion intentionally to support your character, plot, and story world in a way that's appealing to a contemporary audience. As you already know, imagery can get writers into a lot of trouble. If you've done any creative writing training, you've heard of imagery[3] and probably even used simile, metaphor, or other rhetorical devices to convey a specific mental picture (or other visceral experience) to readers. Imagery relies heavily on the senses to describe

---

3. If you're not sure what this means, I'd direct you to do some reading and research, as close explanation of various literary devices is largely outside the scope of this guide. There are entire college textbooks on prosody (the study of poetry, but many verse concepts overlap with prose mechanics) and the various components of sentence-level craft. Pay attention to how other authors use description and invoke comparisons and you'll start to internalize these ideas for yourself. Reading is also just a wonderful habit to get into if you intend to take your own writing seriously.

setting and atmosphere, and the unspoken goal is often to immerse audiences in your story and offer a frisson of enjoyment.

But not all imagery is created equal, and not all moments of emotion (big or small) require it. To me, the most important feature of an image is that it's unexpected but still fits the context. You'll want to stay away from obvious images, such as, "She lit up like a light bulb." Why? Because light bulbs light up (it's right there in the name), so the image doesn't *add* anything to a reader's understanding of the moment or enhance their potential emotional resonance with it. It's a nothing-burger.

You also want to avoid cliché images, which are shorthand attempts to create a desired emotion, such as, "He was giddy as a kid on Christmas morning." This is cheap, we've all heard it a million times, and it has lost any sheen of wonder that it might have once been capable of inducing. (You'll see a cliché leveraged in a particularly clever way in one of our From the Shelves examples in the following chapter. That's pretty much how some writers use familiar images nowadays: ironically or intentionally to make a point.)

Another big error I see in many aspiring manuscripts is reiteration. The writer might not trust themselves to get their point across, so they offer three images when one (more selective and surprising) description will do just fine. For example:

> She sank into the depths of sleep, like a spelunker into a
> shadowy and mysterious cave. No light penetrated her slumber;
> her consciousness was darker than a starless night. She plum-
> meted into dreamland before her head hit the pillow.

I just had to throw a cliché in there, on top of everything else. Is there some writing here? Sure. Are there some images? Yes. But what is the overall effect on the reader? These words are all ringing the same bell, hitting the reader over the head with the same information, being redundant, saying the same thing several times but with different words … do you get the picture?[4]

---

4. Ironic repetition fully intended!

So if you're writing with imagery, you have to aim higher and try harder. Don't reach for the first thing that comes to mind and don't overdo it. I'd much rather see one jaw-dropping image or turn of phrase every few pages than your entire arsenal each time you want to use a description. Not every moment, thought, feeling, or setting flyover needs imagery to support it, either.

An example of a simple image that floored me recently comes from *Whalefall* by Daniel Kraus, which is not technically one of our From the Shelves novels, but I still can't stop thinking about it. In the story, a broken young man, Jay, is grieving his seafaring father. He goes on an ill-advised dive in dangerous waters to try and recover Dad's body. Impossibly, he sees a sperm whale and here's his first encounter with such an epic beast:

> [The whale] holds a pose: a comma in a sentence so large only gods can read it.[a]

WHAT. And I mean *what??????* This sentence stopped me cold[5] in my tracks[6] until I froze like a deer in headlights.[7] Let's see it again:

> [A] comma in a sentence so large only gods can read it.

This image is perfect. It manages to convey the scale, grandeur, and otherworldliness of a whale *and* offers a nod to the whale's shape. It also elicits emotion. At least it did for me. This is the moment Jay encounters the whale who will swallow him. (You read that correctly.) He's getting farther and farther from shore, running on borrowed oxygen, exposed, vulnerable, grieving … then *this thing* rises from the depths.

But instead of "I was so scared to see this giant whale," or anything of the sort, we get an emotional gut-punch of awe, wonder, and, yes, fear (especially when paired with the rest of this passage, in the context of the story's action). And we're treated to all of this by a comparison to

---

5. A cliché image!
6. Another!
7. And another! Have I made my point yet?

something as pedestrian as a comma. I'm serious, y'all. This is an absolute mic drop of an image.

When you're considering your own word choice, syntax, imagery, and emotion, try to make a big effect with a small effort, rather than expending a lot of energy to convey each idea.

Emotion simply means the tone or intended reader reaction you're going for. Words have denotations—literal meanings—and connotations—implied meanings. Those connotations are usually emotional or even subconscious. If you're looking to set a serious scene, let your language and imagery reflect that. As a family sits in a courtroom, waiting to learn if an adoption will be finalized at long last, you'd be remiss to describe the judge's desk as "sparkling" or "glossy," unless those terms are used ironically or to contrast with her serious demeanor. The moment might call for the image of a "dark, heavy mahogany podium with sharp edges." This could be more aligned with what your POV protagonist is feeling as they wait to learn their family's fate.

Of course, the last thing you want is to tell the character's feelings outright, which we discussed in Chapter 2. Words like "nervous" and "scared" have no place in this scene, at least if you really want to render a nuanced character and audience experience on the page. Reach instead for words and images that stir up the same kind of tension, then buttress the scene with interiority that explores the character's wants, needs, wounds, and stakes.

What will happen if this decision goes their way? What if it doesn't? Have them think about the short- and long-term ramifications. What do they say to their spouse? Their lawyer, if they have one? What if the birth parent, who previously signed over parental rights and missed that last three supervised visits, comes storming in?

If you've planned a hard-hitting scene at a crucial point in the story and populated it with characters who want different things and stand to lose a lot, you might find that the storytelling itself doesn't require as much imagery *or* overt markers of emotion to come across as intended.

You might be encouraged to use fewer images and less repetition after reading this chapter, so you can be more selective with your descriptive writing. Do less of it, and when you choose to use imagery, make those words and phrases (and their literal and figurative meanings) accomplish more. You want to wield the language, rather than letting it dictate your choices.

It All Comes Back to Character

Character and voice can't be easily disentangled because they're often one and the same, especially if you're writing in first-person POV. Third-person point of view is also close to the character, but there, we can also get authorial voice, which was defined at the beginning of this chapter. When you think of how old your character is, their cultural context and background, as well as their overall vibe, energy, mood, and position along their growth arc, you will start to tune your ear into what their voice might sound like.

Whether you're aware of it or not, you've already imbibed about 28,000 words' worth of voices from a diverse spread of characters by dipping into our From the Shelves books. And I bet most of the excerpts went down easy.

Discovering and honing a protagonist's voice, regardless of point of view, is really the work of writing a novel from their perspective. What kinds of words and sentence styles do they use? How does their interiority differ from their dialogue? How might they describe the various stimuli in the scene? How could their reactions and interpretations be used to characterize them further?

One thing to watch out for is dry voice, as well as indistinct voices across different point of view characters. To me, dry voice has no place in contemporary fiction, even for academic characters, those involved in STEM, legal, or medical fields, or supposed kids.[8] Not because kids should be speaking in slang and dialect or conveying simple ideas, but because they don't usually say "caused" and "vehicle."

---

8. I cannot tell you how often writers who've created middle-aged-sounding "sixteen-year-olds" come back with, "But my character is *supposed to be a prodigy*, so they can speak like that." If a protagonist doesn't seem young to *me*, an older reader (*ahem* though I'm forever twenty-nine *ahem*), imagine how they'll come across to the actual target audience.

Going to a café and eavesdropping (as long as you're not creepy) might give you a sense of how various demographics speak (and behave) when they're comfortable in their trusted third spaces.

Dry Voice: Overly formal narration and dialogue, often expressing simple ideas with needless verbosity, fussiness, or jargon. Yes, sometimes technical or archaic language is warranted, such as in a police procedural or historical story, respectively, but the overall cadence, sentence structure, and word choice shouldn't be challenging to parse, especially if you're writing contemporary fiction.

For example, let's see some simple scene-setting done in what I'd call a dry voice:

> While they welcomed the extra cover provided by the sunset that caused the street to darken with shadows, they did not welcome the cold that invariably accompanied the arrival of nighttime.

I can appreciate that this example contains some emotional and character layers—the protagonists are clearly looking to stay hidden for a mysterious reason and are physical uncomfortable in the cold.

That being said, this is wordy, tough to read and enjoy, and expresses something simple (night is falling) several ways. Notice that we have "caused" in here, which is one of my least favorite words for creative writing purposes. You'd need a dehumidifier to get any drier. There's also "they did not welcome," which is an overly fussy way of saying that they didn't like something, the word echo of two instances of "welcome," and the ultra-wordy phrasing of "that invariably accompanied the arrival of."

Word Echo: Repeated words or phrases in close proximity. The trick for fixing echo isn't to reach for a thesaurus and simply replace the offending word. Instead, look at your overall sentence structure and ask, "Hey, is there another way I could phrase this so that I don't *have* to repeat myself here?"

How might I rewrite our long-suffering dry voice passage? Maybe something like:

Stella was tempted to take off her hoodie, but the evening brought a chill with it.

However, this revision leaves an important detail out: The character needs cover for something clandestine. Otherwise, we get the darkness, cold, and time of day. I've added a specific point of view, rather than using the joint "they." There's also action here, as Stella physically exists in the scene and considers what she's wearing. But I'm not entirely happy with this revision, so I might add dialogue to inject some energy:

"Hey, put your cloak back on," Colton whispered.

Stella signed. Then shivered. He was probably right. Comfortable as she was in the falling darkness, she knew they'd need cover.

I'm playing with various sentence lengths here, the action of shivering to convey cold, and adding another character to the scene. "She knew they'd need cover" is my attempt to build some stakes and context for their mission, while "comfortable as she was" is a nod to Stella's character. Maybe she's a night owl or feels more at ease in the shadows. "He was probably right" also conveys, with the use of "probably," that Stella might not concede often, as a person, and this says something about her power dynamic and partnership with Colton, too.

So what should you do if you worry your voice isn't working? Sit down and play with it, sentence by sentence. Experiment. See what feels better. Too often, people simply read a writing reference book and bask in the theory, but they don't actually *try* what they're learning. If you recognize yourself in this description, get curious. Why not play around? What's stopping you? Take the pressure to "nail it" away and

have some fun.[9]

My other tip for developing your voice—and making sure it's working as you draft *and* revise—is to read the work aloud. Print the manuscript out and make marks in the margins for anything that sounds weird, or in places where you trip over your words.

Yes, this is a huge pain. It will take a long time. You will probably get a sore throat. And, on top of everything else, your loved ones and neighbors might decide you've finally lost your remaining marbles. But this is a crucial exercise that every writer should do at least once, even if it's with a poem or short story. Voice is meant to be heard. I guarantee you'll learn something about yourself and your work by doing this experiment. (Actually doing it, not just passively filing the tip away for later.)

Odds are you'll spend your entire writing life developing your sense of voice, so there's no endpoint to this journey. Start actively honing your style today. Voice is one of those craft topics you'll be absolutely miserable about unless you relinquish control and enjoy where the ride takes you.

Look, I get it. When I first started doing yoga and heard it called a "practice," I was incensed. A *practice*? No, ma'am. I'm not here to practice. I'm here to *win*. Well, joke's on me, because the most worthwhile skills are often hard to grasp and take lifelong work. It's the same with voice and writing style, which you'll be fiddling with for as long as you're able to sit at a keyboard or notebook. Whew! Okay! Pep talk over.

So far, this chapter has showcased examples I've written (except for that sentence from *Whalefall*), since it'd be bad form to call any of our From the Shelves works out for having voice issues. (A few do, but it'd be unreasonable to expect every sentence to be perfect!)[10] Now let's

---

9. I am absolutely part of this problem as a teacher, editor, and writing reference author myself. I obviously think guides like this one have value, but they're only one part of a well-rounded arsenal of tools and techniques.

10. One of my favorite questions comes from furious aspiring writers who read

explore how voice and interiority harmonize together with some excerpts.

Character Reveals

Both interiority *and* voice offer insight into character. Interiority is *all about* character, after all, and voice can be a delightful accent to really anchor a three-dimensional protagonist on the page.

Let's start with a beautiful image that characterizes an entire person and his backstory. Our first example comes from *Anxious People*, and it's about Jim, the father cop. This is how briefly and elegantly a characterizing detail can be delivered:

> Jim aged badly after [his wife] died, became a lesser man, never quite able to breathe back in all the air that had gone out of him.[b]

Though readers know from their own judgment of Jim that he's not at all a "lesser man," especially after he saves the misguided hostage-taker (which we saw in Chapter 16), this image suggests he will never be as full of air—and, presumably, life—as he was before his wife passed. It's a small but profound meditation on grief and loss. The author also delivers this insight rather plainly, without agony or suffering. It simply is what it is, and Jim is now forever a widower because he has loved and lost.

---

published books and think they're crap. Without fail, they'll go to a conference and ask, "How did *this crap* get published?" (They'll sometimes name the title, too, which is always a fun gamble because the agent or editor of said title could be sitting on the panel.) Well, your idea of crap is another gatekeeper or reader's favorite book. Not everything is for everybody. Publishing is subjective. You might not like romantic comedy because you think it's trite and formulaic … and that's okay. You've developed your own taste, so write toward that taste. Let other people write to *their* taste. Let publishers publish to the tastes of their various editors and marketing departments. What's truly amusing about this question is that, in their frustration, choking on some sour grapes, these writers actually seem to be asking, "So why won't they publish *my crap*?" They're essentially saying, "Just let me publish already, I really, really, really, really want to. I've revised enough and I'm impatient. I'm tired of doing the work so *take my crap*, please." Well, I think everyone should aim a bit higher. (And stop judging other books and authors. That's what Goodreads is for, anyway.)

Let's pivot to another image of grief, this time from *Sing, Unburied, Sing* and Leonie, who is thinking about how her brother, Given's, death has affected the entire family, including Mama, who later dies from cancer:

> Her grief for Given was hungry for life. Sometimes I wonder if
> the cancer was sitting there with us in that moment, too …
> wiggling in the marrow of her bones.[c]

Leonie characterizes the grief itself as "hungry for life," which is intentionally ironic. She seems to believe the cancer and grief combined within Mama, "wiggling in the marrow of her bones," an ominous and unnerving image. Notice how Leonie doesn't really touch her own grief here, but readers can infer that Given's murder has affected everyone, her included.

Here's another passage from Leonie, this time as she considers what it might be like to be rejected by her partner, Michael, who she desperately believes she needs. This excerpt, originally featured in Chapter 6, conveys her self-loathing. The language is beautiful, lyrical, and engrossing, even if the interiority conveys deep unmet need and self-directed violence:

> I would throw up everything. All of it out: food and bile and
> stomach and intestines and esophagus, organs all, bones and
> muscle, until all that was left was skin. And then maybe that
> could turn inside out, and I wouldn't be nothing no more. Not
> this skin, not this body. Maybe Michael could step on my heart,
> stop its beating. Then burn everything to cinders.[d]

It seems Leonie's greatest desire is to "be nothing no more," but I'm not sure she actually wishes to blink out of existence. This seems more like a desperate expression of the need to be loved and valued. She doesn't want to die, she just wants the void filled, the pain gone. Notice how the author uses some shorter sentences and fragments ("I would throw up everything" and "[not] this skin, not this body") interspersed with longer sentences full of visceral imagery. The rhythm suggests a character rocking back and forth, keening. It's plaintive, like a wail.

Another example of a character considering the darkness comes from Atticus in *Lovecraft Country*, but this voice is much more peaceful. Here, Atticus has been tricked into participating in a blood sacrifice. He figures it out at the last minute and is able to stop the ceremony, a moment we saw in Chapter 16. The magic still overtakes him but it doesn't destroy him. Instead, the spell backfires spectacularly and Samuel Braithwaite, the cult leader and antagonist who lured Atticus there, is turned to stone along with his followers. In all the chaos, here's Atticus at the very heart of the paranormal frenzy:

> A veil of protective darkness dropped over Atticus's eyes, shielding him from the light that otherwise would have burned him where he stood. His mind, seeing that the darkness was good, decided to drift off into it.[e]

Though the literal apocalypse is happening all around him, Atticus feels peaceful and covered in "a veil of protective darkness." This is a lovely moment of calm in a discordant scene, and the voice and language help make it so. The magical darkness is "shielding," keeping him from being burned "where he stood."

There's the suggestion of this happening beneath the level of perception, too, as Atticus and "his mind" are described as separate entities. It's almost like the unconscious and the conscious are ensconced in their own bubbles and operating out of self-preservation. But "seeing that the darkness was good" and helpful—a friend, not a foe—the mind steers Atticus toward it.

The entire scene has a very detached, otherworldly tone, and this is likely done on purpose to convey that Atticus is in the thrall of a power much greater than himself. After the horror and high stakes of the nefarious cult reveal, Atticus deserves a lovely break, and that's exactly what this tranquil moment of interiority provides.

A similar breathless, healing pause comes from *Amazing Grace Adams*, as Grace takes a moment with her baby, who we later learn is her second child, who died. (Another cut of this excerpt, which excludes this image, originally appeared in Chapter 5.) Grace looks up at the trees while cradling her daughter and is shocked to see the splendor all around her:

> It's like she's never looked. Like she's gorging on the wonder of
> it for the first time, as though her baby is teaching her how to
> see.... It is beautiful, vital, otherworldly—the beginning of
> something she can barely grasp but that feels like hope—and
> she is dizzy with it.[f]

Grace is not exactly a hopeful character in the present narrative. In fact, she's the opposite: anxious, neurotic, and teetering on the verge of another breakdown. So it's illuminating and bittersweet to see her "dizzy with [hope]" in what must have been a much simpler and more peaceful time. This gorgeous description of how humbled she is that "her baby is teaching her how to see" is indeed so "vital" that readers ache for Grace. This passage seems geared, in part, to make audiences want peace for her again, and to invite them to become even more invested in her story.

August from *One Last Stop* also reveals some voice-driven interiority and vulnerability as she kisses June. Look at where her mind goes, and how she reacts to this moment:

> It reminds her of being homesick for months and tasting some-
> thing familiar and realizing it's even better than you remember,
> because it comes with the sweet gut punch of knowing and
> being known. It melts in her mouth like ice cream at the corner
> store when she was eight. It aches like a brick to the shin.[g]

This openness would've been unlikely earlier in August's character arc, which we saw in Chapter 11, since she kept so much of her heart walled off. Now, her deep and intimate need for "knowing and being known" is expressed by the image of "being homesick for months and tasting something familiar," which evokes pure and elemental ideas of identity. Lest this moment become too sweet and ephemeral, because that's not August's style, the author grounds it with images like "sweet gut punch" and "brick to the shin."

This contrast—so artfully done—reminds readers of both the ecstasy *and* the agony of love without making this swirl of conflicting feelings too explicit. The excerpt demonstrates how to combine both emotional highs and lows using specific voice and imagery.

Let's transition to *The Bodyguard* and Hannah, who deals with her own moment of vulnerability as she arrives, ever the consummate professional, to assume the role of Jake's fake girlfriend. Unfortunately, she must dress the part. While she's technically working, which is her comfort zone, she finds the outfit requirement humiliating. And if we know anything about Hannah, it's that she cannot bear to be humiliated or show any glimmer of her own humanity, especially on the job:

> I guess it's hard to feel professional in a sundress with puffy cap sleeves.... I felt underprepared, a little bit chilly, weirdly naked, and uncharacteristically vulnerable.

> I missed my pantsuit, is what I'm saying.[h]

Hannah is incredibly self-aware but also self-conscious. It's nice to see her admit to having a feeling, though I'd quibble with "uncharacteristically" here. She's felt vulnerable and out of her depth throughout this story, which makes her all the more relatable to audiences. While she tries to play this inner struggle off as a joke ("I missed my pantsuit, is what I'm saying"), savvy romantic comedy readers will know that her feelings of nakedness and exposure are the first cracks in her façade. This audience, especially, will anticipate how Hannah breaks open later in the story—"puffy cap sleeves" and all.

Next let's revisit the amazingly relatable character of Rachel, from *Milk Fed*, as she ... has a burrito for lunch. But because Rachel is a bit neurotic and suffers from disordered eating, she can't simply have a burrito. Instead, she contrives a scenario where she poses with her burrito at the office, eating some, then leaving some, so that she looks "normal" to her coworkers.

This is another great example of a protagonist assuming she has things harder than most and that nobody else thinks like she does. Of course, this mindset makes Rachel accessible, because we all have our individual quirks, even if they don't directly relate to how we eat our food:

> I wanted [my colleague] to absorb my portrayal of ease. Yes, I was performing a one-woman show about a person who could simply take or leave a burrito, no biggie, just coolly have a

burrito at rest on her desk, no obsession, no fear, a sane food woman, a woman to whom food was only one facet of a very expansive life.[i]

My favorite line shows how she's showcasing a "portrayal of ease." She's not *at* ease—heavens no. But she's "[performing] a one-woman show about a person who could simply take or leave a burrito." Not only is this stream of consciousness interiority real and authentic, it's also hilarious. Who among us hasn't wanted to be seen as "a sane food woman" or a sane online shopping woman (that would be me) or a sane plant-collecting woman? A person for whom their foible "was only one facet of a very expansive life"? Rachel so desperately needs to fit in and be perceived a certain way that she twists herself into a pretzel at the office and sits with a half-eaten burrito at her desk for all to see, on the off chance it helps her feel better about herself.

Of course, the amazing irony here is her coworkers probably don't even notice this performance. They're likely wrapped up in their own heads and wondering whether people are judging *them*. She's a "one-woman show" falling in the forest with no one to hear it.

Let's stick with the oeuvre of Melissa Broder for a moment because I have to admit, I'm a fan. This excerpt comes from *Death Valley*. The unnamed narrator is an author, and we're privy to her insightful and irreverent hot takes as the plot unfolds:

The next book I read … described as the tale of a woman "unraveling" after the death of her wife. All I could think was, Who unravels this neatly? There was no mention of fear. Zero messes or catharses. If a feeling did surface, it was an elegant dribble, pristine, assonant. Was this really the inside of a person's head? I've been more unraveled by a yeast infection. It was clear that the author had never, herself, unraveled. Also, she seemed to disapprove of humor in any form, which was another problem, because how could a person unravel so humorlessly and not die? If I saw no humor in my unraveling, I'd have been dead long ago.[j]

This narrator, herself unraveling, perhaps feels especially self-conscious about her downward spiral. She's also potentially planning how she might write an "unraveling" sequence and comparing herself to another author.[11] I also love this as metacommentary on interiority because the character is literally wondering "Was this really the inside of a person's head?" as readers are in *her* head. Interiority-*ception*!

The humor comes out in "I've been more unraveled by a yeast infection," which is such a funny choice of ailment, as it tends to either be a very big deal or simply a minor inconvenience, depending on the person. There's also an element of "toxic vulnerability" here, which is a pop psychology term for oversharing to achieve easy intimacy. Some personalities will tell you their life story within five minutes, including their wounds, the darker the better. There's an element of cheapness and shock value here, as a character angles for sympathy, empathy, and a burst of validation.

Interiority Insight: How does your character get their ya-yas? Do they take any and all shortcuts to knowing others and being known themselves? If they overshare, what do they talk about? What triggers this? Is it a conscious ploy or a genuine (if misguided) bid at connection? Or would they rather die than open themselves up so quickly and easily?

Finally, the narrator calls us back to her humor by expressing that this is, in fact, her very consciously chosen coping mechanism. I found myself in stitches when she asked, "how could a person unravel so humorlessly and not die?" Maybe because I have a warped sensibility and also use jokes as a coping mechanism, I loved being privy to this catty bit of commentary. It helps to lighten and leaven the narrator's experience, maybe in a bid to make it more palatable, or in a play for relatability.

For a certain target audience,[12] this author's work strikes a perfect

---

11. We all do it! We don't all go to a conference and call their work "crap," though!
12. It's me. I'm the target audience.

balance between comedy and tragedy, snark and pathos. Her characters are also almost painfully self-aware, which makes them interiority standard-bearers. The chatty, confessional tone of voice that both Rachel and this narrator use also potentially endears them to audiences, because we feel like we're talking to our best friend about their most unhinged private thoughts. This can help build the character-reader rapport, as long as it's done with some semblance of balance.

Interiority Insight: Voice and humor can be polarizing. If your work is very voice-driven, know it won't be for everyone. But if your choices are consistent, serve the story and tone, and foster reader connection, they're a risk you might want to take, as unique voices tend to stand out.

As you can see here, not every voice fits every reader or story. Sometimes voice can be a big swing, but I often prefer a distinct voice to a generic one, especially if the project or character calls for it.[13]

Just as August from *One Last Stop* remembers that fun is supposed to be fun in Chapter 11, I want to end on an oddball selection of delightful, strange, or masterful From the Shelves voices. Because if writers and readers can't entertain themselves and one another every once in a while, what's the point?

Just for Fun

Voice can have any number of effects on readers, and all of the following excerpts caught my attention, so I wanted to share and analyze them here. As interiority "about" secondary characters tends to reveal more about the protagonist than the other person, I fully

---

13. A notable exception is dialect. Sometimes overdone dialect can really distract. You don't want your style to trump your substance. Instead of veering into caricature territory with gratuitous dialect, add a few flourishes of regional terms and quirks to the writing. You can also consider playing with rhythm and syntax rather than going full-bore.

admit that these selections reflect my individual taste. Read into them what you will!

The first is probably the most bizarre piece of writing sampled in this guide, which makes it noteworthy. It comes from *The Vaster Wilds* and is in the POV of a Spanish priest who landed in America once upon a time and got lost in the woods. Remember when I said Lamentations *especially* fears "strange men" in the previous chapter? This is the weirdest one she stumbles across.

Interestingly enough, we see her—the primary protagonist—through his perspective, instead of the other way around. It's an unexpected choice to switch POVs here. Even less expected, he seems to have merged with the wilderness and lost all sense of context. One has to wonder how he made it this far while still retaining some semblance of structured thought and language. In fact, that he has forgotten what to call Lamentations is the focus of the excerpt:

> This was a thing, a thing; he had lost the name of such things as these, that bleed out of the place of shames. Things of breasts, of holes. Bad things, Eve things, harlot things, mother things, wife things, baby-making things. She things. These not-men things. O it would not return, the name of this kind of human.[k]

It's notable that, while he can't recall the word for "woman," he seems to retain his indoctrinated view of women as shameful "baby-making" factories. If someone asked me what voice was, I could handily point to this example because it's such a showstopper, even though I actively disagree with what he's saying. At least he thinks women are a "kind of human"? Given this time period, I'll take my wins where I can get them.

Subject matter aside, look at this syntax and how easily he calls genitals "the place of shames." Obviously, this is a historical and religious perspective that doesn't really have anything in common with the conversations we're having about gender and identity in today's society,[14] but this viewpoint—you can't accuse this excerpt for not having a

---

14. Not trying to wade into politicized discourse!

viewpoint!—helps to anchor readers in a very specific period and frame of mind.

A similarly patriarchal view of women is demonstrated by our favorite murderer-misogynist, Joe, from *You*. He knows Beck is in dire financial straits and can't help her. Instead, he watches as she tries to return a pair of leggings at the store, which Joe calls "Young Sluts" because he can't be bothered to acknowledge something he believes is beneath him.

Here, he seems to express his admiration for Beck as she moves through a crowd of other young women, but this interiority only underscores his own skewed worldview:

> You take it out on everyone in Young Sluts, plowing through rayon and neon without saying *excuse me*. A couple of bitches say they want to kick your ass, but they won't; they're in high school, they are happy just to call you a *beeatch*. I tell you to slow down and you don't listen and I almost love what a cunt you can be because one of these days you're gonna tie me to a bed and slap me and lord over me the way you lord over all the people who get in your way.[1]

To Joe, Beck is not allowed to be her own woman. She must be observed, herded ("I tell you to slow down"), and judged ("I almost love what a cunt you can be"). Beck doesn't know it, but her every move is being scored according to Joe's approval rubric. Not only that, but her only use to him seems to be future sexual gratification. After watching her walk through a store, he extrapolates she'll be forceful in bed. Yuck. Joe is another very specific character, with a myopic, unmistakable viewpoint.

Let's pivot away from these two sketchy male characters. Maybe their voices come across so clearly because their authors were able to imagine their extreme positions. When we don't have to stay long in such a desolate mental place, we can experiment and have fun writing what that life might be like. (Of course, Joe is the POV character for not only *You* but three additional books in the series. This author took a very deep dive into his depraved world.)

Here's voice that truly lives up to this section's theme of "just for fun." It's from *Milk Fed* again, because I can't seem to quit Melissa Broder. (And I'm not sorry.) As we saw earlier in this chapter, Rachel has some issues with disordered eating. When she starts dating Miriam, her first girlfriend, she goes out to dinner and really lets loose, not denying herself a single thing. The whole sequence is described like a Technicolor acid trip:

> I put the pink straw to my lips and sipped. It was exquisite, like drinking a neon airbrushed rendering of a fruit punch island. It was its own tropical cosmos complete with coconuts, sea, and sunset.[m]

Rachel's exhilaration is perfectly clear here. It's not just the drink, it's the freedom she feels to drop her neuroses and dive right into this "tropical cosmos." Sure, her inhibitions will probably return the following day (as she's nursing a physical and emotional hangover after her binge), but for now, she doesn't seem to care, and the author treats us to descriptions that show just how much both character and writer are enjoying themselves.

We heard from Hannah and *The Bodyguard* earlier in this chapter. In perhaps one of the funniest and most engaging scenes in the novel, she steps out of the car on Jake's family's Texas ranch only to realize she isn't alone.

There are cows. Everywhere.

The voice takes this moment to new and hilarious heights, especially as a sweet and very non-threatening cow comes up and startles her:

> It was close enough that I could feel its humid, otherworldly breath washing over my skin. I don't want to say the cow snuck up on me, but let's just say the field had been empty up to that point and then suddenly—*Boom*.[n]

Though Hannah is trained to notice threats in her environment, as we saw in Chapter 8, she's taken by surprise, which makes this sequence funnier. Something as gigantic as a cow is not supposed to sneak up on an elite security operative and go "*Boom*."

The voice riff, which I'm sure was very fun to write, only continues as she describes the cows:

> [They have] limpid black eyes, and surprisingly feminine lashes, staring point-blank into my soul.[o]

I love the idea of urbanite Hannah, a consummate professional, literally *cowed* in a field in the middle of nowhere. The sweet description of the animals, with their "surprisingly feminine lashes," contrasts with Hannah's acute terror. The combination really lands the moment and makes it memorable.

To round out our chapter on voice, I chose two fun and snarky characters being their fun and snarky selves. Why? Because I relate to them. Were these examples a lowest common denominator play? Maybe. Did I fall for it? Absolutely.

The first comes from *The Villa*, where author Rachel Hawkins really nails the type of contemporary thriller and women's fiction voice that seems to be popular with her target audience. The premise invites this contrast because one of the characters, Chess, is a wildly popular influencer and self-help guru. Of course, Emily, her best friend, sees beneath the façade and resents Chess getting famous for telling people what to do.

In reality, Chess is far from perfect (guess she's still working on her yoga *practice*), especially when she gets drunk and shows her true colors. Here's how Emily takes out her frustration at the dissonance and makes fun of Chess's signature program, the Powered Path, to boot:

> *Jesus, if all those fans of hers who think she's the most enlightened being since Gwyneth Paltrow's vagina could have seen her tonight,* I think as I stand up.
>
> *Powered Path, my ass.*[p]

This friendship is clearly on the rocks, as expressed in Emily's disappointment and judgment. Her interiority also plants a curiosity hook. How far will Emily go to address this disconnect between Chess's true self and her carefully curated public persona? Will she sabotage Chess's self-help empire? Make a video of Chess's *real* self and post it on social media? Though this passage might be good for a chuckle, it also has teeth.

And, finally, as if all the swearing and sarcasm in this section weren't enough, I want to end on a lovely little bit of humor from Sally, who is, appropriately, a comedy writer in *Romantic Comedy*. In this scene, she feels vulnerable as she stands in front of Noah in person for the first time after they fell in love as long-distance pen pals.

He's beckoning her into the bedroom and she cannot handle the intensity of this moment with a straight face:

> "I have something to show you," he said.

> It was because I was a comedy writer, and not because I was
> sexually fearless, that I was tempted to say, "Your penis?"
> Instead, I said, "Is it better than this?"[q]

Here, we get a very endearing moment of Sally not only cracking a joke but engaging in some good-natured self-deprecation. Then, in a satisfying twist, she changes her mind and allows her vulnerability to surface. She could have gotten away with the quip, but instead, she admits to herself—and to Noah—that their budding love is compelling her in ways she never thought possible.

May we all create characters who have their own unique voices, personalities, and layers—with the charm, vulnerability, and relatability to make audiences care deeply and completely. (And maybe laugh and enjoy themselves a little, too.)

Our penultimate chapter is devoted to a few excerpts which really showcase how interiority works within slightly longer scenes. I hope this final exploration will bring home how versatile and powerful interiority can be in conveying both character and story.

20

STACKING THE DECK

In the following sections, I want to simply take a step back and enjoy several scenes where interiority is used to achieve multiple effects and objectives simultaneously. All four "stacking the deck" excerpts come from stories you're already familiar with. They showcase the versatility of interiority and its ability to convey character and inspire audience reaction.

Scene One: *The Cruel Prince*

Let's go back to Jude, the human misfit in a fairy world, in *The Cruel Prince*. She's been put through the wringer by various courtly manipulators. After everything she's experienced, she gets the opportunity to become magical. It's probably a trap, since we know how "fair" fairy bargains are from *Spinning Silver* and *The Fair Folk*. Jude faces a choice. Would she rather sacrifice some status but finally belong in this realm, which has made her life a living hell? Or hold her head up high but remain a "mere" mortal?

That's the surface-level question in this scene, but it turns out Jude is hiding her real desires, even from the reader, for a dramatic reveal. For context, Madoc is her foster father, who brought Jude to the kingdom in the first place:

Could the High King of Faerie really ... make me something

other than human? ... I think of Valerian's words when he tried to glamour me into jumping out of the tower. *Being born mortal is like being born already dead.*

He sees the look on my face and smiles, sure that he has ferreted out the secret desire of my heart.... I am troubled. I should feel triumphant, but, instead, I feel sick. Outmaneuvering Madoc wasn't nearly as satisfying as I wanted it to be, especially since I was able to do it because he never thought of me as someone who would betray him.... The future of Faerie depends on my playing a long game and playing it perfectly.[a]

A few things to notice here. First, we get a mini-flashback as Jade considers what Valerian, a fairy bully, said about mortals "being born already dead." This is her confronting her mortality, literally, and subsuming what it might mean to become immortal herself. It's the dangling carrot being held in front of her, and in this moment, she remembers something which showcases her internal struggle.

But is she really tempted?

We transition to narration as she clocks Madoc's reaction, only her observation is worded very carefully: "sure that he has ferreted out the secret desire of my heart." This suggests Jude is not, in fact, tempted by the dangling carrot, that she wouldn't give up her mortality to become fae.

The author's intention was for Jude to trick her scene partner, Madoc, but she tricks the reader, too (at least for a moment). This is engaging sentence-level misdirection, as audiences are forced to really dig in and figure out what's happening, what the character means, and what she truly wants.

Then things get *really* weird. So far we have some narration about Madoc, paradoxical interiority which shows us what Jude is really feeling and doing, and an interpretation of how it's going.

Remember, Jude has been offered the chance to become fae. She signals that she wants it, or at least pauses long enough to fool Madoc. And when Jude assumes he's content with this false victory, she is ...

Troubled?

Just look at all of these expectation shifts for the reader! Jude won the chess match by acting strategically, but she's not happy. Instead, she feels "sick." Madoc, after all, is supposed to know her better than almost anyone, yet she's able to fool him, too. Her expectations have not been met so she's left with inner struggle.

This truthful interiority is humanizing, relatable, and shows Jude's deep conflict with her own sense of self. Madoc "never thought of [her] as someone who would betray him," and yet she has. What does this say about her reputation, her value system, her old self, and her new self? Is there a tinge of shame? What will she subsume into her identity after this moment? There's also an implied question about the psychic and moral cost of becoming this new Jude.

Interiority Insight: Notice how Jude misleads everyone in the scene. She even misleads the reader for a beat, until she comes clean in interiority. This is key. Most characters lie and dissemble, but interiority is an opportunity for them to expose their innermost selves to audiences. This is an ingenious reader engagement strategy, as we are now held in Jude's strictest confidence and feel like true insiders.

To cap off this character growth arc that takes place over just 123 words, Jude recommits, screwing her courage to the sticking place, when she says, "The future of Faerie depends on my playing a long game, and playing it perfectly."

The message of this interiority is clear. She's going to do what she feels she must because she believes the entire world is depending on her. The fate of Faerie is on her shoulders. Look at those stakes!

Scene Two: *The Final Girl Support Group*

Our next stacked deck of interiority comes from *The Final Girl Support Group* and brings similar gravitas to the table (but with a dash of potty humor). This reaction happens immediately after Lynette kills a fellow final girl, Chrissy, during the epic climactic sequence of the novel. The plot is way too complex to explain here, but the gist is that some serial killers are looking to eradicate a group of notable final girls who have previously survived gristly murder attempts.

Lynette doesn't mean to kill Chrissy, but she does. A sacred bond ruptures when a final girl—a victim of attempted murder herself—kills someone else, especially another victim. Now Lynette reels from what she's done:

> My thoughts feel heavy and absolute, irrevocable and final. I have murdered someone. Whenever I watched a movie and some hero refused to kill the villain because "then I'll be as bad as he is," I dismissed it as a bunch of moralistic hand-wringing by balding Hollywood scriptwriters who had only ever killed the last roll of toilet paper. But they tapped into a universal truth. I'm living in a new world now, and in this world I am a murderer.
>
> I can't take it back, I can't fix it, I can't make it better, but I can do one thing about it.
>
> I can never do it again. I swear harder than I've ever sworn anything since I was a little girl: I will not kill again. No matter how many lives it will save. No matter how much it puts my own life at risk. No matter what. No more killing.[b]

She starts off simply enough by interpreting the quality of her thoughts. They are "heavy and absolute, irrevocable and final," and this imagery is reminiscent of death itself. Chrissy is dead. Lynette has killed her. Those facts hit like bricks.

Then we get some classic Grady Hendrix humorous riffing, which I love, because it's such an unexpected contrast to the soul-baring seriousness of this moment. Lynette leaves the present to muse about heroes refusing to kill villains in movies because of the psychic toll of becoming "'as bad as he is.'" Lynette once assumed this was bullshit "hand-wringing."

However, she's surprised to find those same feelings ringing true within herself now. Readers are very familiar with the moment a hero fills with self-loathing after dropping down to the moral level of a villain. But this is the exact "universal truth" Lynette feels, too, and she wants the freedom to say so without being accused of cheapening the moment with clichés. This is a great strategy to not only disarm any potential recoil of "ugh, how trite," then use the power of the cliché anyway. It's an interesting and clever tactic on the author's part.

When we explored backstory in Chapter 5, I mentioned that sometimes a defining event can cleave a life into a "before" and an "after." This is a common reaction to a huge turning point, and Lynette feels it here. In the "after," she wears a new label: "I am a murderer."

Then we come to a pivot point as Lynette must make a decision. She realizes she can't do anything to change what happened, so how will she proceed? Her solution: "I can never do it again." She vows not to kill, no matter what. Not if it might save lives. Not if it might save *her* life. "No matter what," she says.

This seems like a very straightforward assertion, but then readers remember that we're in the climax and Lynette and her surviving friends are still in acute danger. The curiosity hook is planted in a big way: Will Lynette break this ironclad promise to herself? In our discussion of plot in Chapter 4 and of mentor and ally characters in Chapter 12, I said things often fall apart for protagonists around the climax because assistance is taken away or plans fail. The protagonist is hamstrung in some crucial sense from carrying on as they intended to.

This scene is a fascinating example of this exact moment, except it's Lynette quite literally disarming herself. She may be called upon to kill again, whether to save someone else or herself. Maybe even in the next few pages. But she has made a promise, one upon which her dignity and sense of self-worth rest. Her next choice will be between physical death and soul death. If she keeps this promise, she might not live. But if she breaks this promise, she will not be able to live with herself.

If you're like me, you are frothing to see whether her vow holds up under life-or-death duress.

Scene Three: *Jade City*

We didn't spend a lot of time in the world of *Jade City*, but you might remember the exhilarating magic power of jade, which we saw through the perspective of a street kid in Chapter 14. This society vibrates in constant tension between mob-like ruling families, characters who can wield jade, and denizens of the criminal underworld.

The following interiority puts us in the POV of Lan, the Pillar, or leader, of the No Peak clan. He recently took over for his grandfather, Kaul Sen, but the old man is still actively asserting dominance.

The two meet and Kaul Sen pushes buttons by asking why Lan has chosen not to exact vengeance on his wife, Eyni, for cheating on him. The primary conflicts here are between honor and vengeance, and old and new worldviews. When Kaul Sen implies Lan isn't a man, our POV protagonist reacts in interiority:

> A fleeting and horrible desire to shove his grandfather out of the second-story window crossed Lan's mind. That was what the old man wanted after all, wasn't it? Flagrant egotistical violence. Yes, Lan thought, he could have challenged Eyni's lover— fought and killed him in the way any self-respecting Kekonese man would feel entitled. Perhaps it would have been a more fitting way for a Pillar to act. But it would have been pointless. An empty gesture. He wouldn't have kept Eyni; she was already determined to go. All he could have done was trample out her happiness and make her hate him. And if you loved someone, truly loved them, shouldn't their happiness matter, even more than your honor?[c]

We begin on an arresting intrusive thought: Lan is tempted to shove his aging grandfather (and No Peak don) out of a window. Immediately, this grabs reader attention. Then audiences get a paradoxical reversal— it turns out Lan judges this kind of power play as the old way of doing things, or, as he calls it, "flagrant egotistical violence."

Len disagrees with the established expectations for Pillar behavior and finds himself drawn to a different, more enlightened approach. This could indeed be viewed as less masculine, so Kaul Len's criticism probably bruises. But will Lan's softer sensibility allow him to command power and respect from No Peak clan members who are used to Kaul Len's ways? Such is the bigger question implied in this short sequence.

Lan then thinks about his estranged wife, Eyni, and her lover. The expected course of action would've been to challenge, fight, and kill the man. Part of Lan might have wanted this, purely out of humiliation and spite. Given his role in the community, this bloody vengeance "would have been a more fitting way for a Pillar to act."

No matter how he actually feels about the situation, he finds himself comparing his true self to society's expectations for his role. But Lan finds this duplicity "pointless." Whether the people respect him or not, he doesn't want to make this "empty gesture," which demonstrates an incredibly intricate understanding of the situation, and great empathy for Eyni, even though she deeply hurt him.

Nobody would blame him for exacting revenge. Instead, Lan declares who he really is with this subtle expression of his moral code in interiority. He realizes, likely correctly, that Eyni had already made her decision to blow up the marriage at great risk to herself. After all, in this world, anyone who steps out of bounds is punished. Which is exactly what Lan is risking, too.

But, crucially, he understands that "she was already determined to go," so he takes the high road. Putting an end to the affair and ordering her to stay would "make her hate him." And here is the crux of Lan's selfless decision: He loved her once and might even love her still. This was not a status marriage or a political pairing. Lan can admit that—to this day, and despite her betrayal—her happiness matters to him.

He's expected to rain down vengeance, to protect his honor at all costs, yet has chosen not to. Even if it goes against what a Pillar is "supposed" to do. Even if it hurts him personally. Even if it tramples his image or makes him seem weak. This is a dangerous choice in a society that's all about power and control.

Lan stands by his moral code, though it puts him at odds with his elders (and possibly subservients, once they catch wind of the scandal). This small bit of interiority is a declaration of who he truly is—one that flies in the face of everything he was raised to do and be. What a powerful and, more importantly, humble moment.

Scene Four: *Wellness*

Finally, we'll end on an amazing scene which appears toward the end of *Wellness*. We've only heard about Elizabeth and Jack's marriage and social climbing so far, but the novel ends with Jack going back to his small Kansas town to try and make sense of his past.

Jack has long been unsettled by his sister Evelyn's tragic death, though it isn't revealed until the third act that she's gone, not just estranged, as readers have been led to believe. When his father, Lawrence, dies and Jack goes home, readers finally learn what happened.

The night Evelyn died was a snarl of confusion. Lawrence, a farmer, was doing a controlled burn on the land. Through a series of miscommunications, Evelyn was sent to a field that was soon set ablaze, and died. The parents unfairly blamed Jack.

The truth is that Jack's mother directed Evelyn to the wrong field on purpose, knowing full well where the fire would be. She lied and set her own daughter up to die because Evelyn was talented, buoyant, and full of life—everything Jack's mother wasn't.

The following scene takes place in the present day as Jack and his mother discuss that night. Jack doesn't necessarily go into the conversation thinking his mother did it, but this idea dawns on him as they talk. There's a lot of dialogue here but pay attention to the instances of interiority as Jack attempts to get closure once and for all. These small moments of reflection really elevate the scene. We start with Mom's denial that she sent Evelyn to her death:

"[Lawrence] said Evelyn was popular and happy and I was alone and miserable and that I couldn't stand it. He thought I wanted revenge. He thought I wanted attention. Imagine being married to someone who thinks you're capable of *that*."

Was she capable of that? Was his father right about her? ... Jack didn't know, and maybe he didn't need to know. He had been living with the guilt of his sister's death for so long that this new ambiguity felt like deliverance in comparison.

"I expect you want an apology," his mother said.

"That would be nice."

"... Yeah, well, before you get all high and mighty, just remember all the trouble you put me through...."

"I know. You've told me. I shouldn't have been born."

"That's right.... So the way I see it is, you and I, we're probably even."

Jack had to laugh—at his mother's stubbornness, her audacity, and the grievances she'd collected and nursed in her heart, at her ability to bend history to remain blameless.

"Sure, Mom," Jack said. "Fine. Whatever. We're even."[d]

This scene doesn't actually deliver closure, which is heartbreaking. Jack "has been living with the guilt of his sister's death for so long" he almost can't wrap his mind around the possibility of his mother killing Evelyn instead. Notably, Mom doesn't really deny it. She's purposefully vague, instead taking offense at the implication that Lawrence thought her "capable of *that*." Worse, she plays the victim, asking Jack to "imagine" what it must've been like to receive this kind of blame.

But Jack knows *exactly* what it's like because he's shouldered his misbelief-guided guilt for Evelyn's death since he was a child. Unfortunately, Mom seems stubbornly, maybe even pathologically, unable to empathize with his experience. She's all about her own perspective ... and protection.

What's interesting is that Jack doesn't understand where this nonadmission leaves him, then decides "maybe he didn't need to know." Maybe the very idea that his mother is potentially responsible is "deliverance" enough. The mere possibility of truth, of freedom, may make a material difference in his life.

While this isn't a fairy-tale ending after years of suffering—not only living with his own grief but accepting his family's blame—this scene shifts something within Jack. Maybe it's that he finally got the nerve to have this conversation in the first place, or he received confirmation that his mother is incapable of accountability. *Wellness* is a literary novel, and as such, it's comfortable playing in the gray areas of the human experience.

Of course, readers might be devastated on Jack's behalf, especially as Mom dares to say, "I expect you want an apology." This is also infuriatingly vague. An apology for killing Evelyn? An apology for allowing the blame to sit squarely on her son's shoulders? Her evasiveness strikes me as proof positive that she orchestrated the death, but I'm more upset for Jack, who has this self-serving, miserable woman for a mother.

She continues to sell the victim narrative, clearly terrified that Jack will feel vindicated. She's someone who couldn't let her own "'popular and happy'" daughter *live*, so why would she absolve her son's misery, guilt, and self-imposed shame? So he doesn't "get all high and mighty"?

If anything, she has a very clear value system. She must defend herself at all costs, as everyone else is out to get her. No one is allowed to have better than she did (and she's likely to blame *them* for making her miserable in the first place). Her slippery, noncommittal language continues when she says that "we're probably even." Jack ruined her life by being born, therefore she's justified in killing Evelyn. In her mind, the scales are balanced.

After this, Jack's response in interiority, before he gives his feelings voice, is worth the entire scene. Notice how he summarizes a lifetime of pain and grief in one killer sentence. I'll reprint it here because it bears re-examination:

> Jack had to laugh—at his mother's stubbornness, her audacity,
> and the grievances she'd collected and nursed in her heart, at
> her ability to bend history to remain blameless.

When this realization strikes, he laughs. He laughs! A lifetime of trauma, and he realizes that "the grievances she'd collected and nursed in her heart" and "her ability to bend history to remain blameless" mean these two characters will never get any closer to the truth, or a meaningful relationship.

And yet, maybe there's freedom here. After all, as the wisdom goes, "When someone shows you who they are, believe them."

Jack finally, I think, sees who his mother is. He wasn't mature enough to realize her true nature when he was a teenager and first left home. But life has been one giant wake-up call for him. Instead of giving her any more of his time, emotion, or spiritual energy, Jack might be able to center himself to the point where he doesn't need anything from her anymore.

When he says "Sure.... Fine. Whatever. We're even," he doesn't actually think she's innocent. He simply agrees with Mom because, I believe, he's realized she will never change, won't feel bad for her crimes, and can't see him for who he is. Jack is finally able to relinquish his need to pin her down to reality. Now he can potentially move on with the knowledge that he's innocent.

This isn't a giant moment, nor is it a blinding reveal. But for Jack, this is a watershed confirmation of his own inherent goodness. While his marriage might still be on the rocks, and his artistic aspirations have dimmed with middle age, he can now try to make his life his own rather than carrying the burdens of the past.

He will no longer waste his time on this person because he's unmasked his mother and seen the truth. Jack comes into alignment with his true sense of self as a character, and that is worth everything.

I hope you've enjoyed exploring these excerpts on a deeper level and seeing all the ways in which interiority can function within narrative and scene. Most importantly, I hope you're excited to start using this tool in your own writing. But if you still have questions or want to hear about common interiority pitfalls, I have one more chapter in store.

21

TROUBLESHOOTING INTERIORITY

This guide has been so packed with heady craft concepts and expert excerpt analysis[1] that I wanted to give you—and me!—a bit of a break in this final chapter. I'll structure it as more of a Q & A on common interiority issues I've encountered since I first started working with aspiring writers and their manuscripts in 2009.

Now, I have to level with you: Teaching writing is tough for one very specific reason—every writer is different, so is every story. Sure, there are patterns and categories and writing personality types which tend to have things in common, but I have to figure out how to package writing concepts for maximum applicability, while also considering what individual writers will find relevant to their unique projects. It's a tall order and a fine line to walk, which is why my primary livelihood is freelance editing. Writers can only get so much from general craft teaching. At some point, they want specific advice on *their* manuscripts. You'll notice I've used a lot of hedging language throughout this guide (like "could," "might," or "seems") when talking about various publishing industry topics and offering analysis of the excerpts. This is intentional, as I want to convey that these are *my* generalizations and interpretations. I'd like to think I know what I'm

---

1. If I don't say so myself!

talking about, but I'll still be the first to tell you that publishing is incredibly subjective and I'm not the end-all, be-all.

With this in mind, I can't possibly pre-empt every question or cover every writing topic in a way that's going to be relevant to you. But I will try! And if you feel like you're doing brilliantly with interiority, you can skip this chapter—though I often find that writers really resonate with a concept after hearing it a few times, in different contexts, so the rehash might be worthwhile.

Now, there are two ways to know whether you're having interiority issues—and both are valid. You can suspect something about your own writing that you'd like to improve, or you can start hearing consistent feedback from critique partners, writing groups, freelance editors, or even literary agents or acquisitions editors, if you've already gone out on submission.[2] No matter where you're getting the suggestion to revamp your use of interiority, you've come to the right place!

As you'll see, a lot of common interiority and writing issues come down to the idea of balance. Without further ado, let's get into some specific struggles you might encounter on your own journey with using interiority, and how you might fix them.

Q: What if I don't have any interiority?

This is the good ol' "empty head" syndrome. While I was working on this guide, I had someone write in and ask me something along the lines of:

> I know I should be using interiority, and I can find articles on how to format it, but ... what do I ... put IN THERE? Like, in the character's thoughts?

I have to admit, this was a new one for me. And I'm not making fun of this writer at all. It is a very valid question! When this particular inquiry hit my inbox, I had to unpack some of my own biases. I'm a

---

2. Sometimes this sounds like a critique of your characterization or an inability to "connect with the story."

reader and writer who's interested in character—*clearly*—so my natural assumption is that anyone who wants to write a novel or memoir has an interest in their protagonist. With that, in my mind, at least, comes a natural interest in the character's inner life.

However, I can see this being an issue if a writer comes to the table from a screenwriting background (for reasons discussed in Chapter 7), or with a focus on plot. They want action and probably don't care as much about the person they're putting through the paces of their story. And that's fine—to a point.

I do still fully believe that characters are important conduits for reader engagement in any kind of novel or memoir, even a rip-roaring action-adventure story where the protagonist might as well be a crash test dummy with a Glock. Your audiences in these plot-forward genres might self-select entertainment which doesn't spend too much time navel-gazing, but I'd still challenge you to add some layers and nuance to your protagonist. Most hard-boiled detectives have a wound, for example. Aim a little higher. Dig a little deeper. Push yourself.

Literally the *worst* thing to happen if you do additional character work is a stronger, more compelling protagonist. Not a bad investment of time and creative energy!

If you've read this guide and are still wondering where to start with filling your character's head with thoughts, feelings, reactions, expectations, and inner struggles, my advice is: go slow. Think about what your protagonist wants, which is always a great starting point (go back to Chapter 7 for ideas). What gets them up in the morning, ready to take on the day? What kind of person are they (see Chapter 6)? What do they believe in (see Chapter 10)?

And if you're still totally stumped, do the same for yourself. You know more or less what's in your own head, right? Well, answer some of these questions in journal format. Do some stream of consciousness writing to get into the habit of paying attention to your thought patterns. Once you're in that kind of contemplative mood, try to step into someone else's shoes. First-person POV tends to be better for this kind of work, as it invites you to really empathize with the protagonist. Meander without an endgame. What might you discover? The better you know your fictional person, the more you'll start to feel comfortable slipping into their interiority and filling up the contents of their brain bucket.

Q: What if I'm not using *enough* interiority?

If you suspect, or a qualified reader has outright told you, that you could do *more* with interiority, that's a slightly different issue. Your character might not have a totally empty head going on, but they're still not connecting with your reader, or could be connecting more.

Well, this is a great problem to have because you're clearly already doing *something* right. The struggle here might be that you aren't correctly identifying the parts of your story which could benefit from additional emotional resonance.

Go to Chapter 4 and review your understanding of the seven major tentpole moments. If you aren't able to identify these in your story, that might be a big part of the issue. Even if you're not structuring your plot with a straightforward linear chronology, you'll still want some of these major events or emotional touchstones represented.

Read *Save the Cat Writes a Novel* by Jessica Brody to get your feet wet with plotting. It's a really fun and straightforward way to think about story structure. Some writers find it formulaic and an affront to their free-wheeling pantsing sensibilities, but if you haven't done a lot of robust plotting before, you have nothing to lose by checking it out.

Once you identify the primary plot points in your story, make sure you're supporting them with interiority. You won't want to stop every scene and offer a big character reaction, of course. That's not always appropriate, unless you're in the dark night of the soul, which is pretty much designed as a place for your character to sit and think about how screwed they are.[3]

Consider the balance of action and information, and carving out contemplative moments for your protagonist between dynamic scenes.

---

3. Just kidding! Sort of. Your plot should really put them through the internal and external conflict wringer.

Let your character really feel the impact of what's happening and how it affects them, their sense of self, and their future prospects.

After you do this with all the major turning points in your story, you can identify more events that matter and have protagonists make meaning from *those*. Don't overdo it, though, or you'll be asking me the following question.

Q: What if I'm using *too much* interiority?

This is also, believe it or not, a great problem to have![4] You've done the work! You have the technique! You've developed a ton of insight into your character! All you have to do now is slash it to the ground!

Joking. Kinda. But seriously, you do need to be more selective. This is an issue of pacing and likely means you're interrupting your plot to navel-gaze or not spending enough time in scene. You may also be lavishing interiority in the wrong places and at the wrong times. Something is out of alignment, so you have to put on your detective hat and try to figure it out.

There's more than one way to skin a cat[5] and you can make other changes to your project to influence a reader's *perception* of how much interiority you're using. That's right. The reader's impression of your pacing or storytelling is throwing up red flags, but your volume of interiority might not be the real problem. This complaint could also be exacerbated by other issues.

I'll go back to balance here. Try to really perk up your plot. Add stakes (see Chapter 17). Introduce secondary characters and scenes (see Chapter 12). If there's no white space on your pages because you're just in interiority or narration the entire time, that's a great signal to use dialogue and action to get your POV character out of their head. It is absolutely possible to get too ponderous, and I'd hate for you to gorge on interiority at the expense of other talents you could be developing.

---

4. No, I don't say this about *every* writing problem!

5. But Mary, aren't stories supposed to be about *saving* cats? Also, I'm just using this terrible phrase to make another bad storytelling joke, and this impulse is, perhaps, my downfall. I have never skinned any cats. My cat, Luna, is happy and whole.

You should *also* probably trim some of your existing interiority, while you're at it, because self-restraint is always an option. Just get in there and kill those darlings. If you're struggling with thinning out your prose:

We all have to streamline at some point. The last thing you want to do is over-indulge in any area of your craft. This goes for voice, it goes for bad writing and publishing jokes,[6] and anything else that's out of balance in your storytelling.

If you're leaning too hard on interiority, chances are good you're neglecting other creative elements. This happens to those purple prose enthusiasts I discussed in Chapter 19. They think they're crushing it with all the beautiful imagery, and they truly might be, but imagery is not the only component of a good story.

Imagine yourself as an audio mixing board operator. If you're getting

6. I can clearly dish out advice but can't take it because I'm a ham sandwich.

the "too much interiority" feedback, you need to bring down the interiority volume and bring up the volume on other areas of your craft. There are many to work with. What have you been neglecting?

Q: Can a character be *too* self-aware?

My answer to this question might surprise you: yes! Refer back to Chapter 11 and our discussion of character growth. If the protagonist is already very advanced, self-aware, and able to analyze all aspects of their identity, past context, and future goals, they might be *too good*. Or at the very least, unrealistic. As we talked about in Chapter 2, readers like to relate to characters. This means making your protagonist a little rough around the edges, adding imperfections, and giving them misbeliefs and flaws.

Consider yourself and the people you know. It's very unlikely that any of you are going around saying something like:

> "Well, you see, I'm distrustful and avoidant because of my childhood father wound. But it's nice to meet you."

Most people, for better or worse, have varying levels of self-awareness (as demonstrated in Chapter 9). And even if they have high self-awareness, they probably don't broadcast all of their psychology into a megaphone. These personalities don't read as natural or organic, unless they're very specifically created with this kind of affectation to make a point.

Besides, if a character is so in tune with themselves and can explain their inner lives so easily, you'll end up doing a lot of telling about their deepest identity, which is, as we all know by now, the bad kind of telling.

Give your characters flaws and blind spots. Leave them some room to grow and change. Don't have them explain themselves to everyone (including, by extension, readers) so readily. Audiences want something to do. If the character has done all the work for them already, you might run into connection and relatability issues.

Q: What if people are finding it hard to care about my character?

Is your character active? Are they pursuing an objective? Do they have strong motivations for doing so? Poke around their backstory and need as well. Have you made these compelling enough? Relatable? Remember what I said in Chapter 2: You care about your character. Nobody else does. Outside readers are not yet emotionally invested (and likely never will be *as* emotionally invested as you are, but that's only natural).

Really think about your stakes here. If the protagonist is well-crafted and has been intentionally put together, your stakes may need to be raised. We need those steaks to be a nice, juicy medium-rare, at least, instead of dry and crumbly.[7] Remember, stakes are our way of making meaning for characters *and* readers. If your audience doesn't care, you need to consider the stakes of each event in your story (see Chapter 17). You obviously don't want to have characters react with shock and horror in every scene—that's melodrama (see Chapter 16). You could also run the risk of too much interiority, per an earlier question, if you offer it in every single moment.

That said, when something matters, take that cue to build some stakes into that moment, or after it, at the next opportunity for reflection. What's the best-case scenario? The worst-case? How does an event or internal turning point affect your character? And? So? The more they're impacted by the story, the more the story will capture your audience.

Q: What if I'm really not sure that I'm allowed to break the rule of "show, don't tell," and you will never, ever convince me otherwise?

If you don't do it for me—and if this 500-page ode to telling hasn't swayed you—do it for your characters. They have things to tell you. They want freedom from their never-ending pantomime of hearts fluttering against ribcages and stomachs twisting and turning.

---

7. I'll stop now. I swear.

But seriously, just try it. There's so much fun and interesting nuance in the gray area between showing and telling.

Q: What if my character doesn't experience any meaningful growth or change?

There are indeed writers, characters, and stories that lack a growth arc. As we saw in this guide, *The Guest* features a reverse growth arc. Alex ends up far worse off at the end (by many standards) than she was at the beginning. *Ripe* also showcases a similar trajectory for Cassie. She's not necessarily an anti-hero, she just gets flattened by emotional turmoil (including some of her own making). Leonie from *Sing, Unburied, Sing* could be considered an anti-hero, too.

Read these books and see if you care about the characters. You might find you develop empathy for them despite the fact that they're not redeemed or victorious.[8] This is the trick for anti-heroes and antagonists. You still have to make readers care, and if you're not going to do it with a growth trajectory, what's your plan? Does another character act as a proxy for the story's thematic growth arc?

You can use a lot of the meaning-making and reader engagement tools in this guide to help you. Humanizing the character is one idea. Make your audience relate and care despite themselves. It's your story and you can do whatever the hell you want with it. But the one thing you shouldn't do is waste a reader's time or inclination to become emotionally invested.

Q: What if I'm using too many dialogue tags?

Not an interiority question, but a great writing question overall.

If this is you: stop it.

We don't need "he chortled convincingly" and "she shrieked beseechingly" or whatever. Do less. If you find this is your approach to dialogue and scene, consider having your POV character interpret

---

8. Jury's still out on Alex! Since this book ends on such an unresolved note, she could very well be lounging by Simon's pool to this day!

other characters' actions in interiority instead. Go back to Chapter 12 and see how you might portray the experiences and intentions of your non-point-of-view secondary characters, which should help you cut down on this insecure habit of hitting readers over the head with the emotional tone of beats and scenes.

Q: What if I'm using too many thought tags?

Stop it.

No, but seriously, stop it. Weave interiority into your narration or use italicized verbatim thoughts. Thought tags ("he thought") aren't necessary in most cases, no matter your point of view choices. Go back to Chapter 1 and Chapter 4 for more encouragement to release these inessential filler words back into the creative ether.

Q: What if I'm writing a character outside of my own lived experience?

Enough softball questions and joking around. This is a serious contemporary craft and market question and I'm proud to address it. Diversity and owning one's own lived experience are huge topics of conversation in the current publishing landscape. A lot of well-meaning writers have found themselves in trouble over this issue.

No matter what you personally think about it, or your stance on cancel culture, you need to be aware of this shift in the industry. I'm about to talk about diversity and inclusion as it pertains to publishing. While I'll use race-specific examples, this discussion relates to gender, sexuality, physical and mental differences, body size and function, neurodiversity, and any other axis along which humans can differ from one another.

There are some writers, literary agents, acquisitions editors, and readers who believe everyone must "stay in their own lane," which means only writing from the perspective of their lived experience. There are obvious reasons for this. For example, if you're a white person writing a Black protagonist, you're unlikely to deeply understand some of the broad facets and specific nuances of the Black experience. No matter how much research you do, no matter how you justify it.

There's also an argument that the white person writing a character of color—in a primarily white industry which platforms white voices[9]—is potentially taking an opportunity away from a Black writer to portray a more accurate representation of the Black experience.[10] The current position in publishing seems to say that main characters of color—or of a certain gender, sexuality, creed, etc.—should be written by creators who share that identity. There's tolerance for authors writing outside of their genders,[11] but writers who cross race and disability lines, for example, are seen as much more problematic.

If you choose to write outside of your experience, you may receive pushback. It's as simple as that. This isn't my opinion, either. I regularly speak to publishing house editors and literary agents about what they're seeking and seeing in the market, and the ideas in this section are informed by these conversations.

Do I agree with this state of affairs? It is, of course, an unfailingly positive development for books to reflect the variety of human experiences and the demographic makeup of society. There's no question about it. It's not even a political issue, it's a human issue.

The "stay in your lane" approach does get problematic for me, however, because stepping out of our own lived experience is the absolute cornerstone of both reading and writing. When we write a character, we step into someone else's shoes. Sure, our rendering is informed by our own lives, especially if we "write what we know." But writing is

9. The numbers really are pretty staggering in this day and age. For the latest data, look up the most recent Lee & Low Diversity Baseline Survey, which is done every four years.
10. I want to acknowledge that this is also a double-edged sword. Many writers report feeling pressured to be an ideal representation of their demographic and are expected to write a "Black book" or a "neurodivergent book" when all they really want to do is write … *a book*. But as I first discussed in Chapter 2, publishing is full of categories and labels, and it's hard to get away from them, especially when it comes to DEI conversations. For a great film send-up of this issue, check out *American Fiction*, adapted from *Erasure* by Percival Everett.
11. Right or wrong, love it or hate it, females writing male characters tend to be slightly more accepted than males writing female characters, at least in the cisgender, heterosexual framework.

about taking on other perspectives. If you only wrote your experience, your books would be awfully homogenous. So how does this square with perhaps the most hot-button issue in today's publishing culture?

Well, I do think your protagonist should largely mirror your demographic profile, especially if you're writing and submitting for the first time. You might have opportunities to go farther afield with other characters once you develop a track record. Our From the Shelves authors Matt Ruff (*Lovecraft Country*) and S.A. Chakraborty (*The City of Brass*) have written protagonists outside of their racial demographic profiles, and reactions have been mixed. But that hasn't stopped *Lovecraft Country*, especially, from being a commercial success and getting adapted into an HBO series.

Once we get beyond the protagonist, there seems to be more breathing room. This means you should absolutely fill your story with secondary characters who reflect the diversity of our society, as long as you're able to do it intentionally, respectfully, and without stereotyping.

As I said at the beginning of this chapter, this advice might not be relevant to you, or it might be too general to be helpful. You also might've already thrown this book out the window because you assume I'm a liberal snowflake puppet for the leftist media elite.[12] (There are conservative agents, editors, and publishers who might offer a different take on these issues!) Given how prevalent this exact conversation is in the industry today, however, I'd be remiss if I didn't tackle this extremely polarizing topic in a guide on writing character.

Now that we've had some laughs, answered some questions, and gotten our blood up about a particularly contentious cultural conflict, let's end on one final question.

Q: Do I *have* to use interiority?

I mean, it'd be pretty funny if I said "no, you don't." I obviously believe in this tool to the point of fanaticism. That aside, you don't

---

12. I don't know what to tell you. Californians gonna Californian.

have to do anything you don't want to do. I'm not your mom.[13] It's your manuscript, it's your writing, and it's your life.

However, remember seeing some of our characters get walloped by epiphanies? Once you know, you can't really *un*know. Sure, now that you've metabolized the amazing craft concept of interiority and the scales have fallen from your eyes, you *can* go back to writing the way you always did. You can suppress the blazing a-ha! moments you've had over the last 500 pages. You can absolutely ignore everything you've learned.

But would you want to?

---

13. Joke's on me, because my kids don't do what I tell them to, either.

CONCLUSION

Here's a simple call to action: Care deeply about your characters and make readers care, too! Sink below the surface of your protagonist with interiority, add layers, and ask lots of questions about your characters' experiences in big and small moments.

We're all works in progress, as are our, well, creative works in progress. By using interiority, you'll not only unlock additional insights into your protagonists, you might just live more deeply and richly, too.

The day you sit down to learn and understand interiority is the first day of the rest of your writing life. Storytelling is a journey in external and internal growth, and my most profound hope is that you enjoy the ride.

RESOURCES FOR WRITERS

I've spent almost two decades creating educational materials for writers and designing courses, books, and services focused on craft and industry topics. Please check out my resources and offerings.

Webinars

I regularly teach free webinars about query letters, character, interiority, plot, and first pages. Some webinars offer the opportunity for live feedback. Please check out a current list of my upcoming presentations and workshops here:

https://goodstorycompany.com/workshops

I'm also available to Zoom into your critique group or design a bespoke talk for a writing retreat or conference on any number of industry and craft subjects.

Editorial Services, Ghostwriting, and Writing Workshops

If you enjoyed this book, consider getting personalized one-on-one feedback from me. My specialty is deep developmental editing with a character focus. Alternatively, I am happy to step in as a discrete ghostwriter or offer direct ghost revision to execute any changes to your project. We can also work together in a small group writing workshop intensive setting.

Developmental Editing Services:

https://marykole.com

Ghost Revision and Ghostwriting Services:

https://manuscriptstudio.com

Story Mastermind Small Group Writing Workshops:

https://storymastermind.com

Free Story Mastermind Outline Framework:

https://bit.ly/novel-outline

Courses

It is my (perhaps manic) goal to create as many writing resources in as many formats as possible. I hope you find these courses useful. I'm always so grateful when a written or recorded version of me can be of service.

Writing Mastery Academy Character Class:

With by Jessica Brody, of *Save the Cat Writes a Novel* fame!

https://www.writingmastery.com

Writing Blueprints Submission Resource:

If a deep dive into the submission process sounds helpful, this self-paced course contains over ten hours of instruction. You'll get access to agent interviews, over thirty handouts, and a comprehensive step-by-step submission guide.

https://bit.ly/kolesub

LinkedIn Learning:

My popular Crafting Dynamic Characters class is also available on this platform.

https://www.linkedin.com/learning/crafting-dynamic-characters/

Udemy:

These budget-friendly classes cover assorted writing and publishing topics in an easy-to-digest format.

https://www.udemy.com/user/mary-kole/

Good Story Company

In 2019, I founded Good Story Company as an umbrella brand so that my amazing team and I could collaborate in the service of writing and writers. GSC is where you'll find our most comprehensive library of resources and services. You can also sign up for our email newsletter and follow us on social media to get our most current updates.

Good Story Company:

https://goodstorycompany.com

Good Story Podcast:

https://goodstorypodcast.com

Good Story YouTube Channel:

https://youtube.com/goodstory

Writing Craft Workshop Membership:

https://goodstorycompany.com/membership

Good Story Marketing:

https://goodstorycompany.com/marketing

Workshops and Events:

https://goodstorycompany.com/workshops

Read Like a Writer Book Club:

https://goodstorycompany.com/book-club

The Insider's Guide to Publishing Your Book Substack:

https://goodstoryco.substack.com/

WAIT! BEFORE YOU GO!

If you enjoyed this book, there are **three small things** you can do which would make a big difference to me and Good Story Company. Thank you so much for your time, kind attention, and consideration!

Subscribe to Our Newsletter

Our respectful, short, and non-spammy newsletter features all of our latest and greatest free resources, workshops, events, and critique opportunities. Go here to sign up:

https://bit.ly/hellogsc

Leave an Honest Review

Please also consider leaving a review for this title with your retailer of choice, as well as Goodreads. I love getting feedback of my own, and testimonials help greatly with our discoverability and marketing efforts, so that we can reach more writers.

Reach Out

Finally, I'd love to hear your experience and celebrate your accomplishments. If you run into some trouble in the writing and publishing worlds, don't be a stranger, either. Drop me a line:

mary@goodstorycompany.com

ACKNOWLEDGMENTS

A note of deep gratitude to everyone who's supported my work over the years, whether by reading one of my books, watching a video, working with me directly, showing up at book club, or checking out the podcast. This guide on interiority is the most ambitious and comprehensive project I've attempted, and I truly hope you find it fruitful. Every time I write a book, I become so obsessed with the work that I vow never to write another one. It's draining, everything else takes a back seat, and I slip into an alternate reality (where showers are scarce). By this point, though, everyone in my life knows that I'm lying through my teeth. There will always be another. Sorry, not sorry.

My team at Good Story Company allows me to do the work I love. Thank you to Kristen Overman, Amy Wilson, Rhiannon Richardson, Jenna Van Rooy, Kaylee Pereyra, and Kate London. Thank you also to Kate Penndorf and Valerie Heller: Here's to more community and workshop adventures to come!

To all of my marvelous clients: Thank you for letting me cheer you on from the sidelines, and teaching me about your ideas and passions.

To my business partners at Bittersweet Books, the amazing John Cusick and Julie Murphy: Our work is why I get out of bed in the morning.

My gorgeous, smart, and funny best friends, Lauren Burris and Scott Marasigan: Thank you for putting up with me.

To Todd, Theo, Finn, Ella, Gertie, Olive, and Luna: I love you. That's it and that's all. I'll never stop striving each and every day to give you the best lives possible.

ALSO BY MARY KOLE

Writing Irresistible Kidlit: The Ultimate Guide to Crafting Fiction for Young Adult and Middle Grade Readers

Writing Irresistible Picture Books: Insider Insights Into Crafting Compelling Modern Stories for Young Readers

Writing Irresistible Picture Books Workbook

Irresistible Query Letters: 40+ Real World Query Letters With Literary Agent Feedback

Irresistible Query Letter Workbook

How to Write a Book Now: Craft Concepts, Mindset Shifts, and Encouragement to Inspire Your Creative Writing

Writing Interiority: Crafting Irresistible Characters

NOTES

AI Transparency Statement

a. Brewin, Kester. "Why I wrote an AI transparency statement for my book, and think other authors should too." *The Guardian*, April 4, 2024. https://www.theguardian.com/books/2024/apr/04/why-i-wrote-an-ai-transparency-statement-for-my-book-and-think-other-authors-should-too.

1. What Is Interiority?

a. Ellen Galinsky, *The Breakthrough Years: A New Scientific Framework for Raising Thriving Teens* (New York: Flatiron Books, 2024), 11.

3. Premise and Theme

a. Lauren Blackwood, *Within These Wicked Walls* (New York: Wednesday Books, 2021), 23.
b. Lauren Groff, *The Vaster Wilds: A Novel* (New York: Riverhead Books, 2023), 145.
c. Stacy Willingham, *All the Dangerous Things: A Novel* (New York: Minotaur Books, 2023), 43.
d. Emily St. John Mandel, *The Glass Hotel: A Novel* (New York: Alfred A. Knopf, 2020), 90.
e. Ibid, 114.
f. Emma Cline, *The Guest: A Novel* (New York: Random House, 2023), 73.
g. Su Bristow, *The Fair Folk: A Novel* (New York: Europa Editions, 2024), 52.
h. Naomi Novik, *Spinning Silver* (New York: Del Rey, 2019), 78.
i. Ibid, 377.
j. Kristin Hannah, *The Nightingale: A Novel* (New York: St. Martin's Press, 2015), 533.
k. Ibid, 533.
l. Fran Littlewood, *Amazing Grace Adams: A Novel* (New York: Henry Holt and Co., 2023), 64.
m. Allie Rowbottom, *Aesthetica* (New York: Soho Press, 2023), 14.
n. Ibid, 33.
o. Chelsea Martin, *Tell Me I'm an Artist* (New York: Soft Skull Press, 2023), 268.
p. Sarah Rose Etter, *Ripe: A Novel* (New York: Scribner, 2023), 100.
q. Ibid, 7.
r. Emma Noyes, *Guy's Girl* (New York: Berkley, 2023), 135.
s. Melissa Broder, *Milk Fed: A Novel* (New York: Scribner, 2021), 283-284.
t. Nathan Hill, *Wellness: A Novel* (New York: Alfred A. Knopf, 2023), 246.
u. Su Bristow, *The Fair Folk: A Novel* (New York: Europa Editions, 2024), 252-253.
v. Kennedy Ryan, *Before I Let Go* (New York: Forever, 2022), 262.
w. Sarah Rose Etter, *Ripe: A Novel* (New York: Scribner, 2023), 162.

x. Emma Noyes, *Guy's Girl* (New York: Berkley, 2023), 115.

y. Curtis Sittenfeld, *Romantic Comedy: A Novel* (New York: Random House, 2023), 231.

z. R.F. Kuang, *Yellowface* (New York: William Morrow, 2023), 9.

aa. Chelsea Martin, *Tell Me I'm an Artist* (New York: Soft Skull Press, 2023), 350.

bb. Kristin Hannah, *The Nightingale: A Novel* (New York: St. Martin's Press, 2015), 474.

cc. Tess Stimson, *The New House* (New York: Avon, 2022), 123.

dd. Zoe Hana Mikuta, *Gearbreakers* (New York: Feiwel & Friends, 2021), 14.

ee. Rebecca Ross, *Divine Rivals* (New York: Wednesday Books, 2023), 72.

ff. Melissa Broder, *Death Valley: A Novel* (New York: Scribner, 2024), 2.

gg. Ruth Ware, *The It Girl* (New York: Gallery/Scout Press, 2022), 45.

hh. Tess Stimson, *The New House* (New York: Avon, 2022), 54.

5. Backstory and Wound

a. Yangsze Choo, *The Fox Wife: A Novel* (New York: Henry Holt and Co., 2024), 147.

b. Ibid, 198.

c. Rachel Hawkins, *The Villa: A Novel* (New York: St. Martin's Press, 2023), 37.

d. Fran Littlewood, *Amazing Grace Adams: A Novel* (New York: Henry Holt and Co., 2023), 27.

e. Kennedy Ryan, *Before I Let Go* (New York: Forever, 2022), 167.

f. Ibid, 171.

g. Bryan Washington, *Family Meal: A Novel* (New York: Riverhead Books, 2023), 66.

h. Amber Smith, *The Way I Used to Be* (New York: Margaret K. McElderry Books, 2016), 248.

i. Ibid, 321.

j. Jesmyn Ward, *Sing, Unburied, Sing: A Novel* (New York: Scribner, 2017), 51.

k. Caroline Kepnes, *You: A Novel* (New York: Atria/Emily Bestler Books, 2014), 143.

l. Melissa Broder, *Milk Fed: A Novel* (New York: Scribner, 2021), 18.

m. Colson Whitehead, *The Underground Railroad: A Novel* (New York: Doubleday, 2016), 98.

n. Gail Honeyman, *Eleanor Oliphant Is Completely Fine: A Novel* (New York: Pamela Dorman Books, 2017), 26.

o. Ibid, 51.

p. Ibid, 130.

q. Ibid, 154.

r. Ibid, 237.

s. Tess Stimson, *The New House* (New York: Avon, 2022), 17.

t. Ibid, 79.

u. Ibid, 123.

v. Lauren Blackwood, *Within These Wicked Walls* (New York: Wednesday Books, 2021), 252.

w. Ibid, 257.

x. Katherine Center, *The Bodyguard: A Novel* (New York: St. Martin's Press, 2022), 15.

y. N.K. Jemisin, *The City We Became* (New York: Orbit Books, 2021), 241.

z. Fredrik Backman, *Anxious People: A Novel* (New York: Atria Books, 2020), 284.

aa. Sabrina Imbler, *How Far the Light Reaches: A Life In Ten Sea Creatures* (New York: Little, Brown and Company, 2022), 73.

bb. Emily St. John Mandel, *The Glass Hotel: A Novel* (New York: Alfred A. Knopf, 2020), 89.

cc. Grady Hendrix, *The Final Girl Support Group* (New York: Berkley, 2021), 164.

dd. R.F. Kuang, *Yellowface* (New York: William Morrow, 2023), 206.

6. Sense of Self

a. Emily St. John Mandel, *The Glass Hotel: A Novel* (New York: Alfred A. Knopf, 2020), 14-15.

b. Melissa Broder, *Milk Fed: A Novel* (New York: Scribner, 2021), 151.

c. N.K. Jemisin, *The City We Became* (New York: Orbit Books, 2021), 78.

d. Ibid, 157.

e. Rebecca Ross, *Divine Rivals* (New York: Wednesday Books, 2023), 72.

f. Dizz Tate, *Brutes: A Novel* (New York: Catapult, 2023), 73.

g. R.F. Kuang, *Yellowface* (New York: William Morrow, 2023), 186-187.

h. Chimamanda Ngozi Adichie, *Americanah: A Novel* (New York: Alfred A. Knopf, 2013), 347.

i. Victoria Aveyard, *Red Queen* (New York: HarperTeen, 2015), 43.

j. Ibid, 164.

k. Jesmyn Ward, *Sing, Unburied, Sing: A Novel* (New York: Scribner, 2017), 207.

l. N.K. Jemisin, *The City We Became* (New York: Orbit Books, 2021), 95.

m. R.F. Kuang, *Yellowface* (New York: William Morrow, 2023), 9.

n. Emily St. John Mandel, *The Glass Hotel: A Novel* (New York: Alfred A. Knopf, 2020), 101.

o. Ruth Ware, *The It Girl* (New York: Gallery / Scout Press, 2022), 45.

p. Ibid, 135.

q. Melissa Broder, *Milk Fed: A Novel* (New York: Scribner, 2021), 161.

r. Amber Smith, *The Way I Used to Be* (New York: Margaret K. McElderry Books, 2016), 47.

s. Ibid, 343.

t. Elle King, *Bad Fruit: A Novel* (New York: Astra House, 2022), 7.

u. Ibid, 53.

v. Melissa Broder, *Milk Fed: A Novel* (New York: Scribner, 2021), 206.

w. Zoe Hana Mikuta, *Gearbreakers* (New York: Feiwel & Friends, 2021), 141.

x. Zoe Hana Mikuta, *Gearbreakers* (New York: Feiwel & Friends, 2021), 264.

y. Jessica Knoll, *Bright Young Women: A Novel* (New York: Marysue Rucci Books, 2023), 52.

z. Ibid, 89.

aa. Ibid, 215.

bb. Sonora Reyes, *The Luis Ortega Survival Club* (New York: Balzer + Bray, 2023), 66.

cc. Chelsea Martin, *Tell Me I'm an Artist* (New York: Soft Skull Press, 2023), 308.

dd. Nathan Hill, *Wellness: A Novel* (New York: Alfred A. Knopf, 2023), 407.

ee. Tess Stimson, *The New House* (New York: Avon, 2022), 312.

ff. Emily St. John Mandel, *The Glass Hotel: A Novel* (New York: Alfred A. Knopf, 2020), 73.

gg. Melissa Broder, *Death Valley: A Novel* (New York: Scribner, 2024), 29.

hh. Lauren Groff, *The Vaster Wilds: A Novel* (New York: Riverhead Books, 2023), 145.

ii. Naomi Novik, *Spinning Silver* (New York: Del Rey, 2019), 36.

jj. Matt Ruff, *Lovecraft Country: A Novel* (New York: Harper Perennial, 2017), 221.

7. Objective and Motivation

a. Roshani Chokshi, *The Spirit Glass* (New York: Rick Riordan Presents, 2023), 80.

b. Ellen Galinsky, *The Breakthrough Years: A New Scientific Framework for Raising Thriving Teens* (New York: Flatiron Books, 2024), 357.

c. Matt Ruff, *Lovecraft Country: A Novel* (New York: Harper Perennial, 2017), 128.

d. Nathan Hill, *Wellness: A Novel* (New York: Alfred A. Knopf, 2023), 255.

e. Su Bristow, *The Fair Folk: A Novel* (New York: Europa Editions, 2024), 28.

f. Ibid, 64.

g. Chelsea Martin, *Tell Me I'm an Artist* (New York: Soft Skull Press, 2023), 147.

h. Ibid, 201.

i. Chimamanda Ngozi Adichie, *Americanah: A Novel* (New York: Alfred A. Knopf, 2013), 3.

j. Katherine Arden, *The Bear and the Nightingale: A Novel* (New York: Del Rey, 2017), 98.

k. Talia Hibbert, *Get a Life, Chloe Brown* (New York: Avon, 2019), 22.

l. Gail Honeyman, *Eleanor Oliphant Is Completely Fine: A Novel* (New York: Pamela Dorman Books, 2017), 214.

m. Ibid, 238.

n. Katherine Center, *The Bodyguard: A Novel* (New York: St. Martin's Press, 2022), 5.

o. Jessica Knoll, *Bright Young Women: A Novel* (New York: Marysue Rucci Books, 2023), 27.

p. Melissa Broder, *Death Valley: A Novel* (New York: Scribner, 2024), 5.

q. Rebecca Ross, *Divine Rivals* (New York: Wednesday Books, 2023), 40.

r. Colson Whitehead, *The Nickel Boys: A Novel* (New York: Doubleday, 2019), 64.

s. Holly Black, *The Cruel Prince* (New York: Little, Brown Books for Young Readers, 2018), 288.

t. Ibid, 260.

u. Zoe Hana Mikuta, *Gearbreakers* (New York: Feiwel & Friends, 2021), 77.

v. Roshani Chokshi, *The Spirit Glass* (New York: Rick Riordan Presents, 2023), 3.

w. Ibid, 17.

x. N.K. Jemisin, *The City We Became* (New York: Orbit Books, 2021), 237.

y. Ibid, 258.

z. Casey McQuiston, *One Last Stop* (New York: St. Martin's Griffin, 2021), 226.

aa. Fran Littlewood, *Amazing Grace Adams: A Novel* (New York: Henry Holt and Co., 2023), 9.

bb. Shari Lapena, *Everyone Here Is Lying: A Novel* (New York: Pamela Dorman Books, 2023), 185.

cc. Emma Noyes, *Guy's Girl* (New York: Berkley, 2023), 226-227.

dd. Melissa Broder, *Milk Fed: A Novel* (New York: Scribner, 2021), 122-123.

ee. Stacy Willingham, *All the Dangerous Things: A Novel* (New York: Minotaur Books, 2023), 135.

ff. Sonora Reyes, *The Luis Ortega Survival Club* (New York: Balzer + Bray, 2023), 71-72.

8. Need

a. Gail Honeyman, *Eleanor Oliphant Is Completely Fine: A Novel* (New York: Pamela Dorman Books, 2017), 25.

b. Emma Cline, *The Guest: A Novel* (New York: Random House, 2023), 24.

c. N.K. Jemisin, *The City We Became* (New York: Orbit Books, 2021), 101.

d. Jesmyn Ward, *Sing, Unburied, Sing: A Novel* (New York: Scribner, 2017), 123.

e. Frederik Backman, *Anxious People: A Novel* (New York: Atria Books, 2020), 51.

f. Chelsea Martin, *Tell Me I'm an Artist* (New York: Soft Skull Press, 2023), 168.

g. Su Bristow, *The Fair Folk: A Novel* (New York: Europa Editions, 2024), 184.

h. Katherine Arden, *The Bear and the Nightingale: A Novel* (New York: Del Rey, 2017), 243.

i. Naomi Novik, *Spinning Silver* (New York: Del Rey, 2019), 108.

j. Katherine Center, *The Bodyguard: A Novel* (New York: St. Martin's Press, 2022), 43.

k. Ibid, 86.

l. Tess Stimson, *The New House* (New York: Avon, 2022), 40.

m. Ibid, 73.

n. Bryan Washington, *Family Meal: A Novel* (New York: Riverhead Books, 2023), 12.

o. Ibid, 96.

p. Stacy Willingham, *All the Dangerous Things: A Novel* (New York: Minotaur Books, 2023), 29.

q. Tess Stimson, *The New House* (New York: Avon, 2022), 275.

r. Allie Rowbottom, *Aesthetica* (New York: Soho Press, 2023), 14

s. Dizz Tate, *Brutes: A Novel* (New York: Catapult, 2023), 36.

t. Zoe Hana Mikuta, *Gearbreakers* (New York: Feiwel & Friends, 2021), 25.

u. Katherine Center, *The Bodyguard: A Novel* (New York: St. Martin's Press, 2022), 219.

v. Katherine Arden, *The Bear and the Nightingale: A Novel* (New York: Del Rey, 2017), 88.

w. Amber Smith, *The Way I Used to Be* (New York: Margaret K. McElderry Books, 2016), 282.

x. Ibid, 58.

y. Sabrina Imbler, *How Far the Light Reaches: A Life In Ten Sea Creatures* (New York: Little, Brown and Company, 2022), 39.

z. Ibid, 159.

aa. N.K. Jemisin, *The City We Became* (New York: Orbit Books, 2021), 292.

bb. Ibid, 228.

cc. Rachel Hawkins, *The Villa: A Novel* (New York: St. Martin's Press, 2023), 131.

dd. Dizz Tate, *Brutes: A Novel* (New York: Catapult, 2023), 126-127.

ee. S.A. Chakraborty, *The City of Brass* (New York: HarperVoyager, 2017), 29.

ff. Holly Black, *The Cruel Prince* (New York: Little, Brown Books for Young Readers, 2018), 350.

gg. Ibid, 287.

hh. Emily St. John Mandel, *The Glass Hotel: A Novel* (New York: Alfred A. Knopf, 2020), 44.

ii. Chimamanda Ngozi Adichie, *Americanah: A Novel* (New York: Alfred A. Knopf, 2013), 73.

jj. Elle King, *Bad Fruit: A Novel* (New York: Astra House, 2022), 7.

kk. Fran Littlewood, *Amazing Grace Adams: A Novel* (New York: Henry Holt and Co., 2023), 173.

ll. Grady Hendrix, *How to Sell a Haunted House* (New York: Berkley, 2023), 16.

mm. Yaa Gyasi, *Homegoing: A Novel* (New York: Alfred A. Knopf, 2016), 98.

nn. Sarah Rose Etter, *Ripe: A Novel* (New York: Scribner, 2023), 162.

oo. Sonora Reyes, *The Luis Ortega Survival Club* (New York: Balzer + Bray, 2023), 261.

pp. Lauren Groff, *The Vaster Wilds: A Novel* (New York: Riverhead Books, 2023), 239.

9. Inner Struggle

a. Bryan Washington, *Family Meal: A Novel* (New York: Riverhead Books, 2023), 83.

b. Katherine Arden, *The Bear and the Nightingale: A Novel* (New York: Del Rey, 2017), 109.

c. Talia Hibbert, *Get a Life, Chloe Brown* (New York: Avon, 2019), 88.

d. Holly Black, *The Cruel Prince* (New York: Little, Brown Books for Young Readers, 2018), 308.

e. Gail Honeyman, *Eleanor Oliphant Is Completely Fine: A Novel* (New York: Pamela Dorman Books, 2017), 126.

f. R.F. Kuang, *Yellowface* (New York: William Morrow, 2023), 38.

g. Emily St. John Mandel, *The Glass Hotel: A Novel* (New York: Alfred A. Knopf, 2020), 168-169.

h. Victoria Aveyard, *Red Queen* (New York: HarperTeen, 2015), 202.

i. Tess Stimson, *The New House* (New York: Avon, 2022), 236.

j. Jessica Knoll, *Bright Young Women: A Novel* (New York: Marysue Rucci Books, 2023), 237.

k. Casey McQuiston, *One Last Stop* (New York: St. Martin's Griffin, 2021), 34.

l. Ibid, 137.

m. Kennedy Ryan, *Before I Let Go* (New York: Forever, 2022), 147.

n. Ibid, 278.

o. Lauren Blackwood, *Within These Wicked Walls* (New York: Wednesday Books, 2021), 119.

p. Zoe Hana Mikuta, *Gearbreakers* (New York: Feiwel & Friends, 2021), 77.

q. Jessica Knoll, *Bright Young Women: A Novel* (New York: Marysue Rucci Books, 2023), 22.

r. Ibid, 77.

s. Sarah Rose Etter, *Ripe: A Novel* (New York: Scribner, 2023), 91.

t. Ibid, 125.

u. Melissa Broder, *Death Valley: A Novel* (New York: Scribner, 2024), 20.

v. Emily St. John Mandel, *The Glass Hotel: A Novel* (New York: Alfred A. Knopf, 2020), 139.

w. Tess Stimson, *The New House* (New York: Avon, 2022), 192.

x. Ibid, 157.

y. N.K. Jemisin, *The City We Became* (New York: Orbit Books, 2021), 334.

z. R.F. Kuang, *Yellowface* (New York: William Morrow, 2023), 37.

aa. Shari Lapena, *Everyone Here Is Lying: A Novel* (New York: Pamela Dorman Books, 2023), 212.

bb. Dizz Tate, *Brutes: A Novel* (New York: Catapult, 2023), 191.

cc. Emma Noyes, *Guy's Girl* (New York: Berkley, 2023), 93-94.

dd. Katherine Arden, *The Bear and the Nightingale: A Novel* (New York: Del Rey, 2017), 125-126.

ee. Naomi Novik, *Spinning Silver* (New York: Del Rey, 2019), 78-79.

ff. Katherine Center, *The Bodyguard: A Novel* (New York: St. Martin's Press, 2022), 88.

gg. Ibid, 236.

10. Worldview

a. Su Bristow, *The Fair Folk: A Novel* (New York: Europa Editions, 2024), 36.

b. Victoria Aveyard, *Red Queen* (New York: HarperTeen, 2015), 3.

c. Ibid, 26.

d. Sarah Rose Etter, *Ripe: A Novel* (New York: Scribner, 2023), 100.

e. Lauren Groff, *The Vaster Wilds: A Novel* (New York: Riverhead Books, 2023), 22.

f. Gail Honeyman, *Eleanor Oliphant Is Completely Fine: A Novel* (New York: Pamela Dorman Books, 2017), 224.

g. Grady Hendrix, *The Final Girl Support Group* (New York: Berkley, 2021), 94.

h. Casey McQuiston, *One Last Stop* (New York: St. Martin's Griffin, 2021), 11.

i. Ibid, 57.

j. Tess Stimson, *The New House* (New York: Avon, 2022), 54.

k. Ibid, 249.

l. Ibid, 71.

m. Matt Ruff, *Lovecraft Country: A Novel* (New York: Harper Perennial, 2017), 31.

n. N.K. Jemisin, *The City We Became* (New York: Orbit Books, 2021), 11.

o. Caroline Kepnes, *You: A Novel* (New York: Atria/Emily Bestler Books, 2014), 78.

p. Melissa Broder, *Milk Fed: A Novel* (New York: Scribner, 2021), 17.

q. Katherine Center, *The Bodyguard: A Novel* (New York: St. Martin's Press, 2022), 17.

r. N.K. Jemisin, *The City We Became* (New York: Orbit Books, 2021), 333.

s. Ibid, 236.

t. Fredrik Backman, *Anxious People: A Novel* (New York: Atria Books, 2020), 54.

u. Ibid, 57.

v. Yangsze Choo, *The Fox Wife: A Novel* (New York: Henry Holt and Co., 2024), 248.

w. Ibid, 235.

x. Jesmyn Ward, *Sing, Unburied, Sing: A Novel* (New York: Scribner, 2017), 146.

y. Roshani Chokshi, *The Spirit Glass* (New York: Rick Riordan Presents, 2023), 247.

11. Character Arc

a. Gail Honeyman, *Eleanor Oliphant Is Completely Fine: A Novel* (New York: Pamela Dorman Books, 2017), 8.

b. Ibid, 27.

c. Ibid, 150.

d. Ibid, 220.

e. Ibid, 221.

f. Ibid, 224.

g. Ibid, 260.

h. Ibid, 266.

i. Ibid, 279.

j. Ibid, 294.

k. Su Bristow, *The Fair Folk: A Novel* (New York: Europa Editions, 2024), 18.

l. Ibid, 86.

m. Ibid, 129.

n. Ibid, 271.

o. Ibid, 436.

p. Emma Cline, *The Guest: A Novel* (New York: Random House, 2023), 9.

q. Ibid, 118.

r. Ibid, 139.

s. Ibid, 253-254.

t. Ibid, 285.

u. Caroline Kepnes, *You: A Novel* (New York: Atria/Emily Bestler Books, 2014), 13.

v. Melissa Broder, *Death Valley: A Novel* (New York: Scribner, 2024), 5.

w. Ibid, 11.

x. Emma Noyes, *Guy's Girl* (New York: Berkley, 2023), 24.

y. Curtis Sittenfeld, *Romantic Comedy: A Novel* (New York: Random House, 2023), 26.

z. Bryan Washington, *Family Meal: A Novel* (New York: Riverhead Books, 2023), 123.

aa. Katherine Center, *The Bodyguard: A Novel* (New York: St. Martin's Press, 2022), 222.

bb. Jessica Knoll, *Bright Young Women: A Novel* (New York: Marysue Rucci Books, 2023), 47.

cc. Ibid, 257.

dd. Allie Rowbottom, *Aesthetica* (New York: Soho Press, 2023), 160.

ee. Chimamanda Ngozi Adichie, *Americanah: A Novel* (New York: Alfred A. Knopf, 2013), 136.

ff. Ibid, 190.

gg. Ibid, 358.

hh. Rebecca Ross, *Divine Rivals* (New York: Wednesday Books, 2023), 84.

ii. Lauren Blackwood, *Within These Wicked Walls* (New York: Wednesday Books, 2021), 47.

jj. Ibid, 73.

kk. Ibid, 133.

ll. Ibid, 215.

mm. Sarah Rose Etter, *Ripe: A Novel* (New York: Scribner, 2023), 162.

nn. Ibid, 169.

oo. Ibid, 262.

pp. Kristin Hannah, *The Nightingale: A Novel* (New York: St. Martin's Press, 2015), 4.

qq. Ibid, 212.

rr. Ibid, 474.

ss. Jesmyn Ward, *Sing, Unburied, Sing: A Novel* (New York: Scribner, 2017), 147.

tt. Ibid, 274.

uu. Ibid, 279.

vv. Casey McQuiston, *One Last Stop* (New York: St. Martin's Griffin, 2021), 159.

ww. Ibid, 106.

xx. Ibid, 187.

12. Secondary Characters

a. Colson Whitehead, *The Nickel Boys: A Novel* (New York: Doubleday, 2019), 33.

b. Grady Hendrix, *How to Sell a Haunted House* (New York: Berkley, 2023), 52.

c. Dizz Tate, *Brutes: A Novel* (New York: Catapult, 2023), 210.

d. Jesmyn Ward, *Sing, Unburied, Sing: A Novel* (New York: Scribner, 2017), 269.

e. Ibid, 163.

f. Emily St. John Mandel, *The Glass Hotel: A Novel* (New York: Alfred A. Knopf, 2020), 147.

g. Chelsea Martin, *Tell Me I'm an Artist* (New York: Soft Skull Press, 2023), 191.

h. Gail Honeyman, *Eleanor Oliphant Is Completely Fine: A Novel* (New York: Pamela Dorman Books, 2017), 236.

i. Melissa Broder, *Milk Fed: A Novel* (New York: Scribner, 2021), 237.

j. Zoe Hana Mikuta, *Gearbreakers* (New York: Feiwel & Friends, 2021), 62.

k. Elle King, *Bad Fruit: A Novel* (New York: Astra House, 2022), 18.

l. Ibid, 10.

m. Caroline Kepnes, *You: A Novel* (New York: Atria/Emily Bestler Books, 2014), 7.

n. Rachel Hawkins, *The Villa: A Novel* (New York: St. Martin's Press, 2023), 36.

o. Victoria Aveyard, *Red Queen* (New York: HarperTeen, 2015), 132.

13. The Interiority of Relationships

a. Jessica Knoll, *Bright Young Women: A Novel* (New York: Marysue Rucci Books, 2023), 221.

b. Holly Black, *The Cruel Prince* (New York: Little, Brown Books for Young Readers, 2018), 317.

c. Jesmyn Ward, *Sing, Unburied, Sing: A Novel* (New York: Scribner, 2017), 229.

d. Melissa Broder, *Death Valley: A Novel* (New York: Scribner, 2024), 4.

e. Ibid, 72.

f. Ibid, 206.

g. Yaa Gyasi, *Homegoing: A Novel* (New York: Alfred A. Knopf, 2016), 8.

h. N.K. Jemisin, *The City We Became* (New York: Orbit Books, 2021), 268.

i. Su Bristow, *The Fair Folk: A Novel* (New York: Europa Editions, 2024), 122.

j. Jessica Knoll, *Bright Young Women: A Novel* (New York: Marysue Rucci Books, 2023), 106.

k. Silvia Moreno-Garcia, *Silver Nitrate* (New York: Del Rey, 2023), 35.

l. Rebecca Ross, *Divine Rivals* (New York: Wednesday Books, 2023), 84.

m. Ibid, 306.

n. Jesmyn Ward, *Sing, Unburied, Sing: A Novel* (New York: Scribner, 2017), 54.

o. Katherine Center, *The Bodyguard: A Novel* (New York: St. Martin's Press, 2022), 158.

p. Emily St. John Mandel, *The Glass Hotel: A Novel* (New York: Alfred A. Knopf, 2020), 88.

q. Fran Littlewood, *Amazing Grace Adams: A Novel* (New York: Henry Holt and Co., 2023), 19.

r. Ibid, 167.

s. Su Bristow, *The Fair Folk: A Novel* (New York: Europa Editions, 2024), 252-253.

t. Su Bristow, *The Fair Folk: A Novel* (New York: Europa Editions, 2024), 354-355.

u. Chimamanda Ngozi Adichie, *Americanah: A Novel* (New York: Alfred A. Knopf, 2013), 356.

v. Ibid, 358.

w. Dizz Tate, *Brutes: A Novel* (New York: Catapult, 2023), 180.

x. Rachel Hawkins, *The Villa: A Novel* (New York: St. Martin's Press, 2023), 198.

y. Stacy Willingham, *All the Dangerous Things: A Novel* (New York: Minotaur Books, 2023), 34.

z. Nathan Hill, *Wellness: A Novel* (New York: Alfred A. Knopf, 2023), 429.

aa. Ibid, 432-433.

bb. Curtis Sittenfeld, *Romantic Comedy: A Novel* (New York: Random House, 2023), 223.

cc. Ibid, 257.

dd. Julie Soto, *Forget Me Not* (New York: Forever, 2023), 235.

ee. Kennedy Ryan, *Before I Let Go* (New York: Forever, 2022), 213.

ff. Kristin Hannah, *The Nightingale: A Novel* (New York: St. Martin's Press, 2015), 551.

14. Information Reveals

a. Annie Dillard, *The Writing Life* (New York: HarperCollins, 1989), 78.

b. N.K. Jemisin, *The City We Became* (New York: Orbit Books, 2021), 231.

c. Amber Smith, *The Way I Used to Be* (New York: Margaret K. McElderry Books, 2016), 163.

d. Fonda Lee, *Jade City* (New York: Orbit, 2017), 8-9.

e. Victoria Aveyard, *Red Queen* (New York: HarperTeen, 2015), 136-137.

f. Ruth Ware, *The It Girl* (New York: Gallery / Scout Press, 2022), 72.

g. Gail Honeyman, *Eleanor Oliphant Is Completely Fine: A Novel* (New York: Pamela Dorman Books, 2017), 91.

h. Su Bristow, *The Fair Folk: A Novel* (New York: Europa Editions, 2024), 64.

i. Ibid, 219.

j. Casey McQuiston, *One Last Stop* (New York: St. Martin's Griffin, 2021), 9.

k. Sarah Rose Etter, *Ripe: A Novel* (New York: Scribner, 2023), 151.

l. Emily St. John Mandel, *The Glass Hotel: A Novel* (New York: Alfred A. Knopf, 2020), 57.

m. Rachel Hawkins, *The Villa: A Novel* (New York: St. Martin's Press, 2023), 85.

n. Tess Stimson, *The New House* (New York: Avon, 2022), 30.

o. Ibid, 132.

p. Ibid, 136.

q. Shari Lapena, *Everyone Here Is Lying: A Novel* (New York: Pamela Dorman Books, 2023), 83.

r. Ibid, 98.

15. Character Reactions

a. Yangsze Choo, *The Fox Wife: A Novel* (New York: Henry Holt and Co., 2024), 219.

b. Su Bristow, *The Fair Folk: A Novel* (New York: Europa Editions, 2024), 119.

c. Chimamanda Ngozi Adichie, *Americanah: A Novel* (New York: Alfred A. Knopf, 2013), 192.

d. Ibid, 294.

e. Curtis Sittenfeld, *Romantic Comedy: A Novel* (New York: Random House, 2023), 71.

f. Ibid, 231.

g. Roshani Chokshi, *The Spirit Glass* (New York: Rick Riordan Presents, 2023), 260.

h. Jesmyn Ward, *Sing, Unburied, Sing: A Novel* (New York: Scribner, 2017), 92.

i. N.K. Jemisin, *The City We Became* (New York: Orbit Books, 2021), 377.

j. Sarah Rose Etter, *Ripe: A Novel* (New York: Scribner, 2023), 128.

k. Zoe Hana Mikuta, *Gearbreakers* (New York: Feiwel & Friends, 2021), 71.

l. Melissa Broder, *Milk Fed: A Novel* (New York: Scribner, 2021), 37.

m. Stacy Willingham, *All the Dangerous Things: A Novel* (New York: Minotaur Books, 2023), 73.

n. Chelsea Martin, *Tell Me I'm an Artist* (New York: Soft Skull Press, 2023), 141.

o. Katherine Center, *The Bodyguard: A Novel* (New York: St. Martin's Press, 2022), 85-86.

p. Katherine Arden, *The Bear and the Nightingale: A Novel* (New York: Del Rey, 2017), 166.

q. Gail Honeyman, *Eleanor Oliphant Is Completely Fine: A Novel* (New York: Pamela Dorman Books, 2017), 221.

r. Kristin Hannah, *The Nightingale: A Novel* (New York: St. Martin's Press, 2015), 143.

s. Rebecca Ross, *Divine Rivals* (New York: Wednesday Books, 2023), 55.

t. Ibid, 252.

u. Victoria Aveyard, *Red Queen* (New York: HarperTeen, 2015), 63.

16. The Power of Decisions

a. Katherine Center, *The Bodyguard: A Novel* (New York: St. Martin's Press, 2022), 217.

b. Talia Hibbert, *Get a Life, Chloe Brown* (New York: Avon, 2019), 99.

c. Kennedy Ryan, *Before I Let Go* (New York: Forever, 2022), 252.

d. Ibid, 336.

e. Casey McQuiston, *One Last Stop* (New York: St. Martin's Griffin, 2021), 159.

f. Ibid, 268.

g. Emma Cline, *The Guest: A Novel* (New York: Random House, 2023), 50.

h. Ibid, 289.

i. Sarah Rose Etter, *Ripe: A Novel* (New York: Scribner, 2023), 196.

j. R.F. Kuang, *Yellowface* (New York: William Morrow, 2023), 29.

k. Ibid, 47.

l. Zoe Hana Mikuta, *Gearbreakers* (New York: Feiwel & Friends, 2021), 14.

m. Ibid, 74.

n. Holly Black, *The Cruel Prince* (New York: Little, Brown Books for Young Readers, 2018), 260.

o. Lauren Blackwood, *Within These Wicked Walls* (New York: Wednesday Books, 2021), 17.

p. Ibid, 236.

q. Chimamanda Ngozi Adichie, *Americanah: A Novel* (New York: Alfred A. Knopf, 2013), 345.

r. Matt Ruff, *Lovecraft Country: A Novel* (New York: Harper Perennial, 2017), 102.

s. Victoria Aveyard, *Red Queen* (New York: HarperTeen, 2015), 117.

t. Ibid, 135.

u. Ibid, 228.

v. Naomi Novik, *Spinning Silver* (New York: Del Rey, 2019), 10.

w. Ibid, 18.

x. Su Bristow, *The Fair Folk: A Novel* (New York: Europa Editions, 2024), 86.

y. Ibid, 133.

z. Ibid, 149.

aa. Ibid, 433.

bb. Fredrik Backman, *Anxious People: A Novel* (New York: Atria Books, 2020), 295.

cc. Kristin Hannah, *The Nightingale: A Novel* (New York: St. Martin's Press, 2015), 330.

dd. Ibid, 533.

ee. Ruth Ware, *The It Girl* (New York: Gallery/Scout Press, 2022), 75.

ff. Stacy Willingham, *All the Dangerous Things: A Novel* (New York: Minotaur Books, 2023), 214-215.

gg. Shari Lapena, *Everyone Here Is Lying: A Novel* (New York: Pamela Dorman Books, 2023), 6.

hh. Ibid, 64.

ii. Ibid, 17.

jj. Tess Stimson, *The New House* (New York: Avon, 2022), 193.

kk. Ibid, 292.

17. Leveraging Stakes

a. Fran Littlewood, *Amazing Grace Adams: A Novel* (New York: Henry Holt and Co., 2023), 64.

b. Jessica Knoll, *Bright Young Women: A Novel* (New York: Marysue Rucci Books, 2023), 134.

c. Kennedy Ryan, *Before I Let Go* (New York: Forever, 2022), 116.

d. Katherine Center, *The Bodyguard: A Novel* (New York: St. Martin's Press, 2022), 125.

e. Jesmyn Ward, *Sing, Unburied, Sing: A Novel* (New York: Scribner, 2017), 274.

f. Zoe Hana Mikuta, *Gearbreakers* (New York: Feiwel & Friends, 2021), 141.

g. Julie Soto, *Forget Me Not* (New York: Forever, 2023), 37.

h. Rebecca Ross, *Divine Rivals* (New York: Wednesday Books, 2023), 169.

i. R.F. Kuang, *Yellowface* (New York: William Morrow, 2023), 225.

j. Gail Honeyman, *Eleanor Oliphant Is Completely Fine: A Novel* (New York: Pamela Dorman Books, 2017), 214.

k. Chimamanda Ngozi Adichie, *Americanah: A Novel* (New York: Alfred A. Knopf, 2013), 76.

l. Casey McQuiston, *One Last Stop* (New York: St. Martin's Griffin, 2021), 315.

m. Colson Whitehead, *The Underground Railroad: A Novel* (New York: Doubleday, 2016), 282.

n. Jesmyn Ward, *Sing, Unburied, Sing: A Novel* (New York: Scribner, 2017), 213.

o. Ibid, 271.

p. Emma Noyes, *Guy's Girl* (New York: Berkley, 2023), 191.

q. Caroline Kepnes, *You: A Novel* (New York: Atria/Emily Bestler Books, 2014), 71.

r. Yangsze Choo, *The Fox Wife: A Novel* (New York: Henry Holt and Co., 2024), 107.

s. N.K. Jemisin, *The City We Became* (New York: Orbit Books, 2021), 18.

t. S.A. Chakraborty, *The City of Brass* (New York: HarperVoyager, 2017), 50.

u. Ibid, 29.

v. Victoria Aveyard, *Red Queen* (New York: HarperTeen, 2015), 128.

w. Ibid, 205.

18. Story World

a. Elle King, *Bad Fruit: A Novel* (New York: Astra House, 2022), 22.

b. Tess Stimson, *The New House* (New York: Avon, 2022), 10.

c. Ibid, 70.

d. Caroline Kepnes, *You: A Novel* (New York: Atria/Emily Bestler Books, 2014), 15.

e. Jesmyn Ward, *Sing, Unburied, Sing: A Novel* (New York: Scribner, 2017), 275.

f. Ibid, 89.

g. Stacy Willingham, *All the Dangerous Things: A Novel* (New York: Minotaur Books, 2023), 11.

h. Ibid, 27.

i. Silvia Moreno-Garcia, *Silver Nitrate* (New York: Del Rey, 2023), 35.

j. Dizz Tate, *Brutes: A Novel* (New York: Catapult, 2023), 86.

k. Ibid, 89.

l. Ibid, 107.

m. Allie Rowbottom, *Aesthetica* (New York: Soho Press, 2023), 54.

n. Emily St. John Mandel, *The Glass Hotel: A Novel* (New York: Alfred A. Knopf, 2020), 38-39.

o. Chimamanda Ngozi Adichie, *Americanah: A Novel* (New York: Alfred A. Knopf, 2013), 3.

p. Ibid, 460.

q. Ibid, 404.

r. Colson Whitehead, *The Underground Railroad: A Novel* (New York: Doubleday, 2016), 74.

s. Ibid, 277.

t. Ibid, 124.

u. Lauren Groff, *The Vaster Wilds: A Novel* (New York: Riverhead Books, 2023), 4.

v. Ibid, 198.

w. Nathan Hill, *Wellness: A Novel* (New York: Alfred A. Knopf, 2023), 213.

x. Roshani Chokshi, *The Spirit Glass* (New York: Rick Riordan Presents, 2023), 3.

y. Ibid, 69.

z. Ibid, 45.

aa. N.K. Jemisin, *The City We Became* (New York: Orbit Books, 2021), 105.

bb. Su Bristow, *The Fair Folk: A Novel* (New York: Europa Editions, 2024), 322.

cc. Victoria Aveyard, *Red Queen* (New York: HarperTeen, 2015), 89.

dd. Fonda Lee, *Jade City* (New York: Orbit, 2017), 57.

ee. Katherine Arden, *The Bear and the Nightingale: A Novel* (New York: Del Rey, 2017), 113-114.

ff. Matt Ruff, *Lovecraft Country: A Novel* (New York: Harper Perennial, 2017), 234.

19. Voice and Writing Style

a. Daniel Kraus, *Whalefall: A Novel* (New York: MTV Books, 2023), 83.

b. Fredrik Backman, *Anxious People: A Novel* (New York: Atria Books, 2020), 201.

c. Jesmyn Ward, *Sing, Unburied, Sing: A Novel* (New York: Scribner, 2017), 157.

d. Ibid, 207.

e. Matt Ruff, *Lovecraft Country: A Novel* (New York: Harper Perennial, 2017), 103.

f. Fran Littlewood, *Amazing Grace Adams: A Novel* (New York: Henry Holt and Co., 2023), 27.

g. Casey McQuiston, *One Last Stop* (New York: St. Martin's Griffin, 2021), 143.

h. Katherine Center, *The Bodyguard: A Novel* (New York: St. Martin's Press, 2022), 67.

i. Melissa Broder, *Milk Fed: A Novel* (New York: Scribner, 2021), 67.

j. Melissa Broder, *Death Valley: A Novel* (New York: Scribner, 2024), 38.

k. Lauren Groff, *The Vaster Wilds: A Novel* (New York: Riverhead Books, 2023), 93.

l. Caroline Kepnes, *You: A Novel* (New York: Atria/Emily Bestler Books, 2014), 229.

m. Melissa Broder, *Milk Fed: A Novel* (New York: Scribner, 2021), 85.

n. Katherine Center, *The Bodyguard: A Novel* (New York: St. Martin's Press, 2022), 79.

o. Ibid.

p. Rachel Hawkins, *The Villa: A Novel* (New York: St. Martin's Press, 2023), 151.

q. Curtis Sittenfeld, *Romantic Comedy: A Novel* (New York: Random House, 2023), 231.

20. Stacking the Deck

a. Holly Black, *The Cruel Prince* (New York: Little, Brown Books for Young Readers, 2018), 356.

b. Grady Hendrix, *The Final Girl Support Group* (New York: Berkley, 2021), 265.

c. Fonda Lee, *Jade City* (New York: Orbit, 2017), 37.

d. Nathan Hill, *Wellness: A Novel* (New York: Alfred A. Knopf, 2023), 570-571.

COPYRIGHT NOTICES

This project was truly an undertaking, especially when it came to securing permissions for each excerpt. The following notices are legally required by the publishing partners that helped bring this book to life. All licenses are for the **North American English language** territory rights and have been granted by their respective copyright holders and publishers.

Copyright Disclosures